# STAINED WITH BLOOD AND TEARS

Slain Girl for Whom Negro Was Burned.

MISS ANNA PELLEY

The negro, Will James, who was hung, shot, and burned to death by a mob in Cairo, Ill., last evening, was said to have confessed to the murder of Anna Pelley, a shop girl, who was attacked and killed while returning home from work last Monday evening.

Representation of Anna Pelley appearing in the *Chicago Tribune*, November 12, 1909.

# STAINED WITH BLOOD AND TEARS

## LYNCHINGS, MURDER, AND MOB VIOLENCE IN CAIRO, ILLINOIS 1909–1910

JOHN A. BEADLES

Saluki Publishing

Saluki Publishing
1915 University Press Drive
Carbondale, IL 62901


Printed in the United States of America

ISBN 978-0-8093-7005-4 (paperback)
ISBN 978-0-8093-7006-1 (e-book)

*Cover illustration*: A 1913 postcard (altered) shows 8th Street looking west from Commercial Avenue, Cairo, Illinois. The street intersection, with double arches over it, was the site of the lynching of Will "Froggie" James in 1909. Postcard from the collection of Darrel Dexter.

Printed on recycled paper ♲

*This book is dedicated to my father,*
*the late Thomas H. Beadles,*
*and my sons,*
*John Wade Beadles and the late Andrew Kent Beadles.*
*They loved the Cairo they knew.*

CONTENTS

## ILLUSTRATIONS

## Cairo, Illinois, Map Key

1. Alfred Baltimore's saloon/"house" (3815 Commercial Avenue)
2. St. Mary's Park (north of 28th Street and south of 33rd Street)
3. Cairo Ice & Coal Company (2600–2616 Commercial Avenue)
4. Coffman residence (420 26th Street)
5. Site of Pelley murder (alley between 25th and 26th Streets)
6. Lovie Green residence (2515 Poplar Street)
7. Cairo High School (Walnut and 25th Street)
8. Site of Salzner lynching (Sycamore Street and Washington Avenue)
9. Alexander County Courthouse (northeast corner of 20th Street and Washington Avenue)
10. St. Mary's Infirmary (2025 Walnut Street)
11. St. Joseph's Catholic Church (southeast corner of Cross and Walnut Streets)
12. Red Onion Saloon (1900 Washington Avenue)
13. Site of Salzner murder, Lancaster tenement (208 16th Street)
14. Post office and custom house (1400 Washington Avenue)
15. St. Michael's Episcopal Church Hall (418 14th Street)
16. Myrtle Stevenson's "house" (212 13th Street)
17. Cairo Police Headquarters (1111 Commercial Avenue)
18. Lewis home where Ida B. Wells stayed (612 12th Street)
19. Illinois National Guard Armory (1005–1007 Washington Avenue)
20. Cairo Baptist Church (1000 Poplar Street)
21. St. Patrick's Catholic Church (918 Washington Avenue)
22. Site of James lynching (8th Street and Commercial Avenue)
23. Alexander Club (701–703 Washington Avenue)
24. Pupkin Dry Goods Company (706 Commercial Avenue)
25. Episcopal Church of the Redeemer (northeast corner of Washington Avenue and 6th Street)
26. Site of Maloney purse snatching (Washington Avenue between 5th and 6th Streets)
27. Gus Bourgois's saloon (315 Ohio Street)
28. Illinois Central depot (2nd and Ohio Streets)
29. Halliday Hotel (2nd and Ohio Streets)

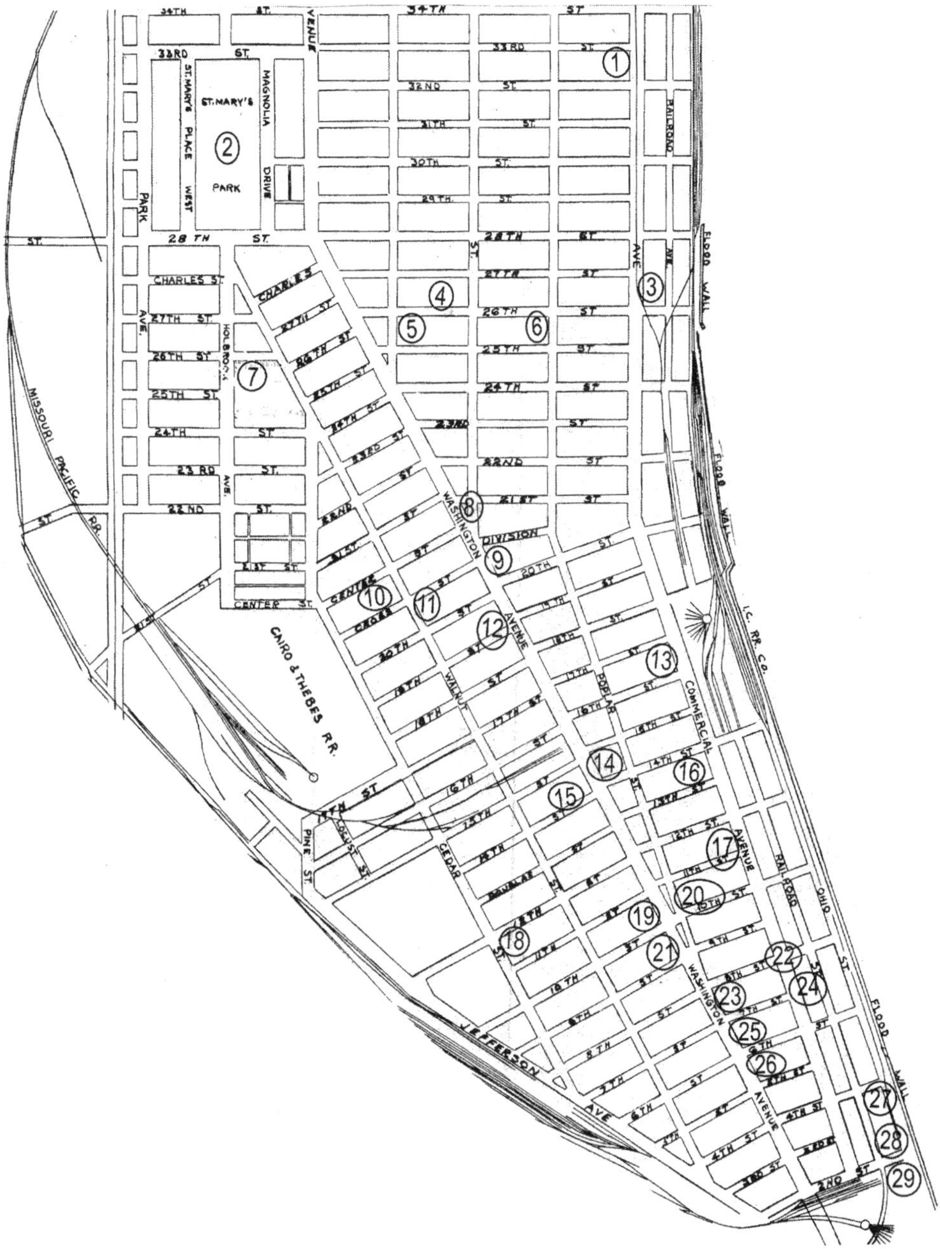
34TH ST
33RD ST
32ND ST
31TH ST
30TH ST
29TH ST
28TH ST
27TH ST
26TH ST
25TH ST
24TH ST
23RD
22ND ST
21ST ST
ST. MARY'S PARK
ST. MARY'S PLACE WEST
MAGNOLIA DRIVE
PARK AVE.
AVENUE
CHARLES ST.
HOLBROOK AVE.
CENTER ST.
CAIRO & THEBES RR.
MISSOURI PACIFIC RR.
WASHINGTON AVENUE
DIVISION ST
20TH
19TH
18TH
17TH ST
16TH
15TH
14TH ST
13TH ST
12TH ST.
11TH ST
10TH ST
9TH ST
8TH ST
7TH ST
6TH
5TH
4TH ST
3RD ST
2ND ST
POPLAR
WALNUT
CEDAR
LOCUST ST.
PINE ST.
COMMERCIAL AVENUE
RAILROAD
OHIO ST.
FLOOD WALL
I.C. RR. CO.
JEFFERSON AVE
1
2
3
4
5
6
7
8
9
10
11
12
13
14
15
16
17
18
19
20
21
22
23
24
25
26
27
28
29

# PREFACE

I began writing this book as a journal article designed for a state historical publication. My intent was to produce a minor but careful study of an incident that had happened in my old hometown during the Progressive Era and that I had heard about for most of my life. But I discovered that reviewers and editors of state historical journals wanted more than an article that might have some state and local historical interest. To these scholars, my work existed in a vacuum; thus, I began to consult several additional secondary sources so that I could provide background and place the story in historical context. This consultation certainly lengthened and broadened my study.

Changes in approach and perspective in my study also altered it from an effort in state and local history to one encompassing a growing body of work on American lynching in particular and American racism in general. As my study developed, the particular lynching I was describing, while still at the forefront of my work, now existed among many such violent acts. Indeed, 1909 and 1910 were a part of the era one scholar has called the "Age of Lynching."[1] Researching American lynching was necessary to my work, but it was an extremely unpleasant and depressing subject.[2]

Abhorrent and distressing as American lynching was, it occurred often in twentieth-century America. A double lynching occurred in Cairo, Illinois, in 1909, followed by an attempted lynching in 1910 and the killing of a city policeman by a county sheriff at the close of that year. These events and Cairo itself at the time are the focus of this work.

# ACKNOWLEDGMENTS

I'm sure writers usually think there are too many people to thank for the launching and completing of their work. I share this thought, but one must begin. The first person who told me about the lynching of Will "Froggie" James was the late Kenny Hendrix, my classmate at Cairo High School in 1959. The first person who told me about the killing of Sergeant Wilfred French by Sheriff Abner Bankson was the late Owen Evers, prominent Pulaski County educator and local historian. These gentlemen, then, started me on the trail that led me to learn more about a violent era in my old home, Cairo, Illinois.

My greatest thanks must go to my editors and my formatter. Jerri Pasborg, my first editor, has been correcting and shaping my writings for over fifty years. She rid my early manuscript of its grammatical errors and set it on a firm foundation toward publication.

My second editor, Darrel Dexter, met me the second time I visited Carbondale to do research at Southern Illinois University. His support from the very first was unconditional. Further, he acquainted me with numerous secondary and primary sources concerning the lynchings and murders of which I was unaware. Unasked, he continually did research he hoped would engender acceptance of my manuscript by publishers. Later, when he became an "official" editor, he became a rewriter and everything else one would want in an editor.

Miho Kuroiwa, my formatter and daughter-in-law, made my manuscript possible. Over a four-year period, she was constantly asked to add, subtract, and rearrange text. As an artist, she also found pictures, maps, and other illustrations for the work. When she could not find them, she often created them herself. She never complained that I or my potential publisher was asking too much. Indeed, she saved my manuscript in the beginning when I wiped out my first two chapters on my laptop. Fortunately, I had printed out the chapters, which she scanned back into my computer.

I will never be able to thank Jerri, Darrel, and Miho enough for all they have done. I will, however, not forget that without their efforts, there would have been no *Stained with Blood and Tears*.

Others who gave me great aid and encouragement should also be mentioned. Jak Tichenor, of radio station WSIU and a former Comprehensive Employment and Training Act (CETA) worker of mine in the 1970s, welcomed me with open arms when I came to Carbondale and got for me the parking passes at SIU that actually made it possible for a man in his seventies to make it from his rental car to the university library. He also told me to call Stace England, a musician and historian, who did everything he could to advance the manuscript, sending me photos and tips at every turn. Whenever my enthusiasm flagged, Stace was there to support me. Constant encouragement also came from my colleague and friend at the State University of New York, Geneseo, Professor Wayne Mahood. I don't remember how many revisions I sent him, but he read them all. His advice was always, "Don't give up and don't give in."

In Cairo, Monica Smith, town librarian, has continually helped me, Jerri, and Darrel with our work on *Stained with Blood and Tears*. We all enjoyed her professionalism and her love for and commitment to Cairo and the city's factual history. Preston Ewing, library board member, also aided me, especially with the absolutely necessary 1910 photo of the Cairo City Council and policemen, and guided me with long telephone conversations about Cairo history.

History as a field of study was constantly the concern of Dr. Karl Kageff, the retired editor in chief of Southern Illinois University Press, who over four years tried to shape my manuscript in a more scholarly direction. I thank him for his efforts and those of Barb Martin, who, at Saluki Publishing, started making the final preparations for the publication of *Stained with Blood and Tears*.

Other librarians who helped me immensely worked at Gwinnett County, Georgia, libraries, especially at the Hamilton Mill Branch, where I spent nearly every day for almost two years. No matter what I wanted, the librarians could find it. I can't count the times the Gwinnett people fixed the microfilm machine and printer as I read the pages of old newspapers and printed them. At the Abraham Lincoln Presidential Library in Springfield, Illinois, where I spent a few days, Jan Perone was extremely helpful and kept in touch, finally sending me vital pictures for the book.

I will always value the assistance of those named and unnamed who have helped me with this work.

# STAINED WITH BLOOD AND TEARS

# INTRODUCTION

## Cairo, Illinois, 1909–1910

Cairo, Illinois, the southernmost city in Illinois, had a population of about 14,000 in 1909. This was a sizable community for the time, and located between the mighty Mississippi and Ohio Rivers, Cairo was still growing.[1] The African American portion of the population was 37 percent in 1910, but in reality this is but an estimate, as there was a considerable "floating" population that came in and out of Cairo on a regular basis.[2] In a letter to the *New York Times*, W. L. Clanahan, a former Cairo newspaperman who had ascended in the realm of journalism to Joseph Pulitzer's *New York World*, pointed out that the estimated 5,000 African Americans in Cairo constituted 5 percent of all the black people in the state of Illinois. Clanahan also asserted that Cairo was probably the only town in the North with a true race problem.[3]

Racial problems in Cairo were intensified, according to Clanahan, because so many black "undesirables" "floated" in and out of Cairo from St. Louis, Cincinnati, Memphis, Vicksburg, and New Orleans, as Cairo was easily accessible by seven railroads and two great rivers.[4] Yet the river city's African American population enjoyed some privileges usually denied to black people elsewhere, even in Illinois, such as an all-black high school, which some claimed was the first of its kind in the United States; and African American justices of the peace, sheriff's deputies, aldermen, policemen, doctors, and clergymen.[5] Cairo's black community was unusually well organized for the time; by 1909 there were 200 identifiable African American organizations.[6] Black Cairo had developed considerable cohesion in the more than forty years after the community had been put in place by the Freedmen's Bureau, which planted large numbers of African American refugees from the war-torn South in the river city. The more established black Cairo, however, like white Cairo, did not welcome the transient population that moved so easily through the city.[7]

Besides this difficult-to-control floating population, there were other stresses on the river city. In the nineteenth century, Cairo had been one of the centers of the hardwood lumber industry in the Midwest with at least thirty-two lumber manufacturing facilities employing over 1,000 men. Wrought iron was the town's second leading industry in the 1800s, followed by grain.[8] Indeed, Wood Rittenhouse, the father of Maud Rittenhouse, whose diaries were published by Macmillan in 1939 and nationally read, tried to control the oats market in the 1880s from his grain silos around Cairo, which were worth millions.[9] Because of excellent transportation to and from Cairo, wholesale trade in groceries and hardware for the region tended to operate in the river city in the nineteenth century and into the twentieth.[10] By 1909–10, however, Cairo had become a center for the wholesale alcohol trade, as prohibition swept the American South and border states. Increasingly, the town's prosperity depended on shipping liquor and alcohol southward, as well as attracting large numbers of persons into the city for the retail alcohol business. Saloons, bars, wine rooms, and "dives" abounded in Cairo. In such establishments, as well as in their own "houses of ill fame," there was an extensive and notorious population of prostitutes. Their existence in Cairo was greatly corrupting, since their "business" was illegal. The police had to be paid off and the city council also placated with monies and privileges.

In his study of Cairo published in 1971, sociologist Herman R. Lantz of Southern Illinois University discussed how dependent the river city was on an economy of liquor and vice in 1909–10, especially for licenses for saloons and wholesale liquor establishments. Lantz also argued that Cairo had possibly the only true upper class in Southern Illinois.[11] Cairo was largely built in the second half of the nineteenth century; indeed, the approximately thirty blocks of buildings along broad Commercial Avenue were used for business until most were demolished in the twenty-first century.[12] By 1909–10, members of the Cairo upper class had acquired a great deal of this property, and much of their income was from rentals, including renting buildings for saloons and houses for prostitutes.[13]

Of course Lantz was not the only scholar to study Cairo in the twentieth and twenty-first centuries. Since the severe racial troubles of the 1960s and 1970s, Cairo, Illinois, has been written about extensively. A documentary film on the distressed town has even appeared. Scholarship, however, has not yet included a lengthy treatment of the Cairo double lynching of 1909 or the attempted lynching of 1910. The killing of a Cairo policeman by the sheriff of a neighboring county is so unknown historically that the victim's name has only recently been added to the honor roll of officers killed in the line of duty.[14]

Cairo's racial conflict in the 1960s and 1970s revealed a national crisis on a small scale; thus, almost naturally great attention was paid to the events. Here was seemingly unusual enmity between the races in an Illinois town and one that had long been notorious for racial conflict and other reasons. In 1909 and 1910, however, there were seemingly fewer reasons why Cairo should be discussed so often and at great length in the American press. After all, 1909 set a record for its time in the number of lynchings that occurred in that year. Cairo's double lynching was just one of about eighty others, and yet it attracted intense national attention.

This national press coverage and commentary on Cairo's double lynching became part of what student of American lynching Ashraf H. A. Rushdy called the "Discourse of Lynching" during what he also called the "Age of Lynching," from 1890 to 1940.[15] According to him, it was in those years that American lynching assumed its most brutal form, occurred most regularly, and became a gauge of that culture. Another scholar of America's racial culture, James W. Loewen, in his book *Sundown Towns: A Hidden Dimension of American Racism*, devotes considerable space to Cairo, Illinois, even though Cairo was definitely not a "sundown town," a community where permanent black residents were not permitted.[16] Echoing most of the national press coverage of the 1960s and 1970s, Loewen is critical of Cairo's white population during both the double lynching in 1909 and the attempted lynching in 1910.

In 1909–10, Cairo was seemingly an easy target for any criticism. Awash in alcohol and teeming with prostitutes, Cairo was regionally, if not nationally, known as a "wide-open" town—one that lacked a strict enforcement of laws, especially pertaining to alcohol, vice, and gambling—and suffered the consequent extremely bad publicity that such a status entailed. The national press, but especially in Chicago and the Ohio River valley, blasted Cairo for the river city's prostitutes, criminals, violence, and general lawlessness.[17] Civic leaders in the town at that time still, to some extent, harbored the dreams of Cairo's founders, which was that the city's location would ensure economic and population growth to rival that of St. Louis or Memphis, or at least that of nearby Paducah, Kentucky, or Evansville, Indiana. Those towns and cities, however, were attracting people from all classes and places, including foreign countries. Cairo, with its bad reputation for liquor, vice, and violence, usually drew distressed rural folk from Southern Illinois, Western Kentucky, and Southeast Missouri, as well as black refugees from the South, principally Tennessee and Mississippi.[18]

Of course this blend of desperately poor southern black people with rural whites, with all their prejudices and educational limitations, created considerable friction from the beginning. For example, some of the white Kentuckians who were living in Cairo in 1909–10 had been Night Riders in the Black Patch Tobacco Wars, which had reached a bloody climax in 1908 with attacks on African American farmers.[19] Others may have been involved in the Charleston, Missouri, lynching in 1910, where two black men were brutally killed.[20] Added to this was the fact that most of the white Kentuckians and Missourians who came to live in Cairo were Democrats and were not used to seeing politics often dominated by Republicans, especially ones whose most faithful voting bloc was black.[21]

Black refugees, as well as economically distressed whites, came to the river city looking for work.[22] Cairo, however, was in the midst of significant economic changes. River trade had made Cairo economically viable, especially the transfer trade across the Ohio and Mississippi Rivers. By 1909–10, however, a railroad bridge crossed the Ohio at Cairo and another crossed the Mississippi a few miles north at Thebes, Illinois, which meant no loading and unloading of cargoes at Cairo. Indeed, cargoes were steadily declining on the Ohio and Mississippi Rivers. The Mississippi carried cargoes of 1,332,855 tons in 1889, 1,244,175 tons in 1896, only 416,855 tons in 1906, and a mere 365,920 tons in 1908.[23] Cairo rivermen also found, to their dismay, that the mass of cotton, which had been shipped to Cairo in the nineteenth century by river and then on to the New England mills, was now going by rail—principally through Louisville or Cincinnati.[24]

The lumber industry was a major Cairo employer in 1909–10, paying relatively high wages, especially for black men, when compared to the porter and attendant jobs in the saloons.[25] Indeed, one of the defendants in Cairo's attempted lynching trial claimed he was transacting lumber business in a saloon the night of the riot.[26] The trees in southernmost Illinois, however, were being cut down rapidly. This continued until the Great Depression, when the remaining forests became more protected as part of the Shawnee National Forest. Unlike during the nineteenth century, great rafts of yellow pine from Georgia and Alabama and poplar from Tennessee no longer reached Cairo. The trees, like much other tonnage, now rode the rails through Cairo bound for another location.[27]

Cairo's economy remained dependent on the rivers. The Ohio and the Mississippi, however, were also a constant threat to the town. As recently as 2011, all 2,800 or so remaining people in Cairo were evacuated because the Ohio threatened to top a second seawall built in the 1950s to protect the town.[28] In 1909–10—as they were even at the town's incorporation in

1859—Cairo's civic leaders were begging first the Illinois Central Railroad and then the federal government for better flood protection. They got much of what they wanted in the 1910s and later in the 1950s, but the town still was not completely safe from its rivers. An industrialist would have to think long and hard about locating in Cairo. The town enjoyed excellent transportation by river and rail, but any investment might be wiped out by flooding at any time. Thus, Cairo had problems that were closely tied to its location between and the Ohio and the Mississippi in 1909–10. Flooding was feared constantly, and pumps had to be run during high water to keep "sipe water" from undermining and flooding the river city.

Cairo, Illinois, was an artificial creation in its beginning. Land speculators picked a spot on the map that seemed ideal for a city. They formed the Cairo City Property Trust hoping to lease—not sell—Cairo's land to various enterprises and persons. They also convinced the Illinois Central, which was building down from Chicago and up from the South, to protect Cairo with levees at the railroad's expense, so the trains could come to the bottom of Illinois with their shipments. A seawall was built after the disastrous floods of 1912–13, which had threatened Cairo with inundation and severely damaged every industry outside the protective barriers, including the jewel of Cairo industry, Sears Roebuck Illinois Lumber Manufacturing Plant. Any property outside the levees and the seawall was almost annually under threat of flooding. The very "land" on which Cairo rested was mostly sand pumped from the Ohio River.[29] Cairo has been fighting against two mighty rivers for almost 170 years.

It is to the credit of the Cairo City Property Trust and others that Cairo was ever established. Five years after the company was formed, Cairo was completely inundated by a flood in 1858, which was duly reported across the United States by the country's newspapers.[30] The establishment of the Illinois Central Railroad with federal government help saved the company and the town. Fifty years later, when Cairo experienced the double lynching of 1909, another wave of terrible publicity bore down on the river city. Reporters from major papers nationwide, wire service men, and writers from many places descended on Cairo. They found not only what appeared to be an unrepentant town but a city now flooded with alcohol, teeming with prostitutes, "wide-open" gambling, and scores of black people, who seemed to be quite independent when compared with the general population of African Americans. The journalists also found municipal corruption, which should not have shocked them. The year 1909 was, after all, right in the middle of the Progressive Era—a time when Lincoln Steffens wrote *The Shame of the Cities*.[31] Yet many of the journalists and other writers *were* shocked by the river city, or pretended to be. From coast to coast, the media printed lurid stories not only of the double lynching but also about Cairo's many problems and its population, black and white.

At the time of the Cairo tragedies of 1909–10, the relations between black and white Americans were growing increasingly strained. According to some historians, white racism in the North was becoming much more pronounced in the time period during which Cairo's lynching and attempted lynching took place.[32] Indeed, a respected scholar on race in America refers to the years between 1890 and 1940 as the nadir of race relations in the history of the United States.[33] After William English Walling interviewed the rioters who participated in the Springfield, Illinois, lynchings and riots of 1908, he found that most of them had no regrets about their actions, and he also detected virulent racism sweeping across the Midwest with whites of all classes expressing enmity toward blacks.[34] At the time of the Cairo double lynching, the *Chicago Tribune* warned that race hatred was growing in the North, pointing out that Ohio black men were being treated exactly as they were in the South. The *Tribune* then compared Cairo to Springfield, saying that both cities had produced "insane and inhuman mobs."[35] Finally, one of the most respected historians of American lynching, Christopher Waldrep, stated that he found little difference in his research as to the way northern and southern newspapers covered lynching.[36]

Even into the twenty-first century, the Land of Lincoln had at least 108 "sundown towns," where no black people were allowed after sunset.[37] White Cairo did not treat black Cairo particularly well in 1909–10 and throughout the twentieth century, but at least black people were not prevented from living there. Here is where racism became a serious problem for Cairo.

Saul Alinsky, a pioneer community organizer and one of the most progressive and radical figures of the twentieth century, recognized that white people in America became extremely agitated if more than 5 percent of their neighborhood became African American.[38] In his efforts with Monsignor John Egan to "stabilize" Chicago's southwest side, Alinsky tried to somehow limit the influx of black people so that they would constitute only 5 percent of the neighborhood.[39] This failed, and in the end southwest Chicago was very much African American.

If the 5 percent population threshold were applied to Cairo, Illinois, in 1909–10, then there was already too high a percentage of black people in town for white comfort. Among the uncomfortable whites was Edward W. Thielecke, the editor of Cairo's leading daily, the *Cairo Bulletin*. As an opinion leader and town booster, Thielecke found Cairo's racial composition very inconvenient. He believed Cairo would be better off without the town's African Americans but never called for "ethnic cleansing," or driving black people out of Cairo. Indeed, he ridiculed press reports of such a thing possibly happening in the river city.[40] He was highly offended, however, by black political power in Cairo and the halting steps black Cairo had made toward equality. He repeatedly warned that no outside white people would want to live in Cairo because there were so many blacks, and bad ones at that.[41]

Thielecke saw Cairo and Alexander County politics as all tied up with race. In an exposé in the *Cairo Bulletin*, he revealed that the local Republican Party was divided into two factions. He believed one faction consisted of Cairo's mayor and the former county sheriff. The other faction was made up of the new county sheriff, the representative in the U.S. Congress from Cairo, and the circuit judge.[42] According to Thielecke, Cairo "negroes," especially a "vicious element" of that race, constituted the deciding factor in any contest between local Republican factions, and most of their votes were bought during an election.

> *The vicious negro has been the primary cause of all of Cairo's trouble. . . . He has found Cairo a pleasant place to live, and has grown bold under this guardianship given to him by the city authorities, with the evident understanding that he must make himself felt in the right way on election day.*[43]

Thus, according to one of Cairo's two daily newspapers, a "vicious negro" element was the basis of "trouble" in town, and since that element dominated at least one faction of the Republican Party in the city and county, the only solution for white Cairoites was to vote the Democratic ticket, especially with respect to any law enforcement officer, such as the sheriff or state's attorney.[44] In Cairo, therefore, as in much of the United States in the early part of the twentieth century, the Democrats became the white man's party. There was also a further split ethnically in the river city in 1909–10. During the mid-nineteenth century, Cairo had attracted numbers of Irish and German immigrants. In 1909–10, the Irish Catholics were almost solidly Democrats, while the Germans, Catholic and Lutheran alike, were more likely to be Republicans.

Political conflict aside, as black and white Republicans struggled with white Democrats and as Irish Americans competed with German Americans,

Cairo was still growing in population, as the 1910 and 1920 censuses would attest. Cairo, however, had developed a very bad reputation because of the town's alcohol economy, which seemed to be spreading the liquor poison southward, especially into Kentucky and Tennessee. There stood Cairo, with access to every possible rail and steamboat line, just north of what was becoming the "driest" part of America, waiting to send the town's considerable alcohol resources to southern bootleggers and citizens alike.[45] Cairo also apparently was ready to accommodate thousands of men, southern or northern, with the river city's scores of prostitutes.[46] In the Progressive Era, therefore, it was hard for other Americans to view Cairo positively. Instead of getting "drier," Cairo stayed defiantly soaked with alcohol. Instead of getting "cleaner," Cairo remained "dirty," filled with prostitutes and their customers.

Worse than the alcohol and sex trade, however, was the violence in the river city. Cairo's mayor in 1909, George Parsons, admitted to the *New York Times* that one would be "tolerably safe" committing murder in the town.[47] Parsons, a native of Kennebunkport, Maine, graduate from Harvard University in 1876, and a banker in Cairo, was first elected mayor in 1905. A couple of days after Parsons's quotation appeared in the *Times*, an editorial in the New York newspaper charged that Cairo people "have been inclined to think the killing of human beings a thing of no great moment."[48] Former Cairo newsman W. L. Clanahan, whose writings appeared in the *New York Times* in November 1909, charged that murders by either white or black men were "alarmingly frequent," with the killer escaping across one of the rivers to Kentucky or Missouri.[49] Harry Eichoff, a railroad worker in Cairo, told a Cairo chronicler in 1909 how one Sunday morning on the way to work he saw three dead bodies in a four-block area, one a woman with her throat cut. Eichoff also told about bartenders taking out life insurance on railroad section hands and riverboat workers without their knowledge, which was permitted at the time, and then urging the hands to get into barroom fights or seeing that the rivermen ended up in the Ohio when they were dead drunk.[50] Even if Eichoff was exaggerating to shock a reporter writing about Cairo, this is a chilling portrait of the river city during the first decade of the twentieth century. There seemed to be general agreement among Cairo officials, the national and local press, and ordinary citizens that violence to the point of frequent homicide was rife in Cairo.[51] And, things were about to get worse, as some Cairoites developed their own solution to perceived violence and racial problems through lynching.[52]

## Lynching and White Supremacy in America and in Cairo, Illinois

Statistics on lynching in America are notoriously unreliable. One of the foremost scholars of lynching, Christopher Waldrep, even came to the conclusion that "lynching" cannot be defined.[53] Most students of this horrifying practice that will be forever associated with the history of the United States believe the illegal murder of people by hanging and other means was probably most prevalent during Reconstruction.[54] Such scholars and statisticians also usually agree that American lynching remained generally common through the 1880s and 1890s before starting to decline somewhat after 1900.[55] Yet in 1908 there was a dramatic rise in recorded lynchings in the United States, undoubtedly helped by several lynchings in the northern part of the country, including the traumatic killings in Springfield, Illinois, during the epic race riot in Abraham Lincoln's hometown.[56]

The *New York Age*, an influential black newspaper, which had been edited and published until 1907 by the famous civil rights leader Timothy Thomas Fortune, asserted that there were eighty-seven American lynchings in 1909, the year that a double lynching occurred in Cairo.[57] Another widely used source states that eighty-two people were lynched that year.[58] Only fifty miles south of Cairo was Fulton, Kentucky, whose county was tied for twenty-fifth place for having the most lynchings in the United States between 1877 and 1950.[59] No wonder Cairo newspapers attempted to blame the town's own double lynching on Kentuckians. No doubt there were numerous Kentuckians in Cairo's lynch mob in 1909 as spectators and "mobbers," if not leaders.[60] Obion County, Tennessee, had as many lynchings from 1877 to 1950 as Fulton County, Kentucky. It was from this county, as well as others in west Tennessee, that a noticeable number of black people had migrated to Cairo, including a well-known police officer.[61]

Cairo, therefore, was near border state counties where lynching was prevalent, and there were probably a number of white migrants and black refugees in the river city from those counties. Such whites had belonged to a society that easily practiced lynching, and the African Americans had firsthand knowledge of the effects of the brutal vigilantism upon their people.

According to the latest study of lynching in the South and earlier works, white supremacy was the basic motivation for lynching in America during the "Age of Lynching."[62] White supremacy, however, was interpreted differently in various places. In the Deep South, according to Ida B. Wells, white supremacy meant black people had no rights that the law would enforce.[63] In 1950s Osceola, Arkansas, where a white grandfather might take his grandson to check on his "cotton land," white supremacy meant that black people would literally jump off the sidewalks to clear the way for an elderly white man and a young white boy. In Reevesville, South Carolina, in 1904, the consequences of white supremacy led to a black man being lynched for knocking on the door of a white woman's house.[64] What could white supremacy have meant in 1909 Cairo, and what was the lynching of a black man in that year supposed to further in that realm?

At the turn of the twentieth century, there was a "rough accommodation" between whites and blacks in Cairo. Black and white families lived in the same neighborhoods and in the same buildings. Black people could attend white-owned theaters, stay in "white" hotels, and eat in "white" restaurants and drink in saloons. Black professionals worked in Cairo, and blacks had been elected to the city council. There was also an African American middle class of postal workers, teachers, and clergy.[65] Additionally, racially mixed marriages were not unheard of, with black husbands and white wives.[66]

Yet, white Cairo was richer than black Cairo, with some leading citizens extremely well off. The mayor and the police chief were white, as were the majority of the city councilmen. In Cairo could be found the usual American pattern of white dominance and black subordination. White teachers earned more than black teachers, and the schools and churches were segregated. Worst of all in some minds, the purity of the white race was being compromised in Cairo—white females had black lovers and husbands.[67] Racial purity leagues thus formed in the river city.[68]

The aim of the racial purity leagues in Cairo and elsewhere was to prevent interracial sex and marriage between black men and white women. The best means for achieving this "racial purity" was widely believed to be racial segregation. Under segregation or "Jim Crow," whites and blacks were kept as separate as possible; white women especially were to have no social contact with black men. In Cairo, however, there were examples of white women who were married to black men and of African American men who apparently thought little of accosting white women in town.[69]

The white people in Cairo who were concerned with matters of race and "racial purity" and who probably made up the vast majority of the town population in 1909–10 had sufficient reasons for fearing interracial sex and its consequences. The most extreme form of interracial sex was the rape of white females by black males. In Cairo in 1909, a white woman was raped and murdered, and almost all sources agreed the assault was by a black man or men.[70] This rape and murder fed into the "rape myth" that was sweeping America in the early years of the twentieth century, which broadcast the idea that the only way to protect white "girls" from rape was to lynch the rapacious black "fiends," "brutes," and "beasts."[71]

The southern lecturer and writer Rebecca Latimer Felton declared, "If it needs lynching to protect a woman's dearest possession . . . I say 'lynch' a thousand times a week if necessary."[72] U.S. senator Ben "Pitchfork" Tillman of South Carolina said that he would rather have one of his virgin daughters killed by a wild beast "than to have her crawl to me and tell me the horrid story that she had been robbed of her jewel of womanhood by a black fiend."[73] The rape of a Cairo store clerk named Anna Pelley in 1909 was a fact; she had been sexually assaulted.[74] Was the lynching of her accused rapist and murderer, a black man named Will "Froggie" James, designed to give a graphic demonstration to black Cairo that contact between the races, especially with regard to females and males, was now to be severely limited? We do know that by 1915 Cairo was as rigidly segregated as any town in the North, or probably in the border states.[75] Black Cairo withdrew protectively into itself and diminished, as at least 1,700 African Americans left the river city between 1910 and 1920.[76]

Many of the African American Cairoites who fled by 1920—numbers of whom were from families who had been settled in the town since the 1860s—may have been trying to escape a town where their legal and political rights were fast eroding. Even some of the white people in Cairo, who were firmly convinced that Will James was guilty of rape and murder, began to admit that the case against him was circumstantial in a sense.[77] The problem with lynch law was that the victim never received a trial where guilt was proven beyond a reasonable doubt. In his pioneering study of American lynching, Arthur F. Raper found that on numerous occasions the wrong suspect was killed.[78] Black people in Cairo in 1909 and into 1910 could count on reasonably fair treatment in the courts, sometimes before magistrates of their own race.[79] In 1910, however, the Democrats in Cairo and Alexander County swept into power. All black deputy sheriffs were removed from their positions, and no new African American justices of the peace were appointed.[80] The Democrats remained in power for almost ten years, and their rallying cry was to remember Anna Pelley's rape and murder at the hands of the "brute" Will "Froggie" James and to vote as white citizens for their community for the sake of their wives and daughters.[81]

For these white wives and daughters to be safely separated from the likes of Will James and to be free of the temptation provided by more appealing

African Americans, the Alexander County Democrats made changes in the county courts and the courthouse. Water fountains became separate, as did seating both inside and outside courtrooms. Almost no black men were chosen for juries.[82] Separate never meant equal in America, and many if not most black people in Cairo who had been struggling for a rough kind of racial equality must have realized that their condition had worsened materially on Election Day 1910. White Cairoites, and especially white women, were now urged to view the typical black Cairo male as Will "Froggie" James, not as the African American doctor or councilman or polite patrolman or postal clerk whom they had met previously almost daily.

Alexander County, Illinois, was ensuring white supremacy, at least the segregationist aspects of the concept. The city of Cairo would soon follow the county. In 1913 Cairo adopted the commission form of government. Cairo added a twist to this political system, however: all four commissioners and the mayor would be elected at large. If white people voted as a bloc, as they apparently did for the next seventy years, there would be no black people on the city council.[83] During those seventy years, Cairo ranged between 20 percent and 49 percent African American, yet they had no political representation.[84] Thus, Cairo's black citizens could not stop the local ordinances legalizing stringent segregation and ensuring racial separation and hopefully reserving white women for white men only. Now everything was segregated—schools, parks, streetcars, public restrooms, hotels, restaurants, swimming pools—all public accommodations.

If the Will James lynching was part of the process of bringing what one author has called "virulent segregation" to Cairo, that would not be surprising, since segregation and lynching were intimately tied together in 1909–10. In 1905 there were sixty-two lynchings in the United States; the annual average for American lynchings from 1910 to 1919 was also sixty-two.[85] By 1923, however, the number of lynchings had markedly decreased. Various theories try to explain why American lynching declined, but scholars still disagree. Some of the most prevalent notions are that in the 1920s and 1930s, southern elites realized that lynching was bringing unwelcome attention to the way of life in the American South and that it must be curbed before the North and West acted to impose legal controls on Dixie. Some scholars see southern urbanization in the 1920s and 1930s and into the 1940s as the underlying cause for less lynching in America, believing lynching was primarily a rural phenomenon. Others see World War I and its aftermath as the cause for a decrease in the act. As a result of the war, poorly trained and poorly armed state militias became better trained and much better armed National Guard divisions. When the military was called out, lynchings were less likely. Also, after 1919 and the terrible race riots and lynchings of that "Red Summer," southern newspapers began to denounce lynching.[86] A respected student of lynching in American society, Michael J. Pfeifer, largely attributes lynching's decline from the 1920s and beyond to the states' increase in capital punishment, which continued at a high level well into the 1940s.[87]

Cairo, Illinois, had only the one night and morning of lynching in November 1909, although in February 1910 the river city experienced an attempted lynching. Both a black man and a white man were killed that November, but it was the black man's lynching that was ever after associated with the Cairo tragedy of 1909. On the night of November 8, 1909, Anna Pelley, a sales clerk working in Cairo, was raped and murdered. On November 11, 1909, a black man named Will "Froggie" James was lynched for the assault and murder. Those three days may have been the most tragic of the many tragic days in the history of Cairo.

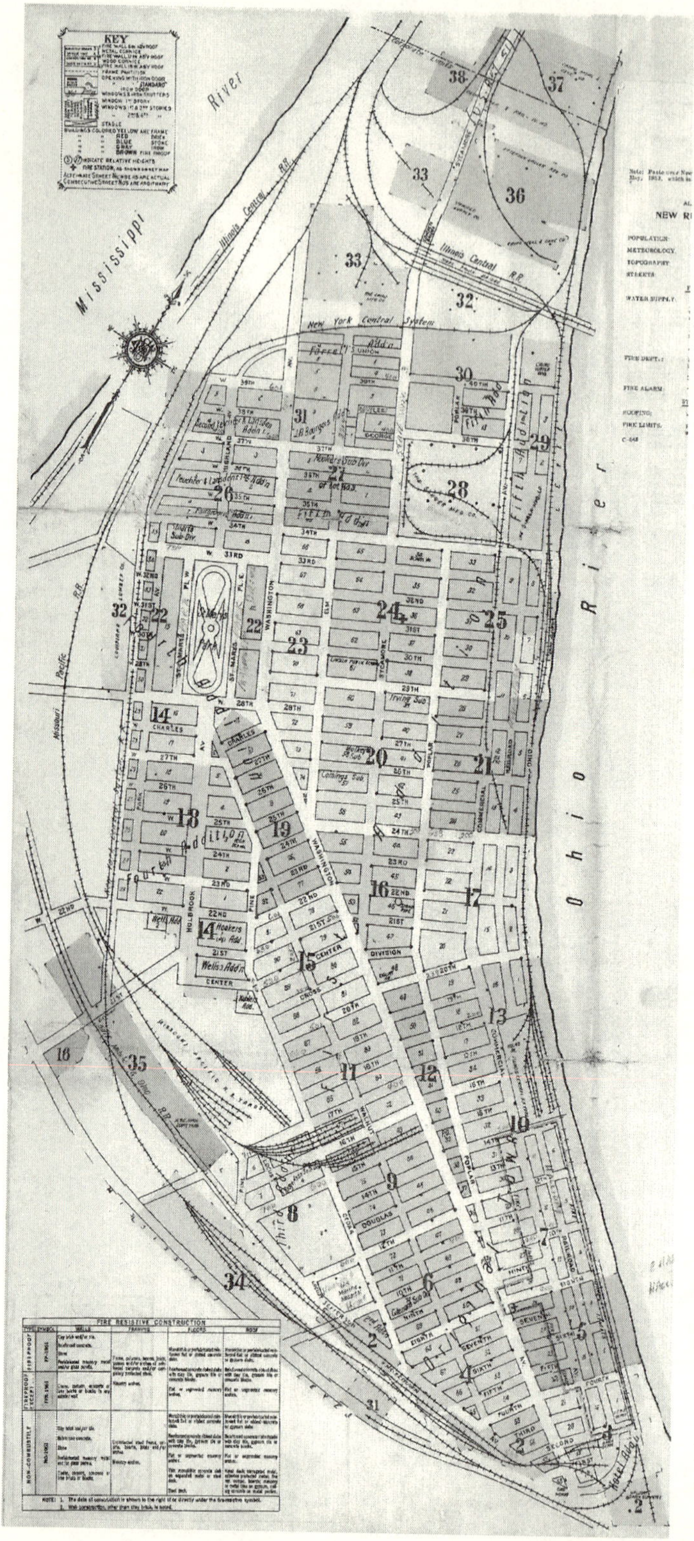


Insurance map drawn in July 1914 by the Sanborn Map Company showing the city just five years after the Pelley murder. Geospatial Resources Collection, Morris Library, Southern Illinois University, Carbondale.

CHAPTER ONE

# ANNA PELLEY'S LIFE AND DEATH

Anna Pelley was only twenty-four years old at the time of her tragic death. She was the youngest of eleven children of Joseph Pelley, an Irish immigrant, and Mary Margaret Frances Anders, a native of North Carolina. Anna's parents had met in North Carolina, married there after Joseph's service in the Confederate army, and settled in Anna, Illinois, a small community in Union County along the Illinois Central, about 1872.[1] Joseph had been a farmer near Hendersonville, North Carolina, and in Illinois he supported his family by keeping a garden and selling its produce. His daughter Anna was born January 16, 1886, in the town of Anna, where she attended school and spent all of her young life until her removal to Cairo in 1907. She was described as "a young lady of a sweet disposition and queenly appearance, with large black eyes and an abundance of beautiful black hair that was the admiration of all her friends."[2]

Anna Pelley, or "Annie," as she was also known, was in many ways an extraordinary woman for her time. Although both of her parents were illiterate, she was a high school graduate and while in school was active in extracurricular activities, even playing on the girls' basketball team. She was competitive and athletic, and a sports reporter noted that in a game with the rival Carbondale team, she was one of only two players from Anna who scored.[3] Most extraordinary, however, especially for a young Catholic woman, was Anna Pelley's involvement with the largely Protestant Woman's Christian Temperance Union (WCTU), primarily focused on prohibition. Three years before her death, Anna Pelley submitted a story to the WCTU about a young Irish American immigrant named "Robbie" who was enticed into underage drinking by an evil saloon owner.[4] The story won Anna a silver medal from the WCTU. She became known at least as far north as Chicago for her anti-saloon work, and the *Daily Herald* of one of that city's suburbs stated after her death that she was "well known in her home city as an earnest and concerned Christian, an active worker in the temperance cause, a prominent member of the WCTU, and the holder of a series of oratorical awards, including a diamond medal in the White Ribbon series of public contests."[5] Indeed, Miss Pelley was prominent enough in the WCTU that in December 1909, under the direction of the state president of the organization, memorials for her were held throughout Illinois.

One of Anna's brothers, Joe Pelley, was known to frequent saloons and even owned a tavern in Kelso, Missouri, in 1910, but it is not clear what role alcohol abuse might have played in her own Irish American family.[6] Regardless of the cause, something motivated Anna to become a WCTU crusader. In whatever ways Anna Pelley differed from the rest of her seven surviving brothers and sisters, she was obviously an integral and beloved part of her large family. After her parents died, she went to live with an older sister and brother-in-law, Kathryn "Kate" and John M. Coffman, a railroad worker, who lived at 420 26th Street in Cairo. As evidence of her commitment to keep the memory of her beloved sister alive, Kate Coffman

Images from the November 10, 1909 (*above*), and November 12, 1909 (*right*), issues of the *St. Louis Post-Dispatch*. Anna Pelley was pictured in many national newspapers after her murder.

named the child born to her on July 26, 1910, Anna Pelley Coffman in honor of Anna.[7]

Anna Pelley's large family could not shield her from all danger, and her short life ended violently on November 8, 1909. After leaving work at Pupkin Dry Goods Company at 706 Commercial Avenue, where she was a clerk or shopgirl, Anna stopped to talk briefly with her friend Ella Dolan.[8] She then boarded a streetcar at 14th Street and Washington Avenue, where she was recognized by the conductor, Robert Dainsworth, and by Alexander Wilson, the Alexander County state's attorney.[9] When the streetcar stopped at 28th and Elm Streets, it had been raining and was already getting dark. Elm Street was not her usual stop, but the sidewalks on that street, although darker, were better, and she wanted to avoid the mud. Anna left the trolley and apparently walked down Elm Street to 26th, where Judge W. S. Dewey resided, and then headed for the Coffman house, where she lived, just a few blocks away. She wore a hat and was carrying an umbrella, her alligator purse, ten yards of red cloth, a dress pattern, and a postcard.[10] Seemingly heading home in the dark on a rainy night, Anna Pelley was attacked by one or two men and apparently broke her umbrella defending herself, because its handle flew off into the nearby yard of the residence of Harry Lipe at 424 26th Street. It was believed at the time that Anna Pelley's assailant or assailants gagged her and then dragged her to the alley between

One of the few remaining structures on Commercial Avenue in Cairo is the site of what was once Pupkin Dry Goods Company. The advertisement comes from the 1908–9 Cairo city directory. Photo by Darrel Dexter.

Pupkin Dry Goods Co., EXCLUSIVENESS, QUALITY, DRESS GOODS, TRIMMINGS, NOTIONS.
CAIRO, 706 Commercial Avenue, ILL.

While walking along 26th Street in front of a row of cottages, Anna Pelley was attacked. The cottages are still there although now abandoned. Photo by Darrel Dexter.

25th and 26th Streets, behind the home of George E. Atcher, the city health officer, at 438 25th Street.[11]

The county coroner, Dr. James McGriffen McManus, reported that there was no question that she had been raped.[12] Marks on the ground apparently showed that she had been dragged seventy-five feet around the corner, where she was assaulted and murdered. Anna's clothing was torn to shreds.[13] The marks from the fingers that strangled her were clearly evident on her throat.[14]

The Coffmans were worried when Anna did not come home, because she usually called when she would be out overnight. It was not until about eight o'clock the next morning that Anna Pelley's body was discovered. A four-year-old child named Katherine Boren, living at 433 25th Street, was going to her grandfather's house through the alley, but she came back home, frightened by something she had seen there. An older child was sent with the little one, and both returned saying, "Papa, there's someone dead out there."[15] "Papa," W. C. Boren, told the mail carrier, Thomas P. Carraher, who then phoned in the discovery to the police. When they arrived, the police saw that Anna Pelley's body was already rigid and beside her was a broken umbrella. The umbrella handle was found only two doors from

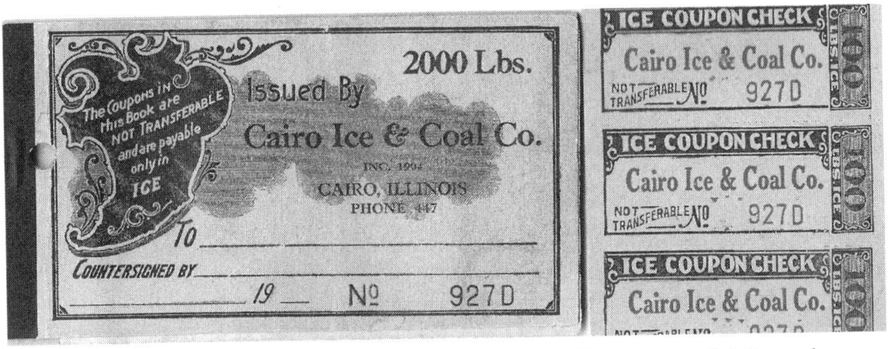


Will "Froggie" James worked for the Cairo Ice & Coal Company and delivered ice to the Coffman house, where Anna Pelley resided. Regular ice customers, like the Coffmans, purchased coupon books like the one pictured here. From the collection of Darrel Dexter.

the Coffman home, where she was first attacked.[16] The policeman on the scene, William Henry French, thought he recognized the body and went to the Coffman home and requested Mrs. Coffman to come to the alley to see if she knew the woman. She did not at first suspect it would be Anna, but "her shock was great when she recognized in the dead and bruised form that of her sister."[17]

The November 12, 1909, *St. Louis Post-Dispatch* printed a photograph of the alley where Anna Pelley was murdered and one of William James, the supposed murderer. The photograph on the right shows how the alley looks today.

Anna Pelley's nightmare and suffering is often overshadowed by the more popularly known and gruesome story of the lynching that followed. Yet the streets of Cairo in 1909 were not safe for this young woman walking home from work who was sexually assaulted and murdered only two doors away from her own home. The citizens of Cairo would grapple for years over the question of who should share in the blame and guilt over the loss of Anna's life. Was it only her attacker or attackers who were to blame, or did the city leaders, police officers, lawyers, politicians, businessmen, and all citizens share the responsibility? In the meantime, outrage and fear spread quickly throughout the communities in Cairo as the story of the assault and murder swept over the town.

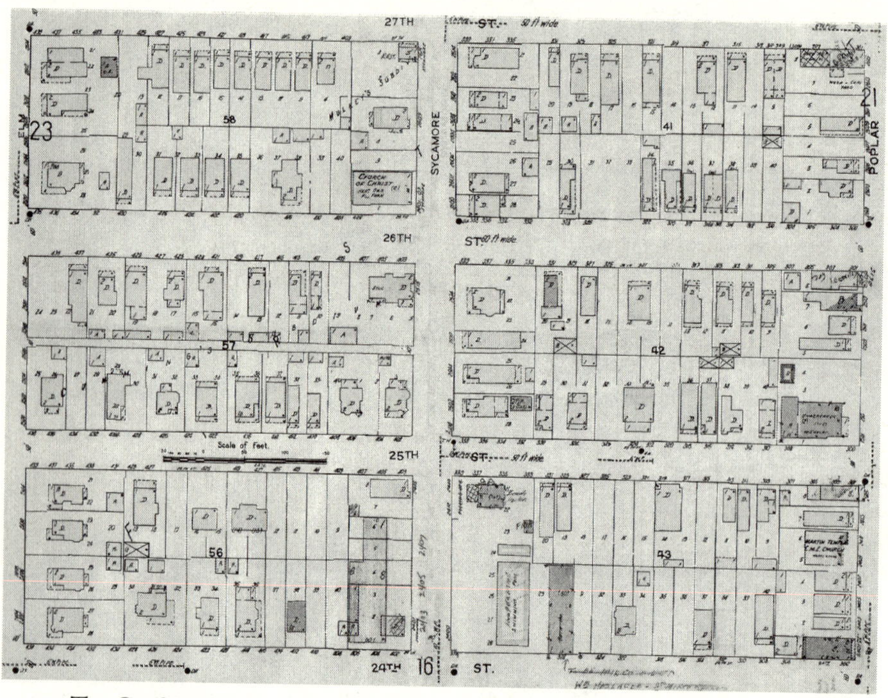


The Coffman residence, the site of the attack of Anna Pelley, the alley where she was murdered, and the Lovie Green home at 2515 Poplar can be found on this 1914 Cairo city map by the Sanborn Map Company. Geospatial Resources Collection, Morris Library, Southern Illinois University, Carbondale.

CHAPTER TWO

# THE CRIME INVESTIGATION

In Anna Pelley's mouth was a dirty cloth that had been stuffed inside so tightly that the police had some difficulty removing it. This gag was given in the afternoon to a pair of George Rufus Riley's bloodhounds that had been brought in from Wickliffe, Kentucky, a town across the Ohio River from Cairo. The dogs got a scent and led the police to a dwelling variously described as a "shack" and a "ramshackled house."[1] The dwelling was kept by Lovie Green, an African American woman who was suspected of operating a house of prostitution there. "Mr. Riley's Wickliffe dogs" were taken back to the crime scene and repeated their chase to the same house at 2515 Poplar Street, "a tenement house occupied by several black families."[2]

Jailer Melchor Lutz (*second from left*) and Cairo police chief Martin S. Egan (*far right*) with bloodhounds used to help find Anna Pelley's killer. From the author's private collection.

Sheriff George W. Cupp arrived from Charleston, Missouri, and his dogs made two more trips to the exact same place.[3]

More bloodhounds were used—those of William Kenner of Harrisburg, Illinois. The dogs also followed the scent to 2515 Poplar, Lovie Green's dwelling. That made five times in all that dogs went to the same house.[4] This place was sometimes home to three men—William (usually called "Will" or "Froggie") James, Arthur Alexander, and Ed Thomas (also known as Will Thomas).[5] All three were brought in by the Cairo police for questioning.

The first two times the bloodhounds came to the tenement house, it was locked. On the third trip, an unidentified "negro woman" brought Cairo police chief Martin Stephen Egan a key and entered the dwelling. Only one suspicious article was found at first—a muddy coat, which was seized as evidence. The renter of the property, Lovie Green—described by the *Cairo Bulletin* as "a negress of bad repute"—was found in a shed by two Cairo police officers. She was discovered washing a piece of cloth similar to the gag in Anna Pelley's mouth, which was seized by Chief Egan. Lovie Green was arrested, as had been "her lover," Will "Froggie" James.[6]

Altogether there were now six people in Cairo police custody, four of whom had at some time been residents of the dwelling at 2515 Poplar Street: the three men—Alexander, James, and Thomas, who were described in the local press as "rounders" and, concerning Alexander at least, as "bearing a bad reputation";[7] two women, Lovie Green and Georgia Cooper, sometimes known as Catherine Cooper; and Cooper's twelve-year-old son, James Drain. Most suspicion focused on Will "Froggie" James, especially when he was put in a cell at police headquarters and bloodhounds were brought in. The animals became frenzied, barking furiously and leaping in the air around James's cell.[8] Earlier bloodhounds had followed a trail from Lovie Green's dwelling to the Cairo Ice & Coal Company at 2600 Commercial, where James worked, and to Paul Cody's saloon at 2515 Commercial, where James was located and arrested at 5 p.m. on November 9, 1909, by Cairo police officer James Casey.

"Froggie" James is variously described in accounts at the time as unusually large, muscular, and powerful.[9] James was only 5'4½", but made strong by his job of shoveling coal and lifting heavy blocks of ice, he could have overpowered and assaulted Anna Pelley, who weighed 140 pounds. Will James was illiterate and moved around frequently. He was in Fort Wayne, Indiana, working construction a few months before Anna Pelley's murder and seems to have come in and out of Cairo over a period of several years.[10] James was not in much trouble in town before the Pelley murder but yet was always considered a "bad man" by the police.[11] When the police questioned

A photograph of Will "Froggie" James was taken about 1907. It was widely published in newspapers after his lynching. From the author's private collection.

James, it was determined that he knew Anna Pelley, having delivered ice to the Coffman house daily during the summer. Because of his ice deliveries, it was also revealed that James was aware that Anna usually arrived home at about 6:30 p.m., which was after dark in Southern Illinois in November.[12]

At the time of his arrest, James's landlady of record was Georgia Cooper, now in custody, of 211 30th Street. She told police that on the night of the crime, James came home from work around 6 p.m., changed his clothes because they were wet, left, and did not return until at least 8 p.m.[13] Being "sweated" by the police, James could not account for his whereabouts during the time the crime was committed. Lovie Green, the other woman in custody with Will James, seemed to be trying to protect him, but under interrogation by Cairo's police chief, the county coroner, and state's attorney, her story greatly disagreed with that of James.[14]

Besides the behavior of the bloodhounds, which was amazingly consistent, the strongest piece of physical evidence against James was the piece of cloth used to gag Anna Pelley. In the minds of the Cairo press, "there is no question at all that it is identically the same quality of cloth as was the piece of cloth found in possession of the negro woman with whom he was stopping."[15] Testimony from James Drain, Georgia Cooper's young son also taken into custody, additionally revealed that "Froggie" James used such a piece of cloth as a handkerchief.

In questioning Will James, State's Attorney Alexander Wilson was most suspicious because of James's appearance and apparent fatigue.

> *The negro showed every evidence of having spent a wakeful night. He answered the questions asked him in a hesitating manner, yawning at every answer he made. "You seem to be sleepy," said State's Attorney Wilson. "Naw, I slep all last night," was the reply. "Are your eyes always red when you sleep all night?" asked the attorney. "My eyes ain't red, is dey?" said the negro. Yet his eyes were badly blood shot—a sure symptom of sleeplessness and unusual excitement.*[16]

Among the other men arrested with James, Ed Thomas, also known as Will, was hardly referenced after the news of his custody was reported.[17] Arthur Alexander is more prominently mentioned. Like James, Alexander worked as a teamster—for the Scudder-Gale-Warren Company—and his reputation with the Cairo police was also negative. Alexander was taken into custody because he had lived at the Poplar Street address where the bloodhounds went five times the day the body of Anna Pelley was found. In fact, 2515 Poplar is listed as the residence of George and Callie Alexander and their children, including Arthur Alexander, in the 1908–9 Cairo city directory. By the time of Anna Pelley's murder, Alexander's parents and siblings were living elsewhere, but he occasionally stayed at the same house, now kept by Lovie Green. Under questioning, Arthur Alexander claimed that he had not been at 2515 Poplar for a couple of weeks. Alibis were provided for Alexander by one of his little sisters and by Ada Ross, the wife of a local pimp, Dave Ross.[18] Rather strangely for that time, this was enough for Arthur Alexander to be released by the Cairo police.

With Alexander released, Will "Froggie" James became the chief suspect in Anna Pelley's death. Indeed, the *Cairo Evening Citizen* published an article with the title "Searching for Evidence against Will James."[19] Crowds began to form in Cairo, the first at Lovie Green's dwelling on Poplar Street. A man no one recognized stepped forward and repeated the story of the crime. He then offered to head a "crowd" to go to jail and hang "the negro" James.[20] More discussion followed and someone called, "Come on boys." In an instant everyone in the crowd responded, and they ran down Sycamore Street toward the county courthouse. Upon reaching it, the men talked more, discussing whether James was there or in the city jail. When it was determined he was in the city jail, the crowd took off for police headquarters at 1111 Commercial.[21]

By the time the crowd reached the police station, it numbered fully a thousand persons. Now a mob, the members roared in unison for the police to hand Will James over to them. A crush of men went into the jail and strained its main door. At that point, Chief Egan and a squad of policemen fought their way through the crowd to the steps of police headquarters. After several attempts, the chief made himself heard, pleading with the mob and saying that the police might not have the right man. Egan warned that it would be a grave mistake to do violence to an innocent person. Seeing a man in the mob wearing a mask, Egan ripped it off, and the individual ran away. Chief Egan then went into the police station for some time, but the chance of a lynching seemed to him to be subsiding, so he departed in the early evening, leaving the regular night force in charge.[22]

A statement had been issued to the press by Chief Egan that James had refused to confess but that police had increasing evidence against him. The gag found in Anna Pelley's mouth, which had been carefully crafted to silence the victim, had been positively identified as belonging to James.[23] Witnesses stated that James left work before 6 p.m. on the night of the murder and that he was inquiring for Lovie Green at the restaurant where she worked at 7 p.m., leaving his whereabouts unaccounted for at the time of the murder. Seeking still more evidence, State's Attorney Alexander Wilson also told the newspapers that the authorities were turning Lovie Green's dwelling and the nearby area upside down in an effort to find a missing purse, gold chain and cross, and a roll of red cloth, which Anna was said to be carrying at the time of her death. The investigation continued, but as far as the lynch mob was concerned, the investigation was over.

CHAPTER THREE

# THE FLIGHT AND PURSUIT OF WILL "FROGGIE" JAMES

By the afternoon of November 10, 1909, if not sooner, Alexander County sheriff Frank E. Davis realized that Will "Froggie" James was in danger from Cairo's population and the thousands of people streaming into town from across the Ohio River in Kentucky, from across the Mississippi River in Missouri, and from Southern Illinois, especially Anna, which was Anna Pelley's hometown. For half an hour the police tried to clear the area around the city jail of gathering crowds. At this point, Cairo police chief Martin Egan suddenly emerged from the police station and jumped into "McDaniel's automobile" and sped down Commercial Avenue.[1] This was a ruse to take the crowd away from the city jail. The car was faster than people on foot, and it met a patrol wagon at 12th and Ohio Streets. Chief Egan then got in the patrol wagon, and he and the driver returned to the police station.

Chief Egan and the driver were in the wagon when it drove up in front of police headquarters, as if to deliver a plain drunk. Jailer Melchor Lutz had been standing in the doorway, with his keys in hand, but as the wagon appeared, he rushed to the jail. Half a dozen officers appeared as if they arose from the floor, and in less than a minute after the patrol wagon halted, it was gone again with "Froggie" James and the officers.

The No. 8 passenger train on the Illinois Central was heard coming up the levee, and past 12th Street to the levee went the patrol wagon on the run. A yell went up from a small crowd of people, who had gathered quickly when they saw the purpose of the swift action of the officers and the wagon.[2]

Chief Egan and the police officers drove rapidly to 14th Street, where the No. 8 train had stopped.[3] Sheriff Frank Davis was already on the train, having boarded at the main depot on 2nd Street in another ruse. Indeed, so as to not arouse suspicion that he was moving James from Cairo, Sheriff Davis did not purchase the train tickets for himself, Deputy Thomas Andrew Fuller, and Will James in the city. Their destination, according to the *Chicago*

Sheriff Frank E. Davis boarded the Illinois Central train at the 2nd Street depot (*pictured*), but Will "Froggie" James and Deputy Thomas Fuller boarded at 14th Street so as not to attract attention. Postcard courtesy of Darrel Dexter.

*Tribune*, was Murphysboro, Illinois, where one of the most impenetrable jails in Southern Illinois was located.[4] As soon as the train carrying James left Cairo, a dozen men hurried to the freight house near the station. They made calls to Mounds, Mound City, and Anna, Illinois, anywhere they thought the train would go, hoping it would be intercepted.[5] According to the *Cairo Bulletin*, a large crowd had already gathered at Anna, which was not disorderly but more curious than potentially violent.[6] Some regional papers disagreed, saying that Union County, where Anna was the largest town, was "practically in a state of general uprising" and that the people were gathered there with the express purpose of lynching Will James.[7]

Only minutes after James left 14th Street, a mob gathered at police headquarters. Leaders came forward and appointed a committee to search the jail. Chief Egan said there was no reason for any searches because James was not there, but the crowd did not believe him. Angry shouts to produce the prisoner filled the air.[8] Joe Pelley, brother of the murdered woman, confronted Egan and said, "Chief, I am a brother of the girl. I want to look through the cells."[9] Chief Egan then consented to a search. Several African Americans in the cells lay quietly on the floor or in bunks, "their shining eyes expressing terror."[10] The men who searched the cells struck matches and held them so as to better see the features of the prisoners. Joe Pelley lived in Illmo, Missouri, but the other "committee" members were from Cairo, and they knew Will James on sight. Joe Pelley and the "committee" were satisfied and reported to the gathering that James was not in the jail.[11] A more thorough search was made later, looking for any secret crawl spaces or passageways where James might be hiding, but he was nowhere to be found.

The gathering then became extremely agitated and denounced Chief Egan and Lutz the jailer, threatening to lynch them if they could not produce James.[12] This threat may not have been idle. In this time period, lawmen who tried to protect their prisoners were frequently attacked and physically abused.[13] For an hour, threats were hurled at the Cairo police chief and the city jailer from the thousand or so who had gathered. Joe Pelley broke the tension and ended the immediate crisis by waving his hat and saying, "Come on boys, we'll go to the courthouse!"[14]

Now a mob, the group went up Commercial Avenue to 14th Street and turned west toward Poplar Street. The men grew more angry and violent as they marched, shouting and cursing, and fifty or more shots were fired from revolvers as the crowd moved toward the courthouse.[15] Going north on Poplar, the group went to 15th Street, then to Washington Avenue, and then to the courthouse on 20th Street. Three or four men were delegated to enter the courthouse and demand a search. The jailer, Edward Washington Abernathie, consented to a search, and every occupant of the county jail was inspected. Among them was Henry A. Salzner, who was alleged to have murdered his wife and was awaiting trial. There was some talk among the mob outside the courthouse of lynching him, but nothing came of it at that time. When the "delegates" returned, the mob moved east on 20th Street.

Rumors drove the mob one way and another. Word began circulating that James had been taken to the Pulaski County jail in Mound City, about five miles by train from Cairo. Upon reaching Commercial Avenue, part of the mob commandeered an interurban streetcar for Mound City. About 125 men got aboard, packing it full inside, with some hanging on the steps and some even climbing on the roof. The motorman was ordered to "go ahead and run her like hell."[16] Word of this sortie spread over the city, and several automobiles started for Mound City, carrying more men to the Pulaski County seat.

At the Pulaski County jail, the jailer assured the group that the man they wanted was not there. Another "delegation" was selected to inspect the cells, but they did not find James. Frustrated and at a loss to know what to do next, that portion of the mob began to wander around Mound City.[17] Realizing that this was a potential lynch mob, the *Cairo Bulletin* tried to put some distance between the town and the mob, even though the paper had

The current Pulaski County Courthouse was built in 1912. Before that the upper story of the Blum building on Main Street in Mound City served as the courthouse. Postcard courtesy of Keith Vincent.

previously revealed a definite Cairo presence at the city jail. The morning daily asserted, "The mob was composed almost entirely of strangers, or men not well known in the city."[18]

When the Illinois Central train carrying Sheriff Davis, Deputy Fuller, and Will James stopped at the Cairo junction, just outside of town, to allow Chief Egan to return to Cairo, a telegram was given to Sheriff Davis. The telegram warned that a mob was forming in Anna, Illinois, where the feeling for the former resident, now murdered, was intense.[19] Davis and Fuller took James from the train at Dongola, about twelve miles south of Anna.[20] Even in Dongola, however, a small mob had formed, and the two lawmen and the prisoner were forced to immediately make for the woods at the edge of Dongola, which they did successfully. A call, however, went out from Dongola, right away tipping off those in Cairo who wanted to lynch James.[21]

In Cairo, many of those determined to kill Will James decided that Sheriff Davis, having abandoned the Illinois Central, would try to catch the Mobile & Ohio passenger train at Mill Creek, a small village about five miles west of Dongola. Sheriff Davis, however, was nowhere to be seen around Mill Creek, even as hundreds of men combed the area. Rather, when Davis, Fuller, and James fled the Illinois Central train at Dongola, they headed east toward the settlement of Cypress in Johnson County. The

The Illinois Central depot in Cairo along Ohio Street, taken about 1909. Photo courtesy of Knox College Special Collections and Archives, Galesburg, Illinois.

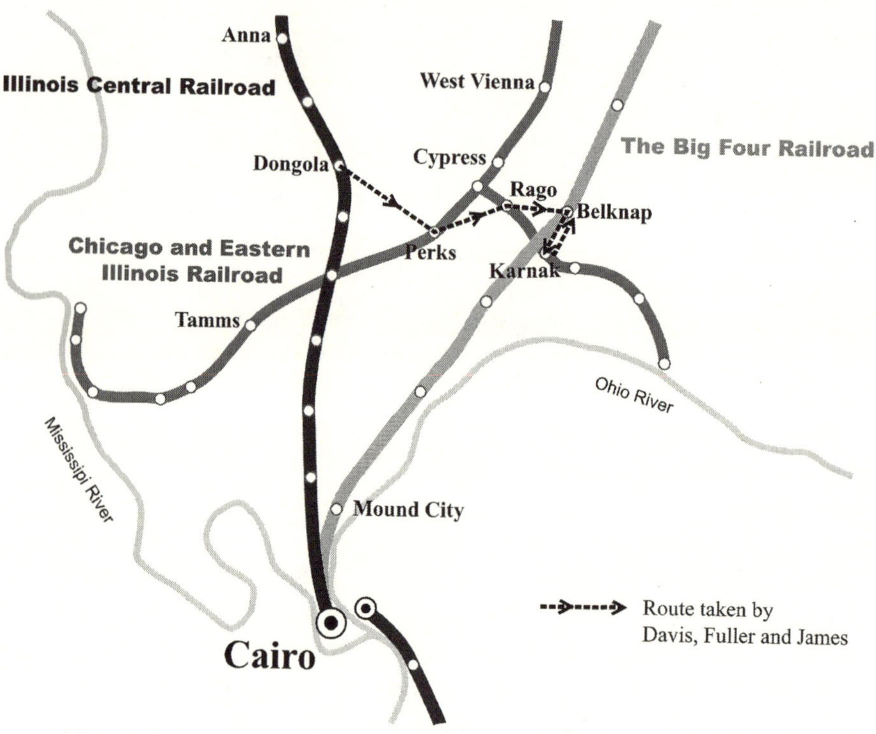


Map of the route taken by Sheriff Davis, Deputy Fuller, and Will James. Drawn by Miho Beadles.

sheriff, however, lost his way in the woods, and the men came to the small village of Perks, in Pulaski County, which was on the edge of Cypress Swamp. At Perks they found a boy with a wagon and persuaded him to take them to the lumber camp called Rago. From Rago to Karnak, the trek was made in mud and water that was sometimes waist-deep. Around midnight of November 10, 1909, the three men slept some before continuing their ill-fated journey.[22] In commenting later on his attempt to flee to some sort of safety with James, Sheriff Frank Davis said, "News had spread over the country and the farmers knew the crime the negro had committed and I could not get assistance and hardly anything to eat."[23]

Early in the morning of November 11, 1909, Davis, Fuller, and James left an abandoned dwelling where they had taken shelter. They were hurried on their way when a Belknap resident, who had given them the shelter, told them that trains were coming in both directions with mobs aboard. The lawmen took the handcuffs off James so that they would not attract attention, and as they walked along the railroad track, they spaced themselves far apart so they would appear to be tramps.[24] The trio finally reached Karnak, where they hoped to catch a Big Four passenger train, but they had just missed it.

James's doom was sealed when Sheriff Davis went to a store in Karnak to buy food and drink for the men. First, Davis was recognized by Joseph Herrin, a Cairo streetcar conductor who was hunting in the area and who reported having seen Sheriff Davis in Karnak as soon as he returned to Cairo.[25] Then a Big Four train crew sent a report to Cairo that Davis and the prisoner were seen going north

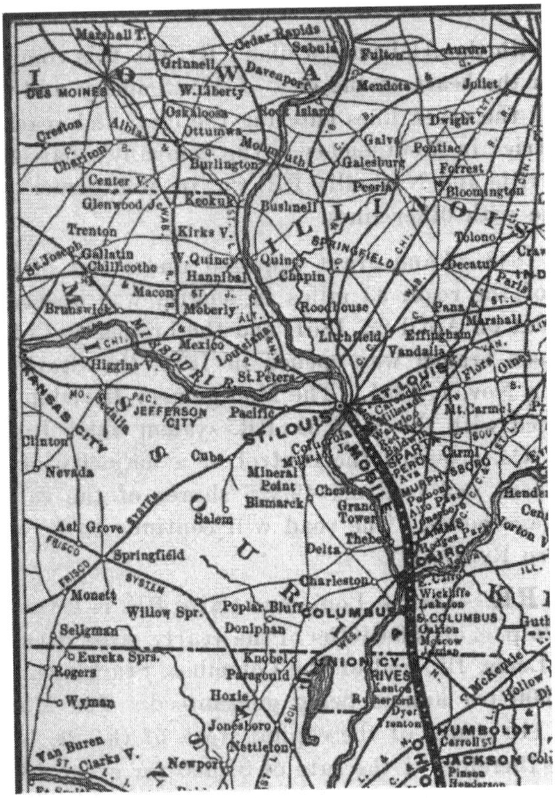


Map of the Mobile & Ohio Railroad and connections. From Poor, *Poor's Manual of the Railroads of the United States 1903*.

just below Belknap in Johnson County, Illinois. John D. Copeland, the postmaster in Karnak, sent a telegram to Cairo that the sheriff and James were at the town.[26] Finally, the sheriff was seen at the Big Four and Chicago and Eastern Illinois junction in Karnak by Philip Preetorius Jr., a Joppa lumberman who was often in Cairo on business and knew the sheriff well.[27]

On the morning of Thursday, November 11, 1909, while Sheriff Davis and his deputy and prisoner were desperately trying to evade the vigilantes, in Cairo hundreds crowded into St. Patrick's Church for the funeral mass for Anna Pelley. The day before, a constant stream of friends and relatives had passed by the casket at the home of her sister, Mrs. John Coffman. "We could stand it if she had died a natural death," one relative said, "but to have her die in this horrible manner is too much to stand."[28] At the funeral in Cairo, Father James J. Downey officiated and spoke the following words:

> *The world has nothing superior to a virtuous and upright young lady. She is the light and comfort of the home. She is the consolation of parents. She is the guardian angel of the family. She is the pride and honor of companions.*
>
> *Her words, her actions, her ideas, kindle truth and affection in all hearts, and my dear friends, you will bear me out, such a young lady was Miss Pelley. She was a credit to any home. From the very day she became a member of the congregation until she was struck down by this wretched assassin, her conduct was such as any congregation might feel proud. She represented the splendid class of young ladies who make their living by honest endeavor and effort. She had the inestimable advantage of good home training and she certainly was true to the traditions of her home.*[29]

After the morning funeral, the body of Anna Pelley was taken by the 11:15 Illinois Central train to Anna, Illinois, accompanied by family and several hundred Cairoites. A large crowd met the body at the Anna depot and escorted Anna Pelley's remains to St. Mary's Church. Her burial beside the graves of her parents in Anna City Cemetery was one of the most well attended in the town's history. So many floral tributes were sent that a large wagon had to be used to bring them all to the gravesite.[30] After the services, the return train brought hundreds back to Cairo at 6:35 in the evening.

While the funeral service was being conducted in Cairo, a telegram was received there from a railroad conductor in Karnak that said Sheriff Davis, his deputy, and Will James were in the vicinity of the town.[31] A mob of

Funeral services were held for Anna Pelley in St. Patrick's Catholic Church in Cairo (*left*) and in St. Mary's Catholic Church in Anna (*right*). Postcard courtesy of Darrel Dexter. Photo from the *Anna (Ill.) Gazette-Democrat.*

300 men then seized Big Four freight train No. 82 in the yards at Cairo and forced the train crews to take them to Karnak.[32] There was one lone woman in the mob, seen wearing a long brown ulster coat and scarf and standing on the train car, waving a handkerchief as they passed through Grand Chain and other towns and by train stations along the way.

Only the *St. Louis Post-Dispatch* identified the standout as "one woman whose name was said to be Maloney," saying that she had "clambored up on the caboose" with the men at Cairo.[33] In an interview with the newspaper a few months later, Rosa K. Maloney confessed to being the lone woman, the "Joan of Arc" of the lynch mob.[34] She was proud of her role in the mob and said that from atop a boxcar in Mounds she had harangued a crowd, begging the people to enlist.

Men were coming north from Cairo and Mound City and south from Anna to find the Davis party. There were so many of them that they covered the landscape between Karnak in Pulaski County and Vienna in Johnson County—a distance of sixteen miles.[35] Mobs, or at least hostile groups, had stopped Davis, Fuller, and James from boarding any train in Southern

Illinois, and farmers in the area either were after James themselves or would not aid Sheriff Davis in any way.[36]

Sheriff Frank Davis, Deputy Fuller, and Will James left Karnak and headed back toward Belknap, hoping to catch what the sheriff knew to be a five o'clock train to Danville. They spent some time in an abandoned house, and at dusk they were trying to walk the last mile and a quarter to Belknap. The following is Sheriff Frank Davis's account of his and Will James's capture.

> *[We] went two miles through the corn fields into the timber and seated ourselves on a log, were looking at our watches, expecting that the crowd from Cairo would come up on the afternoon passenger trains.*
>
> *We expected to get further into the woods, but had to cross a clearing when we noticed three men coming along. We crouched in the weeds when three other citizens came along. One of them had a gun. I arose to meet him and found that it was the man who had sold me some food in Karnak in the morning. The man passed by and we still crouched when we saw five men.*
>
> *One of them stood upon a stump and looked intently in our direction. Then he stooped down and we knew he was telling the other man that he had seen us. I went to him and said: "This man is in my custody, and nobody has a right to molest him."*
>
> *Then I saw a man I know. He stood with his arms folded. I said: "If you hang this man. . . ." He said: "We don't intend to hang him; we want to take him to Cairo, so that he can get a speedy trial."*[37] *Then five men fired their guns in the air and all around squads of men took up the signal and fired their guns in the air.*
>
> *At this signal, men from all directions came running toward us, and I began to recognize the Cairo crowd. Previous to that the men were all strangers to me, except the one I was talking with.*
>
> *When the Cairo crowd gathered around us, two Cairo men came and attempted to take the negro. We hung on to him until we were overpowered, and then, as the march to Belknap began, we followed after.*
>
> *Two or three struck the darky in the face, and I was pleading all along with them not to do so. When we reached the deserted*

> *house* [where they had rested], *it was afire, and the crowd yelled, "Burn him alive!"*
>
> *Again I pleaded, and one of the men who had been most insistent on mob violence, came clear over to my side, and he rendered me a great deal of assistance.*
>
> *By the time we had reached the depot the crowd was pacified, and brought us food and water. At the suggestion of some of the number, I selected a committee to take the prisoner into the depot to try to get a confession.*[38]

Will "Froggie" James was now under the control of the mob, which had complete power to determine his fate. Sheriff Davis's latent response to get custody of James from the Cairo police and then out of Cairo to save him from a lynch mob had come too late to save James. The main criticism of Davis was that he had not acted soon enough, and now it appeared that would cost James his life. Davis's political career was over, but he would spend many more years in Cairo wondering, "What if I had taken charge of Froggie James sooner?," "What if we had not missed the train at Karnak?," "What if I had not gone into the store at Karnak and been recognized?," "What if . . . ?"

## CHAPTER FOUR

# THE LYNCHINGS OF WILL "FROGGIE" JAMES AND HENRY A. SALZNER

"With ghastly solicitude," the mob of at least 1,000 took Will "Froggie" James back to the freight train they had commandeered, having decided to return him to Cairo rather than burn or hang him at Belknap.[1] According to one source at the time, women in Belknap came out as James was being led to the train and hissed and spat at him.[2] Sheriff Frank Davis, who had been disarmed, pled for the return of his gun, and it was given back to him. Davis stayed next to James and sat with him on the return trip to Cairo. The train started back for the river city about 6 p.m. By this time at least 6,000 people had formed a mob in Cairo, and another train had been hastily made up, drawn by a switch engine. This improvised train was totally packed with men and at least one woman.[3]

Sheriff Davis had not contacted the governor of Illinois, Charles Deneen, to discuss calling out the National Guard, one company of which was located right in Cairo, but the mob members on the train heading to town with James were unaware of that. According to Davis, the mob members feared the "militia" would be waiting at the Cairo depot. The sheriff said the men on the train were continually pulling on the cord and the train kept stopping.[4] "Daddy" Bishop, the leader of the men in the second train car, lamented that he was not in charge of the lynch mob but advised his men as the train pulled into Cairo "to be orderly and not to shoot unless compelled to."[5]

The lynch mob may have been uncertain about what awaited them in Cairo, but there seems to have been little doubt that James would be wrested from Sheriff Davis and Deputy Thomas Fuller and killed. The groups that pursued the doomed man and his legal captors in Alexander, Pulaski, Johnson, and Union Counties were organized at four or five locations, and they interchanged messages as the trail of the trio grew "hot or cold."[6] Communication was also constantly maintained between Cairo and Anna, especially information as to passenger trains that Davis, Fuller, and James were on or could possibly board.[7] One regional newspaper commented on the "cool planning" of the lynching.[8] Cooperation with the mob seemed to be nearly universal in the state, and its leaders received messages all along the Illinois Central and Big Four lines that James was not jailed anywhere in Illinois.[9]

The first lynching on the evening of November 11, 1909, was set in motion when the first train seized at the Big Four depot arrived in Cairo at 8:45 p.m. A rope was placed around the neck of James, but Sheriff Frank Davis removed it and was struck in the face by another mob member. Davis made one last plea for Will James's life, but he was firmly pushed away in such a manner that he knew further resistance would be dangerous.[10] The train had stopped at 10th Street, probably so that Will James would be close to Eighth and Commercial, "the most important corner in the city."[11] James and the vigilantes were met by individuals selected to carry out the actual killing; they had been informed that "the coast was clear" for their violent intentions.[12] The plan appears to have been to hang James from the illuminated steel arch at Eighth and Commercial, which had been erected the year before for the Egyptian Hustlers convention.[13] When James had been forced beneath the arch, he was made to climb on a barrel in order to confess, but he refused, saying he was not guilty. "Many in the great mass of people became impatient. . . . 'We don't want to hear him! String him

The intersection with double arches over 8th Street and Commercial was the site of the lynching of Will "Froggie" James. Postcard courtesy of Edward Oliver.

up! Kill him! Burn him!'"[14] This became the steady roar of the crowd: "Burn him! Burn him! Burn him!"[15]

At this point James, who had already been threatened with being burned alive, may have decided that being hanged was the better death and confessed. He said, "I killed her, but [Arthur] Alexander was with me and took the lead."[16] This was James's first and only confession. Sheriff Frank Davis had never gotten him to admit to the killing, nor did the Cairo police or the mob members who had questioned him near Belknap.[17] Others standing near James, though, said he never confessed but "protested his innocence until blows and bullets silenced his protestation, declaring that he saw Alexander in the commission of the crime."[18]

While Will James was being abused by the mob, a man had climbed to the top of the arch and let down a rope to the men below. The following is the *Cairo Evening Citizen*'s account of how James was killed.

> *One man climbed up the iron post nearest the Alexander County bank and a shout went up: "Turn on the light!" The switch box where the incandescent lights are controlled is at the corner. He did not turn them on. But later on the lights were flashed on and*

Alistes Leonard and Hollie S. Blockley, photographers at LeBlock Studio, 209 8th Street in Cairo, took nearly two dozen shots associated with the Will James and Henry A. Salzner lynchings. The *Cairo Evening Citizen* said of this image, "No one need have any fear of being identified and connected with the lynching. This precaution was taken by Mr. Leonard" (November 13, 1909). The photo was taken by prolonged light exposure and not by flash.

> *their light threw a glare that revealed the great crowd packed in that street intersection. Another man climbed up another post and a rope was lowered in readiness to raise the negro and make him pay the penalty for what the crowd fully believed was his crime. . . .*
>
> *Occasionally James was raised up so that even those on the outskirts of the crowd saw his head and shoulders all bound with the rope that held him. A dry goods box was used as a scaffold and a rope that dangled from the steel arch overhead was put around his neck, and an attempt was made to haul him up. But the rope was not strong enough to sustain his weight. Then he was dragged toward the river and a volley of shots fired into his body, ending his miserable life.*[19]

According to Cairo's other daily newspaper, the *Bulletin*, the great majority of the throng at the lynching were "silent spectators," and the few who supervised the actual lynching were quiet and earnest. In the *Bulletin*'s account, besides the onlookers and the determined killers, "there were many women in the crowd, and they all seemed to look approvingly on the work."[20]

Will James's dead body was dragged by mob leaders up the Ohio levee with the intention of throwing it in the river. A change of plans brought them to 12th Street, by the police station, and then west over Washington

Site of the James lynching showing an active street even at night under the lighted arches. Postcard courtesy of Edward Oliver.

After Will "Froggie" James was shot, his dead body was dragged up the Ohio levee toward 12th Street. This postcard view shows an Ohio levee scene south from 8th Street. Postcard courtesy of Darrel Dexter.

Avenue, and finally to the site of Anna Pelley's murder.[21] As the mob went, they gathered boards, boxes, a ladder, and other inflammable material to use as kindling. When the mob reached the alley where Anna Pelley's body had been discovered, they built a huge pyre. Kerosene was brought in and poured over the pile, and Will James's body was thrown on it. An unidentified "young lady" was given the opportunity of setting the fire.[22] An eyewitness recounted that "the flames revealed thousands of people on streets, on roofs of houses, at windows, and the streets and sidewalks[—] a mass of humanity."[23]

Even before James's body was burned, the typical lynch mob abuse of his remains began. A man slashed at his body, and the rope that had been (unsuccessfully) used to hang him was cut into pieces and soaked in his blood.[24] As the fire was dying down, the mob began to clamor for even more souvenirs of the lynching. Mob members cut out James's heart, carved it into pieces, wrapped them in newspaper, and distributed them. One person who had cut off one of James's feet took it away as a great prize.[25] Several of his bones were taken from the pyre.[26] Most ghastly of all, a man took an ax and after three blows severed the head of James and carried it off.[27]

An African American undertaker, L. S. Williams, who had recently opened a business at 1913 Poplar Street in Cairo, was directed by the county coroner, Dr. James McGriffen McManus, to clear away the ashes of James's body from the alley. Williams found the charred skull of James on an eight-foot pole standing upright against a fence at Candee Park at the southeast corner of 25th Street and Washington Avenue, about fifty yards from the scene of his burning.[28]

LeBlock postcard showing the "half-burned head of James" atop an eight-foot pole in Candee Park, close to the site of the Anna Pelley murder.

If there were 10,000 people in the lynch mob that killed Will James, many must have been "satisfied with the night's work," because only 2,000 of them took out on a hunt for Arthur Alexander.[29] Luckily for him, the Cairo police found him first and locked him up for his own protection.[30] Another 1,000 or so, directed by mob leaders, went the five blocks to the county courthouse where Henry Salzner, a white man, was being held in the county jail.[31]

Salzner, a photographer, had been charged with killing his wife, Mary E. Salzner, with an ax on August 15, 1909, almost three months before the rape and murder of Anna Pelley.[32] The couple's two children were found playing in their mother's blood on that day. Suspicion immediately fell on Salzner, who was known to be a wife beater and a poor provider for his family. He had his wife living in a shed-like building, known as Lancaster tenement, at 208 16th Street with their two children—one a baby—while he spent most of the time living more comfortably with his parents, William F. and Emily

Salzner, at 226 16th Street.[33] Though Mrs. Salzner had a fractured skull, she regained consciousness long enough to tell her sister, Daisy DeLoach, and another woman who was caring for her, "Henry did it, when I refused to yield to him that night." She died August 18, 1909, at St. Mary's Infirmary, and immediately afterward, at the foot of her bed, Sheriff Davis placed Henry Salzner under arrest and took him to the county jail on a charge of murder, where he had remained for several months awaiting trial—until the lynch party arrived.[34]

A part of the James lynch mob was "casting about for a suitable victim," and some of the men had already suggested that Salzner should be lynched.[35] Armed with a sledgehammer, other hammers, and chisels, the mob and its leaders entered the courthouse through the south basement, where the jail cells were located. Then they began to attack a wooden door that protected the jail cells. Sheriff Davis was in his office upstairs in the courthouse and heard a "dull thumping" below him. He went out on the porch and asked the intruders, "What is it, gentlemen? What do you want?"[36] He received no reply. Davis went down to the basement of the courthouse, where he found approximately twenty-five men battering at the wooden door leading to the jail cells. The sheriff went among the men and pleaded with them to stop. They quietly told him that they wanted Salzner. None of the deputy

St. Mary's Infirmary, where Mary E. Salzner was cared for before her death. It was established by the Sisters of the Holy Cross in Cairo in 1867. The brick additions were made in 1893 and 1901. Postcard courtesy of Darrel Dexter.

The mob broke through the door of the courthouse in search of Henry Salzner. Postcard courtesy of Darrel Dexter.

sheriffs were in the courthouse at the time except Thomas Fuller, who had been with the sheriff and Will James at Belknap. Trying to get a story, the editor of the *Cairo Bulletin*, Edward W. Thielecke, was also in the building.[37]

Sheriff Davis went to his office and called the police in an effort to stop further violence, but the Cairo police stayed in their headquarters. He next called on deputies to report for duty. None of them came.[38] Deputy Fuller, already present, was an extremely brave man, as later events in Cairo would prove. We do not know what counsel he gave Frank Davis, but the only other lawman in the courthouse, jailer Edward Abernathie, hid somewhere in the building with his family and was not found, nor were the keys he had to the cells.[39] Davis and Fuller had not had much sleep for two nights and had been walking the woods and swamps of Union and Pulaski Counties, but once again Davis tried to save a prisoner. He finally telephoned Governor Charles Deneen and told him that a mob was storming the jail and that his call for deputies and volunteers had yielded none.

Sheriff Davis pleaded with the governor for troops, saying that the streets of Cairo were filled with crazy people.[40] The time was approximately 11 p.m. on November 11, 1909. Governor Deneen decided to check the situation and called the Cairo police station. As the governor later said, the night sergeant "deceived" him, saying that Cairo was becoming quiet.[41] Many members of the Cairo police force were in sympathy with the lynch mob, and one St.

Louis reporter wrote, "The regret of the policemen was that their uniforms rather made it in poor taste for them to participate."[42]

The absence of troops gave the mob the opportunity to lynch Salzner. The county courthouse doors had been quickly broken, as had been the heavy wooden door leading to the jail cells, which were supposed to be mob-proof. Perhaps giving credence to the assertion that the mob leaders were outsiders or men new to Cairo, they expressed doubt as to which cell was Salzner's.

Two LeBlock postcards feature the cell at the Alexander County Courthouse in Cairo, from which Salzner was taken to be lynched by the mob on the night of November 11, 1909. The two men are unidentified.

A call was raised for someone to identify him, and the answer was, "Here's someone who knows him."[43] A man with his face partially covered came in and identified Salzner. Henry Salzner was in a "steel cage," and breaking into it required repeated blows with a sledgehammer, while others in the mob went after the cell with hammers and chisels.[44] The hammering and chiseling sounded loudly throughout the courthouse. Jailer Abernathie's family, consisting of his wife and eight children, ranging in ages from one to seventeen years old, were still in the basement of the building and quite afraid, although they were told that no harm would come to them.[45] It took between thirty minutes and an hour for the mob to open the cell, and during this time Salzner crouched in one corner and did not utter a sound.[46] The *Chicago Tribune* believed he was a "frightened wretch . . . reduced almost to a state of idiocy by his terror" as his cell was being broken into.[47]

When the door was opened he was roughly dragged out and taken to 21st Street and Washington Avenue, where an effort was made to make him confess. Instead, he protested his innocence, changing his earlier story that four men were responsible for killing his wife to accusing his own sister.[48] He then seemed to give in and said, "Do what you want with me. I don't care."[49] At this point local and national accounts of the lynching differ. Supposedly an old man came forward and said he believed Henry Salzner was innocent. The man was immediately attacked, hit, kicked, and knocked down, and calls were made for a second lynch rope.[50] In these accounts, the cooler heads in the mob had a hard time saving the defender's life. The mob made the man beg for his life and shout that Salzner should be lynched, but following the beating and the humiliation, he was let go and dragged away by his friends.[51]

A rope was brought to the scene and thrown over the crosspiece of a telegraph pole at the south end of a grassy plot that divides Sycamore Street and Washington Avenue. When the rope was thrown over the pole, the *Chicago Tribune* stated, "Crying and mumbling like an idiot, the doomed man managed to utter an accusation that his sister killed the woman."[52] Salzner was asked to pray, and he again protested his innocence.

> *Then he was standing there in that awful scene, he lifted up his voice to the Almighty for salvation and peace for his soul. While he did so the crowd stood with uncovered and bowed heads. But it was not for long. They grew impatient, and cutting his almost incoherent prayer short, they pulled him up into the air. A volley of bullets was fired into his body and one of them*

A contemporary view of the site of Salzner's lynching. Photo by Darrel Dexter.

> *cut the rope that held him suspended in two, and he fell to the ground. But the mob was not satisfied.*
>
> *Another volley was fired into him as he lay prostrate upon the earth. Then the savage nature of his slayers was revealed. Someone slashed his throat and another grabbed the rope around his neck and cut it into souvenirs for the crowd. Then the body was left lying on the ground and an hour later, upon orders from the dead man's father, it was taken charge [of] by undertakers Burke and Blaine.*[53]

The burning of Salzner's body was prevented only by the intervention of Cairo alderman Edward A. Burke of Burke and Blaine Undertakers.[54] The time of Salzner's lynching was established as 11:46 p.m.

Henry Salzner did not receive much mercy from the mob, nor did he get much sympathy from the press. The local and regional press saw Salzner's

The intersection of Washington Avenue and Sycamore Street in Cairo, the site of Salzner's lynching. Postcard courtesy of Edward Oliver.

lynching as an example of justice delayed, because here it was November, nearly three months after the murder, and Salzner had not been tried in a court of law. The Cairo public was apparently incensed at the delay in a trial.[55] Some would later point to the lynching of Henry Salzner as reassurance to the black community that the lynchings were not about race but about protecting women.[56] It is doubtful that many were reassured, and if the lynchings had anything to do with protecting women, it was only about protecting white women.

Drawing of Anna Pelley appearing in the *Portsmouth (Ohio) Daily Times* on November 12, 1909.

LeBlock postcard photo of black and white children viewing the ashes of Will James. The *x* in the background represents the location where Anna Pelley's body was found.

## CHAPTER FIVE

# A THIRD LYNCHING PREVENTED

At 10:30 p.m. on November 11, Governor Charles Deneen received the first telegram from Sheriff Frank Davis that informed him that Will James had been taken from him and lynched. The message read in part, "Am unable to preserve order. Send troops."[1] This finally moved the governor, who was in Chicago, to call out the state troops. Governor Deneen first wired Captain William P. Greaney in Cairo to turn out Company K of the Fourth Regiment of the Illinois National Guard. Greaney mobilized the company at the armory at 1005–1007 Washington and informed the governor that he and his men were ready, even though he saw no further danger of an uncontrollable situation. Cairo's company of citizen soldiers was divided into five squads. One guarded the homes of Mayor George Parsons, another police chief Martin Egan's house, and a third Captain Greaney's own home. Two squads patrolled up and down Washington Avenue, hoping to prevent arson and property crimes.[2]

Governor Charles Deneen was first advised of the situation in Cairo after the lynching of Will "Froggie" James. From *Governors of Illinois, 1818–1918*, 44.

At 4:30 in the morning on November 12, Sheriff Davis asked that twenty-five men from Company K be sent to the courthouse because about fifty men were demanding to go through the jail to look for

Arthur Alexander, whom Will James had implicated in Anna Pelley's rape and murder. Captain Greaney reported that he went there with some of his soldiers and found thirty-five intoxicated men, whom he dispersed and sent on their way.[3] According to the *Cairo Bulletin*, Alexander was five minutes from death, as he had been identified by the other prisoners and members of the mob were trying to break into his cell when Captain Greaney and some of his men surprised them and made them desist.[4] This sensational report seems false, as Alexander was actually being held at the city police department and not at the county jail.

Ten more companies of militia soldiers were on the way by train to Cairo from all over the state to try to maintain order. Company C from Carbondale was put on a special train and arrived first at 6 a.m. on November 12. They were followed at 12:20 in the afternoon by Company G from Effingham, Company M from Champaign, Company B from Newton, Company F from Mount Vernon, Company I from Vandalia, and Company L from Olney.[5] An hour later Company D of Paris arrived, followed by Company H of Shelbyville at 4:05 and finally Company A of Casey at 6 p.m. Including Cairo's own Company K, this placed 362 enlisted men and 45 officers on duty in the town.[6] National Guardsmen soon surrounded the lockup at Cairo Police Headquarters, which held Alexander, dressed in a police uniform to disguise him from easy recognition.[7] The soldiers also patrolled the surrounding streets so crowds could not gather.[8]

Tension in Cairo remained high as the word was passed: "Wait until the soldiers go." Some people wanted to send them on their way as soon as possible, hooting and jeering at the troops on patrol.[9] A streetcar conductor, John Pearl, was arrested by the militia and placed in the city jail for heckling the soldiers and calling them "nigger lovers."[10] Company C from Carbondale, not having local ties, fanned out across town and cleared the levee district of crowds. These Illinois soldiers were hoping to encourage potential lynchers from Kentucky and Missouri to leave town.

Sheriff Frank Davis said he feared "wholesale murder" when he made the first request for troops, and at least two Chicago newspapers worried about a race riot in Cairo of the magnitude of the one that had struck Springfield, Illinois, in 1908. The question arose whether James's lynching had been aimed primarily at a man or at a race.[11] The memory of the Springfield race riot haunted Illinois, if not the entire United States. At least one historian has stated that the Springfield riot led to the formation of the National Association for the Advancement of Colored People. A prominent journalist at the time, William English Walling, interviewed Springfield rioters and found them showing no remorse or shame for the barbaric bloodletting and property destruction they had inflicted on Abraham Lincoln's hometown. Walling further discovered a contagion of racism sweeping across the Midwest, with whites of all classes warring against African Americans.[12]

Cairo might have become another Springfield. After all, rioting and killing had continued in the Illinois capital the year before, even after the state soldiers arrived. Some regional papers discounted the possibility. The *Cincinnati Enquirer*, which had its own reporters in Cairo and did not rely on the wire services, argued, "The fact that the mob wreaked summary vengeance on a white man as well as upon the negro James is taken by the negroes here as proof that a law-abiding member of their race have no race war to fear."[13] A southwestern Illinois daily even claimed that black people were in the crowd that viewed the James lynching, and a few even saw Henry Salzner put to death. The *Alton Evening Telegraph* concluded its observations by stating, "There is no ill feeling between the races." *The Fort Wayne Daily News*, which also had its own correspondents in Cairo, observed,

> *The city is quiet and the thing which the officers feared most—a riot of race against race—seems a remote possibility.*
>
> *During the disturbances no demonstration has been made against the negroes as negroes, and the whole fury of the mob spent itself in the lynching of Will James (colored)* alias *"Frog," believed to have murdered Anna Pelley Monday night, and Henry Salzner, (white) alleged murderer of his wife.*[14]

It is doubtful that there was no friction between the races in Cairo. Nevertheless, the incidents of November 10 and 11, 1909, in that town were not directed at the local African Americans as a group. Indeed, at the time it seemed more likely that Cairo mayor George Parsons would be attacked rather than any particular black person, except for Arthur Alexander, whom Will James had accused in his confession as being a co-attacker in Anna Pelley's assault. At 2 a.m. on November 12, 1909, Captain Greaney wired Governor Deneen: "One Negro for rape and murder and one white man for wife murder lynched tonight. Situation in hand. No necessity for additional troops. No disorder, and perfect quiet prevails at this hour."[15] Captain Greaney seems to have judged the lynched men guilty and the lynching justified. He may not have been the most reliable judge of law and order in Cairo, since he had his own home under guard for good reason. Regardless, there had been no property damaged in town. As the *Cairo Bulletin* emphasized, there was "no thievery, pillaging, or fighting."[16]

There were, however, two lynchings in Cairo on the night of November 11. There was also a racial difference in the designs of the mobs. Henry Salzner (white) was never threatened with being burned alive; Will James (black) came close to being immolated twice—once before he was brought to Cairo and as at least part of the mob surrounding him yelled, "Burn him! Burn him! Burn him!"[17] Will James was not burned alive, but he *was* murdered after being taken from the care of Sheriff Frank Davis.

The primary task of local officials and the Illinois National Guard now was to prevent Arthur Alexander from also being "injured to death" by "persons unknown," as the coroner's jury would characterize James's death. In furtherance of this goal, Brigadier General Frank P. Wells left Decatur, Illinois, at 4 a.m. Wells was experienced in restoring order, having served as a young officer in railroad strikes in the 1880s and 1890s; in riot duty in Pana, Illinois, during the fierce mine strikes; and in the horrible race riot in Lincoln's hometown the previous year.[18] Having dealt with violent racism and the aftermath of lynchings, General Wells decided that the best way to quell disorder in Cairo was to get Arthur Alexander out of town as soon as possible. A special Illinois Central train was ordered for that purpose.[19]

Late in the afternoon on November 13, 1909, the removal from Cairo of Alexander, now viewed by many as "the negro accomplice of James," began. Rumors circulated that "a large body of armed men from Anna" would storm the jail in Cairo that evening and try to lynch Alexander. The troops were sufficient to guard Alexander, but a clash between them and the civilian mob, it was feared, would bring "wholesale bloodshed."[20]

The angry mob was further infuriated as the press reported false rumors that Alexander had made a partial confession to the police, "admitting that he stripped jewelry from the lifeless body of Miss Pelley." When it was leaked that the militia troops intended to move Alexander from town, the crowd grew angrier and larger. "Only the triple ranks of soldiers with rifles loaded and gleaming bayonets held menacingly breast high held the crowd back," the *Waterloo Evening Courier* reported.[21]

There then occurred an incident that had the potential of leading to a third lynching. A gray-haired woman of "refined appearance" stepped from the crowd. She addressed those assembled, "Men, men—and you women too—will you be cowards? Will you see the black demon escape? Will you see your daughters murdered by a black fiend? I call on you to take this negro murderer and give him the fate he deserves."[22] A sullen roar rose from the crowd and yells and jeers were directed at the soldiers. The troops, however, at this point stepped one pace forward, thrusting bayonets in the faces of the crowd, and any potential crisis quickly passed.

Two companies of guardsmen stood before the courthouse steps as Arthur Alexander emerged handcuffed, escorted by Sheriff Frank Davis and two deputies. Soldiers surrounded the lawmen and the prisoner on their way to the special train that was brought to the 12th Street stop, which was closest to the county jail. Alexander could hardly be seen by the mob, as he was completely surrounded by troops. He was stolid, showing no sign of fear, except his hand twitched slightly. The crowd got in some final shouts: "Hang the murderer!" "Kill him!" "Burn the black fiend as we burned James!" There were also curses and calls to rush the soldiers.[23]

When the train was reached, Alexander was hustled into the rear coach, and two companies of guardsmen—Company G of Effingham and M of Champaign—filled two coaches and a baggage car. When Alexander and the guardsmen pulled out at 4:30 p.m., the remaining troops in Cairo had to constantly push the crowd away from the tracks until the train was well underway. Apparently Alexander still was not safe. Orders for "slow running" through the towns of Pulaski, Dongola, and Anna were given, rather than orders to stop, because of fear that the inflamed people in those towns might be alerted by telephone that Alexander was being removed from Southern

View of 8th Street, looking toward Commercial Avenue. Postcard courtesy of Darrel Dexter.

Illinois and attempt to derail the train. This fear had been aroused when crowds in the neighboring towns had yelled jeers and curses at the soldiers' special trains when they passed through on the morning of November 12 on their way to Cairo.[24] The report of the Illinois National Guard to the governor said large crowds were assembled at Mounds, Anna, Carbondale, and Centralia as the train went through with Alexander, but they did not stop at the depots.[25]

The troops, lawmen, and Alexander were on a fast train, and only necessary stops were made. A mob of perhaps 500 gathered at Centralia, when it was reported that Alexander would go through there. Centralia was in fact originally the destination, but the yardmaster had alerted the general and the sheriff before the special train left Cairo. The special raced up the line and only slowed at Centralia, where the crowd had to be satisfied with hoots and jeers as the train passed.[26]

With Arthur Alexander gone and saloons closed, the authorities were not too afraid of further rioting. By November 16, 1909, less than a week after the double lynching, there was little for the troops to do. Order had been restored in Cairo. The soldiers were quickly sent home, but the turmoil in Cairo continued, and for a short time, the entire nation seemed focused on the small city.[27]

# CHAPTER SIX

# THE NATIONAL SPOTLIGHT ON CAIRO

In the glare of countrywide focus, the national press began to look for the officials on whom they could place the responsibility for the November 11 lynchings.[1] Nationally recognized newspapers solicited the views of Cairo mayor George Parsons on the events in the river city. The *Washington Post* quoted him as saying, "A regiment couldn't have stopped the work of last night's night."[2] In the same article in the *Post*, Sheriff Frank E. Davis echoed this sentiment: "There would have been wholesale bloodshed had the soldiers been here last night."[3] In an interview with the *New York Times*, Mayor Parsons excused himself, Davis, and Cairo from responsibility for the lynchings.

> *Though the protection of the men who were lynched here was in no way under my control, no one can regret the affair more than I do. I do not think blame attaches to any official. The entire community was working up to such a pitch that no other termination was possible. I believe that the majority of the citizens are pleased at the turn of affairs, and while they deplore the disgrace to the city and state, they believe the result will be salutary.*
>
> *There has not been an official execution in Cairo for 10 or 15 years, and the city has had its share of murders. Juries have failed to convict . . . or have convicted in only a minor degree, and it has been possible for murderers to escape. In fact, I regret to say murder in Cairo has been tolerably safe. The feeling against crime that has so long been suppressed has found vent, and I believe Cairo will be peaceful and law abiding hereafter.*[4]

The *New York Times* in a sarcastic editorial answered Parsons's explanation for the lynchings in Cairo: "Having now calmed down—with the help of a few hundred rifles ready to be aimed their direction—the people

Mayor George Parsons. John M. Lansden Collection, Southern Illinois University Special Collections Research Center, Carbondale.

of Cairo, Ill., have promptly thought up an excuse for the little orgy of blood and murder with which they recently indulged themselves."[5] Having established that the *Times* viewed the Cairo lynchings as extremely serious crimes with wide local support, the eminent New York daily continued, "The best excuse they have been able to invent happens to be a pretty bad one."[6] The *Times* described Mayor Parsons as "a man with such a fine capacity for sleep that he never once woke up during the night when his fellow citizens were all out firing guns and therefore knew nothing of the sanguinary barbarities until the next morning."[7]

The "bad excuse" offered by Parsons was that Cairo juries habitually acquitted murderers or "let them off with light sentences" and delayed justice "until public patience was exhausted. At last the people rose in their might and virtuous indignation to inflict the justice that had been denied." The *Times* called this excuse "all nonsense from one point of view . . . and a further indictment of Cairo people from another." In that same vein, the *Times* judged,

> *If there have been no hangings in Cairo it was because the people there have been inclined to think the killing of human beings a thing of no great moment. The courts, too, in the matter of granting postponements must have been acting in accordance with general public tastes. . . . The law in Cairo has been just as efficient and prompt in its actions against crime as the residents of Cairo have chosen to make it.*[8]

Willis Leonard Clanahan, a former Cairo resident and past editor of the *Cairo Bulletin*, now working at the *New York World*, answered the editorial and the coverage of the lynching by the *New York Times*. Clanahan's lengthy and racially charged letter was printed in the *Times*.

It is uncertain whether Mayor Parsons actually slept through the lynchings, but the mob's initial plan to parade Will "Froggie" James by Parsons's house at 604 28th Street was canceled, and he was taken directly to 8th and Commercial. Postcard courtesy of Edward Oliver.

> *As a former resident of Cairo, Ill., where I was the editor of a daily newspaper for three years, I crave a word, not in defense of the double lynching which occurred there a few days ago, but in explanation of it. Cairo, at the extreme southern point of Illinois, at the junction of the Ohio and Mississippi rivers, is peculiarly located. Across one river is Missouri; across the other is Kentucky, and Tennessee is only 50 miles away. Cairo thus becomes a buffer between North and South. It is probably the only town in the North which has a true race problem to deal with. . . . Out of a population of 13,000 in 1900, 5,000 of the inhabitants of Cairo were Negroes. Of the 100,000 Negroes in the State of Illinois 5 per cent are in this one little town.*[9] *Aside from this, the floating colored population is unusually large, and Cairo, at some time or other, harbors most of the "bad niggers" from St. Louis, Cincinnati, Louisville, Memphis, Vicksburg, and New Orleans. It is these whom citizens fear the most, and for whom they are constantly alert. Murders by either white men or Negroes are alarmingly frequent, but the murderer*

> *usually escapes to Kentucky or Missouri, and is never heard of again. Thus crime after crime is recorded against the name of Cairo, with no recompense in the name of the law. On the other hand, there is hardly a time when there are not forty or fifty Cairo Negroes in the Southern Illinois Penitentiary, all convicted of theft or burglary.*
>
> *The white people of Cairo have dealt indulgently with the Negro. For years it has been the policy to keep two Negroes on the small police force, and there have been Negro Justices of the Peace. A Negro physician once came near to being elected a member of the Board of Education. While they pay but little taxes, the Negroes are provided with three public schools. The Sumner [High School] was the first colored high school ever established in the United States. Yet this Negro population, coddled as it is, is a constant menace to the town. No white woman dare venture outside of the house at night alone for fear of assault. Many outrages of which the world has never heard have been attempted. This is why, as Mayor Parsons says, the effect of the recent lynching will be "salutary."*
>
> *Altogether it is not surprising that a lynching took place in Cairo. The only wonder is that one did not take place long ago.*[10]

Even though he denied it, Clanahan was obviously defending Cairo, Mayor Parsons, and the double lynching. He was also using race as a factor in interpreting crime in Cairo and hinting that the assaults against white women were more serious than the world outside Cairo could know. Unlike Mayor Parsons, however, Clanahan did not blame crime conditions in Cairo on acquittals and postponed trials. Instead, he was arguing that Cairo's African Americans were largely responsible for Cairo crime and that the river city's geographic location made it extremely difficult to catch either black or white murderers.

An examination of the *Cairo Evening Citizen* files reveals reports on eighty-one homicides that occurred in Cairo between 1904 and November 1909.[11] In many cases, the courts declared the alarmingly frequent homicides were justified by self-defense, but in some instances the guilty parties fled Cairo to escape prosecution and were never apprehended. From the eighty-one homicides, twenty-nine murder cases came before the circuit court in Alexander County, of which nineteen resulted in convictions. All of the convicted were sent to the penitentiary; none were hanged. The most notorious verdicts of "not guilty" all involved white defendants. One of the accused released by an Alexander County jury, Walter Davidge, had shot and killed Eugenie McClarney, the mother of a sixteen-year-old girl he was with when she surprised them near the high school and tried to persuade the girl to come home.[12] As to attacks on white women in Cairo, there is one piece of hard evidence: between November 1908 and November 1909, four assaults were committed or attempted in the alley where Anna Pelley was killed.[13]

In the autumn of 1909, Cairo was a city where an accused murderer had an almost 50 percent chance of being acquitted and where a white man could shoot to death a white woman for trying to prevent the "dishonoring" of her daughter and be declared "not guilty." The river town also had a number of homicides where no one was ever indicted, and public hangings at the courthouse, as mandated by law, had not been carried out in ten years.[14] Finally, criminal assaults against women could occur in the same place over a year's time and nothing would be done about it, such as lighting the area to discourage criminals.[15]

Yet these facts of Cairo life were not enough to condone the double lynching of November 11, 1909, according to most national newspaper editors. The *New York Times* emphatically refused to overlook the lynchings and satirized Cairo and the town's excuses for them. Illinois's own eminent newspaper, the *Chicago Tribune*, an American pioneer in anti-lynching news

Cairo High School was completed in 1897. Postcard courtesy of Darrel Dexter.

coverage, also could not excuse the double lynching and blasted the people of Cairo, particularly city and county officials. In an editorial titled "The Terrible Combination of Official Weakness and Mob Ferocity," a writer not only condemned Cairo and its officials but also warned of the growing racism in the northern states and the consequences for the nation.

> *From the moment it was known that the mutilated body of a white girl had been found in a Cairo alley and that bloodhounds in repeated trials had traced the crime to a negro shanty the people of the state knew what to expect. They could see the streets of that southern Illinois city filled with a crazed, brutalized, inhuman mob, the body of a negro swinging in the air, the local authorities cowed and submissive, and the state troops rushing in on special trains.*
>
> *The sheriff of Alexander County and the mayor and police of Cairo must have had this prophetic picture before their eyes. They could not have been deceived during the few hours which were given to them to act after the arrest of the murderers. They knew their own town with its dangerous element of river rats. They knew how the temper of an American community manifests itself after a crime of this nature. They knew that every ruffian would be yelling at the heels of that portion of the respectable population which yielded to the passions kindled by the unspeakable outrage and which for the moment was willing to throw aside every consideration of law, decency, and civilization to make punishment swift and sure.*
>
> *They knew these things. They knew also, that they would not protect the law by force against their fellow townsmen. They knew that their only hope lay in beating down the mob before it could gather headway and getting their prisoner out of town. . . . The police might as well not have been in existence—better not have been—for then there would have been no open confession of incapacity on the part of those sworn to maintain the law. The feebleness of officials and ferocity of crazed or ruffianly men make a terrible combination, with the consequences of which the north is coming to have disastrous experience.*
>
> *It is useless to ignore the fact that race hatred is growing in the northern states, which once cast reproach on the south for the horrors of mob violence. It is worse than useless. It may be*

> *dangerous to ignore it. The criminal negro class with which the south has had to deal is finding its way northward. . . . Two of the cities of Illinois have been handed over to the mercies of insane and inhuman mobs within a little over a year. The north, once so strong for negro rights, even when the possibility of negro domination in some states was involved, now is indifferent or hostile. . . .*
>
> *The north is finding a new problem in the vicious and criminal negro, and if such outbreaks of lawlessness and bestiality, almost incredible in their details, are to be avoided, the men to whom the protection of law is entrusted must be of better caliber than those who permitted the Cairo mob to disgrace the state.*[16]

The *Chicago Tribune* argued that it was the lynchings in general by the Cairo mob that had disgraced Illinois and not the particular lynching of a black man. The *Tribune* argued that "the criminal negro class" was coming northward, presenting a "new problem" for Chicago. The newspaper was blasting Cairo and the town's authorities but was also warning its readers of an invasion to the north of violent and unlawful African Americans. In some sense the *Tribune* editorial was not so different from Willis Clanahan's letter to the *New York Times*, as both the letter and the editorial spoke of a growing African American presence in Illinois viewed as transient, criminal, violent, and at times murderous. The letter and the editorial appear to be largely in agreement on race; their disagreement was on lynching. Clanahan "explained" and seemingly excused the lynchings in his letter, while the *Tribune* editorial strongly condemned them.

An even stronger condemnation of Cairo in particular, and all of Southern Illinois in general, came from Massachusetts, the home of American abolitionism and apparently a state where African American human rights were still considered more than forty years after the Civil War. The *Boston Herald* stated that "Egypt" (Southern Illinois) was racially contemptuous.

> *But the Cairo mob has not drawn the line at race, and a white murderer, as well as a negro suspect[,] have been exterminated by the collective action of men and women who in a twinkling dropped the veneer of their religion, their reverence for law, their respectability, and started out for blood.*

The Boston newspaper judged that the nation was "mortified over the scandal," which, if it had happened in Asia, would have been seen as barbarism.[17]

Another Massachusetts paper, the *Springfield Republican*, condemned not only Cairo and Southern Illinois but also the entire state.

> *If the South ever yielded up a more horrible story of human savagery than comes from Cairo, Ill., we do not recall it. Indeed, it is impossible that any Southern community could have done so; for how to surpass in deviltry and bloodthirstiness the hanging and shooting and burning of the victim, the soaking of pieces of rope in his blood, the beheading and parade of the head, and the cutting out of the heart and chipping it into pieces for souvenirs? . . . It is altogether as revolting an exhibition of human degradation as this country ever saw, or as Illinois ever saw, and Illinois has of late been given several exhibitions of the kind. The ease with which public authority broke down is a particularly discreditable feature of the case. That spectacle of the sheriff fleeing with the prisoner through the woods and over fields, with the mob in full pursuit—how hollow is shown to be the pretension of Cairo to a civilization worthy of the name!*[18]

Either from a sincere feeling of horror at the double lynching in Cairo or a desire to show that the American South was less barbaric than Illinois, or a mixture of both, leading southern newspapers the *New Orleans Times-Democrat* and the *Memphis Commercial-Appeal* strongly condemned the Cairo lynchings.[19] The New Orleans paper saw the Cairo lynchings as going beyond what could possibly be justified.

> *Even among those who defend the rough justice of lynch law when it is invoked to avenge outrages of the type that stirred the citizens of Cairo to fury will hardly find excuse for the mob leaders who conveyed the negro James to the city's public square, urged women to officiate as spectators, and later dragged the body of the dead brute for more than a mile through the public streets.*[20]

According to the New Orleans daily, the problem with the Cairo mob was that it acted too publicly, allowed women to witness the lynchings, and desecrated the body of the victim. It was not the lynching itself that was so deplorable but the way it was done. In that newspaper's opinion, "if the mob leaders upon overtaking the sheriff and his prisoner in the woods had quietly put the fiend to death, there would be no very strong censure of their actions by anyone fair enough to consider the provocation."[21]

The *Memphis Commercial-Appeal* was less restrictive in deploring the double lynching in Cairo, citing the enormity of the outbreak of lawlessness, which the Memphis daily had been fighting against for some time. The *Commercial-Appeal* then blamed conditions in Cairo on the local citizens' indifference to the law.[22]

In terms of a newspaper with national impact, the *New York Age* also condemned the events in Cairo in mid-November 1909. The *Age* was an influential African American weekly edited by Timothy Thomas Fortune, one of the most prominent activists of the twentieth century. Even the *Age*, however, did not argue that lynching was intrinsically wrong. In its headline concerning the Cairo incident, the paper emphasized that Illinois law would force Alexander County to pay out thousands of dollars in compensation to the victims, as Springfield, Illinois, had been forced to do the year before.[23] Monetary cost was in the forefront, even in the *Age*, and not the human cost to black people and the nation.

Another newspaper with influence beyond its city of publication was Joseph Pulitzer's *St. Louis Post-Dispatch*. The *Post-Dispatch* saw "madness" in the Cairo mob. The St. Louis newspaper, however, acknowledged that the mob's motive could be found in the horrible crime. The *Post-Dispatch*'s editorial placed the ultimate blame for the double lynching in Cairo on Sheriff Frank Davis but also expanded responsibility to Governor Charles Deneen. According to the St. Louis daily, Davis should never have "taken to the woods where capture was certain."[24] As to Governor Deneen, the editorial charged him with negligence—not keeping informed of the Cairo situation and not keeping in communication with Sheriff Davis. In conclusion, the *Post-Dispatch* declared that Cairo had reverted to barbarism.[25]

As major American newspapers were condemning the lynchings in Cairo and those responsible, other press organs, particularly in downstate Illinois, either condoned the lynchings or actually praised them. The editors of the *Bloomington Pantagraph* said, "So the greater shame and disgrace in the whole affair was the act of a brutal negro in murdering a young woman." The *Champaign Gazette* added, "As long as the outraging and murder of women continue, so long will lynching continue. . . . The outraging and murder of Anne Pelley in Cairo by William James was, from the very first report of it, a case in which Judge Lynch was almost certain to take a hand."[26]

The *Peoria Journal* also upheld Cairo's response to Anna Pelley's murder: "Mob law is a fearful thing. It is not defensible. But if there ever was a case in which a man met a righteous fate by unrighteous means, it was the case down at Cairo, in which a black brute followed up his crime of outrage by killing his victim to cover up his crime."[27] And the *Southern Illinois Herald* opined, "The killing of a brute in human form, after satisfactory evidence that he had committed the most heinous crime that the human mind can conceive[,] is a credit to Cairo and Cairo people."[28]

One might expect that unvarnished racism would emerge sometime in the debate over the Cairo lynchings, and it did in an editorial in the *Belleville News-Democrat*. The editor of this southwestern Illinois newspaper not only made an extremely racist observation on the Cairo event but also managed to give the oft-repeated justification for lynching in twentieth-century America—that is, due process of law was untrustworthy for achieving justice.

> *Save your sympathy for the girl who was murdered and her family and friends. . . . Don't waste it on the cowardly coon, the brutal beast who strangled her to death.*
>
> *The city of Cairo will be better for the fire test and the ordeal through which she just passed. She saw times that try men's souls. They will not be bothered with any Anna Pelley outrages and murders soon again. The cheeky niggers down there, the rankest in the state of Illinois, will be much tamer for a while and will know their place much better.*
>
> *In also stringing up the bloody handed and dastardly wife murderer* [Henry Salzner] *the alleged mob in Cairo purged itself of race prejudice, race persecution and race hatred. . . . It played no favorites. It showed no partiality to the white malefactor available for the scaffold. It acted on the fact that a white cutthroat is no better than a black one and deserves the same fate.*
>
> *Law's delays, wearisome technicalities of legal procedure in criminal trials, manufactured testimony, the spinelessness of juries, and weak and vacillating governors ever ready to commute sentences or to pardon thugs altogether create mobs, mob violence. Because of the lynchings there will be better order in Cairo hereafter and greater security.*[29]

Security given by lynch law, as opposed to the due process of law, was also defended by the *Muncie Press* of Indiana. The *Press* argued, "Conditions sometimes exist in a community, which make it seem farcical to plead that the law should be allowed to take its course. It doesn't take its course."[30] The Muncie paper went on to explain the Cairo lynchings by stating that lawlessness ruled in the river city, giving as evidence the now widely circulating fact that three women had been sexually assaulted at the same spot where Anna Pelley was found dead, with no rapists ever punished. The Indiana newspaper concluded by asserting, "Give us laws that must take their course quickly. And give us officials who will see that they do take their courses. Then lynchings will cease."[31]

The emotions aroused in Southern Illinois by the double lynching in Cairo were intense. As an example, the *Belleville News-Democrat* could not be content with the paper's initial support of Cairo. In a follow-up editorial titled "Cairo Redeems Herself," the editor spewed hostility at African Americans and reformers and lauded young women workers and the people at large. The editorial ends with a political theory of rather extreme popular sovereignty:

> *A so-called mob, without due process of law, executed the negro fiend who from the vilest of motives foully murdered an unprotected and innocent white working girl on the public streets and alleys of that city last Monday night.*
>
> *Every prude and every hypocrite and every sentimental reformer in the country is today hurling his anathemas against the city of Cairo for thus outraging propriety and imprudently setting the law of the land aside. Public officials will be blamed for not performing physical impossibilities and preventing that which heaven itself was powerless to prevent. . . .*
>
> *So long as virgin girls are ravished and murdered by human hyenas, so long will there be hangings to hold, and even Judge Lynch will be asked to get busy once in a while.*
>
> *That Anna Pelley, the innocent girl, working hard in a store to make an honest living, and on her way home after her day's toil, outraged by a fiend and then brutally murdered had been your sister or your daughter, what say you then should be done with the beast, the frightful monster, the hideous abortion of nature who committed the bloody and cowardly deed? Hanging is too good for him and burning too full of tender mercy.*
>
> *What is the sense in raving and panting against a people, vulgarly called a mob, who have temporarily taken the law into their own hands and avenged an awful crime and meted out rough justice? They are the state. They are simply resuming the reins of government which for considerations of expediency they gave up originally when they entered the civil compact and*

> *social contract. They have performed the supremest function of organized society, and we do not doubt they did it in the most effective way possible.*[32]

Opinions in defense of the Cairo lynchings from Belleville, Illinois, and Muncie, Indiana, and those deploring them in Chicago and New York were part of the intellectual and cultural conflict in America during the "Age of Lynching." The small-town and southern newspapers often defended the practice, and the more urban and northern press usually condemned lynching.[33] The Cairo press representing white Cairo also weighed in on the historical event that had gained the river city notoriety across America.

One of the letters to the editor of the *Cairo Bulletin* was titled "People Not to Blame." The letter writer observed "that no more God-fearing, cultured, kindly disposed, law-abiding, and better people exist on this broad continent, than do in the city of Cairo." The writer then claimed that the Cairo people were victims and that state laws were not enforced locally because of corrupt or incompetent officials. The greatest problem, however, according to the writer, was juries composed of "illiterate, incompetent, weak-minded, unsophisticated men who are hunted up by hirelings of the officers and made jurors, who weigh the evidence, but who are not competent to judge it and are easily swayed by lawyers, who scorn and laugh at justice."[34]

Another writer denied the worst aspects of the lynchings that were reported by the national wire services. Declaring that every report that went out of Cairo was full of misrepresentations, the writer stated that no women took part in lynching Will James, that there was no possibility of a race war, and that there was almost no disorder. The letter criticized the sensationalism of the accounts of the double lynchings in the national press, saying, "The ghastly and bloodthirsty details as given to the press were for the most part pure myth."[35] Finally, the letter writer used the unreliability of the due process of law, especially in Alexander County, as sufficient justification for the lynchings.

> *James and Salzner were undoubtedly guilty of crimes unspeakably horrible, the evidence, however, in both cases was largely circumstantial, and it was felt that both might go free, as other murderers have done here before. Blood hounds may not testify before juries and the strongest evidence will avail nothing against unscrupulous lawyers and packed juries. Mob law is wrong and is to be deplored—but there is a limit to human patience. The blood of Anna Pelley, Mrs. Salzner, poor Mrs.*

*McClarney (shot dead by the adult bar tender lover of her 16-year old daughter), and other martyrs was calling aloud, and who should say the answer to the call was not justified.*

*Ninety-nine out of one-hundred in Cairo have no regrets over these executions in Cairo. Let it go at that. Another thing: not the sheriff, the chief of police, or the captain of militia should be criticized for their inaction on the night of the executions. No power on earth could have saved these men; they were doomed, and to have offered resistance would have been to cause the loss of many lives.*[36]

The double lynchings took place on a Thursday, and the next Sunday all but one of Cairo's white ministers and priests commented on them. The Reverend Smallwood C. Ohrum of Cairo Baptist Church told his congregation that the worst class of criminal was the criminal Negro and that the local politicians had "patted this class on the head, as one pats a dog on the head to make him do his bidding."[37] He spoke of "real men," whom the women of Cairo were expecting to squelch the "dive" saloons, which were in his opinion the breeding places for Cairo crime. Reverend Ohrum completed his sermon by saying Cairo needed to be a safe place for women to live.

Cairo Baptist Church, pastored by the Reverend Smallwood C. Ohrum in 1909. Postcard courtesy of Darrel Dexter.

The Reverend Charles H. Armstrong of Immanuel Lutheran Church also attacked saloons, "where negroes are educated . . . for these crimes." Reverend Armstrong additionally criticized local courts, stating, "The failure of the courts to execute judgment caused people to take vengeance into their own hands." The Reverend August S. Buchanan of First Presbyterian Church echoed Reverend Armstrong, blasting dens, gambling rooms, and honky-tonks

Immanuel Lutheran Church, pastored by the Reverend Charles H. Armstrong in 1909 (*left*). Photo by Darrel Dexter. Cairo First Presbyterian Church on Washington Avenue, pastored by the Reverend August S. Buchanan in 1909 (*right*). Postcard courtesy of Darrel Dexter.

as "schools to educate criminals and have more graduates than the high schools."[38]

The Reverend George M. Babcock, Cairo's Episcopal priest, asked the members of his congregation to look at themselves and their fellow citizens to blame for crime in general and for Anna Pelley's death in particular. Reverend Babcock was one of the first to reveal that there had been four assaults or attempted assaults at the same spot where Anna Pelley was found. "The expense of a few dollars to place lights here would have made it an impossible hiding place for evil minded men," he declared.[39] He also asked his congregation about their love for their fellow man. The priest spoke of the African Americans migrating to Cairo from the South and asked if they were being offered a chance to live decent lives in Cairo: "Were they given an environment that would lift them up, or were they encouraged to live like dogs in miserable shanties, to pay big rents and ask for no repairs; to work for low wages?"[40] Reverend Babcock told his flock that African Americans in Cairo were encouraged to participate in vice for profit and that their political participation was a commodity to be bought and sold for a dollar or a drink. He concluded with the question, "Are your dives and hell holes a necessary evil or are they rather profit makers, vote getters and stock in trade for commercial privileges?"[41]

At least one white Cairo clergyman recognized that black people were mistreated and exploited in the town. Reverend Babcock's attempt to shame his congregation into deeper consideration for African Americans was, however, not recognized in America's urban press. The headline in the *Chicago Tribune* was that the Cairo clergy condoned the lynchings.[42] Chicago's *Inter Ocean* declared that "half a dozen" Cairo ministers intimated that the lynchings were a blessing in disguise.[43] The headline in the *Los Angeles Herald* was "Pastors in Cairo Approve Lynching."[44] None of the three mentioned Reverend Babcock's recognition of racism in Cairo. The city newspapers, however, showing the influence of the wire services on news stories at the time, all gave the same quote from editor Edward W. Thielecke of the *Cairo Bulletin*: "Cairo's disgrace is not the mob, but the conditions that made the mob necessary. For these conditions the authorities, from the judge on the circuit court bench down to the deputy sheriffs and bailiffs and the police department of the city[,] are responsible."[45]

The Church of the Redeemer on Washington Avenue and 6th Street, pastored by the Reverend George M. Babcock in 1909. Postcard courtesy of Cairo Public Library.

In an editorial in his own newspaper, Thielecke expanded on his defense of the town and identified what he saw as the long-range causes of the double, interracial lynchings. First, Thielecke argued that the thousands of people who had surged through Cairo streets were not a mob at all in the ordinary sense of the term. He pointed out that this throng was not motivated by racial prejudice, and it did not wantonly destroy property and take lives like the real mob in Springfield, Illinois, had a year before.[46]

> *From its beginning to its terrible end, the work of that awful night proved that the men engaged in it were sober, earnest, determined men—not bent on murder, but on punishing murderers, which the properly constituted authorities for years failed to do. It was a protest against lawlessness, a lawless protest to be sure, still a protest and one which struck terror into the hearts of the weaklings and corruptionists in official circles in the city and county, who had for years sneered at milder expressions of disapproval from the people.*[47]

The *Cairo Bulletin* editor concluded the piece by declaring that the problem with most Cairo critics was that they could see the town only as it was on the Thursday night of the lynching, not as it was on the Tuesday when Anna Pelley's body had been found or on "a long list of mornings in Cairo, whose history is written red in innocent blood unavenged."[48]

CHAPTER SEVEN

# THE REMOVAL OF SHERIFF FRANK E. DAVIS

Among the people most adversely affected by the lynchings, after Will "Froggie" James, Henry Salzner, and their families, was Frank E. Davis. Davis, the sheriff at the time of the lynchings, was born in 1863 in Cairo, Illinois, the only child of E. F. Davis, a merchant, and Julia Davis, a socialite and leader of the Cairo Benevolent Society. His New England–born parents had moved to Cairo before the Civil War, and his father died when he was a boy. Frank Davis, a bachelor, lived in Cairo all of his life, except for a time in the 1880s when he and his mother moved to Chicago, where he found employment as a clerk in a dry goods store. He worked as an accountant in railroad offices in Illinois and "was more at home with a long row of figures than he is anywhere else."[1] He was a "union man," being a member of the Brotherhood of Railway Clerks, which appealed to the many other union members who voted in Cairo. After returning to Cairo, he was elected to a term as county treasurer and assessor.[2] Next, Davis was overwhelmingly elected county sheriff in 1906 as a Republican, the Democrats not even running a candidate against him, and he was serving his first term at the time of the lynchings.[3]

Campaign picture of Frank E. Davis, appearing in the November 3, 1906, edition of the *Cairo Evening Citizen*, when he was running for sheriff of Alexander County.

For about a week after the lynchings, Frank Davis had possessed almost complete governmental powers in Cairo and Alexander County, but the Democratic county officers, coroner Dr. James McGriffen McManus and State's Attorney Alexander Wilson, were not happy with the situation. Even though he denied in press interviews any responsibility to investigate the double lynching, Wilson had demanded that Governor Charles Deneen declare the sheriff's office vacant and install McManus, a native of Cairo and the son of Irish immigrants.[4] Wilson quoted the law to the governor of Illinois: "The law provides that when a man is taken from a jail or the possession of a sheriff and lynched by a mob, the governor of this state must make a declaration or proclamation declaring the office vacant."[5]

Governor Deneen thus sent word to McManus, "I have at 5 o'clock issued a proclamation declaring the office of sheriff of Alexander County vacant and proclaimed you to be sheriff of Alexander County, Illinois." A Democrat, McManus revoked the commissions of fifty deputy sheriffs appointed by Davis.[6] Only two or three of the deputies were salaried, but the position conferred some power and prestige. Then, Dr. McManus appointed Alexander S. "Cot" Fraser, another Democrat, as his chief deputy and Alderman Frank Gorman as office deputy.

As Alexander Wilson had done, the Chicago *Inter Ocean* newspaper argued that under the 1905 law the governor must remove the sheriff from office but pointed out that Davis might be reinstated, if he could prove he had done all in his power to protect his prisoner. The *Inter Ocean* emphasized that pressure from Alexander County Democrats had forced the Republican governor's hand and expected Davis to be returned to his sheriff's post in a few days.[7]

The *Cairo Bulletin*, which had defended Davis's courage at the time Will James was taken from him and lynched, could not excuse his conduct as sheriff in the long run. Cairo's oldest daily charged Davis with appointing corrupt deputy sheriffs whom "he persisted in keeping in his employ to interfere with and thwart the administration of justice in important murder cases and in other cases civil and criminal."[8] The *Bulletin* saw no promise of betterment after judging the interviews given by Davis when he was in Springfield trying to get his job back.

Henry Salzner's death may have been more important than Will James's in causing Republican governor Deneen to permanently remove Frank Davis as sheriff of Alexander County. This was because Davis had been in the courthouse when a portion of the lynch mob broke in, and he had been armed and had an armed deputy with him. It was argued that local officials should have taken more precautions to ensure the safety of the suspect, as a portion of Cairo's population, referred to by some as "river rats," was known to be volatile and at times unlawful.[9] Perhaps Governor Deneen decided that if Davis had done all he could, the mob would never have gotten inside the courthouse.

This raises the additional question of how armed resistance to the lynchings might have changed things in Cairo on the night of November 11, 1909. After Frank Davis was removed from office, the *Cairo Bulletin* discussed Davis's role in the double lynching. At the outset of the editorial, the *Bulletin* declared that Davis had done everything reasonable to protect his prisoners. The Cairo paper then wrote that Davis could not have done more without sacrificing his own life, "to no purpose whatever," and that the people of the town credited Davis with preventing the loss of countless lives and a riot, which would have engendered huge damages to property, by not using his guns.[10] Another river city, Cincinnati, much larger but perhaps equally troubled and corrupt, had suffered forty-five lost lives and great property damage, including the burning of the county courthouse, when that city defended an accused murderer with armed force twenty-five years earlier in March 1884.[11] It certainly could be argued that Sheriff Davis's lack of resistance, and that of the Cairo police and the local National Guardsmen, saved considerable bloodshed, because the lynch mob may have numbered 10,000 and was certainly well armed—hundreds of shots were fired. Frank Davis had observed the day after the lynching that it was a good thing outside soldiers had not arrived on November 11, because there would have been wholesale bloodshed.[12] Mayor George Parsons declared, "A whole regiment of soldiers couldn't have stopped the work of last night."[13]

Although Frank Davis may have done "everything reasonable to protect his prisoners," he was still removed from his position as sheriff of Alexander County and was not reinstated, but it was not for lack of trying. On November 18, 1909, a week after the double lynching, he was in Springfield, Illinois, conferring with Governor Deneen. A petition was then filed with the governor for reinstatement. For about three weeks Frank Davis had hopes of getting his job back, both because Illinois's 1905 anti-lynching law provided a hearing for a removed sheriff and because Davis had the support of prominent citizens in Cairo, both white and black.[14]

The *Bulletin*'s criticism of Frank Davis was mild compared to the opposition marshalled by Ida B. Wells-Barnett, the most prominent female African American enemy of lynching in the United States.[15] A native of Mississippi and a resident of Tennessee and eventually Chicago, Wells-Barnett was asked to go to Cairo by her husband, Ferdinand Lee Barnett, who worked in

Ida B. Wells-Barnett visited Cairo in 1909 to investigate the lynching of Will "Froggie" James. Photo taken in 1909 courtesy of University of Chicago Library.

the Cook County state's attorney's office in Chicago as one of the few African American lawyers in Illinois. Hers was to be a fact-finding mission, but Wells-Barnett had already made up her mind as to what was at stake. She reasoned that if Frank Davis was reinstalled as sheriff, it was as good as condoning the lynching, which would mean that no black prisoner in Illinois would be safe.[16]

It was more than a 400-mile train trip from Chicago to Cairo, and Wells-Barnett arrived after dark on Sunday, November 28. Arrangements had been made for her to stay with Elder Thomas Andrew Head, an African American pastor and former deputy, and his family, who resided at 2611 Commercial.[17] Elder Head's wife, Bertha Avington Head, was prominent in the African American community in Cairo in her own right and had been printer of the *Cairo Standard*, an African American newspaper, until it closed after its printing office was burned in 1905.[18] After introductions, the clergyman told Wells-Barnett that Will "Froggie" James was probably guilty as charged.[19] Wells-Barnett then asked him why he believed that. Head replied, "Well, he was a worthless sort of fellow, just about the kind of a man who would do a trick like that."[20]

Wells-Barnett jumped up and heatedly told the preacher that condoning James's lynching meant that black people of all social classes and degrees of innocence would be exposed to mob violence. She refused to stay in his house. An African American druggist named Will F. Taylor lived in Cairo; Wells-Barnett had known him in Chicago, and the wife of the pastor accompanied Wells-Barnett to his house at 1313 Washington. From there she was sent to the home of John C. and Cordelia C. Lewis, who lived at 612 12th Street and were both teachers in the all-black Sumner High School.[21]

"They gave me a bed," Wells-Barnett wrote in her autobiography, but the next morning Mrs. Lewis telephoned Taylor that they could not keep her any longer.[22] They were afraid of the ramifications they would face if word got out that Wells-Barnett was staying at their home.

That night she and Taylor organized an "emergency meeting" for the next day.[23] At the meeting, Wells-Barnett learned that many black people had already signed petitions calling for Frank Davis's reinstatement. Furthermore, Davis had appointed black men as his deputies and was seen as popular and useful by the African American community. Fortunately for Wells-Barnett, two of the deputies, who had been fired by the temporary sheriff, Dr. McManus, were at the meeting. She called them out, and under her questioning they admitted that Davis had not done all he could to protect Will James. The Chicago anti-lynching crusader wanted to give the impression that black Chicago was supporting her and that she realized how difficult it was for black Cairo to want a Republican sheriff removed. She tried to reassure her audience that all she needed was some evidence of local support. At that point Wells-Barnett called for a resolution against the reinstatement of Frank Davis as sheriff, and it passed.[24]

Ready to board the train for Springfield and the Davis hearing, Wells-Barnett heard of a meeting of African American Baptists in Cairo and instead attended that. Allowed to address the meeting on November 29 at St. Michael's Episcopal Church Hall at 418 14th Street, Wells-Barnett says in her autobiography that she moved the presiding clergyman, the Reverend Thomas C. Graves, to tears, even though he had already signed a petition calling for the reinstatement of Frank Davis as sheriff. This man and others then signed the following resolutions now opposing Davis.[25]

> *Whereas the state of Illinois in less than two years has been disgraced by four lynchings of indescribable brutality;*
>
> *Resolved, that we call upon our public officials to use the militia before, rather than after, lynchings; and we demand the impeachment of officials guilty of criminal neglect of duty who rely upon lynchings "to clarify the atmosphere."*
>
> *Resolved, that the statute directing the governor to remove a sheriff who permits a prisoner to be taken from him and lynched is a wholesome incentive to effective service which should be vigorously enforced, and we call upon Governor Deneen to do his plain duty under the law.*

> *Resolved, that this mass meeting of fifty of the representative negro citizens of Cairo demand the permanent retirement of Sheriff Davis for failure to do his sworn duty under the law to protect the prisoners Will James and Henry Salzner in his charge who were lynched on the night of November 11. Every man, woman and child in Cairo knew 48 hours before the lynchings took place, that Will James was to be lynched. Yet not once did the sheriff swear in any deputies to aid him, nor call on the governor for assistance.*[26]

The reaction by the local press to Ida Wells-Barnett's descent into Cairo's black community was immediate. The *Cairo Evening Citizen* explained her foray into the river city:

> *Cairo negroes are by no means united in approval of the action of Mrs. Ida Barnett in resisting the reinstatement of Sheriff Frank Davis. Some of the most prominent colored people of Cairo discouraged the action of the meeting at St. Michael's Hall Monday night at which resolutions were adopted against the reinstatement of the sheriff.*
>
> *George E. Jackson is one of the outspoken colored men against stirring up race feeling at this time. He says that a large number of the better class of Cairo negroes do not approve of the action of the meeting, and that they feel that they are able to take care of themselves without the aid of any* Chicago negroes.[27]

Although admitting that she presented a strong case, the *Cairo Bulletin* called Wells-Barnett a "female race agitator" and expressed doubt that Governor Deneen would take her seriously.[28] Neither of the Cairo dailies recognized Wells-Barnett's hyphenated last name; both referred to her as "Mrs. Barnett."[29] Elder Head, who later testified in Springfield, questioned Wells-Barnett's right to be involved in the Davis hearing, saying that her views might be all right for Chicago but would not do in Cairo.[30]

Upon arriving at the state capital in Springfield, Ida Wells-Barnett faced formidable opposition to her objective of preventing Frank E. Davis's reinstatement as sheriff of Alexander County. After its ordeal of the previous year, she might have expected considerable support from Springfield's black community. In the hearing room, however, there was just one other black person favoring Davis's permanent removal, Abraham M. Williams, an attorney who came to give her legal advice.[31] Officially arrayed against her were Alexander County state's attorney Alexander Wilson and Walter Warder, an attorney and former state senator.[32] Also appearing in Davis's defense was the aforementioned former deputy under Davis and pastor Thomas A. Head and another black man, Thomas W. Warrick,[33] along with a priest, merchants, and businessmen. Mayor George Parsons sent a statement endorsing Davis. Warder presented a petition signed by nearly 500 African American men that had been circulated in Cairo barbershops.

Ida Wells-Barnett began by establishing her credentials as an advocate for her race in Illinois. She said that she had been appointed by a meeting of black citizens at the Institutional Church in Chicago to investigate the Cairo lynching. With that commission she had gone to Cairo and interviewed both black and white citizens, finding that Davis had "utterly failed" to protect his prisoners William James and Henry Salzner. She argued that the prisoners could have been protected if Davis had called on the police, gathered his deputies and appointed special deputies, and called on National Guardsmen in Cairo as soon as a suspect in the Anna Pelley murder was arrested. Wells-Barnett contended that if Davis didn't know a lynching would be attempted many hours if not days before James was killed, he was the only one. She revealed that a man was openly going about Cairo with a megaphone trying to form a lynch mob several hours before one actually coalesced. Then, to what was probably the astonishment of all present, Wells-Barnett stated that Will James was an "industrious negro" who had never been in trouble before. She further declared that there was no proof that James had known the murdered girl. Concluding this part of her argument, Wells-Barnett said that the only evidence against James was "the testimony of a dog," which had followed the trail to James after being given one of his coats to sniff.[34]

Returning to the concept that Frank Davis should have known there was to be a lynching, Wells-Barnett said that every police officer had warned of just such an event forty-eight hours before it occurred, and just about every adult male in Cairo also knew of the potential lynching. In addition, she criticized Davis's decision to take James out of town, chiefly because hundreds of Cairoites knew Davis, James, and Deputy Thomas Fuller were on an Illinois Central train out of Cairo as soon as it left, and when they learned the trio's location they went and captured them.[35]

Wells-Barnett then charged that Frank Davis and his supporters had made tools of Cairo's black population by frightening them with the prospect of a Democrat, Dr. McManus, becoming sheriff. According to Wells-Barnett, the African American people in Cairo believed "Davis would be easier with the colored people than McManus."[36] At that point in her presentation, Wells-Barnett spoke of the epiphany experienced by Cairo black people at the emergency meeting the previous Monday night. In her account, many at the meeting had realized that their letters to the governor or signatures on petitions to reinstate Davis were mistakes, and they were sorry. She then presented a list of 150 names of prominent Cairo citizens who had refused to sign the petition to reinstate Davis, followed by a copy of the resolution by the Negro Ministers Alliance of Cairo signed by eight black clergymen, including Presiding Elders McCracken and J. F. Duke of the Christian Methodist Episcopal Church. Completing her opposition to Davis's return, she told the story of the Reverend Thomas C. Graves, who was moved to tears by her words at the Baptist meeting in Cairo and renounced his previous strong and outspoken support of Davis. Senator Warder had just praised Reverend Graves, saying he had known him since he was a boy and "he has such a standing for truth and veracity in the community that if he were to tell me that black was white, I would believe him."[37]

Perhaps lost in the oratory over who supported Frank Davis was Ida Wells-Barnett's purpose both for her trip to Cairo and for her almost lone opposition in Springfield to Davis. She recognized, even if the majority of black people in Cairo initially had not, that here was a singular opportunity for Illinois's 1905 anti-lynching law to be enforced.[38] If a sheriff was removed permanently from office for losing a prisoner to a mob, every prisoner in the state after that time would be more strongly protected by the sheriff who had that person in custody because the sheriff's job would be at stake.

Frank E. Davis lost his job as sheriff of Alexander County when Governor Charles Deneen chose to permanently suspend him from office. Deneen stated, "The law may be severe; whether severe or not, it must be enforced."[39] According to the governor, his decision was based on several factors. The first was that Anna Pelley's murder had excited great public outcry, creating the climate for mob action, and yet Sheriff Davis did not enlist special deputies or make any other moves to resist a potential mob. Second, with Will James in custody and violence threatening, Davis did not contact the governor or alert him that troops were needed, although a company of militia was present in Cairo itself. Third, on his own initiative and almost without protection, he took James outside Alexander County, and when forced to leave the train at Dongola, Illinois, he contacted neither the governor nor the sheriff of nearby Union County for aid.[40] Finally, according to Governor Deneen,

> *after the execution of James the mob repaired to the county jail. Although cognizant of the temper of the mob and knowing that it was seeking [Arthur] Alexander, another colored man suspected in being implicated in the assault and murder of Anna Pelley, and whom the mob believed to be confined in the county jail, no effort whatsoever was made to place additional guards about the jail, [and] neither the sheriff or his deputies made any show of force. The most that was done was to ask for volunteers. Although it must have taken some time to beat down the cell door,* yet the sheriff is unable to identify a single person composing the mob, or to identify a single person whom he asked to aid him in suppressing the mob. *After [Henry] Salzner was taken from his cell, no effort was made to follow up the mob and rescue Salzner.*[41]

This official statement by Governor Deneen shows that it was obvious to him that Frank Davis was an accessory to the James-Salzner lynchings after the fact if not before. When Davis was interviewed after the double lynching, he had identified a Cairoite and two residents of Karnak, Illinois, as mob participants, yet Davis never again pointed them out to any official source.[42] He seems to have had political amnesia, as he realized that his town had sanctioned both murders of the suspects. In addition, he could not prove he had contacted a single person to come to his aid.

Former sheriff Frank E. Davis was not one to vacate his office easily. He did not accept Governor Deneen's decision and brought suit to test the constitutionality of the law under which the governor acted. In the circuit court, the judge ruled against Davis, who then appealed.[43] Davis rejected an offer of the position of county collector and treasurer, then held by Fred D. Nellis, who was likely to be appointed to replace Davis, as his lawyers advised him it would weaken his case.[44] The case was fought through the courts of the state of Illinois, and more than a year later Deneen's actions were affirmed by the Illinois Supreme Court.[45]

When he discharged Frank Davis, Governor Deneen set a new standard for Illinois sheriffs threatened with attempted lynchings. The standard required sheriffs to resist mob violence, even to the point of taking human life.[46] It is remarkable that the *Cairo Evening Citizen* endorsed Governor Deneen's action, although regretting Davis's removal. In doing so, the *Citizen* recognized the governor's courage, denied he was seeking the African

American vote in removing Davis, and asserted that mob lawlessness was still lawlessness and not likely to help the overall crime situation in Cairo.[47]

In her daunting literary study of lynching, Jacqueline Goldsby argues that Ida Wells-Barnett's political effectiveness was at an end very close to the turn of the twentieth century.[48] It should be noted, however, that had Wells-Barnett not gone to Cairo and argued in Springfield, Governor Deneen would have had a difficult time in not reinstating Frank Davis as sheriff of Alexander County. Wells-Barnett was the only opposition present at the hearing, and because of that, she had significant political impact. The 1905 anti-mob law was upheld, and Illinois sheriffs were put on notice that the loss of a prisoner meant the loss of a job.

Ida Wells-Barnett and others have brought to our attention that the James-Salzner lynchings in Cairo in 1909 were the last lynchings in the state of Illinois.[49] The removal of Frank Davis as county sheriff by Governor Charles Deneen and the upholding of the 1905 anti-lynching law encouraged and perhaps was the chief cause for Illinois sheriffs' successful resistance to lynching after 1909.[50] We know that about six weeks after the first Cairo tragedy, Sheriff Charles Cashel of St. Clair County strongly resisted a possible attack on his jail. An African American man had shot and killed a streetcar motorman and wounded the conductor. After the assailant was identified and taken to the county jail in Belleville, the sheriff quickly secured twelve riot guns and called on the governor for troops. There was no lynching in Belleville.[51]

Similarly, in neighboring Vienna, the county seat of Johnson County, Sheriff John B. Mathis took immediate action on January 12, 1910, calling Governor Deneen and requesting troops to check a mob and "forestall lynching" of three African Americans accused of killing Allen Clark, a white mail carrier from Carrier Mills, on a Big Four train.[52] Governor Deneen ordered four companies of the National Guard to Vienna "at once." Company K of Cairo was the first in Vienna and arrived within hours of the death of Clark, yet another example of quick action that was missing in Cairo in November 1909. Even the railroad cooperated with orders from Governor Deneen to not transport large crowds to Vienna. Lessons were learned from the Cairo double lynching, and sheriffs in St. Clair and Johnson Counties knew they needed to take speedy action not only to protect their prisoners but to save their jobs.

## CHAPTER EIGHT

# LOVIE GREEN AND HER HOUSE

Vengeance was still on the minds of Cairo people and others in the region in the few short days after the double lynchings, and the crime against Anna Pelley still haunted even the most humble citizens of the river city. Their letters to the *Cairo Bulletin* not only expressed the usual themes justifying the double lynchings but also added some chilling new details about Anna Pelley's death and revived focus on one of the original suspects in the murder, Lovie Green.

Little is known about Lovie Green outside the comments made about her in contemporary newspapers, which typically portrayed her as a villain and conspirator in the murder of Anna Pelley. Lovie Green was born about 1881 in Mississippi and claimed she moved to Cairo in August 1909; she somehow acquired property at 2515 Poplar Street, previously occupied by the parents of Arthur Alexander. The *Cairo Bulletin* said she came from Murphysboro, Illinois, where as a young girl she was known as Lovie Gray and had served time in the county jail for snatching a purse from a white girl.[1] At the time of the murder, she was working in a restaurant at 26th and Commercial in Cairo.[2] She had at least one sister living in Cairo, who Green said after the murder "would go downtown and hear stories" and come back and advise her to leave town, which she refused to do.[3]

A letter to the editor of the *Cairo Bulletin* on November 15, 1909, from a mother of five repeated the judgments of some of Cairo's clergy that saloons and other "dives," gambling houses, and "bad houses" were the cause of crime, such as the Pelley murder. She also argued that such establishments were not only tolerated in Cairo but encouraged. She added that "all the entertainment Cairo needs is a clean city." In this vein she said Mayor George Parsons should be impeached if he could not initiate the cleanup.[4]

At that point, the letter writer introduced stories that must have been circulating around Cairo but were nowhere in the newspapers. This is a reminder of Christopher Waldrep's frustration with historical research in the period—almost all historians' information about lynchings comes from what small-town newspapers were willing to print, and many of them sanctioned local lynchings, as did both of the Cairo dailies.[5] In her letter, the mother of five writes of the "living death" of Anna Pelley:

> *In the last nine or ten hours of her life [she was] in a filthy den, then not quite dead dragged into an alley where she made one last convulsive effort, clutching at the ground and drawing up one knee, exposed, mutilated horribly.... The negress who kept this dive was worse if possible than the frequenters of her place.*[6]

The "negress" she is referring to was Lovie Green, who managed the dwelling at 2515 Poplar Street, which was variously described as a house of prostitution, a disorderly house, and an assignation house.[7] An assignation house was a place where couples could meet and for a fee be given a private space, usually for sex. Cairo had not only prostitutes in the "houses of ill fame" along 13th Street and elsewhere in the city but also "street walkers," especially in the railroad yards and saloons, who sometimes needed a place to take their customers. The dwelling operated by Lovie Green was described in the *Cairo Bulletin* as the "barracks" to which the bloodhounds tracked the murderers of Miss Pelley. According to the *Bulletin*, complaints had been made against the house by black and white people who "were frequently

LeBlock Studio photograph of Lovie Green's house at 2515 Poplar Street. The *x*'s represent the entrance to the house and the shed where Green was discovered washing the rag of Will "Froggie" James.

annoyed by the disgusting practices and loudly disorderly conduct of the inmates of the house. Dissolute negroes and dissolute whites made it a nightly rendezvous for drunken carousing."[8] Across the street diagonally from Lovie Green's was Mt. Moriah Missionary Baptist Church at 2610 Poplar, and the pastor, John H. Knowles, also lived in the neighborhood and was doubtless distressed at the goings-on at 2515 Poplar. When a Citizens' League for Law and Order was established after the double lynchings in Cairo, the league listed nine demands, and among them was the suppression of assignation houses in Cairo, which were apparently springing up all over town.[9]

An oral history taken in 1975 claimed that Anna Pelley had a suitor at the time of her death, a white Cairo policeman, and that they met in "colored town," presumably at Lovie Green's place.[10] There is no evidence that Anna Pelley was at Lovie Green's dwelling on November 8, 1909, but rumors were flying, and this makes the hatred of Green in Cairo and in Union County, Illinois, better understood. Some people in Cairo, such as the "mother of five" who wrote to the *Cairo Bulletin*, seemed to believe that Anna Pelley had been forced to go to 2515 Poplar on the night of her murder.

The building used by Mt. Moriah Missionary Baptist Church was dedicated June 24, 1882, and is still standing but sits abandoned in Cairo. Photo by Darrel Dexter.

It was obvious that this letter writer believed Lovie Green was deeply involved in Anna Pelley's assault and murder, as did the *Jonesboro Gazette* in Union County, which called Green "the she nigger accomplice" and said things occurred on the night of Pelley's murder that were too horrible to print.[11] After all, Lovie Green had been caught washing stains out of Will "Froggie" James's handkerchief the evening the bloodhounds went to her dwelling. According to circuit judge William Nichols Butler, the public believed Lovie Green to be guilty, and the authorities were severely criticized for allowing her to remain at large.[12]

Two of those apprehended the day after Anna Pelley's murder, Georgia Cooper and her son, James Drain, left Cairo as soon as they were released by the police; friends had made it possible for them to flee. They returned to Cairo after the town had quieted down; in June 1910 they were living on Commercial Avenue, and Drain was working in the veneer mill. Cooper died in St. Louis in December 1910 and her remains were brought back to be buried in the cemetery at Mounds, Illinois.[13] Unlike Cooper, Lovie Green, at the time, refused to leave Cairo.[14]

On November 29, 1909, Green was called to testify before the police, jail, and fire committee of the city council. It was alleged that she gave five dollars per week for police protection, allowing her to run a "disorderly house" at 2515 Poplar, "where the hounds tracked when hunting the slayer of Miss Anna Pelley."[15] But Lovie Green denied everything. "I never gave a policeman a nickel in my life and I never run any house," she claimed. Upon further questioning by city attorney Angus Leek, Green stated that John R. Magee, "the negro lawyer," had advised her on several occasions to leave town and "go back up of Mound City and stay awhile," but she refused. "I haven't done nothing. I went on about my business, went wherever I wanted to go." Lovie Green remained defiant, saying that no police officer or deputy sheriff, like Elder Thomas A. Head, had ever asked her to leave Cairo. She admitted knowing the "negro" police officers John Wade and Luther Lewis and that "Mr. Gus" (Officer Johnson) had brought her to the current investigation.[16]

Lovie Green was then freed to go about her business. She was not arrested, because there was no evidence presented that she had committed a crime. She could have been easily run out of town under the climate of criminal justice existing at the time, but this was not done. If she kept a "disorderly house," she could have been forced to move it to 13th Street, Cairo's center for such places, but the 1910 census shows that all of those houses were inhabited by whites only.[17]

Lovie Green's time in Cairo is mostly an enigma. There are only a few remarks in the local press and an oral history interview made decades later that give researchers glimpses into her life. But a few facts about Cairo are relevant here. First, at the time of the lynchings, the municipal government and especially the police were branded as corrupt. It was becoming relatively clear that the Cairo police were being paid off to allow brothels and assignation houses to exist and that some officers used such places for personal sexual activities.[18] Second, a grand jury had been called to investigate not only the lynchings but also corruption and other crime in Cairo and Alexander County. The city and county officials and the police could have feared what Lovie Green might have to say. Finally, the purpose of an assignation house was for lovers or potential lovers to meet privately, and there is evidence of interracial affairs in town at the time.[19] Cairo policemen, as well as city and county officials or their relatives and friends, could have been using Lovie Green's dwelling. Thus, no matter what Green had done or helped others to do, or what she had concealed from the police, she still might have known far too much about the private lives of Cairo authorities and lawmen for them to be comfortable with her upcoming testimony before the grand jury. Of course, there is also a very simple explanation for Lovie Green not being arrested: the Cairo police and Alexander County lawmen did not want to risk another lynching, having been powerless to prevent the last ones.

As might have been expected, the *Cairo Bulletin* had no doubt about Lovie Green's guilt and why she was not being charged with anything.

> *The house to which the murderer or murderers of Miss Pelley were traced by blood hounds was a viciously disorderly house, and the police knew it to be such. It was a trysting place for bad negroes, men and women who engaged in boisterous conduct almost nightly, one of the many places in this city which attract and hold dissolute and desperate negroes and whites to the city. . . .*
>
> *Where is Lovie Green? Why not bring her before a grand jury and make her tell whether or not she paid $5 per week for the privilege of conducting her dive, in spite of repeated protests of the decent people of the neighborhood permitting the murderers of Anna Pelley to come and go at will and conduct themselves as they pleased, finding refuge in her resort safe from police interference.*
>
> *The circumstance in this case plainly indicates graft.*[20]

Lovie Green remained in Cairo for at least a short time after the murder, professing her innocence. A grand jury questioned her in December 1909 but found no evidence on which it could base an indictment against her. The 1910 census shows her still in the Sixth Ward on 25th Street with a man named John Merriweather, a street worker. The census taker called him her husband, although he was listed as single and she is listed as Lovie Green, a "mulatto," widow, and the mother of two living children, neither living with her. She left Cairo some time later and moved to East St. Louis, where she found work in a freight house and took in boarders. Her house on Poplar Street was purchased by James A. and Eva Woodward and served as their grocery as well as residence.[21] Lovie Green's only known involvement in the rape and murder of Anna Pelley was an intimate acquaintance with Will "Froggie" James and being caught in the act of washing a rag from a meal sack that matched the one used to gag Anna Pelley. It was generally believed she kept an assignation house, although she denied it. What Lovie Green testified before the grand jury investigating her involvement and that of Arthur Alexander in the murder of Anna Pelley is unknown, and what additional light she could have shed on the case, if any, she took with her when she left Cairo.

The site of Lovie Green's house in 1909 is now a vacant lot. Photo by Darrel Dexter.

## CHAPTER NINE

# THE GRAND JURY'S REPORT AND CORONER'S VERDICT

A grand jury had been impaneled on December 8, 1909, to investigate the deaths of Anna Pelley, Will "Froggie" James, and Henry Salzner and to identify and indict members of the lynch mobs who had killed James and Salzner.[1] Judge William N. Butler, who gathered the grand jury, seemed to be somewhat solitary in his hope that mob members would somehow face justice. There was some excitement also in mid-December when the rumor was circulated that Gertrude Maude Crabtree, the wife of Isaac W. Crabtree, a Mobile & Ohio Railroad conductor living on 30th Street, was said to have seen Will James at the corner where Anna Pelley got off the streetcar on the night of her death and recognized him because he was the "ice man" for uptown Cairo.[2] Her later testimony in court, however, was only that she had seen a "low, heavy set negro" at the location and "was afraid and hurried away."[3] She did not recognize the man as James, whom she knew "from his being on the ice wagon."[4]

Judge William N. Butler. Photo from Smith, *History of Southern Illinois*, 814.

On January 8, 1910, two months to the day after the rape and murder of Anna Pelley, members of the grand jury issued their report of the Pelley murder and the James and Salzner lynchings:

> *We find that Miss Pelley was the victim of said William James, who was taken from the custody of Sheriff Davis by a mob on the 11th of November, 1909, aforesaid, was executed by said mob about nine o'clock in the evening of said day near the corner of Eighth Street and Commercial Avenue. Immediately after his death the body was dragged to the spot by said mob or a portion of it. . . .*
>
> *It is evident to us that the mob was not composed entirely of the so-called "lawless element," as it was entirely directed toward the punishment of the two murderers aforesaid. No other person, white or black, was molested and no property was destroyed.*
>
> *The morning after the lynching the city was quiet and peaceful with no indication of the terrible work that had been done the night previously, and while the lynchings were contrary to the statutes of the state of Illinois and greatly to be regretted, we believe no innocent man met his death at the hands of said mob.*[5]

No members of the mob were named in the grand jury report, although Sheriff Frank E. Davis had mentioned three to the press by name or by reference through which their names could easily have been determined: George William Logan of Cairo, John D. Copeland of Karnak, and one of the storekeepers in Karnak had been in the mob that took James from Davis in Pulaski County, he claimed.[6] Yet despite this identification by Sheriff Davis, the Alexander County coroner's jury also had named no one in James's death. Instead they gave the usual verdict that Will James "came to his death by injuries at the hands of persons unknown to us."[7]

The coroner's jury was still to deliver a final report on Anna Pelley's death. Mayor George Parsons continued to offer a $1,000 reward for information pertaining to her rape and murder, which suggests that he still believed Arthur Alexander or someone else had been Will James's accomplice, or he believed that the Cairo citizenry thought so.[8] Finally, on January 25, 1910, the coroner's jury returned a verdict.

> *We, the undersigned jurors sworn to inquire into the death of Miss Pelley on oath[,] do find that she came to her death by strangulation and suffocation at the hands of William James and at least one accomplice whose identity is unknown to us. We further find that the deceased was attacked in front of No. 424 Twenty-sixth Street, then carried to the alley-way between*

> *Twenty-fifth and Twenty-sixth streets near Elm Street where she was criminally assaulted and killed. This happened between the hours of 6:30 and 8 o'clock p.m., November 8th, 1909.*[9]

The opinion of the inquest, therefore, was that Will James did not act alone. The grand jury, however, had previously refused to indict Arthur Alexander and explained why. Bloodhounds had been taken to Arthur Alexander's house several times, but the dogs had refused to take up his scent at any time.[10] Alexander had been released from the Champaign County jail at Urbana on January 10, 1910, before the inquest report was issued.[11] The release was on the orders of Alexander County state's attorney Alexander Wilson and the county's new sheriff, Frederick Daniels Nellis. Wilson and Nellis added a "postscript" to the release order: the Champaign County sheriff was told to warn Alexander that it would be unsafe for him to return to Cairo, as public sentiment was not satisfied that he was innocent. Will James's confession implicated Alexander, and some circumstantial evidence tied him to the crime. The *Cairo Bulletin* also stated that Arthur Alexander's character condemned him as "a mean negro, bad on general principles, frequently involved in disturbances of the peace. His presence in any community is therefore a menace to law-abiding people."[12] Alexander said in a press interview in Champaign that he was never going back to Cairo.[13] He went to East St. Louis, the same place Lovie Green sought refuge, and died there in 1916 at the age of thirty-eight years.

## CHAPTER TEN

# THE ANNA PELLEY AND MARY E. SALZNER MEMORIALS

The *Cairo Evening Citizen* was the first to report that a "prominent citizen" had proposed that a collection be made to mark the scene in the alley where Anna Pelley lost her life. It was to be "a testimonial from the people of Cairo of their deep sorrow over her awful death and a standing reminder to the vicious element of the community that Cairo will not tolerate a repetition of such crimes."[1] The choice of location aroused considerable controversy; the Pelley family opposed the idea of a memorial in Cairo, as did the people living near the site of the killing.[2]

John Jeremiah Pelley, a brother of Anna Pelley, became the spokesperson for the family and its wishes for the memorial and where it would be located. Pelley was, at the time of his sister's murder, roadmaster for the Illinois Central in McComb, Mississippi. He eventually became general manager for the Illinois Central and continued to rise in the ranks of American railroading until, by 1934, he was president of the American Association of Railroads and chairman of its board of directors, which controlled 63 percent of all railroads in the United States.[3] He expressed the Pelley family wishes, as well as his own, in the following letter to the *Cairo Bulletin*, the newspaper selected by the family to supervise the collection of contributions:

> *If the people of Cairo wish to give some testimonial of their appreciation of my sister's noble character and life rather than to commemorate the manner of her death and what followed it, I would much prefer that they do so by erecting a monument at the cemetery where she lies buried.*[4]

John Pelley's plea must have had great influence in Cairo because the collector for his sister's monument fund immediately acceded to it. The *Cairo Bulletin* proposed, as an alternative to the *Citizen*'s original plan, a public subscription for a monument on Anna Pelley's grave in Anna, Illinois, which was accepted by her family. And to commemorate Pelley's violent death, the *Bulletin* proposed the following:

> *On the 10th day of November each year every man in the city should wear a small knot of rope in the lapel of his coat as a quiet and dignified manifestation of the end of evil doers of any kind and all races, who outrage or insult pure womanhood. Every white and colored man of the city can thus place himself on record for law and order for a day each year, and it is believed that no object lesson could be more impressive or permanent.*[5]

One could easily deny that there is any dignity in the display of a symbol of a lynching rope, and it is doubtful whether any "colored man" in Cairo wore "a small knot of rope in the lapel of his coat" on November 10, 1910. One could also argue that the "object lesson" was not law and order but the reverse, mob rule and riot. Anna Pelley's death was on November 8, and the Will James lynching was on November 11, so the choice of November 10 was doubtless intended as both a memorial of her death and a celebration of his.

The Anna Pelley monument in Anna City Cemetery reads "A Life Sacrificed but Remembered by Friends." Photo by Darrel Dexter.

The *Cairo Bulletin* collected over $1,000 for a monument for Anna Pelley's grave. The marker was made from a huge block of granite, featuring a cross before which knelt a female figure in an attitude of deep grief. More than 1,500 people contributed, with gifts ranging from five cents to ten dollars.[6] On January 24, 1910, a monument company in Centralia, Illinois, having submitted the lowest bid, was selected to make Anna Pelley's marker by the committee composed of Julius P. Schuh, Fannie Brandis (Mrs. John A.) Miller, and Judge

A. J. Pickrell, the postmaster in Anna.[7] An unveiling of the marker and memorial service was held at the gravesite in Anna on Sunday, October 17, 1910, before a crowd of several hundred; 150 attended from Cairo alone. Miss Ella Dolan, an intimate friend of Anna Pelley in Cairo, pulled the cord and uncovered the stone.

There was already a campaign for legal funds to be used to convict the alleged murderer of Mary E. Salzner, which had been started at the time of her death. By November 24, 1909, $82.50 had been collected, and it was originally also going to be added to the Pelley memorial fund. But the *Cairo Evening Citizen* spoke out:

> *It has been suggested that while we are honoring the memory of the girl whose life was taken that Cairo might be aroused from her lethargy, we should not forget the woman who suffered such indignities and died from cruelty and neglect—Mrs. Henry Salzner.* The Citizen *believes that while we are remembering the one, we should not neglect the other, who leaves fewer friends to perpetuate her memory.*[8]

Mrs. Salzner's funds were kept separate and a committee was formed to select a stone to mark her grave.[9] Ironically, the fund was held by Cora

The marker over the grave of Henry A. Salzner can be found only two rows from the Anna Pelley monument in Anna City Cemetery. The original monument for his murdered wife, Mary E. Jones Brown Salzner, which was erected in 1910 in Oak Grove Cemetery in Paducah, Kentucky, is gone, and her grave is now marked by a simple stone. Photos by Darrel Dexter.

Bails Zanone, the wife of a notorious saloonkeeper, Louis Zanone. Mrs. Zanone, however, kept the fund well and added to it, so a $100 monument was erected, but not in Cairo. It was raised over the Salzner grave in Paducah, Kentucky, but has since disappeared.[10] What became of that original marker is unknown, but today only a small replacement marker identifies the Salzner grave.

Although Anna Pelley could not be buried in Cairo, some physical remembrance of her was still sought by women in the city. One suggestion was that a memorial window be placed in St. Patrick's Church, but the fund was eventually used for the "working girls' rest room" at the interurban trolley car station in Cairo. A plea for this shelter was presented in the *Cairo Bulletin*, the newspaper describing "several hundred young women equally faithful in business and upright in character, co-workers and in some cases warm friends of Miss Pelley."[11] The piece went on to remind the readers that "working girls" labored early and late, in heat and cold, to serve the public and that they needed a place of refuge from fatigue, exposure, and danger. Some $119 was collected for the facility, and there were many in-kind contributions: a ton of coal for heat by the Cairo City Coal Company; furniture and toilet articles by the Schuh family, drug wholesale and retailers; a rug by Ladies of the Church of Redeemer; a sofa and pillow by the Ladies of the Presbyterian Church; a gas range by Mrs. Leo McDaniel, an alderman's wife; draperies for all windows by Pupkin Dry Goods Company; and soap, cleaning tools, dishes, silverware, curtains, and other necessities by various other businesses.[12] The rest area opened in the cold of December in 1909.[13]

The late Miss Anna Pelly, whose noble life was sacrificed to corrupt government in Cairo, Monday, Nov. 8th, 1909.

Photo of Anna Pelley that ran in the *Cairo Bulletin* for several consecutive days as money was collected for her monument. Notice the crucifix, which was one of the items stolen after her death. *Cairo Bulletin*, December 15, 1909.

Many people of Cairo were anxious to donate to the memorials to honor Anna Pelley and Mary E. Salzner, partly to pay tribute to the character and memory of the women and partly as a sign of regret that Cairo had not been a safe place for them. One could easily argue that the remorse was over the fact that the city had not been safe for white women, as there had been little outcry or remorse shown for the fifteen African American women who had been slain in Cairo between the years 1886 and 1909, some of them as violently as Anna Pelley and Mary Salzner. Yet Anna Pelley's murder was the only one committed in the city by a black man against a white woman. Regardless of the motivation, there was a rising voice that began to call for the cleanup of the city that would curb the violence of Cairo. How committed would the leaders of Cairo's business community be to this movement if it began to reach deep into their pockets?

Postcard view of Commercial Avenue looking southeast from 9th Street in Cairo. Postcard courtesy of Darrel Dexter.

CHAPTER ELEVEN

# LIQUOR, VICE, AND CORRUPTION IN CAIRO

In December 1909, a living memorial to Anna Pelley was operating in Cairo as a rest area for working women. In that same month, memorial services were held for Pelley throughout the state of Illinois, on the official order of Mrs. Mary E. Kuhl of Chicago, president of the Illinois Woman's Christian Temperance Union.[1] Both in Decatur, where Mrs. Martha Litts received Mrs. Kuhl's order, and in Cairo, Anna Pelley's murder was blamed on the "saloon element." In Cairo, the WCTU memorial service contained the following charge:

> *Miss Pelley's life was sacrificed as a result of the conditions which put money and the traffic in body and soul destroying vices above decency, honor, and virtue.*
>
> *Miss Pelley's life was taken as the fruit of laxity in law enforcement and disregard of the public welfare.*
>
> *Miss Pelley's life was cut short because beings in the semblance of men connived for money at the miscarriage of justice. Finally, the death was caused because the "self-respecting" members of the community have not held politicians responsible for conditions in the city. To keep such a crime from happening again, we can abolish the dives and dens, and compel the saloons to adhere to the law or vote them and the dives out altogether.*[2]

It is obvious that the WCTU would condemn the alcohol trade in Cairo as elsewhere because that was the organization's purpose, but the tying of Miss Pelley's murder to the town's considerable trade in alcohol and other vices such as prostitution and gambling had merit. Cairo was a "wide-open" town with a vengeance. The saloons never closed. Indeed, they stayed open the night and morning of the lynchings and could not be closed, despite the orders of Governor Charles Deneen, until the National Guardsmen arrived.[3] In his official report to Governor Deneen, Brigadier General Frank P. Wells, commanding the National Guard in Cairo, stated that he had advised Mayor George Parsons the day after the lynchings that the governor wanted all the saloons closed. Parsons had replied that "he would think over the matter and do as he thought best in regard to keeping the saloons closed."[4] General Wells informed the mayor that it was an order and not a request, but Parsons still exclaimed he would "do as he pleased." Lieutenant Colonel Claude E. Ryman, who commanded the remaining three companies of soldiers in Cairo, was ordered by General Wells to keep the saloons closed as long as the troops were there, regardless of Mayor Parsons's wishes.

When the *Cairo Evening Citizen* began a reform drive after the lynchings, one of the first things the newspaper called for was the Sunday closing of establishments that sold alcohol. In the body of the article advocating Sunday closing, the *Citizen* asked, "What is going to be the result of this terrible sacrifice of pure life in Cairo?"[5] The *Citizen*, therefore, saw a relationship between Anna Pelley's death and Cairo's alcohol trade. To further inform or shame its readers, the *Citizen* claimed that the state was watching Cairo and that the foremost daily in Illinois, the *Chicago Tribune*, was saying that Sunday closing would be the first step in bringing about a better Cairo.[6]

The scope of the alcohol business in Cairo in 1909 and 1910 was almost incredible. In 1909, seventy-six saloons (taverns, bars, and the like) operated in Cairo—a town whose population was about 14,000 men, women, and children.[7] In addition, the *Cairo Bulletin* claimed that the "liquor houses" (wholesalers) brought more money into Cairo than any other business, noting a post office flooded with money orders, banks flooded with deposits, and express companies almost swamped with packages.[8] An estimated 200,000 packages of liquor shipped from Cairo in one week. The American Express mail business in Cairo was the largest in the state outside of Chicago, and the Southern Express Company added two special cars on the Mobile & Ohio Railroad every day and on one day added four. A week earlier the *Cairo Bulletin* observed, "From the day and night shipments from Cairo's mail order liquor houses for the week past, it may be assumed that many a dry town will have a wet Christmas."[9]

Every Sunday, railroads ran special excursions to Cairo, which became a mecca to surrounding communities. There were even runs on the Sunday following the double lynching, but numerous visitors complained because the saloons were closed and they did not enjoy themselves. A day later, however, when National Guard companies from disinterested Effingham and Shelbyville were withdrawn, the saloons, often known as "dives," on Ohio Street by the levee opened their doors. Many other saloons "back in town" also opened and did a "rushing business" until Mayor George Parsons, on Governor Deneen's order, had the Cairo police close everything down again. The very next day, however, Deneen lifted his closing order and saloons, bars, dramshops, wine rooms, and taverns reopened.[10]

Cairo stayed awash in alcohol in the succeeding years. The city ordinance allowed one saloon for every 300 residents, but the ratio of establishments to the population in 1910 averaged out to one saloon for every 190 people.[11] A new ordinance for one saloon for every 500 people was introduced but was tabled.[12] Additional reform was attempted in 1911 when it was proposed that "disorderly houses"—houses of prostitution—be denied a liquor license. The *Cairo Bulletin* cynically commented that if keeping a "disorderly house" meant revocation of liquor licenses, there would be no such houses in Cairo.[13]

Prostitution was another vice that contributed to the wealth of Cairo. Nearly ten years earlier, in 1901, when Marion C. Wright was elected mayor of Cairo, he had attempted to abolish organized prostitution, with the support of the *Cairo Evening Citizen*.[14] Wright had great business interests at stake in Cairo, being president of the City National Bank and the Cairo City Coal Company and vice president of the Cairo City Gas Company and Cairo Electric and Traction Company during his tenure as mayor.[15] When the newspaper started exposing "Thirteenth Street," the heart of Cairo's "red-light district," the *Citizen* claimed the street was notorious throughout the state if not the nation. Thus, not only had Wright's attempts to attack prostitution in Cairo failed miserably, but Cairo's main center of prostitution was known far and wide.

Mayor Marion C. Wright. John M. Lansden Collection, Southern Illinois University Special Collections Research Center, Carbondale.

Cairo, according to John M. Lansden, author of *A History of the City of Cairo, Illinois*, "had long borne a hard name."[16] A few days after the double lynching, the *Louisville Courier-Journal* stated that Cairo was known all over as a "tough town."[17] Sixty years later, Herman R. Lantz of Southern Illinois University, in his historical and sociological study of Cairo, argued that the city at the time of the notorious lynchings had an economy based on liquor and vice.[18] Lantz further asserted that the trade in alcohol, and especially prostitution and gambling, because they were illegal, led to an atmosphere of crime and violence. This was because the police had to be paid off and the city administration had to look the other way for prostitution and gambling to exist.[19] The continuation and even the spread of these vices in Cairo were symptomatic of a decline in public safety. Four women had previously been attacked in the exact same place where Anna Pelley was raped and murdered, possibly by the same person or persons, and no suspects were identified. Even Mayor Parsons admitted after the double lynching that it was relatively safe to commit murder in the river city.[20]

Cairo's gambling problem in late 1909 was intimately tied to the town's problem with "dives"—saloons where patrons could be drugged, robbed, assaulted, cheated, and more. Such places existed all over Cairo and were operated by both white and black people, but the *Cairo Bulletin* considered Gus Bourgois's "dive" at 315 Ohio Street the worst.[21] Augustus or "Gus" Bourgois was born in Cairo in 1884, the son of John A. Bourgois, a native of Paris, France, who served as Alexander County commissioner, Cairo city alderman from the northwest part of the city, and owner of a saloon there called the Half-Way House.[22] Gus Bourgois's place was called a "strong-arm" establishment, because if all other methods to relieve a customer of his money failed, a patron might simply be beaten up and robbed. Gus Bourgois sent "cappers" to the principal Cairo streets to lure in transients and strangers in town, and, according to the *Bulletin*, "the victims have been many."[23] Once someone was enticed into the Bourgois "dive," the two favorite schemes for robbing them were the dice game and the assignation room. The dice game allowed the player to win a few throws, and then a button was pushed under the dice table, which activated an iron plate attached to a battery underneath. The dice had metallic spots, which made them move as the button was pushed. Bourgois's "assignation rooms" featured prostitutes armed with knockout drops who would "roll" the victims—that is, take their money and valuables after they had been rendered unconscious.

Because of the political and economic circumstances in Cairo, the local reformers saw little hope of positive change, although they were still fighting rather valiantly for it. Indeed, the *Citizen* headlined the arrest of Lu Vaughn, Dave Ross, and seven others for being inmates or "frequenters" of assignation houses as "Another Cleaning Up Stunt by the Police."[24] Arresting Lu or Lulu Vaughn, an African American keeper of an assignation house on 15th Street, however, proved to be a mistake. Angry that her trade was interrupted, she said she had paid off a policeman and allowed him and his partner to entertain women there. Such police protection of prostitution made combating "the social evil" difficult. When Ethel Wells, Myrtle Stevenson, and Rose St. Clair were fined for allowing fourteen-year-old boys to use their houses, the *Citizen* once again raised the call for reform.

> *The revelation that boys under age have been frequenting houses of ill fame and have contracted diseases that they may never rid themselves of shows that there must be more safeguards thrown around the boys. . . . No matter what is done with the scarlet district . . . it must be better policed than it has been, if we are to have any reform here.*[25]

The *Cairo Bulletin* was less discreet in publicizing why Rose St. Clair and others were arrested and fined:

> *It has been developed in the course of the investigations . . . that nineteen young boys had been in the habit of patronizing the houses on the street and twelve of them needed the attention of a physician, as a consequence. It is stated that in one case a boy of 14 years was picked up by one of the women and carried in her arms to her room and there debauched.*[26]

The barriers to alcohol and prostitution reform were political and economic. Mayor George Parsons had been recently reelected as a "wide-open town" candidate and had done nothing to disappoint his supporters. The *Citizen* pointed out the economic ramifications:

> *Is it not a fact that there are those who condone the red light district because of the profit there is in it? Is it not a fact that the high rentals from property occupied by these unfortunates and the trade of these people and the male element that is attracted by them is the real reason why it is tolerated in any community? Is it not a fact that just, as in the white slave traffic, there are those who want revenue from it, and for that reason it is permitted to exist?*[27]

The problems of "disorderly houses," drinking establishments that were so dirty and dishonest that they were called "dives" or "dens," and illegal gambling in Cairo seemed to make the river city ripe for reform in the winter of 1909–10. In addition, Anna Pelley's rape and murder and the double lynching that followed turned state and national attention to Cairo. This was also the Progressive Era, and reform was everywhere in America. Might reform also touch Cairo? As might have been expected, the more legitimate business interests in Cairo along with the daily newspapers made an attempt at reforming prostitution, dives, and illegal gambling in the river town, but there was strong resistance.

CHAPTER TWELVE

# CORRUPTION AND REFORM

Eleven days after Anna Pelley's assault and murder, the Cairo Board of Trade named twenty-five men to explore constituting a "Law and Order League."[1] The Board of Trade called on the Commercial Club, another business organization, to name an equal number of men to help form such a league. Less than a week after the league was formed, Commercial Club president Egbert A. Smith issued a statement that conditions in Cairo were bad and had been for many years.[2]

Alderman James Meehan attended the meeting of the Commercial Club, but his statements to the potential reformers must have discouraged the clubmen, if they expected cooperation from city government. First, Meehan echoed Mayor George Parsons's earlier defense of the two lynchings, saying that since the mob action, the city had been quieter than ever before. Meehan went on to declare that this quiet would have remained had it not been for the Cairo newspapers, whose editorials aroused the people. The newspaper influence, in the alderman's account, did great harm. Then Meehan challenged the commercial men, declaring that there was no need for any "Law and Order League." The alderman continued, "What do we want a Law and Order League for? Who wants it? The newspapers want it."[3] Becoming steadily more heated, Meehan threw in the face of the Commercial Club men the assertion that if the law were enforced, some of them would be in jail. The alderman's conclusion was that the town was being killed through the newspapers.

Despite Alderman Meehan's tirade before the Commercial Club, that organization and the Cairo Board of Trade each selected twenty-five men "to explore the possibility of bringing better government to Cairo."[4] At the first meeting of the committee of fifty, Mayor Parsons himself attended and spoke briefly. He, like Meehan, did not want a "Law and Order League." As a counteroffer, the committee for better government in Cairo offered to work in an advisory capacity to the city government, which met with agreement from Mayor Parsons.

The *Cairo Bulletin* saw Parsons's compromise as a tacit admission that better government was needed in Cairo, and the morning paper called on the mayor to lead the movement for municipal reform. The *Cairo Bulletin* then suggested that the mayor should get rid of his "false friends" who for years had been deceiving him about conditions in the police department. The crusading Cairo daily added, "This would be assuming that the mayor is really ignorant of the conditions in the police department."[5]

Much of the reform effort had to center on eliminating corruption and complicity in the Cairo police department. For example, Lovie Green was keeping an assignation house at 2515 Poplar Street, where Will "Froggie" James and Arthur Alexander usually lived when they were in Cairo. Black families in the vicinity of the dwelling were disturbed by the noise and activities at 2515 Poplar, which was disorderly almost every night, and complained to the police, but nothing was done.[6] On three occasions young white ladies were insulted as they passed the house. The *Bulletin* exclaimed sadly, "If the place had been suppressed or legally regulated, perhaps the insults would not have taken place, and Miss Pelley might not have been murdered."[7]

Links between the Cairo police and prostitution went beyond not shutting down assignation houses and brothels. Some policemen also fraternized with prostitutes. Two Cairo officers were so drunk and disorderly in rooms over a saloon at 15th and Commercial Avenue in November 1909 that the bartender called Police Chief Martin S. Egan. Suspecting the worst, the chief tried to telephone the policemen to warn them that he must come answer the complaint. They were still there, however, when he arrived and were with "dissolute women."[8] This was not all. It was later learned that one of the policemen "was in the act of defiling the person of a young girl, the daughter of a respectable family of this city."[9] A male friend of the girl had been looking for her and found her in the rooms over the saloon at 15th and Commercial. The man asked the girl to leave with him, whereupon one of the police officers threatened to arrest him and ordered him to leave. Egan suspended the officers for a few days with pay. One of them, "having been led by his previous experience to believe that he might do what he pleased without danger to himself, grossly insulted one of Cairo's highly respected young ladies on her way home from church" and was dismissed.[10]

In late 1909, police behavior to a large degree determined the behavior of Cairo's prostitutes. Cairo police chief Egan apparently wanted to protect his officers and the women they were consorting with, even those who were prostitutes. He did not seem interested in closing down assignation houses, which were obviously a serious public nuisance. That is one reason why the

*Cairo Bulletin* called for Egan's immediate removal from office, along with four police officers whose behavior with "dissolute women" was offensive both to public decency and public safety.[11] Egan was not immediately removed as chief, but at the end of 1909, he was ordered by Mayor Parsons to close down all assignation houses in Cairo because of an agreement between the mayor and the newly forming Citizens' League.[12]

Prostitution was an attraction for Cairo, with the hub of the town's sex trade on 13th Street known nationally, but the alcohol trade, especially the wholesale trade, was a vital part of Cairo's economy. The regulation of the alcohol business, therefore, created considerable controversy in the river city. By December 1909, assignation houses were out, but twenty-four-hour saloons were still in, much to the disappointment of Cairo's afternoon daily, the *Evening Citizen*. Less than a week after the double lynching, the *Citizen* called strongly for the closing of saloons at least on Sundays. The newspaper warned that all the evils that had beset Springfield, Illinois, because that city had rejected the Sunday closing of saloons would strike Cairo if saloons were left open on the Sabbath.[13] The *Cairo Bulletin* differed with the *Citizen*'s position to the point of ridicule. The *Bulletin* compared Cairo and Springfield:

> *The people of Springfield are probably just like the people of Cairo and of other cities, in this: they do not favor extreme restrictions which will hamper them in their harmless liberties, recreations and amusements—on Sunday or any other day. And it is safe to assume that here, as in Springfield and elsewhere, any man who shall announce himself in favor of such restrictions could not be elected mayor. But are we justified in declaring that, because the people of Springfield defeated [Lawrence Yates] Sherman on the issue of Sunday saloons, therefore they must want bad government? Would we be justified in saying that because the people of Cairo might defeat a man for mayor on the issue of general Sunday closing therefore they want and approve unrestrained and unpunished murder?*[14]

Of course, the debate over Cairo's alcohol situation did not end with the dailies sparring. At a meeting of the Commercial Club late in November 1909, some of the "saloon men" of Cairo threatened to organize in opposition to new attempts to regulate the alcohol situation in Cairo, especially with respect to Sunday closing.[15] They were opposed by the Reverend S. C. Ohrum of Cairo Baptist Church, who called for the "peace of Sunday" not to be destroyed by the opera house and saloons being open, which encouraged the "rougher sort from the surrounding country to spend their day here in drunken carousels and terrorizing the people. . . . A proper regard for the good of all would close up the saloons on Sunday."[16]

Three weeks later, at a special city council meeting, the saloon closing issues came to a head when the Citizens' League Executive Committee called for the closing of all Cairo saloons from midnight to 5 a.m. every day. The first to reply to this was Mayor George Parsons, who said there was no state law against saloons being open twenty-four hours a day and to close them for five hours daily would require a vote of the city council. The mayor was followed by Alderman Patrick Scullin, a saloon and restaurant owner who wanted saloons open at all hours for humanitarian reasons, because they "afforded shelter to poor fellows who had no other place to stay."[17] Scullin also expressed sympathy for Cairo's saloon men, who were heavily taxed by new licensing fees of $1,000 each. According to Scullin, it would be a "great hardship" if they had to close at midnight. As it was, Scullin claimed, half the saloon men in the city needed to borrow money to pay the new license fees. Joseph A. Curry, another saloon owner, spoke next, declaring that closing saloons at midnight would throw fifty men out of work, most of them family heads.

Curry need not have worried; the alcohol trade in Cairo remained the same, with saloons, taverns, bars, dramshops, and wine rooms remaining open twenty-four hours a day. All that had been done in Cairo in 1909 in the way of reform was the closing of known assignation houses. Gambling, however, was next to come into the crosshairs of the Citizens' League in Cairo.

Because gaming house owners paid off policemen to operate and an officer could get ten dollars per week from each protected "game," Cairo gamblers had extraordinary privileges in 1909. Henry Lisle, a "notorious gambler" from Marion, Illinois, ran a game at 6th Street and Commercial Avenue in Cairo and there had a physical altercation with another gambler and pickpocket named "Red" Johnson. Lisle filed a complaint, and the Cairo police put out a warrant for his apprehension. Johnson was duly arrested after he fled, and a Cairo police officer was sent to return him to town. Lisle was informed and lay in wait at the Illinois Central station and shot at Johnson when he and his police escort got off the train, "trying his best to kill him."[18] Luckily for Lisle, he hit neither his intended target nor anyone else on the crowded platform. Lisle was brought to the Cairo police station but never jailed. He was fined five dollars and costs for "disorderly conduct" and sent on his way.

Perhaps emboldened by this permissive police behavior, Lisle entered Gus Botto's saloon at 613 Commercial and opened fire on the bartender, who apparently had offended him. The barkeep had a gun behind the bar and returned fire, but Lisle quickly ran out of the saloon, pursued by the bartender. By the time the barkeep was at the door of the saloon, Lisle was well down Commercial Avenue. He turned and fired several shots, hoping to hit the bartender as he emerged from the saloon. Once again, Lisle was arrested but not jailed. He was allowed to give bond and go free, and his case was continued. The bartender was approached by Chief Egan and asked not to testify against Lisle, was paid, and did not appear in court as a witness.[19] Lisle returned to Marion, where in December he shot Dick Adams, who then made a deathbed will, instructing his infant son to kill Lisle when the boy reached the age of twenty-one.[20]

Privileges and protection for gamblers were also extended to African Americans. Henry Small, twenty-two, described in the Cairo press as a "habitual offender, carrier of concealed weapons, frequent disturber of the peace, gambler, and a desperado," shot and killed another black man named Will Polk because Small believed Polk had insulted "his woman," Fannie Blanton, by exposing himself.[21] Small said in his statement before his sentencing that "he had a quarrel earlier in the day over a discussion of the lynchings, and that when he killed Polk he had been drinking."[22] Small claimed he told Polk that Will "Froggie" James "got what he deserved," which made Polk mad.[23] Polk was in Will Walker's barbershop at 1909 Poplar when Henry Small entered and cursed him and said he had "no respect for ladies." Polk denied he had insulted any ladies but offered to apologize and tried to leave the shop, but Small followed him outside, took deliberate aim, and shot him. Polk crawled four feet and died.[24]

This rather crude murder of an unarmed man in broad daylight revealed certain facts about Henry Small. The *Cairo Bulletin* offered a blatantly racist description of Small as "one of the hordes of dissolute blacks who infect the negro dives of the city."[25] The newspaper then revealed that Small was a "petty ward politician . . . and sort of 'boss' among his dirty clan."[26] Small's criminal record was also printed, including the fines he received in city and justice of the peace courts, the twenty days he served in jail for carrying a concealed weapon, and the time he was arrested for "shooting at several negroes" and charged with attempted murder. No one appeared in court against him that time and the case "fell through." The *Bulletin* then commented, "Not surprising when arrested for murdering the other negro he asked to be charged with disorderly conduct—his idea of fit punishment for the crime."[27] Lending some credence to earlier newspaper reports that black Cairoites had participated in or at least witnessed the lynchings, it was reported that "the working negro population was much incensed at the murderer who had been a tough character nearly all his life; and threats of violence were heard."[28] The threats were credible enough that Deputies Edward Washington Abernathie and Thomas Andrew Fuller took Henry Small to the Union County jail at Jonesboro for safekeeping.

In late November and into December 1909, therefore, there were attempted murders by black and white gamblers with one finally succeeding. Seeing law and order in near shambles in Cairo, State's Attorney Alexander Wilson used sheriff's deputies to raid the gambling "dives" and rooms in town. Gus Bourgois's place on Ohio Street was the first to go, when Bourgois and two of his gamblers were indicted and readied for prosecution in county court.[29] Four Cairo policemen immediately signed up to testify on Bourgois's behalf. The gambler Henry Lisle was apparently run out of town and sent back to his home in Marion, Illinois.[30] Henry Small was ordered to the Chester penitentiary for life in January 1910, having pled guilty to murder.[31]

By the time the executive committee of the Citizens' League met in late December with Mayor Parsons and many of the Cairo aldermen, the committee acknowledged that gambling had been checked in Cairo and called for it to be stopped completely. At the end of 1909, therefore, assignation

Gus Bourgois's saloon (*right*) was adjacent to the Illinois Central Railroad. Postcard courtesy of Darrel Dexter.

houses in Cairo were being closed, the serving of alcohol remained the same—that is, constant—and gambling was being attacked by county officials, if not at the city level. The most important developments since Anna Pelley's death and the double lynching were the formation of the Citizens' League to promote reform in Cairo; the decision of the *Cairo Bulletin* to crusade against Cairo's "dives," illegal gambling, police corruption, and unlimited alcohol availability; and, of course, Governor Charles Deneen's removal of Sheriff Frank Davis from office.

While some were connecting the lawlessness in Cairo to alcohol, prostitution, gambling, and a corrupt police force, the *Cairo Bulletin* began to charge that the circuit court was either corrupt or incompetent for allowing murderers to escape justice and thus encouraging further homicides. Indeed, on the day following the double lynching the headline in the *Bulletin* proclaimed, "Cairo Reaps the Fruit of Many Murders Unpunished—Rope, Fire and Shots Means of Avenging Mob."[32] The headline appeared on page 1, and an editorial inside directly linked the lynchings and Anna Pelley's death to the "rank" miscarriage of justice in the local courts. The *Bulletin* charged that Anna Pelley "was the latest victim of the reckless and vicious element in the city, made bold by long continued official pandering, indifference, and corruption."[33]

Only two days after the double lynching, the *Cairo Bulletin* recalled earlier murder trials and blasted the circuit court for allowing not guilty verdicts in five trials of white men, who the *Bulletin* claimed were "all unquestionably guilty of the crime with which they were charged." The morning newspaper pointed out glaring errors by the circuit judges and bold corruption on the part of sheriff's deputies and bailiffs, who, according to the pioneer Cairo daily, colluded with friends and relatives of defendants to pack juries and give perjured testimony. The *Cairo Bulletin* also placed personal responsibility on then sheriff Frank Davis for deputizing men he knew to be rogues and murderers: "These corrupt underlings of his, not satisfied with skulking in the dark while performing their treacherous work against the people who pay them, have boldly appeared on the witness stand and perjured themselves."[34]

The cause of Cairo's perceived problems, as far as the *Bulletin* was concerned, always seemed to lead back to the mayor and the police. The newspaper again attacked Mayor Parsons's assertion that the acquittal of the five "actual murderers" was the only relevant cause of "Cairo's black Thursday" (the double lynching) and blacker Tuesday (the rape and murder of Anna Pelley). The morning paper declared that not even the mayor could deny that corruption on the part of the Cairo police was a major contributor to violence and crime in the river city.

> *A series of smaller wrongs may have had a collective effect as a few larger ones; and he cannot successfully deny that his police department has furnished a long list of these during the past four or five years. The existence of foul dives for the wild revelries of dissolute negroes, and wide open gambling—these are but minor things when considered in the abstract, while grow in importance when considered as the natural breeding places for greater crimes.*[35]

About a month later, the *Bulletin* printed sworn testimony as to the specifics and scope of police corruption in Cairo. The sworn statement was from a "Kentucky farmer," who according to the *Bulletin*'s account was of considerable standing in his own community—sober, industrious, and truthful. According to the farmer, two friends of his had recently visited Cairo and had a drink at an Ohio Street saloon. After one drink they left and were walking along the street quietly when they were accosted by a Cairo police officer. He asked them whether they had been drinking, and when they said yes, the policeman said, "Come along with me."[36] The two were taken to police headquarters, where one friend had a pistol and twenty dollars confiscated. They were offered the choice of going home or going to jail. They decided to go home.

The unnamed Kentucky farmer continued with his testimony. He had been on his way to visit relatives in Missouri but missed a train connection at Bird's Point, Missouri, and decided to walk the seven miles to his destination. During the walk, he met a "neat looking young man" who was also walking. The Kentuckian asked, "Why don't you ride?" The young man replied that he was broke and explained that he had been in Cairo the day before and asked a police officer where he could find a hotel. The policeman instead took the young man into custody, keeping him in jail Saturday night and all of Sunday. The young man was then fined precisely all the money he had, thirty dollars. He begged for enough money to take a train home, but he was told to get out.[37]

Individual cases revealed police corruption in Cairo, but the Cairo police could apparently organize significant "shakedowns" on special occasions. For instance, according to the Kentucky informant, a great many other Kentuckians had been arrested when they came to Cairo to attend the circus that had set up in town. The farmer said he knew of at least twenty men who were taken in on circus day, searched, and divested of all money and valuables. The fines were always exactly the amount of cash the defendants had in their possession. The Kentucky informant then said he knew of numerous similar cases. Being familiar with both states, the man declared that the farmers of Kentucky and Missouri were afraid to go to Cairo for fear of being robbed by the police. The *Cairo Bulletin* then offered all information in the newspaper's possession to the grand jury upon request.[38]

Cairo's morning newspaper had constantly bombarded its readers with charges of corruption against the Alexander County sheriff and his deputies and bailiffs, Mayor George Parsons, Chief of Police Martin Egan and the Cairo Police Department, and especially circuit judge William N. Butler. From the day after the double lynching through November and December 1909, the *Bulletin* was relentless in its exposure of corruption and crime in the river city. At one point Mayor Parsons even made a thinly veiled threat that the *Cairo Bulletin* could be sued for libel because of the stories and editorials it was printing attacking city and county officials, the police, and the courts.[39]

When threats did not stop the *Cairo Bulletin*'s crusade for local reform, someone decided that the newspaper's editor, Edward W. Thielecke, must be stopped from writing ever again. On Christmas Eve 1909, at 11:30 p.m., someone shot through the front door of the editorial office of the *Bulletin* at 6th and Ohio Streets while Thielecke was seated at his desk. The force of the bullet was considerable, but fortunately for the editor, the glass of the newspaper's front door was a heavy plate. After blasting a large hole in the door glass, it tore past Thielecke through a heavy wooden door into a stockroom and finally plowed into a pile of papers stored there.[40]

On Christmas morning, Thielecke and the directors of the Bulletin Company met at the newspaper office and decided that the shot through the window had been no accident and that someone was trying to kill Thielecke. A $500 reward was offered for information leading to the prosecution of the assailant, which was a year's income for a skilled worker at the time.[41] The newly formed Citizens' League added to the reward money, as did the Southern Illinois Press Association.[42] Various press opinions in Southern Illinois blamed lowly thugs, officials of the city of Cairo, or "gamblers" for the shooting. The *Herrin News* made the following comments:

> *Cairo seems bent on keeping herself before the people of this state in a sensational and lawless manner. . . .* The Bulletin *has been using much of its editorial space lately denouncing crime*

Assalto alle prigioni di Cairo (Illinois), difese dalla polizia, per impadronirsi d'un negro reo di furto e quindi linciarlo.

Drawing appearing in a weekly Italian newspaper, *La Domencia del Corriere* (February 27–March 6, 1910), above the caption translated as "Assault on prison in Cairo (Illinois), defended by the police, to take over a negro guilty of theft and then lynch him." The happenings in Cairo had made international news. Courtesy of Darrel Dexter.

> *and corruption, which for a long time have been running riot in that city, and it is supposed that this cowardly bullet was meant to sound a warning to the paper that it had proceeded far enough on its program of urging reform.*
>
> *A low type of American citizen surely he must be who chose a missile of lead to silence the voice of the free press. It is, to say the least, discouraging even to entertain the thought that newspapers are published and circulated in this free and enlightened age in a community in which live people who chose assassination of an editor. . . . The savage who sent a bullet into* The Bulletin *office evidently aimed at the life of Editor Thielecke, and should be apprehended at all costs.*[43]

Unfortunately, apprehension of the shooter was probably a moot point, because the Cairo police, whom Thielecke and the *Bulletin* were ruthlessly attacking for corruption, dereliction of duty, and incompetence, were unlikely to investigate too closely what seemed to be attempted murder. It is even possible that the potential assassin was a Cairo policeman. The *Cairo Bulletin* continued to strongly urge local reform, especially against corruption in the police and courts, throughout 1910 and was joined by the *Cairo Evening Citizen*, Cairo's other daily. The shooting at the *Cairo Bulletin* in December 1909 would remain, like the double lynching of November 1909, ascribed to persons unknown. Editor Thielecke kept the bullet on his watch chain as a souvenir and reminder that there is always a price to be paid by those brave enough to stand up against local government corruption, especially when they sometimes seem to be standing alone.

CHAPTER THIRTEEN

# A NEW SHERIFF, A PURSE SNATCHING, AND ANOTHER LYNCH MOB

The new Alexander County sheriff, Frederick Daniels "Fred" Nellis, was a Republican, as had been Frank Davis. One of the problems Republican governor Charles Deneen had had with the county coroner, Dr. James McManus, who initially became sheriff upon Davis's dismissal, was that he was a Democrat. Governor Deneen gave the Alexander County Board of Commissioners, a majority of whom were also Republicans, the power to appoint the new Alexander County sheriff, pointing out that there was less than a year remaining in Frank Davis's term in office.[1] A former steamboat captain, coal dealer, county treasurer, and city alderman, Fred Nellis was also the presumptive Republican nominee for sheriff to replace Davis for the upcoming 1910 election.[2]

Nellis made a number of quick reforms after assuming office. The most important one, politically, was that he ordered the black deputies who had been removed by McManus back to duty and appointed more African Americans besides. He also fired the jailer Edward Abernathie, took weapons away from the prisoners in the county jail, tried to disinfect the jail, and had it whitewashed.[3] He requested the purchase of riot guns to be used in the event of a reoccurrence of mob violence, but the county commissioners denied his requisition.[4]

Sheriff Fred Daniels Nellis. From *Memoirs of the Lower Ohio Valley*, 2:365.

The reform movement in Cairo to control vice was overshadowed by a desperate attempt to maintain basic law and order by newly appointed Sheriff Nellis. Yet, another tragedy occurred in Cairo just three months after the double lynching of Will James and Henry Salzner.

There had been a string of unsolved purse snatchings in early 1910 in Cairo. On Wednesday, February 16, 1910, at about 6 p.m. on Washington Avenue between 5th and 6th Streets, John Pratt, an African American man, snatched a purse from a white woman, Mrs. Rosa Maloney, who was unaware of his approach because of a blinding snowstorm. Ironically, Maloney was the sole female who had participated in the Will "Froggie" James lynch mob and the one woman Pratt should have avoided. Mrs. Maloney had a pistol in her fur muff, which she had carried since the Pelley murder, and fired at Pratt but missed.[5] She then saw an African American man enter a two-story tenement house on 5th Street. The newspaper described it as one of the "worst dives, if not the worst in the city," filled with "negroes" from top to bottom and the scene of many crimes.[6]

The morning after the purse snatching, Pratt went into Will F. Taylor's drugstore at 1313 Washington in Cairo and purchased an envelope, paying for it with a silver dollar that had two postage stamps on it. He removed one stamp but left the other. A quick-witted "young negro drug clerk" had heard that the silver dollar in Mrs. Maloney's purse had stamps on it and immediately called the police and tipped them off. The *Cairo Citizen* stated, "The young man should be given credit for his act, the more so because he was bringing to justice an offender of his own race."[7] The clerk, whom the *Citizen* failed to identify, was twenty-one-year-old William Bricie "Will" Scott, a grandnephew of prominent black Cairo politician, saloonkeeper, and gambler William

Rosa H. Kratky Maloney, purse-snatching victim. *Fort Wayne (Ind.) News*, February 28, 1910.

Thomas Scott, who in 1904 became the first African American to be nominated for president of the United States by a national political party.[8]

Rosa Maloney and her husband, William, owner of an automobile garage in Cairo, were at the police station when Scott's call came in, and they joined the police who were directed by Scott to the post office in Cairo. The police and the Maloneys found John Pratt standing at a desk, writing a letter to his mother in Atlanta, Georgia, saying he had gotten rings from a sweetheart, including a diamond ring, which he asked his mother to sell for thirty dollars and then to send him the money.

Pratt was arrested, and a small procession, consisting of the prisoner, two police officers, and the Maloneys, headed east from the post office on Washington Avenue to the police station on Commercial Avenue. William Maloney walked behind the rest to observe Pratt. At 13th and Poplar Streets, Pratt dropped a small box in the snow that contained a diamond ring all packed for mailing. At police headquarters Pratt was asked for the rings, which had been in Maloney's purse, but he said he didn't have them. Then William Maloney produced the jewelry box and Pratt told his story. He was a paroled convict from Menard Prison in Chester, Illinois, and he had taken Mrs. Maloney's purse. The police chief personally went to where Pratt had been staying and found the overcoat that other purse-snatching

The post office and custom house at 1400 Washington Avenue, where John Pratt was arrested, now the Cairo Custom House Museum. Postcard courtesy of Darrel Dexter.

victims had described and a set of spoons belonging to Mrs. Margaret Accord, who had been robbed a week earlier near her home at 606 Jefferson.[9] Pratt, in his confession, implicated his companion Lincoln "Link" Wilson in the Maloney purse snatching, claiming he had helped him dispose of the purse in a water trough behind Burke's stable.[10] As for Will Scott, there is no record in either the *Bulletin* or the *Citizen* of him receiving a reward from the Maloneys or the police, or even their thanks.

Talk of another lynching began to circulate through the city. Joe Pelley, the brother of Anna Pelley, who had been murdered only three months earlier, allegedly arrived in Cairo from St. Louis the evening of February 17, after the arrest of the purse snatchers.[11] Pelley, according to the *Chicago Tribune*, "immediately began making the rounds of the saloons, crying for vengeance for this second attack on a woman of his family."[12] Newspaper reports that he was a brother-in-law or relative of Rosa Maloney provided an interesting twist to the story for their readers, but there was no truth in the statements. Pelley's involvement in the case may have been exaggerated or even mythical. More substantiated is the claim that Alexander "Spinney" Halliday, an old schoolmate of Rosa Maloney, told her the evening after Pratt's arrest that he intended to lead a mob against Pratt to avenge her.[13]

Ironically, Sheriff Nellis was supposed to leave for Belleville, Illinois, that evening to be a witness at the execution by hanging of Willis Clark, a black man who had shot and killed Eugene V. Goudy, a white streetcar motorman. Before he could leave, "tips" began to come in that there was "talk of lynching, and he better watch out."[14] Since the "tips" were from "prominent citizens," the sheriff visited several saloons to confirm what he had been told.[15] The sheriff then went immediately to the Alexander County courthouse and there found Deputy Tax Collector Ben Jones, janitor Henry Reeves, Judge William Sabin Dewey, and attorney Angus Leek. On the advice of friends, at about 10:10 p.m. the sheriff called Governor Charles Deneen, who asked if Judge Dewey and Angus Leek were still in the courthouse, but Sheriff Nellis replied that they had made a getaway. Deneen then advised Nellis to locate Captain William Greaney, the commander of Cairo's Company K of the National Guard, and to keep him informed, but the sheriff had difficulty finding Greaney, who was a Cairo alderman as well as a guardsman. The adjutant general of the Illinois National Guard could not locate Greaney either but finally found Lieutenant Arthur Thistlewood, who was instructed to aid Sheriff Nellis in any way he could. Finally, the sheriff called Cairo's mayor, George Parsons, to ask for assistance. Parsons's only response was to say that he would notify the night sergeant.[16]

By this time, Chief Deputy Thomas A. Fuller was at the courthouse and Nellis told him to telephone other deputies for assistance. Every one of the nine African American deputies Fuller called reported for duty, according to the sheriff. Jerry Dunning, a white deputy from Olive Branch, had been on duty in the grand jury room at the courthouse and was stationed in the county clerk's office "with a cheap pistol he was not sure would shoot."[17] Nellis himself called for outside help—presumably white—and got one response. Benjamin F. Thompson, a seventy-three-year-old Civil War veteran who was "quite deaf," came from his home on Park Avenue and was placed to guard the basement stairs.[18] Company K did not arrive.[19]

Sheriff Nellis had thirteen men to protect the courthouse and its jail, which held three prisoners: John Pratt and his alleged accomplice, Lincoln Wilson, and a black man charged with having set fire to more than twenty-two tenements in Cairo.[20] The volunteers, some of whom Nellis did not even know, were scattered all over the building. He placed his deputies throughout the courthouse, including the sheriff's office and the circuit clerk's office. Two deputies were stationed at the front door—Thomas Fuller, white, and veteran lawman and ex-soldier George Jackson, black.[21] The lights in the courthouse were then turned out.

Deputy Thomas Andrew Fuller left Cairo in the 1920s and moved to Monmouth, Illinois, where he died in 1944. Photo courtesy of Jacqueline Short.

Sheriff Nellis's most trusted deputy was Thomas Fuller, the same deputy who had been with Sheriff Frank Davis when he had tried to get Will "Froggie" James out of harm's way in November 1909. Upon taking office, Nellis had promoted Fuller to chief deputy and jailer. This time Deputy Fuller was prepared with a .32-caliber Winchester rifle and a Colt revolver. His place was right behind Sheriff Nellis.[22]

Ben Jones, who would later become Nellis's chief deputy, came into the courthouse specifically to tell Deputy Fuller that there was talk of forming a mob. Jones stayed and later testified that Nellis took his family from their living quarters in the basement to the courtroom on the upper floor and told them to stay in the middle of the room.[23] Jones was then stationed in the sheriff's office at a window.

Of the thirteen men defending the courthouse, jail, and prisoners, eight were identified as "negroes" and five as white. Charles Hudson, identified as "negro county constable," was stationed at a window at the corner of the building. George Jackson, one of the oldest African American deputy sheriffs, stood in the courthouse door exposed to gunfire from outside. The former regular army soldier and New Yorker later testified that bullets "came by him."[24] Henry Douglass, "a negro constable," was placed at the window of the circuit clerk's office with a revolver, and his brother, James Douglass, was in the sheriff's office. Edward H. Henderson, "colored deputy sheriff," was stationed in the sheriff's office with his "old style 44 Colts." Thomas A. Head was another African American deputy sheriff who was on duty when trouble was sensed. Regularly armed with a pistol, Head had a shotgun at home, and he got it and returned to the courthouse and took up a place at another window in the circuit clerk's office. The other two African American deputies were identified as Charles Bolar and a man named Mitchell.[25] The sheriff advised the men in the courthouse, "Don't be hasty. . . . Shoot in the air first, if they keep coming we'll have to stop them the best way we can."[26]

At 12:45 at night, a mob of anywhere from 75 to 200 men came up the east side of Washington Avenue and approached the jail. Back on the phone with Governor Deneen, the sheriff saw the men in the mob start through the gates of the courthouse, with some even climbing over the fence, and begin to ascend the courthouse steps. Sheriff Nellis left the phone and went to the door of the courthouse, flanked by Deputies Fuller and Jackson (whom the newspaper in parentheses identified as "colored"). Even though stormy with snow, the night appeared bright to Sheriff Nellis, who had darkened the courthouse.[27] The men at the front of the mob were masked with handkerchiefs, and Nellis later recalled, "There was no yelling and no noise save that of their feet crunching in the snow."[28] The lawman addressed the mob: "I am Fred D. Nellis sheriff of this county, and am here to protect the courthouse and jail and the prisoners in my charge. Please go away."[29] The cry came back from the mob, "To hell with you!"[30] A tall man disguised behind a flour sack in which holes were cut for his eyes said, "We've come after the niggers, and we expect to get them."[31] Someone shot at the sheriff and a bullet slightly grazed his pistol hand, raising a blister. Then other shots were fired. These may have been the shots that Deputy George Jackson later said "came by him." Later testimony by the sheriff and deputies was that the first shots came from the mob and then firing became general.

Bullets were now raining on the courthouse porch. The little force in the courthouse fired directly into the charging men; one or two fell and some others dropped back. Some witnesses described these shots from the courthouse as the "second volley."[32] Even on the day after the mob was repulsed, the *Cairo Bulletin* asserted that no shots had come from the mob and that all wounds were caused by one volley of shots.[33] Whoever fired, the rioters attempting a lynching were immediately deterred, and they fell back out of the range of most of the pitiful arsenal of Sheriff Nellis's men. When the mob retreated, one body was left in the snow on the south side of the steps leading to the courthouse door.[34] Quite soon after the mob retired, the sheriff got a phone call from Eugene E. Ellis, city editor of the *Cairo Bulletin*, who was at the Red Onion Saloon, asking if men could be sent to retrieve the fallen body. Quickly Nellis called Governor Deneen, who Nellis said told him to stay put until reinforcements arrived and to not allow anyone to enter the courthouse yard.[35]

Much was made of a body left in the snow, both at the time and for some considerable time afterward. "It was still warm," erroneously stated the *Cairo Bulletin* when describing the corpse after troops took charge of it several hours later. From the accounts from Cairo and elsewhere, it appears that allowing a dead man to lie where he fell was worse than killing him in the first place.[36] At the coroner's inquest, Sheriff Fred Nellis defended his action on the night of February 17–18, 1910:

> *I want to further say in connection with the removal of the body from the courthouse yard at the particular time and before the arrival of Company K, which I expected every minute, that those of the general public who may wish to criticize my action in that matter may overlook the fact that I had allowed it to be done, knowing the conditions existing, it would have in my opinion, been the jeopardizing of not only the lives of my deputies and myself, but the prisoners confined in the jail, and if the body had been taken away and recognized by friends, it would have caused another attack, which I would have been powerless to repel.*[37]

Sheriff Nellis had waited. No police came, and Company K of the Illinois National Guard—although located only minutes away—did not arrive until 4 a.m., hours after the attack. The lack of action from Company K guardsmen was more than a little suspicious. The *Chicago Tribune* asked if they had been hiding on the night of the attack, and Sheriff Nellis charged that the citizen soldiers did not come because they had relatives in the mob and wanted it to succeed.[38]

Then the body in the snow was removed, with Cairo guardsmen falsely saying it was still warm.[39] It was the corpse of Alexander "Spinney" Halliday, son of Thomas W. Halliday, former mayor of Cairo and state legislator and a member of Cairo's leading family.[40] Halliday's body was taken to St. Mary's Infirmary, where Dr. John T. Walsh pronounced death. The bullet had entered his neck below the right ear and came out under the left shoulder, severing the jugular vein and the main artery, so the body couldn't have been warm as the guardsmen claimed.[41] The mob men injured in the attack were Horton Crehan and George B. Walker, both wounded in the leg; John Maloney, shot in the head; and Sam Wissinger, shot in the shoulder.[42] All had been hit with "duck shot" and were taken to Rudolph Carl "Rudy" Laurent's saloon, the Red Onion, at 1900 Washington, where Dr. Edward Everett Gordon was called to dress the wounds. At 5 a.m., Sheriff Nellis went to his old residence, where he had likely sent his family, to get some rest.[43]

The elusive Captain Greaney and thirty National Guardsmen of Cairo's Company K now guarded the courthouse and its prisoners. By the next day

The childhood home of Alexander "Spinney" Halliday was built by his father in 1876 on Washington Avenue in Cairo. Photo by Darrel Dexter.

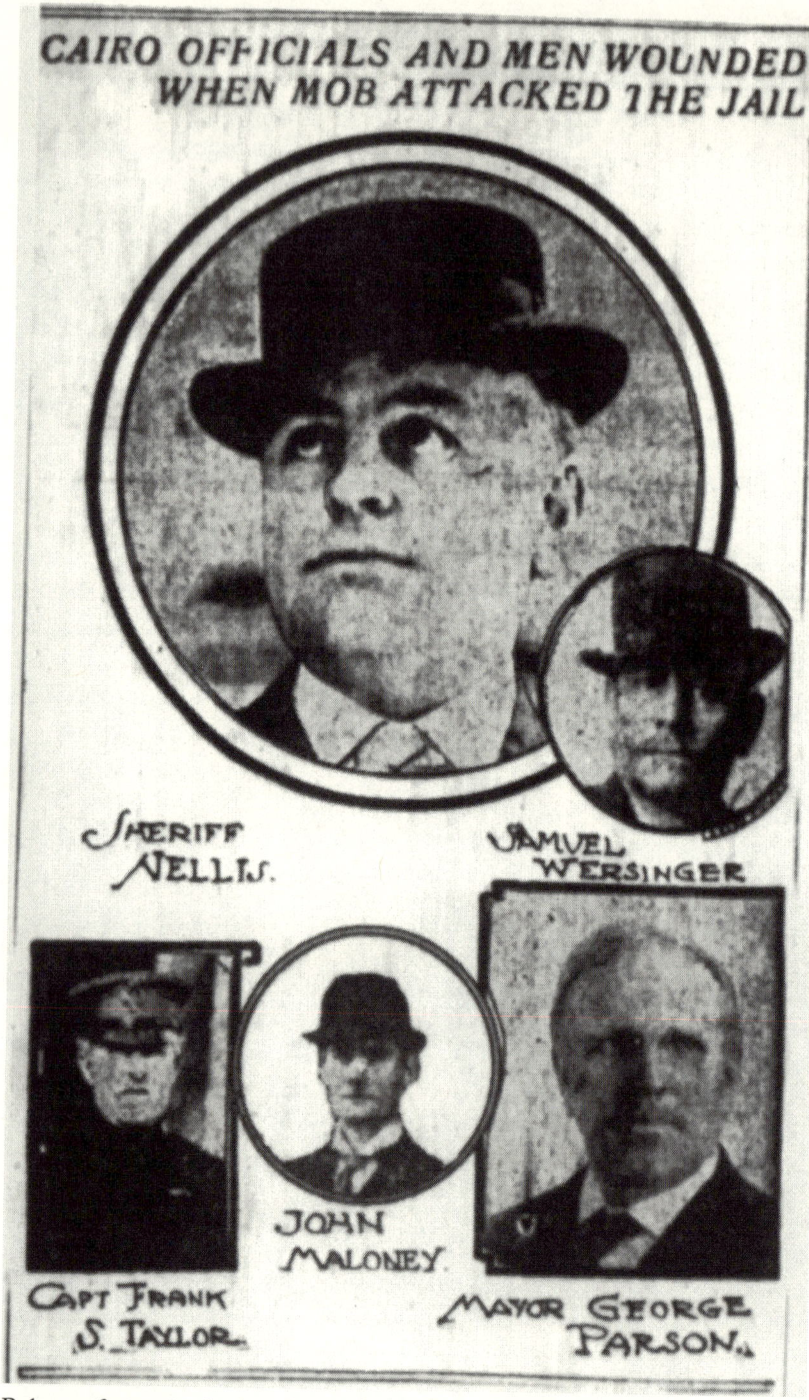


Relevant figures in the courthouse attack. *St. Louis Post-Dispatch*, February 19, 1910.

three companies of militia were guarding the courthouse and jail under command of Adjutant General Frank S. Dickson.[44] It seems like it was easy duty for the militia guards at the courthouse, as Captain Frank L. Taylor had to issue an order that soldiers there must not gamble. "Come seven, come eleven" games in the sheriff's office, circuit clerk's office, and lobby were how some soldiers had been passing time.[45]

A fourth company of National Guardsmen arrived in town the next day, February 19, with orders to enforce Governor Charles Deneen's order closing all retail liquor establishments in Cairo. At that point, Mayor George Parsons finally acted, sending police around to the saloons to see whether they were indeed closed. They were not. Mayor Parsons then threatened to revoke the license of any establishment that remained open. "They must keep closed until I advise them to open," said the mayor. "It is my intention to keep them closed until that man [John Pratt] is taken out of town."[46]

Now it seemed that closing saloons had become a major priority in the affair of the attempted lynching and subsequent killing and wounding of Cairoites. General Dickson and Lieutenant Colonel Claude E. Ryman of Effingham issued a statement to be circulated in the local press:

> *Soldiers will remain as long as the sheriff feels they are needed to maintain order. If the talk against officers who are trying to do their duty does not subside, the troops will be kept here and the saloons closed until it does. Agitation will do more to prolong the state of affairs than anything else. The sheriff has it in his power to keep the saloons closed thirty days if necessary.*[47]

If the retail alcohol trade was suspended for any length of time, Cairo would face a major blow to its economy. What could be done to preserve Cairo's economy and the rule of law—not to mention human life? Steps were already being taken the very day of the attempted lynching.

Judge William N. Butler, who had been a judge in Southern Illinois since the 1890s, took care of the John Pratt case in about twenty minutes and criticized Cairo's mob violence. Pratt was hustled into court before Judge Butler, where he quickly pled guilty and admitted he was on parole. For parole violation, he got fourteen years and another fourteen years at hard labor for the purse snatching. Then Judge Butler lectured those assembled in the courtroom. He said, "We had hoped that there would be no further recurrence of the events of last November."[48] He informed them it was the duty of the sheriff to protect prisoners and that the rioters were guilty of committing a felony. He told those in the courtroom that the guilty parties should be found. "This thing has got to be stopped," he said. "The law, if not enforced, is without power at all."[49] The *Cairo Bulletin* wondered at Butler's resolve because the paper saw him as a Republican machine politician who used "questionable practices" to get elected.[50]

Then Judge Butler spoke of the strain upon Sheriff Nellis and his men in the courthouse during the previous night's attack, comparing the stress upon Nellis to that upon President Lincoln during the Civil War. Concluding, the judge stated, "If a mob can take the law into its own hands, the individual can do so also."[51] He called attention to the fact that there had been five murders in Cairo since the November 11 lynching, showing that lynch law had utterly failed to deter the crime of murder.

Lynch law, however, was still a possibility in Cairo on February 19, 1910, so the local authorities, with the help of the state military, removed John Pratt from town on that day. Deputies James Barrow and Joseph Mulhan (neither of whom helped defend the courthouse the night of the attack) were given charge of twelve prisoners, including John Pratt, who were shackled together at the ankles.[52] Lieutenant Albert H. Gravenhorst of Company G, Fourth Regiment, Illinois National Guard, a corporal, and five privates helped guard the dozen prisoners to prevent their escape and protect them from outside interference. The prisoners and deputies, escorted by the soldiers, left the courthouse at 4:10 a.m., "floundered" through the snowdrifts to the Illinois Central station, and left for Menard Penitentiary in Chester, Illinois, on the 5 a.m. train.

The prisoners waited, seated together on a long bench, about ten minutes for the train to arrive. A few men asked the guards to point out Pratt, and one heckler yelled, "Good bye nigger; that's the only way you can get out of this town alive."[53] But other than the verbal ridicule, no action was taken against Pratt. The main concern the militia had after Pratt left Cairo was that threats of violence against the African American deputies or their property would be carried out.

The *Cairo Evening Citizen* commented approvingly on the Pratt case:

> *In the case of John Pratt, Cairo and Alexander County has a precedent for prompt rendering of justice. On Wednesday evening a negro held up and robbed Mrs. Maloney. Thursday morning John Pratt was arrested by the police, identified by two women he had robbed and confessed to the robberies. His case was presented to the grand jury Thursday, and within 20 minutes Pratt pleaded guilty. In both cases was sentenced*

> *to prison for the limit of law in each case. Before daylight on Saturday morning he was on his way to the penitentiary to serve 28 years.*[54]

For a few days in February 1910, the river city was a positive example to the entire United States. That is when Sheriff Fred Nellis and his determined band of interracial lawmen defended the Alexander County Courthouse against a mob bent on lynching two accused purse snatchers. Indeed, it would be hard to overestimate the attempted contribution to law and order that Nellis and these thirteen deputies made. In the same year in Dallas, Texas, a black man accused of molesting a white child, although defended by 70 armed deputies and police, was taken from a courtroom by a mob of 200 men (similar to the estimated number of the mob in Cairo) without a shot being fired. The elderly African American victim was thrown from the courtroom with a noose around his neck to the street below. Still alive, he was kicked and beaten into a bloody mess and then dragged to a decorative steel arch (such as the one used in the 1909 Cairo lynching). The dragging was so brutal that most of his clothes were torn off. At the arch, a debate broke out between hanging and burning the victim. Mercifully he was hanged.[55]

Because of the example of Fred Nellis and his men, other sheriffs realized that resistance to mobs was not futile and lynchings were not inevitable. As argued in the *New York Times*, the important feature of the "little battle" was that it demonstrated that any sheriff who wanted to defend his prisoner could do so.[56] There were no more lynchings in Illinois after Nellis's stand, although some were attempted. There were, however, numerous lynchings in Texas and the American South for the next forty years; there were even lynchings in Missouri.[57]

If one looks at Nellis's "little battle" as a battle for due process of law against a vicious kind of popular sovereignty, then certain facts become clear.[58] First, Fred Nellis and black and white deputies were risking their own lives to save African American prisoners and to defend the jail where they were being held. Second, this was a rare if not unique event, where black lawmen were able to defend black prisoners. In America, black men were usually excluded from law enforcement in what has been called "the era of lynching."[59] Might history have been slightly different if this was not the case? Might a black lawman be more inclined to risk his own life and use deadly force to battle to save a black person from a lynching than would a white lawman?

At the center of the controversy is the fact that the prisoner being targeted was African American. Rosa Maloney, whose attack had led to the attempted lynching and who said she received telephone reports of the lynch mob's progress, likely echoed the feelings of many whites in Cairo. She said Pratt "deserved to be lynched" and even went so far as to make an unsubstantiated claim that he was implicated in the death of Anna Pelley.[60] Maloney said, "I do not envy Sheriff Nellis the load that must be on his conscience tonight. Think of having to remember that you shot down a white man in defense of a negro."[61]

Fred Nellis and his men at the courthouse were not saints; Nellis was later indicted for embezzlement when he was county treasurer, as was his apparently fearless sometimes chief deputy, Ben Jones. But when confronted with a threat, they did not hesitate to use their guns to meet it. As Nellis said after the successful defense of the Alexander County Courthouse, "My conscience is easy over the entire affair. They were determined to get me unless I got them. I got them, and I did my duty in protecting prisoners at any price."[62]

## CHAPTER FOURTEEN

# ANOTHER CORONER'S INQUEST AND INVESTIGATION

John Pratt was in prison and Lincoln Wilson was freed and sent on his way, so the next thing for the county authorities in Cairo to do was to hold the coroner's inquest to see what could be determined about Alexander Halliday's death. The coroner's jury of six Cairo residents opened on February 19, 1910.[1] The first witness was Sheriff Fred Nellis, then Deputy Sheriff Thomas Fuller and the other deputies who defended the courthouse testified. The physicians testifying were Dr. William Clarence Clark and Dr. John Thomas Walsh, both of Cairo.[2] The testimonies of the deputies were the most illuminating. They all agreed that Sheriff Nellis had told them to fire in the air first, and all but Deputy George Jackson said shots had come from the outside, as evidenced by the broken glass that covered the office floors in the courthouse.

Charles Hudson, an African American deputy sheriff, testified that Sheriff Nellis had said that the man lying in the snow after the shots would stay there even "if he were my brother."[3] Hudson further stated that he did not know the man in the snow was dead until Captain William Greaney and his bugler, Fred Lind (whom Hudson called "his toots man"), came to the courthouse and told the defenders. Finally, Hudson did not think he had killed Halliday. When asked about press reports of events during the mob attack, Hudson said newspaper men were here and there and "[I] guess they print what folks tell them."[4] When asked how he knew it was Captain Greaney informing the defenders of the body in the snow, Hudson said he had known Greaney since he was a boy. Deputy George Jackson was positive that the mob would have taken the courthouse if the defenders had not been serious in their shooting, because the mob kept coming after warning shots were fired in the air.

After the deputies testified, bystanders came before the coroner's inquest. George B. Walker, one of the wounded men, explained his presence in the "crowd" by the fact that he was a correspondent for the Associated Press and was in Swoboda's saloon when Deputy Charley Hudson came in and told him "there was something doing at the court house."[5] Walker followed the "crowd" when he saw it going up the street and was outside on the pavement when he was hit by "the first volley."[6] He testified that he did not see any shooting from the "crowd" and heard Sheriff Nellis addressing the crowd as the shooting began. He estimated their number at 100 to 150 and said that few of them got into the courthouse yard. Walker thought several volleys were fired. Richard Fitzgerald was in his saloon across the street from the courthouse and testified that he saw flashes of gunfire from the courthouse windows—the shots fired in rapid succession. Both Walker and Fitzgerald tried to distance themselves from the mob because Judge William Butler had days earlier impaneled a grand jury to name mob members and bring indictments against them.[7]

Nineteen-year-old Horton Crehan testified before the coroner's jury that he had been at a dance at the Alexander Club and was on his way home and in the middle of the street when the shooting started. He ducked into an alley and stayed there about fifteen minutes until all was quiet and it was safe to come out. His father, John R. Crehan, stated in the *Citizen* that Horton was not hit by a bullet during the attack, as was generally believed.[8] Finally, definitely not wanting to be numbered among the band of men who defended the seat of justice and its prisoners were Amos C. Dennis and Joseph Gotthart, who made a sworn statement to the *Cairo Bulletin* emphasizing that they were not members of Nellis's posse and that neither of them were deputy sheriffs under him, as had been reported previously in the newspaper.[9]

Captain William P. Greaney testified that he was the one who telephoned to advise Sheriff Nellis not to go to Belleville, as Nellis had originally intended, "as he heard rumors of trouble."[10] Greaney did nothing, however, to prepare Company K for possible trouble, and the men had had a "smoker" (a party suitable for men only) that night at the armory until 10:30. When Nellis telephoned Greaney at his home and "informed him he was short of ammunition and that he needed help as quick as he could get it," Greaney stopped at Fitzgerald's saloon to get a drink before going back to the armory. Captain Greaney then testified that he "made the rounds of the saloons and Thirteenth Street resorts looking for his men."[11]

When the coroner's jury made its verdict, no individual deputy sheriff was named in the death of Alexander Halliday. It found that Halliday died due to a gunshot wound caused by a weapon in the hands of one of Sheriff Fred

D. Nellis's deputies from the north window of the circuit clerk's office.[12] The jurors did not comment on the role that the slow arrival of Company K may have played in the death of Halliday, perhaps because they did not think it was an important factor or perhaps because Captain Greaney's brother, Joseph Greaney, had been selected by the coroner as a juror.[13] The *Citizen* headlined "Tension Relieved by Verdict of Coroner's Jury."[14] The newspaper went on to say that anxiety over possible wording of the verdict gave way to relief, because the verdict offended no one. The paper also tried to dispel rumors that Governor Charles Deneen and Sheriff Nellis had trouble between them by stating that the governor gave the sheriff all possible support and that Nellis appreciated it both at the time of the attack and at the present moment.

The *Cairo Bulletin*, however, which proclaimed itself as independent politically, said that the Illinois adjutant general denied that Governor Deneen had ordered Sheriff Nellis to leave Halliday's body in the snow until the "militia" came to secure the courthouse. The *Bulletin* said that Nellis had stuck to the story before the grand jury and said there was no way of knowing for certain unless there was a record of the Nellis-Deneen long distance telephone conversation.[15]

Before the judgment by the coroner's jury, Alex Halliday, or "Spinney" as he was more popularly known, was buried. He was twenty-nine years old when killed and had a regional reputation as a baseball player. Yet, as a son of a former Cairo mayor and a member of the town's prestigious Alexander Club, a social and athletic organization, Halliday's jobs were not what one might expect. For several years he drove a streetcar, then he owned a saloon and then tended bar and "railroaded."[16] After being shot and killed, Halliday's body was taken to the home of his brother, Parker Halliday, on 27th Street, where it was viewed by the coroner's jury.[17] Burial was in Beech Grove Cemetery, with the service conducted by George M. Babcock, Episcopal rector. The service was standard, attended by several hundred people, and "the funeral passed off quickly with no incident to disturb its solemnity."[18]

With Halliday buried and the coroner's jury verdict delivered, the press and people began to register their beliefs concerning the attempted lynching and those involved with it. The *Cairo Evening Citizen* gave judgments about Sheriff Nellis, John Pratt, and Alex Halliday on the very day of what the newspaper called the "terrible tragedy." The paper said that those who took the law into their own hands forced the sheriff and his men to go to extreme ends to do their duty.[19] As to Pratt, the *Citizen* declared that had

Rosa Maloney succeeded in putting a bullet into him after he tried to snatch her purse, justice would have been done, but Mrs. Maloney missed and Pratt instead was sentenced to prison. As to Halliday, the Cairo newspaper said the community had the deepest sympathy for the family, but "had he been conducting himself as a law-abiding citizen, he would be living today."[20]

The *Citizen* reserved praise in what the paper called the "dreadful affair" for Sheriff Fred Nellis:

> *There was no other course open to Sheriff Nellis than to fire upon the mob which attacked the jail. There was no other course open to him but to swear in whoever he could get to aid him. There were few he could reach at that time of night to come to his assistance. Those few he summoned. He appealed to the police and they failed him. He appealed to Company K, the governor and Captain Greaney, and they were a long time coming. With only a handful of men he had to protect that jail with his life if necessary. He ordered the mob to disperse. They scorned him. He gave orders to fire, not to kill but to let the mob know that he would meet force with force. They still came on, firing as they came. There was only one thing more to do and that was to stop the advance of the mob with cold lead. He did this.*
>
> *Probably no one regrets what has happened more than Sheriff Fred D. Nellis. It is not a pleasant thing to take the life of a fellow being. And yet Sheriff Fred D. Nellis was sworn to perform his duty and did not propose to be a coward.*[21]

The dutiful Sheriff Nellis did elicit praise from many quarters but certainly not from all. The coroner's jury was divided, because some jurors wanted a severe censure of Nellis for having a majority of black deputies and for his refusal to let Halliday's body be touched.[22] The *Cairo Bulletin* admitted that Sheriff Nellis had stood for law and order and that the mob had no business being where it was under the circumstances. The *Bulletin*, however, declared that Nellis could not be absolved of his "egregious blunders" and argued that the sheriff and his deputies had done almost all the shooting from the first: "The deputies shot to kill the men in the mob, not to scare them, in wanton violation of the sheriff's orders."[23]

One of the sheriff's harshest critics was Henricus H. "Harry" Roseman, a high-level manager for the Illinois Traction Company, which had interests in streetcars throughout the state of Illinois. Roseman was in Cairo on the Saturday following the attempted lynching. In reporting to Decatur's

*Daily Review*, Roseman claimed that condemnation of Nellis was almost universal in Cairo because the sheriff used "negro" deputies to defend the attack and because Nellis allowed Alex Halliday's body to lie in the snow for almost four hours before it could be recovered by doctors and the coroner.[24] Roseman also told the central Illinois newspaper that if the coroner's jury had named any "negro" deputy as the one who shot Halliday, another lynching would have occurred. Finally, almost hysterically, Roseman said that the only actions Sheriff Nellis could take to escape with his life were to resign and leave Cairo.[25]

According to Roseman, Nellis's problem and that of all Cairo politicians derived from the fact that all of them competed for the "negro" vote. The source of the trouble was traffic in "negro" votes and the complicated nature of Cairo politics. To Father J. J. Downey of St. Patrick's Church in Cairo, though, local politics were not so complex.

> *Politics is the ruin of Cairo, the white purchase of negro votes and that is what brings them here. To my mind it is a brand of disgrace that a white man should climb into office by the rotten votes of negroes. But as long as the negro can vote in Cairo there will be trouble.*[26]

Reverend Downey's solution to Cairo's high crime rate was black disenfranchisement. Mrs. Rosa Maloney, whose purse Pratt had tried to steal, which led to the attempted lynching, was a member of Father Downey's parish and had a more extreme remedy for Cairo's problems. She wanted Cairo's black population driven out, as did her brother-in-law John Maloney, who had been wounded at the courthouse.[27] The rumor that the black people of Cairo were to be attacked, driven from their homes, or worse quickly spread across the country.[28] The *Cairo Bulletin*, however, said that talk of "burning out" Cairo's "negroes" was "not taken seriously" and was "groundless."[29]

The *Cairo Evening Citizen* never mentioned black expulsion but did report on a series of destructive fires of "negro tenements" under "suspicious circumstances" in January 1910, a month before the attempted lynching.[30] Six "substantial negro tenements" were burned on the east side of Commercial, known as "Pidgeon Roost," leaving thirteen families homeless on January 29.[31] The firemen even asserted that someone tampered with the hydrant and partially turned off the water to the hoses. The *Citizen* went further by stating, "The frequency of tenement house fires lately is likely to arouse suspicion" and that some insurance companies had canceled policies on tenements in Cairo.[32] After eight separate fires were set to tenement houses by the "firebug," amounting to losses of about $20,000, a $450 reward was offered for the arsonist's apprehension.[33]

After more than two months of uneasiness and fear among African American tenants and white property owners, a suspect was arrested by police chief Martin Egan. Circumstantial evidence against Essie Taylor, alias Doughbelly, of 513 19th Street, was that he had purchased several containers of coal oil at different stores in Cairo, which could have been used to start the fires; additionally, other tenement occupants where he lived said they "began watching for a fire in the city after every time he left late at night."[34] By the time the evidence was placed before the grand jury in May 1910, jurors refused to indict the African American man, but the fires seemed to have stopped.[35]

If Cairo's black people were not to be burned out, expelled, or disenfranchised, what was to be done with them? Father James Gillen of St. Joseph's Catholic Church said they should be pitied: "They are poor, intellectually, morally, and often physically. They are shiftless and improvident, and hence more susceptible of influence of the bad rather than the good members of their race."[36] In 1910, words of racism dripped from the mouths of the press and the pulpit.

Also seeing it as unfortunate that "negro" deputies were the majority among the defenders at the attempted lynching in February 1910 was one of America's most eminent newspapers, the *New York Times*. The newspaper, however, welcomed Cairo back to the category of civilized cities.

> *What can be done by a sheriff with a realizing sense of official duty and the obligations of his oath was illustrated at Cairo, Ill., Thursday night, when a mob attempted to lynch a negro. It is not long ago that another lynching party in Cairo encountered only a pretense of resistance when it attacked the same jail, took two prisoners and murdered them. Sheriff Nellis did not pretend to resist, nor did he decide resistance was useless.*
>
> *After warning the mob that his deputies would fire on them if they attempted to invade the jail, he carried out his announced purpose as soon as the attempt was made. As a result one rioter was killed and four wounded by a single volley which, after one had been in the air, proved enough to cool the zeal of the attacking party. It is an unfortunate circumstance that the majority of the twelve deputies who won the little battle were negroes. That will add bitterness to the episode and distract*

> *from its one important feature, which is the evidence it gives that any sheriff who really tries to defend his prisoner can do so. The usual course, unfortunately, is for the sheriff to yield to force which he calls overwhelming, to let the mob work its will, then bring a few militiamen on the scene for no other reason, apparently, than to see to it that the selected victim is not killed again.*
>
> *Cairo, thanks to Sheriff Nellis, can now consider itself freed from its deep disgrace and is entitled to number itself among civilized cities. It owes little gratitude, seemingly, to its mayor, and none to its police.*[37]

Other major newspapers, while praising Sheriff Fred Nellis, condemned his use of "Negro deputies" to drive back Cairo's attacking mob. The *Louisville Courier-Journal* in Kentucky asserted, "It is better for a mob leader to be killed than for a mob murder to be allowed to take place. . . . A sheriff who will not shoot to defend a prisoner—however guilty and depraved—is not worthy of the office."[38] The *Courier-Journal* went on to applaud the Illinois law that had removed Cairo and Alexander County's previous sheriff, Frank Davis, for not preventing the double lynching in 1909. Davis's and Nellis's practice of appointing a number of African American deputies, however, was seen as fundamentally wrong. The *Courier-Journal* pointed out that deputies were "peace officers," but racial friction in Southern Illinois made the employment of black deputies a future cause of ill will between whites and blacks. "And peace officers who menace the peace, regardless of their freedom and equality and their right to office under the Constitution and the law, are failures."[39]

Echoing the Kentucky newspaper was one of Illinois's most eminent press organs, the *Chicago Tribune*. While admitting that Sheriff Fred Nellis had shown more courage than Sheriff Frank Davis, the Chicago paper observed, "If colored deputies were employed, short of absolute necessity, this too is an inexcusable mistake. It cannot but add fuel to the flames of race hatred and seriously retard measures for any fundamental treatment of the situation."[40]

Other newspapers throughout the country praised Fred Nellis without criticizing his choice of deputies by race, saying that Cairo at last had a sheriff with a backbone, one who took his oath seriously and was "a good deal of a man."[41] Nellis's example was also emphasized. "Men are imitative creatures, and many another officer will find just the extra stiffness necessary in order to uphold the law in a crisis imparted to his resolution by the example of Sheriff Nellis."[42] The *Denver Republican* also made Nellis a hero:

> *One man stands out sharp and clear against the background of that picture of the storming of the Cairo jail. That is Sheriff Nellis as he faces the frenzied mob with drawn gun and warns that he will shoot to kill. There stands the law; the law of the state, the law of the nation, the law of man, demanding justice without regard to race, color or previous condition of servitude.*[43]

While not paraphrasing the Fourteenth Amendment like the Denver newspaper, the *New York Age*, a widely read African American weekly newspaper, also lauded Sheriff Nellis and Governor Charles Deneen: "Sheriff Nellis and Gov. Deneen are the heroes of Illinois. The former is being praised by all citizens opposed to mob law for his prompt action in preventing another lynching in Cairo and Gov. Deneen is having many nice things said about him due to the prompt manner in which he sent the militia to preserve order."[44] These words appeared on the front page of the *Age*, with a formal picture of Sheriff Nellis accompanying the article. In an editorial on the inside of the paper, the *Age* asserted, "Sheriff Fred D. Nellis of Cairo, Ill., deserves the thanks of every lover of law and order throughout the country for his brave and successful defense of his Negro prisoners."[45]

The opinion of the *New York Age* differed greatly from that in the several newspapers that lamented Alex Halliday's death at the scene in Cairo. "The killing of the son of a former mayor by the sheriff's deputies is regrettable only in that the lynchers numbered among themselves so prominent a citizen," the *Age* stated. The New York City weekly saw Halliday's death and the wounding of four mob members as an object lesson to those who would defy the law in Southern Illinois. Finally, unlike almost every white newspaper that commented on the "colored" deputies who defended the courthouse in Cairo, the *Age* praised them as "good and courageous Negroes."[46]

Cairo may have had good and courageous African American deputies, but the regional press vehemently attacked Cairo for the city's failings in the lynchings of 1909 and the attempted lynching in 1910. In an editorial titled "The Carnival in Cairo," the *Fort Wayne Daily News* in Indiana assigned the blame for the failed lynching to the grand jury that was convened after the double lynching in 1909. The jury recognized no crime in the killings but instead reported that the lynchings represented the will of the community. The *Daily News* then elaborated on the result of the grand jury's actions:

> *And from every dive and den in Cairo went up the endorsing cheers of thugs and hoodlums. Anarchy had been vindicated and awaited only the opportunity to vaunt itself. This opportunity came Thursday when two negro lads were arrested. . . . But before evening came it was talked about in the slums of the rotten river town that there would be some rare sport when night came, as a mob would visit the jail to "get the niggers."*[47]

Fort Wayne's weekly newspaper also blasted Cairo:

> *Cairo, as may very well be supposed from its situation, has a bad lot of negroes, but infinitely worse are the lawless whites as they swill their rotgut in Cairo's dives. The November riots were marked by atrocities that have given them exclusive class and Cairo will not survive long enough to live down the shame of them.*[48]

The *St. Louis Globe-Democrat* called Cairo a "lynching center" and a place where mobs had become fashionable.[49] The *Chicago Post* called Cairo a "mob-ridden" city.[50] "This is the price of lynch law—loss, disgrace, anarchy, wounds, death. . . . Assuredly the lynchings of last November have not reformed the laws, nor uncovered a way whereby two races may dwell together in harmony," commented the *Denver News*.[51] Echoing this commentary was the *Mansfield News Journal* in Ohio, which said that the mob spirit had never died in Cairo since the November 1909 lynchings and that racial conflict aroused then had culminated in the attempted lynching.[52]

The *Cairo Evening Citizen* recognized the racial conflict and discussed the situation in an editorial. First, the newspaper said that because of the large "negro" population in Cairo, which had long been a part of the town, there was nothing to be gained by exciting racial prejudice in Cairo. Second, the paper pointed out that lawbreaking was not confined to one race. Third, Cairo had many hard-working, law-abiding black citizens, and it was outside "negro" riffraff who floated in and out of Cairo causing the trouble whom the police should be able to handle. Finally, the paper argued that "negroes" had the same interest in law enforcement and punishment of crime as whites.[53]

On the same day as the *Citizen*'s editorial, the grand jury was excused. The jurors, of whom the foreman was a relative of Alex Halliday, did not want to investigate the "mob."[54] Without a grand jury, what was Cairo to do? The *Cairo Bulletin* stated, "Cairo's name has been dragged in the mire from ocean to ocean and from the lakes to the gulf; a community to be shunned by people who would live in peace and prosper."[55] The *Citizen* asserted, "For the good of Cairo, mob law must be put down. We cannot have a recurrence of these outbreaks every little while. If we do we will only ruin our city. . . . [The] only way to put down mob law is to have the laws enforced."[56]

Who was going to enforce the laws? During the lynchings of 1909–10, completed and attempted, the Cairo police had been largely absent from the scene. During the 1909 disorders, Chief Egan had helped get Will James on the train and out of town and had dressed Arthur Alexander in a police uniform, which may have saved his life. At the times of the actual lynchings, however, the police were holed up in their station making no effort to protect the Alexander County Courthouse, which was also located in Cairo. During the attempted 1910 lynching, Mayor George Parsons had been alerted by Governor Charles Deneen, and yet no Cairo police were present when the mob attacked the courthouse. Indeed, the feeling in town was that the police were in sympathy with the mob spirit, and those inciting mobs believed they were in no danger of interference from the police.[57]

Because of the lack of a police presence to deter mobs, there was a call for the conservative and prominent citizens to come forth to join any sheriff's posse in time of need. Citizens were asked to make an oath that "no matter who is sheriff, I agree that I will respond promptly to his call for help in defending the county jail, should he need my services."[58] According to the *Cairo Evening Citizen*, if a hundred prominent men would sign up to support the sheriff to deter mob violence and he could call on them at any hour of the day or night, there would be small danger of further assaults on the jail.[59]

Cairo business, not surprisingly, was opposed to the mob activity in town over the past three or so months. The Cairo Board of Trade and the Commercial Club issued the following joint statement of resolutions:

> *That we believe that it is the duty of every citizen of Cairo to support the civil authorities of the city and county in every lawful undertaking to preserve the peace of the community and protect the lives and property of our citizens;*
>
> *That we do discourage in every possible way the spirit of mob rule as being wrong in principle and destructive to the advancement of the highest order of civic prosperity and*
>
> *That we do hereby pledge our moral and physical support to our civil authorities in the discharge of their sworn official duties.*[60]

With Cairo businesses and newspapers supporting the sheriff, there was still uneasiness about the town's future. Cairo, after all, was known nationwide as the city where a mob stormed the county jail in an attempt to lynch a purse snatcher. Such lawlessness was bound to have a harmful effect on the city's image.[61] Thus, the question for Cairo's future appeared to be how to keep the "misguided and hotheaded element" in the community from taking the law into their hands on the slightest pretext and bringing "disgrace, trouble, and sorrow" to the city.[62] The answer lay with the city government and the police.

CHAPTER FIFTEEN

# THE CAIRO POLICE AND A NEW REFORM EFFORT

The *Cairo Bulletin* boldly declared that Mayor George Parsons and his police were the major cause of disorder and lack of law enforcement in Cairo, which had allowed the lynch mobs of 1909 and 1910 to form. The *Bulletin* argued that there was no question that there would have been "no mob and no tragedy had the city police done their duty. . . . The chief and two police officers on the courthouse steps in a firm attitude could have prevented the tragedy."[1] Then the *Bulletin* revealed what it saw as the secret behind Cairo and Alexander County politics: there were two rival factions in the local Republican Party. One faction was led by Mayor George Parsons and the former county sheriff Frank Davis, who were concentrating on defeating U.S. representative Napoleon Bonaparte Thistlewood, their fellow Republican from Cairo. The other faction was the Alexander County Republican organization, which the *Bulletin* called "the machine," led by Judge William Butler and Thistlewood. Sheriff Fred Nellis was identified with this faction. The *Bulletin* reported that Mayor Parsons had tried to keep on "friendly terms" with Cairo's "vicious element," allowing them "all manner of liberties" against the repeated protests of the "good people."[2] The county Republican organization, on the other hand, and presumably Sheriff Nellis, believed the "vicious element" should be curbed when they were "particularly bold."[3]

Napoleon Bonaparte Thistlewood served in Congress from 1908 to 1913. Harris and Ewing Collection, Library of Congress.

According to the *Bulletin*, Cairo's "negroes," especially the "vicious element" among them, constituted the deciding factor in the contest between the local Republican factions, and most of their votes were bought during elections. The newspaper further asserted that Mayor Parsons's police element of the local Republican Party pandered to lawless African Americans, who became increasingly uncontrollable because of police leniency and prosecutorial protection.[4] Thus, stated the *Cairo Bulletin*,

> *the vicious negro has been the primary cause of all of Cairo's trouble. . . . He has found Cairo a pleasant place to live, and has grown bold under this guardianship given to him by the city authorities, with the evident understanding that he must make himself felt in the right way on election day. . . . Crap shooting, petty larceny, burglary, street brawling, actual murder, and insults to white women have been his diversions.*[5]

The *Bulletin*'s assessment of the relationship between African Americans voting in elections and their increasing boldness in their interaction with whites, and a consequent perceived threat to whites by growing black criminality, had been shared by the Springfield, Illinois, press in 1908 during the race riot in Illinois's capital city.[6] Apparently there was a widespread belief among whites in the state that voting by black men made them bold and arrogant and more likely to be "criminals, drunks, and hoodlums."[7]

The *Cairo Bulletin* and some of the Springfield newspapers argued that the African American male franchise and consequent political protection made black people more likely to be criminals and "drunks." Political developments in Cairo following the attempted lynching in 1910 were not encouraging to reformers who wanted city government to control the "drunks" among the criminal element. For six days after the county courthouse was attacked in February 1910, saloons in Cairo were closed. When a sixth "dry" day passed, a rope, chisel, and sledge were found by police chief Martin Egan and Sheriff Nellis at 19th and Washington in Rudy Laurent's Red Onion Saloon, almost immediately opposite the Alexander County Courthouse.[8] It was believed that the riotous mob had hatched the plot to attack the county courthouse in Cairo's saloons. Here, then, was direct evidence of the connection between the alcohol trade and mob violence. And yet on the day after the rope was found at Laurent's saloon, Mayor Parsons removed the order that saloons be closed.[9] Apparently neither Governor Charles Deneen nor Sheriff Nellis objected.

At the same time, the Louis Zanone case came to light. Zanone was a fifty-five-year-old native of Italy who had immigrated in 1873 and moved directly to Cairo, where he went into the saloon business. National Guardsmen had heard that Zanone was selling liquor at his establishment despite the ban. A soldier in civilian clothes was sent to the Zanone saloon, where he bought a bottle of liquor. As soon as the liquor sale was completed, soldiers rushed in to arrest the saloon owner. Zanone pulled a gun, but seeing it was soldiers doing the arresting, he put it away. Mayor George Parsons immediately revoked his liquor license, but less than twenty-four hours later, the city council overruled the mayor and renewed Zanone's license.[10] Alderman James Meehan said that Zanone should not suffer such a severe penalty for the small offense of selling half a pint or so.[11]

The Zanone case demonstrated at least two truths. The first was that the alcoholic beverage industry was extremely important and influential in Cairo. The second was that local politics in Cairo could not be depended on to produce outcomes that supported law and order. Cairo had experienced two nationally known lynchings and an attempted lynching in less than three months, and yet a barkeep who defied the military, the governor, and the mayor of Cairo was not punished for his defiance of the law and executive orders. The lesson was clear for Cairoites and those who came into town from other places in Illinois, Kentucky, and Missouri: there was little need to respect the rules of law and order in Cairo, because many local politicians had scant regard for them.[12]

Local officials were back in control of Cairo, as the *Cairo Evening Citizen* headlines asserted: "Normal Conditions at Court House Restored: Soldiers Who Crowded County Building Last Week Have All Vanished; Officials Were at Their Usual Tasks; Every Trace of the Soldiers Who Held the Place for Ten Days Removed."[13] One of the tasks that Cairo and Alexander County officials faced was removing the Cairo police chief, Martin Egan. Twice during murderous riots in town the Cairo police force was nowhere to be seen. Someone had to take the blame for police inaction in the face of very serious civil disorder, and Egan was selected.[14] Egan's removal was largely political and not punitive, as immediately after leaving office he was appointed to the position of wharfmaster at the Cairo city wharf. Now the "right man" had to be found to replace Egan, a man who would do what was right, perform his duty fearlessly, restore the "right conditions" to Cairo, and prevent further disorder.[15]

The *Cairo Bulletin* expressed an opinion of whom it did not want as Cairo's new police chief—anyone who had been associated with the Cairo police previously.

> *The inefficiency of the Cairo police department in maintaining order was lamentably if not criminally demonstrated in February, meaning that anyone associated with the Cairo police cannot be chosen as the new chief. If such a man is chosen the public can only see that as evidence that the mayor is satisfied with what has been and wants it to continue.*[16]

Mayor Parsons must have wanted Cairo policing to remain substantially the same, because he named Sergeant James Graham Cowell as police chief. Cowell was the night sergeant whom Mayor Parsons "notified" on the night of the attempted lynching and who had done nothing to aid Sheriff Nellis. Yet Cowell was unanimously confirmed by the city council.[17] More police and firemen were also added to the force and department. The *Cairo Bulletin*'s comments on Cowell's appointment were negative:

> *Parsons said Cowell was the logical man to be new chief. He's only the logical man if present policies (now five or six years old) are to be continued. Cowell is harmoniously and intimately identified with the "old regime," which has dragged the community through blood and tears at home and infamy abroad. But* The Bulletin *is willing to judge Chief Cowell on the record he shall make, realizing that while he must be rather timid about making any changes that will mean better government so long as the mayor stubbornly refuses to see anything in the awful record of the past that calls for a change of police policy in this city.*[18]

The *Cairo Evening Citizen* was also disappointed in the selection of the new chief, who it claimed would be controlled by the same people who had put Egan in office, and warned of future trouble.

> *If so soon after the dreaded disorders of last November and only last month, we are to return to the order, or rather the disorder of things of which these outbreaks are but the natural sequence, then our city will be in a bad plight indeed. We shall go rapidly from bad to worse, just at the time when we are hoping to see the city take a new lease of life. . . .*
>
> *It would appear that the Chief of Police is powerless to carry out your wishes because of powerful interests that are opposed to your platform.*[19]

Despite the *Citizen*'s misgivings about the Cairo police, the newspaper applauded their record in the first few weeks with the new chief. In a two-day period, nine inmates of "houses of ill fame," seven vagrants, and one concealed weapons violator were arrested. The prostitutes were all fined ten dollars or jailed. Three of the vagrants were heavily fined and given an hour to get out of town.[20]

The *Cairo Bulletin*, however, did not share the *Citizen*'s appreciation of the police cleanup, at least insofar as the concealed weapons charge was concerned. In that case J. M. Curtis, the chief of the Cairo Loan Office, was fined twenty-five dollars for carrying a concealed weapon. He was stopped on the street by Officer French (probably William French) and told that the chief wanted to talk to him and was taken to police headquarters. There he was searched, a gun was taken from him, he was placed in a cell for a few minutes, and despite protests of not being ready, he was taken upstairs for his trial. The *Bulletin* said that there was no reason for the arrest, because the man was minding his own business and needed a gun since he handled so much money. At the end of an editorial on the affair, the *Bulletin* asserted,

> *If the law can be enforced in the case of an offender who is otherwise a law abiding citizen quietly walking down the street, in pursuit of his legitimate business, it is many times easier if against the pistol toting "bad niggers" who have been so much in evidence in Cairo during the last five or six years, to the community's great injury.*[21]

In the space of a few days, the *Cairo Bulletin* had gone from discussing "vicious negroes" to gun-carrying "bad niggers." The implication for black Cairo must have been apparent: the *Bulletin* was a white man's newspaper and certainly not above blatant racism.

In the first days and weeks of Chief Cowell's being on the job, both black and white Cairo citizens began to press for better law enforcement in the city, especially with respect to the saloons and the "red-light district." First, a coalition of "Colored Women's Clubs" stated, "We know there are many colored people in Cairo who are law-abiding, upright, honest, and a credit to their race. . . . And, we greatly deplore the license which is accorded this unfortunate lower element by the city."[22] The "license" of which the African American clubwomen spoke was allowing children and women in Cairo's saloons. The clubwomen wanted this stopped and the curfew for minors strictly enforced. Further, the city authorities were to suppress immorality, crime, and lawlessness wherever found. Added to these law enforcement steps, to which most white reformers in Cairo could agree, were calls for the building and renting of "shacks" to be somehow curbed, as these were "veritable incubators of crime and immorality." Finally, the "colored" women and men of Cairo were admonished to change certain behaviors, including frequenting saloons, "going upon the streets in dirty garments and head rags," and voting for officials who were not scrupulous about law enforcement.[23]

Almost exactly two weeks later, a group that the *Cairo Evening Citizen* called "the colored preachers" presented a petition to the city government that echoed many of the concerns of Cairo African American clubwomen, including a prohibition of women and children from saloons. The petition also called for the Sunday closing of saloons and for them to be shut down from 11 p.m. to 5 a.m. each day. Saloon closing was something that the newspaper had promoted at least as far back as the previous year. Following the "colored" women, the "preachers" advocated a strict enforcement of the curfew for minors but added a call for the complete abolition of gambling in the city. The black pastors then made blunt suggestions concerning Cairo's serious social problem: "That assignation houses be prohibited anywhere in the city limits and that houses of ill fame be not scattered all over the city. And, if they must exist, that they be confined to one district irrespective of race or nationality."[24]

Also, apparently irrespective of race was the reform impulse in Cairo. Both black and white citizens recognized not only that the unrestricted alcohol trade was damaging the town but also that prostitution "scattered all over the city" was giving Cairo the wrong kind of publicity, as well as contributing to lawlessness, corruption, and the destruction of human lives. White pastors and other members of the Social Purity League met at the Presbyterian church one Sunday afternoon in March 1910. They discussed setting up a rescue house in Cairo's red-light district so that women who wanted to leave prostitution would have some place to live.[25] Money was immediately collected for that purpose. If the city government would not act, there were steps the clergy and women of both races could take to deal with Cairo's problem, and they had the support of the *Cairo Evening Citizen* and the *Cairo Bulletin*.[26]

Both Protestant and Catholic clergy in Cairo spoke against conditions in town. Reverend S. C. Ohrum said he had never seen a community where the churches had so little influence as they did in Cairo. He called for the establishment of men's Bible classes, saying, "These organizations of earnest men are chained lightning for the devil and his works and the dynamite of God to wake up and restore the community to nobler ideals." They would make Cairo a good place to live.[27] Father James Gillen even hosted a meeting of the Social Purity League at St. Joseph's parish hall to condemn not only prostitutes in Cairo but also their male customers. Gillen said, "I have as much disrespect for the prostitute young man as I do for the prostitute young woman. Where is there ruin, if this is not a ruin? Where is there vice, if this is not vice, and it should be fought to the end."[28]

There were, however, still officials in Alexander County who were not willing to let the clergy, women, and newspapers fight vice and lawlessness without government help. Sheriff Nellis himself had raided the Bourgois and Richard "Dick" Taylor "dives" in Cairo's First Ward, which enraged former police officer James Casey. Casey was under indictment for accepting bribes and was identified as one of the mob members who had attacked the courthouse in 1910.[29] Sheriff Nellis also gathered 100 names, addresses, and phone numbers of members of the Board of Trade and the Commercial Club, who were sworn to come to his aid in an emergency. The sheriff also had the county board buy him ten twelve-round-magazine lever-action Winchester rifles, "with a sufficient amount of ammunition to resist any attack upon the jail."[30] In addition, "the Sheriff also had chains and locks to put on the gates at the court yard, which, if locked, would compel members of the mob to climb the fence, which would make them easy targets for men inside the building."[31] Judge William N. Butler also pressed for better law enforcement by convening the third grand jury within ninety days, with the purpose of probing Cairo's "disorders" and "lawlessness."[32]

That Cairo suffered from "lawlessness" became a constant theme for the *Cairo Bulletin* in the spring of 1910. The newspaper asserted, "There is a lawless element in Cairo. Officials have favored that element in their official conduct—ignoring their oaths of office."[33] Two days later, the *Bulletin* headlined, "Four Negro Highwaymen in Police-Protected 'Dive' Rob Young Negro of Money."[34] In an editorial on that same day, Cairo's oldest daily continued to lay the blame for the town's lack of law enforcement on the city government.

> *The Cairo police are contemptuous of citizen complaints, inefficient in dealing with negro vagabonds and criminals—from whom the community have suffered so much in the last six months.... The 5th Street dive where the robbery took place has been the subject of complaints for many months. The mayor and the chief of police have been complained to about it repeatedly. The fact that the "negro wenches" who reside there are daily parading the streets soliciting strangers to go with them; the*

> *fact that the strangers, who have yielded to such solicitation have been robbed in the den by what is known as the "panel game"—all this is known to the mayor and to his police—has been known for many months, if not years. But they have done absolutely nothing to break up this nest of criminals. . . .*
>
> *The proprietor of the "dive" is the negro who has long figured in some of the cases of police graft that have come to light in the lower part of the city. He is a recognized "police-go-between"—one who conducts negotiations between the police and their victims permitting the police to stay in the background. He was a good witness for the gang before the grand jury of some months ago, which investigated police graft, returning a true bill against Officer Casey—he knew absolutely nothing.*[35]

John M. Lansden was an attorney in Cairo and author of the 1910 *History of the City of Cairo, Illinois.* John M. Lansden Collection, Southern Illinois University Special Collections Research Center, Carbondale.

Here is Cairo's pioneer paper charging the city government with protecting the lawless, especially "negro" criminals and tramps; with criminal enterprise involving soliciting "negro wenches" and the "panel game"; and with engaging in graft, concealed by a career criminal and "police-go-between." The newspaper's condemnation of Mayor Parsons's administration could not have been much more severe. If the city government was protecting criminals and crooked police officers, however, many of Cairo's citizens were at the same time trying to shield members of the February mob from the force of the law.

Despite efforts by Alexander County state's attorney Alexander Wilson, the townspeople did not seem willing to punish or even reveal very much about past mobs. Wilson called twenty-five people to testify before the latest grand jury. A number of them were prominent citizens, including attorney and author John M. Lansden. And yet, evidence "came slowly," because the witnesses claimed they knew very little of what had happened during the lynchings or attempted lynching, or they "suffered a lapse of memory."[36]

Almost pleadingly the *Cairo Evening Citizen* speculated that surely this "handpicked" grand jury, whose members were "leading businessmen," from "the top of the barrel," and among the "best citizens," would bring troublemakers to justice. While indicting such troublemakers, the grand jury still surprised many in Cairo when it brought a certain class of "law violators to the bar of justice."[37] These were the owners, operators, and inhabitants of the houses of ill fame on 13th Street and elsewhere in town. The list of those indicted and liable to fines of up to $200 included Mabel McFarland, Leonard A. Rink, Joachin Murat Guion, John Walter, John Sullivan, Robert Jones, Hattie Barrow, and Alfred Baltimore.[38] Baltimore, who came to Cairo a few years earlier from Nashville, Tennessee, was singled out for running a disorderly house at 3815 Commercial. He had also been exonerated for killing former "negro" police officer and partner George Bradley on January 15, 1909, the coroner's jury calling it justified "gunplay."[39]

Judge William Dewey quickly disposed of those associated with Cairo's many houses of ill fame. The fines he levied were from $75 to $150, followed by a lecture to the defendants:

> *I had rather break up your business than to fine you. But the law prescribes a fine on the theory that by imposing it, it will make the business unprofitable, and so I shall fine you $75 and costs, and the State's Attorney asks that you stand committed until the fines and costs are paid.*[40]

All white keepers of the "houses" pleaded guilty, but three alleged black owners or operators demanded trials. The article that identified the owners and operators of Cairo's houses of ill fame also revealed the names of the "mistresses," women who today might be called "madams." These were Myrtle Stevenson, of 212 13th Street; Myrtle Ward, 214 13th Street; Dot Wade, 210 13th Street; Ethel Wells, 228 13th Street; Alice Parham, 225 and 235 13th Street; Rose St. Clair, 217 13th Street; and Willie Estelle, an African American "madam" on 17th and Cedar.[41] The indictments were made and fines levied, but the grand jury also delivered a report on the sex trade in Cairo, with particular attention paid to "satellite" houses spreading out over town at 15th Street between Commercial Avenue and Washington and along 18th Street.

> *The latter is even worse than the former. The latter seems to make a specialty hellishly catering to the school boys from 13 to 16 years of age. It is too vile to mention and almost incomprehensible.*
>
> *These resorts (to say nothing about others scattered about town) and the actions therein and thereafter are a menace, and worse than a disgrace to any community, civilized or otherwise. The more we probe, the worse it gets.*[42]

This report confirmed earlier charges by the Cairo newspapers and some of Cairo's clergy that underage boys were going to the city's brothels in significant numbers. Neither prostitution nor the almost unbelievable alcohol trade in town, however, was the most severe problem identified by the grand jury. That problem was that the city government did not enforce the law, nor maintain order, even in the face of mob violence and riot.[43] Those on the grand jury boldly stated these facts in their final report:

> *This jury being convinced from evidence at hand and heretofore submitted and disregarded, that the city authorities are either unable or unwilling to bring about that much needed and continuously solicited reform; feel it incumbent upon themselves to apply more strenuous measures, and such as cannot be misconstrued or ignored. Recommendations are good only when accepted in good faith and when executed, which unfortunately has not been the case.*[44]

As might have been expected, the *Cairo Bulletin* gave a somewhat strident response to the grand jury findings. Not only that, but the older daily reviewed the reports of previous grand juries under the headline "City Officials Denounced by Four Cairo Grand Juries." In 1906 the grand jury called for "these evils so fatal to the honor and citizenship of our youth, so dangerous to the safety of the community[, to] be forever abated."[45] In both 1906 and 1909 the grand juries complained of "grievous wrongs, disorder, unlawfully conducted places and the like."[46] In those years, the city authorities were admonished to abolish or at least correct wrongs, disorders, and abuses, but it was not done.

To correct the problem of being practically ignored by the Cairo city government, the March 1910 grand jury made specific recommendations, and they cost money.[47] First, a separate fund was to be created so that Sheriff Nellis could hire "reliable, fearless and discriminating deputies to enable him (the sheriff) to enforce the laws."[48] Next, the state's attorney was to have a hired assistant ready by the next term of the circuit court. The grand jury then reviewed the formation of the mob, with Rudy Laurent's Red Onion Saloon again being given prominence as the place where the mob came together and the attack on the county courthouse originated.

The members of the grand jury delivered twelve indictments of men in the mob and complained that they had been hampered, as had several juries before, by the "witnesses' reticence and unwillingness to impart information and tell the truth."[49] They went on to comment on Cairo's Company K (which they called militia) and the citizen-soldiers' late arrival at the courthouse, blamed on the very bad weather and on poor communication.[50] The grand jury, therefore, suggested a modern electric alarm system be installed in Company K headquarters, as well as in the police station and fire stations. Then the jurors made a final summary of the Cairo situation:

> *We sincerely deplore that facts and conditions, coupled with past experiences and a preponderance of evidence force upon us any such actions as contemplated . . . but we feel in duty bound to endeavor in some positive and unequivocal manner to offer what we hope to be a remedy for the evils that exist and have existed, without any apparent abatement, for some years.*[51]

When would "abatement" of lawlessness and disorder come to Cairo? The *Cairo Evening Citizen* and other Illinois newspapers discussed the issue on the day of the grand jury indictment and the following day. *Evening Citizen* "dispatches" sent to the metropolitan newspapers generally stated that Cairo, as a community, was largely in sympathy with the men indicted for participating in the mob.[52] Who were these men? A chilling "confession" concerning their identities and purpose emerged in at least two regional newspapers in the days after the attempted lynching. A mob member said the mob had been composed of "business men," who had expected that other crowds would join them at the Alexander County Courthouse to form a throng "in the hundreds."[53] This did not happen, so according to a mob member, a determined group, originally numbering only thirty-five, marched to the courthouse. The man then said, "We expected to carry out the lynching quietly. We intended to . . . take the negroes out and hang them. We were never more surprised in our lives than when Sheriff Nellis and the guards fired on us."[54] Were these cold-blooded potential lynchers of purse snatchers indeed "business men" who reflected the Cairo white population's "sympathies"? The *Cairo Evening Citizen* wasn't sure. The *Citizen* asked rhetorically how many grand juries it would take before the mayor would realize that there were real evils in Cairo that must be corrected. The newspaper further commented that the organization of various citizens' groups, such as the Citizens' League, the Pure Ballot League, and the Social Purity League, would not have been necessary if Mayor Parsons had upheld his oath in the first place.[55]

Other Illinois newspapers commented on the indictments of alleged rioters. The *Chicago Journal* said they were a hopeful sign. "If the prosecutor shows as much determination as Sheriff Nellis displayed, Cairo may be taught a lesson, and cease to be a disgrace to a law-abiding state." The *Quincy Whig* said that Cairo had done herself proud.[56] Of course, the proof of whether the Cairo majority supported the sheriff and the criminal justice system depended on at least two outcomes. The first would be conviction of some or all of those indicted for participation in the mob attacking the courthouse. The second would be the reelection of Fred Nellis for sheriff in the November election.

Until the trials and elections were held, the progressive and reform element in Cairo concentrated on the municipal elections of April 19, 1910. The Citizens' League, with the support of the *Cairo Evening Citizen*, endorsed a candidate for each of the town's seven wards. The *Cairo Bulletin* warned that Mayor George Parsons had a scheme to elect men to the city council who would be his henchmen and that he must be stopped.[57] The newspaper then discussed what was believed to be the situation in each of Cairo's wards. First Ward alderman James Meehan was unacceptable to the *Bulletin* because his ward was seen as a "hotbed" of police corruption and because Meehan and Officer James Casey had tried to resist raids in the ward by county officers. In discussing the Fourth Ward, the *Bulletin* called former police chief Egan, who was expected to run for alderman, a thief. Such samples of the *Bulletin*'s opinion of the Parsons administration clearly showed the depth of local press opposition to the mayor and his men.[58] Both Cairo dailies opposed them.

The opposition of the press and the Citizens' League was expressed in the league's platform, with nine "planks." The platform called for the enforcement of vagrancy laws and concealed weapons laws. It also called for the suppression of gambling, prostitution, and dance halls, known as "honk-a-tonks." Saloons were to be forbidden to women and children and closed from midnight until 5 a.m. Finally, "we object to the indiscriminate scattering of houses of ill fame in our city."[59]

What the Citizens' League and other opponents of vice and the extreme alcohol trade were facing in Cairo in 1910 can possibly be illustrated by one incident. Charles Adkins of Frederick, Kentucky, twenty-three, had secured eighteen-year-old Lottie Whitlock of New Albany, Mississippi, and brought her to Cairo with the promise of marriage. Instead, because of the town's reputation, he took her straight to 13th Street to a "bawdy house."[60] His plan was to take her to a room, "ruin her," and then sell her to the woman running the brothel. His proposal to the "woman of the town" and proprietor of the house was not well received, because she wanted nothing to do with "white slavery." She called the police and held the couple in the house until they arrived. The couple then came to the attention of county authorities and both were arraigned. Judge William Dewey frightened Adkins and told him what happened to persons charged with "white slavery." At that point the man decided to wed the young woman, and they were married in the court. The *Cairo Evening Citizen* commented on the case:

> *The agitation for moral improvement may have been in a measure responsible for the prompt action in this case. If so the gain is worth the cost. There have been similar cases in the past, and in some instances the police have rescued girls from a life of shame after they have been deserted. But this is probably the first time the man in the case found himself pinched in a trap of his own setting.*[61]

How were the "agitation for moral improvement" and other reforms going to turn out for the Citizens' League and other Cairo progressives? According to the reformist *Cairo Evening Citizen*, "If there is any issue in this campaign, it is or should be this issue of reform in the civic affairs of Cairo."[62] The *Cairo Bulletin* as usual was more aggressive than the *Citizen* and was out to expose the depth of the corruption in Cairo.

On March 22, 1910, the *Bulletin* headlined, "Blind Tiger Is Discovered Adjoining Police Station, Conducted by Assyrian Under Cover of Grocery Store—Opium Joint Also."[63] The story under the headline went on to tell that George Maloof, a native of Mount Lebanon, Syria, had been selling liquor next door to Cairo Police Headquarters with no license.[64] Maloof was fifty years old and a member of Cairo's "Syrian Colony" who had immigrated to the United States in 1895. It was Sheriff Nellis and Special Deputy Thomas Fuller who raided Maloof's "store" and not the Cairo police. During the lawmen's search, they found an opium pipe. Apparently Maloof's activities were so well known that the special grand jury had already issued a true bill for Nellis and Fuller to enforce.[65] Maloof was found guilty of selling liquor without a license and fined twenty-five dollars plus fees but left the country without paying and when last heard from was in Jerusalem.[66]

While showing that alcohol and drugs were illegally peddled in proximity to the police, the newspaper made a rare positive mention of Cairo's African Americans in its pages. The *Bulletin* emphasized that the strongest protests against "dives" came from "law-abiding negroes." The newspaper went on to say, "A very large proportion of the negroes of Cairo are law-abiding people. That so many of them are not and are so often in evidence as disturbers is due principally to the criminal want of police control, as exemplified in the case of the Baltimore dive and numerous others."[67]

It seems that the *Cairo Bulletin* had particular enmity against Alfred Baltimore for his role as a successful saloon and dance hall operator and friend of the Cairo police. A few days after saying that Baltimore's "dive" exemplified Cairo's African American crime problem, the daily headlined, "Nightly Carousals Occur at Baltimore's Negro Dive under Police Protection, Notorious 'Honky Tonk' Sells Liquor to Negro Boys and Women—Headquarters for Police on That Beat." The *Bulletin* claimed that Baltimore's place was filled with scores of black women and girls who mingled with the men and boys, drinking and engaging in "lewd dancing." Officer John Wade, who was black, and his partner used the phone at Baltimore's place at 39th and Commercial Avenue to check in at the police station, and when they left the yelling and fighting would usually begin.[68]

The *Cairo Bulletin*'s stand for the forthcoming city elections was clear: liquor and drugs were being illegally sold, saloon operators were corrupting women and the youth, and the Cairo police knew about it and protected the offenders—indeed, they worked together. To the *Bulletin*, the remedy was clear; the aldermen who supported Mayor Parsons must be defeated. The Citizens' League and its candidates won the *Bulletin*'s support because their purposes were the same: eliminate the saloon dives and regulate liquor traffic so it was lawful.[69] The *Cairo Evening Citizen* had also endorsed the Citizens' League's candidates but worried about the quietness of the campaign and wondered whether the voters generally had forgotten Cairo's disorders and the resolve immediately after them to bring about "better conditions."[70]

Hopefully, the "better conditions" in Cairo were on the way. Six of the seven candidates of the Citizens' League were elected.[71] To the reformers, the defeat of James Meehan, First Ward alderman, was particularly gratifying. Meehan had led fights for Mayor Parsons in the city council and was in favor of a "wide-open town" to the end. Bold to the point of recklessness, he had expressed long and loudly his opinions in the city council, even when no one agreed with him.[72] Meehan left Cairo and moved his family to Chicago, where he operated his own private detective agency through the 1920s.

The progressive *Cairo Evening Citizen* rejoiced at Meehan's defeat and at the victory of the Citizens' League's candidates. "Cairo has shown that she is determined to carry reform into the election of honest men for office," the paper exclaimed. The newspaper further stated that the town owed the Citizens' League a debt of gratitude. The *Citizen* further argued that former alderman Meehan, and by extension Mayor Parsons, should have learned that reform in Cairo was not just "newspaper talk." There were conditions in Cairo that the "better element" would not tolerate.[73] Finally, the *Citizen* publicized the virtues of the Pure Ballot League and the election commissioners, saying that Cairo at last had a clean election. This was the first year of voter registration and that procedure had severely lessened, if not absolutely stopped, for the time being, election fraud in Cairo.[74]

Reformers hoped that, with honest elections and honest men in office, Cairo was on the threshold of an era of reform and progress. The Social Purity League in town was certainly optimistic that the city could be "cleaned up." Members asked for information on any houses used for immoral purposes in Cairo, especially ones "scattered over the city," that is, not on 13th

Cairo's Commercial Avenue, north from 6th Street. The arches at 8th Street can be seen in the background. Postcard courtesy of Darrel Dexter.

Street. The Reverend George M. Babcock, rector of the Episcopal Church of the Redeemer, said that the Social Purity League was watching a house on 23rd Street and another on 10th Street, where it was rumored that parties had moved in from the infamous 13th Street. As information was gathered and evidence procured, the Social Purity League would have the authorities move against the owners of any properties used for immoral purposes and fine them. Reverend Babcock also proposed to clean up Cairo by rescuing prostitutes from their way of life. He stated that if any of the women who left the street cared to lead a different life, the league stood ready to help them to begin anew, with a place to live and a job.[75] One of the indications that a "clean up" was wanted by the majority of Cairo's people or that considerably better law and order were coming to the river city would be the outcome of the trials of those charged with attacking the county courthouse with the intention of lynching John Pratt, as would the county elections later in that year.

## CHAPTER SIXTEEN

# THE RIOT CASES

If Cairo was to be "clean" and lawful after the April 20, 1910, city election, did that mean the majority of the townspeople wanted such a community? One test of community sentiment would be the trials of those indicted for attacking the county courthouse the previous February. The *Cairo Evening Citizen* called the trials the "riot cases," and the first one began May 11, 1910.[1] The state of Illinois brought in June C. Smith[2] from the attorney general's office and James Lingle of Union County for the trial. Walter Warder, state senator and attorney from Cairo, was also part of State's Attorney Alexander Wilson's prosecution team.[3]

Warren Webster Duncan, of Marion, Illinois, was the judge in the riot cases and went on to become a justice on the Illinois Supreme Court. Courtesy of Marion Illinois History Preservation.

For the defense there were Angus Leek and Reed Green of Cairo. They argued that the indictments under which the "rioters" were charged were faulty and that all should be thrown out. Circuit judge Warren Webster Duncan, of Marion, Illinois, took the matter under advisement. Confidence in the judge was shaken when on the same day the rioters' trials started, the judge declared the grand jury drawn in December 1909 to investigate the November lynchings of that year to be illegal because it had been selected by the county commissioners and not by Sheriff James McGriffen McManus, as it should have been.[4] Judge Duncan's decision freed a person charged with two counts of bribery (ex-policeman James Casey), one charged with manslaughter (John Mitchell), and two for assault to murder (Will O'Donley and ex-policeman Luther Lewis), all of whom had been indicted by the "illegal" grand jury.[5]

The bribery case was immediately dropped by State's Attorney Wilson, but he quickly gathered documents so the new "legal" grand jury could reindict the three men charged with manslaughter and assault to murder.[6]

With Alexander County's always-busy court docket, Sheriff Fred Nellis did not get a chance to testify as to the February attack on the county jail until the middle of July 1910. His testimony was coordinated by June C. Smith, the lawyer sent from the Illinois attorney general's office. The others testifying for the prosecution included the deputy county clerk, several black deputies, Captain and Alderman William P. Greaney, Lieutenant Arthur Thistlewood, and saloonkeeper Rudy Laurent.[7] State's Attorney Alexander Wilson made the opening statement for the prosecution, which was not very ambitious. He said he would submit evidence that the defendants were guilty of being parties to a mob and refusing to disperse at the command of the sheriff.

Sheriff Fred Nellis's testimony must have been riveting, as he told the story of the attempted lynching. Other prosecution witnesses directly identified mob members. Those named were Frank J. Gorman, George B. Walker, James B. Scott, Sam Wissinger, Camelous O. Foster, and Cairo police officer James L. "Jim" Casey, who was in the front ranks and recently charged with bribery.[8] Others charged with being a part of the lynch mob were Lee Watson, W. H. Simpson (foreman of the coroner's jury that investigated the death of Anna Pelley), William C. Charles, Oliver P. Hurd Jr., John Maloney, and James M. Davidge.[9] The witnesses also corroborated Sheriff Nellis's testimony that the lawmen had fired in the air first and that the initial shots had come from the mob. Added to the sheriff's sworn statements were the facts that the mob made no hesitation after coming through the courthouse gate and that "as many as could jammed the steps to attack the courthouse." James B. Scott was directly identified by a prosecution witness who saw him remove his mask. In cross-examination, attorney Reed Green somewhat impeached the testimony of the prosecution's witness, because he had said that Frank Gorman was smoking a cigar and Green claimed Gorman had not smoked for two years.[10]

June Smith was able to get the sledgehammer, cold chisel, and rope found in Rudy Laurent's saloon admitted as evidence. These were said to have been supplied by Scott, a blacksmith, and would have been used to enter the cell that held purse snatcher John Pratt. Thomas A. Head, "another negro deputy," stated that he saw a mob forming at Laurent's Red Onion Saloon for some time before the attack. Head also said that about an hour before the attempted lynching, he saw Frank Gorman cross Washington and take a look at the courthouse. The defense argued, however, either that the twelve men indicted for the attack on the courthouse on February 17 were not at the location or that, if they were, they had a right to be there. Scott, previously identified as a masked mob leader, was home with his wife, Hattie Scott. George B. Walker was a wire service reporter for a news service; he was a permanent resident of Cairo, a job printer and publisher of the Cairo city directory. Camelous O. Foster was nowhere near the attack; he was at 18th and Cedar. Jim Davidge was at Riddle's saloon, at 714 Commercial near 8th Street, during the attack, playing cards. John Maloney was an "innocent bystander" who was shot when he ran after the crowd to see what was happening. James Casey was in the Red Onion, at 1900 Washington Avenue, during the disturbance.[11]

It was Rudy Laurent who testified that Oliver P. Hurd Jr., W. H. Simpson, William C. Charles, Lee Watson, and Jim Casey were all in his saloon at the time of the attack and remained there from the time other men left to attack until they returned with Sam Wissinger and George Walker limping in wounded. Peter Lind Jr. provided an alibi for Frank Gorman, saying that he was in front of the Red Onion when Gorman and Dick Fitzgerald ran past him and ducked into an alley, where he joined them. The three then went to the saloon, where they were joined by Horton Crehan. When Crehan was called, he echoed Lind's testimony. Then attorney Lingle cross-examined him as to the gunshot wound on his ankle, but Crehan said it was a bruise. Lingle then said, "But you noticed the 'bruise,' as you call it, after the shooting took place?" Crehan admitted it was about the time of the attack that he noticed the bruise.[12]

Lieutenant Thistlewood and Captain Greaney were in the Red Onion about one o'clock in the morning on February 18 when they heard defendant Frank Gorman say to someone who had phoned him, "Hold the receiver and listen, and I'll telephone you some noise."[13] Then Gorman went outside and fired several shots into the air with a rifle. Thistlewood's testimony was corroborated by another witness. Gorman, under cross-examination, said he had walked up the west side of Washington Avenue to Division Street and then crossed the street and walked down the east side of the avenue, past the courthouse to Rudy Laurent's saloon. He admitted he saw none of the defendants there.

When coroner and former sheriff James McManus testified, he said that at his inquest Sheriff Nellis, Ben Jones, and the deputies did not testify that they recognized any of the defendants in the mob that made the attack. The negation of the prosecution's cases went on and on. More testimony that Jim

Davidge was in Riddle's saloon far from the courthouse almost all night was heard. Robert M. Jeffries was with defendant Foster on February 17, and he claimed that they knew nothing of the mob until the next morning. Finally, Jim Davidge took the stand and stated that he was in Riddle's saloon all night playing cards. Attorney Lingle then asked how he could remember his movements on February 17 so exactly, when he couldn't remember being at the Bijou picture show or the arcade. Davidge then said he did go to a picture show but couldn't remember which one. The *Cairo Evening Citizen* reported, "Attorney Lingle has questioned nearly every defendant and witness especially as to why they would remember so well the exact time of their movements on the night in question, and all had some excuse or another on their lips ready to offer."[14]

Ready to excuse his patrons was Rudy Laurent, keeper of the Red Onion. He was serving a particularly heavy crowd on the night of February 17, 1910, many coming into his place after a dance at the Alexander Club closed. He said he heard a heavy volley of shots, after which Sam Wissinger and George Walker came in wounded. Laurent further testified that five defendants were in the bar drinking before Wissinger and Walker arrived. About fifteen or twenty minutes before the attack on the courthouse, the crowd in the saloon grew so large that it was unusual. Laurent said he asked someone what was going to happen and that person replied, "We're going to hang a nigger." Upon being asked by the prosecution who made the remark, the barkeep replied that he thought it was the man who was killed, Alex Halliday.[15]

James Casey told the familiar defendant story. He was in Laurent's saloon until after midnight, and what was more, Hurd, Simpson, Charles, and Watson were with him. Lee Watson's testimony that followed would be amusing if the charges against him and others were not so serious and the verdicts in the trials not so important for law and order in Cairo. Watson said he visited John F. Ashley's saloon at 911 Commercial and Frank Sebille's saloon at 215 8th Street on the night of the riot, as was his custom almost every night. Watson came into the company of defendant Charles, and they visited Peter Day's Popular Saloon at 1200 Washington between 10:30 and 11:00. But they weren't finished; they went from Day's saloon to Laurent's at 19th and Washington and stayed there from 11 to 11:30. When they heard shots, Watson and Lee were at the bar drinking, and not surprisingly from all other defendants' testimony, they were with the others charged with riot—Hurd, Simpson, Charles, and Casey. Defendant W. H. Simpson portrayed the night of the attempted lynching as just another night on the town for him and Lee Watson at Sebille's saloon, where they met Oliver P. Hurd. Simpson claimed there was no "mob talk" at Sebille's, where they stayed until about 11:30 p.m. At that time, the trio took a "leisurely walk" to the Red Onion. Simpson said he often visited that saloon "on his way home," and there was no particular reason why he was there that night. He said he certainly did not have a mask and was not on the courthouse steps. Of course, when shots rang out, he was at the bar drinking with Hurd, Charles, Watson, and Casey.[16]

Samuel Wissinger testified that he was working at the Mobile & Ohio yards the night of the lynching when he received a call that he was wanted at the courthouse as a deputy sheriff. He left work, but instead of going directly to the courthouse, he stopped to eat at Hank's saloon, where he saw Captain Greaney, who also told him Sheriff Nellis wanted him at the courthouse. He was on his way to report for duty when he got caught in the crowd and was subsequently wounded.

Every witness for the defense testified under oath that the huge crowd at "Rudy's" (the Red Onion) on the night of February 17 was not unusual (even though it was contradicted by Laurent's own testimony) and that all the defendants frequented that saloon. They all supported each other's testimony. No one saw any masks at any saloon or chisels or sledges. Most of the defense witnesses knew Alex Halliday but couldn't remember if he was at Rudy's on February 17. The one who did remember Halliday, Rudy Laurent himself, supported the testimony of every defendant who said he was in the Red Onion at the time of the shooting at the courthouse, and Alex Halliday was dead and couldn't be tried. Defense witnesses and defendants all swore that they were regular patrons of Rudy's, that it wasn't unusual for them to be there at any hour, that they didn't hear any talk of a lynching while they were there, and that Sebille's saloon and the Red Onion were often used as business places. Oliver P. Hurd Jr., for example, used it as a sort of "lumber exchange."[17]

The closing for the prosecution was handled by former state senator Walter Warder and James Lingle. Senator Warder explained the law as to the two counts of the indictments and then talked about the fact that Sheriff Nellis couldn't find any more than a few people to come to the courthouse before the attack. He then pointed out that Judge William Dewey and defense attorney Angus Leek were in the courthouse at the time of the attack and as attorneys were duly sworn to the law, and yet they at the time discounted the possibility of a mob forming and left the building. Warder then mentioned the wounded Sam Wissinger and asserted that if Wissinger's presence at the courthouse was because he was a duly sworn deputy, then all the other men with Sheriff Nellis were duly sworn law officers under the

Walter Warder (*left*) was president pro tempore of the Illinois Senate. From *Official Directory of the Fortieth General Assembly of Illinois*, 62. James Lingle (*right*) was state's attorney for Union County, Illinois, and helped prosecute the "riot cases." From *Standard Atlas of Union County, Illinois*, 65.

sheriff's commission and were doing their duty. Prosecutor James Lingle, although not from Cairo, talked about the situation in the town.

> *The chief excuse of the mob is that the courts do not do their duty, and yet they come here and ask you to discharge these defendants. The best thing to tell the people of Cairo or of Alexander county is to tell them that here is a jury that holds that law is supreme.*[18]

Lingle went on to point out that the witnesses gave so many conflicting statements that the whereabouts of the defendants at the time of the riot would be impossible to prove by the defense and that their alibis were suspect to say the least, especially that of James B. Scott. The prosecutor spoke of alibis in general, saying they were easy to provide and hard to disprove. Lingle then singled out defendant Sam Wissinger and argued that Wissinger's story that he was at the courthouse to report for duty was unbelievable. Lingle said Wissinger was part of the mob before the attack and that after he was shot, he returned to Laurent's saloon, where the mob started and where it disbanded.[19]

Then Lingle went after John Maloney's claim of being an innocent bystander and said that such claims could not be credited. Lingle said Maloney was in the mob, going the way of the mob, and, as the evidence showed, was as guilty as any of them. The attorney said to be an innocent bystander, one must be passing and must stop to see what is going on—not be a part of the mob itself.

James Lingle then talked of coincidence, referring to defendants Hurd, Simpson, and Watson. He said it was strange that these three were all attracted to a particular saloon at that time of night. Next, Lingle revealed information that was well known in Cairo: young men in the Alexander Club, of which Alex Halliday was a member, had heard a mob was forming, and several of them came together to Rudy Laurent's saloon. They were aware of the situation, and if they did not actually join the mob, they knew what was going on and encouraged it.[20]

Referring to attorney Angus Leek's charge that Nellis put the lights out in the courthouse so his deputies would be in the dark, Lingle said Leek should be the last man to make such a charge, because he was in the courthouse that night and "ran away."[21] According to the prosecutor, Sheriff Nellis did the natural thing—not making targets of his men. "A mob is war," declared the attorney. Lingle was aware that defense attorney Leek

The prestigious Alexander Club at 701–703 Washington Avenue attracted members from Cairo's leading white families. Postcard courtesy of Darrel Dexter.

had tried to arouse "race prejudice" during the trial, and he said, "God pity us if you twelve cannot convict because race prejudice has been stirred up so you cannot do your duty."[22]

Perhaps knowing his jury, defense attorney Angus Leek did not waste much time on his closing. He ridiculed Senator Warder for talking about the Constitution, the Statue of Liberty, and the "Star-Spangled Banner" and said the prosecutor had evaded the evidence. Then Leek attacked Sheriff Nellis's character and openly appealed to the racist prejudice of the jurors. He said that Nellis was "no gentleman" because of the way he conducted himself before the mob and after the gunfire. Leek said the sheriff had set up a "death trap" manned by "treacherous negro deputies" who were armed with revolvers and shotguns loaded with buckshot. These deputies had fired almost before the sheriff could open his mouth to warn the "mob."[23] Leek further ridiculed and condemned the sheriff's deputies because their testimonies were contradictory and because they claimed that the mob had fired first. At the end of his closing, Leek returned to the sheriff's leaving of Alex Halliday's corpse in the snow for four hours. Judge Duncan "called him down" on bringing up the body in the snow again, saying it was irrelevant; it did not matter if the body lay there for four or 400 hours. Then the virulent racism came out. Leek retorted, "It is up to you, judge, whether you believe these white men or whether you believe these niggers."[24]

Whether it was racism on the part of the all-white jury, who simply could not get past the fact that it was the sheriff's black deputies in the main who defended the courthouse against a white mob, killing a prominent white man and wounding others, or other reasons, not a single defendant in the "riot trial" was convicted. The twelve of them found a large automobile, probably from the Maloney garage, and rode around town in celebration of their triumph.[25]

Judge Duncan, who seemed to be more in tune with following the letter of the law rather than the spirit of the law, spoke in the county courtroom after the "riot" defendants were acquitted. Duncan said he had discovered an unhealthy sentiment in Cairo with many believing that mob law is sometimes justified. He said they were wrong for themselves and wrong for Cairo. "Under no circumstances does mob law better conditions," he declared.[26]

The acquittal of the rioters in the attempted lynching of 1910 was not unusual. What would have been unusual would have been more than one conviction. Springfield, Illinois, the state capital, experienced not only lynchings fewer than two years before the Cairo attempt but also a full-blown race riot. There had been sixty-seven indictments in Springfield but only one conviction—for stealing a sword—and none for murder, assault, or arson.[27] Possibly the only surprising aspect of the mob members' acquittal in Cairo, after the jury in the twelve-day trial deliberated only three hours, was that four jurors in the beginning were adamant that two of the rioters be convicted but were beaten down by the remaining seven jurors. (One juror had been excused because his wife was dying.)[28]

The action of the Cairo jury should not have been surprising, and neither should have been the reaction of Cairo's two daily newspapers after the verdict on the rioters was in. The *Cairo Evening Citizen*, a reformist law-and-order newspaper, did not criticize or condemn the freeing of the defendants. Indeed, the newspaper argued that the trial proved that the local courts were capable of exacting justice. The *Citizen*'s solution to the events of February 17–18, 1910, was to forget: "Now let us settle down and forget the whole unfortunate affair, nursing no grudges, holding no scores, forgetting, if possible, that it ever happened."[29]

The *Cairo Bulletin*, always more critical of city and county authorities, reviewed the events of February 1910 for the paper's readers. First, the daily argued that no one in town could deny that "on the night in question" there was a lawless demonstration whose purpose was to enter the courthouse by violence and lynch a prisoner there "for a paltry offense" and that they were repulsed by lawful authority.

> *Nor will it be denied that the community has suffered greatly because of this lawless demonstration by a few of her citizens. What it suffered in money spent in the trial is nothing; what it suffered in reputation as a law-abiding community, with the resultant set-back in the way of commercial and industrial prosperity may not be calculated.*[30]

The *Cairo Bulletin* granted that some of the men accused were not guilty but pointed out that the men who were guilty were not convicted, showing once again that the police and judicial power of the state of Illinois was miserably weak.[31]

Not everyone in Cairo felt the same remorse over the jury's decision that the *Cairo Bulletin* expressed. The accused parties were no doubt elated and thought a celebration of their acquittal was in order. Ten of the twelve alleged "rioters" and about a hundred of their friends assembled at Gorman's Park on the banks of the Mississippi River after the trial concluded for a picnic and barbecue. The *Citizen* reported, "All had enough to eat and drink and all had a good time."[32]

CHAPTER SEVENTEEN

# THE CONTEST FOR ALEXANDER COUNTY SHERIFF IN COURT AND AT THE POLLS

Sheriff Fred Nellis was in a weakened position in the summer of 1910. On the very day the "riot case" was opened for trial, circuit judge Warren Webster Duncan delivered an opinion that Fred Nellis had obtained his office illegally. Nellis was appointed to his post by the county commissioners, but Duncan ruled that the sheriff's office had become vacant when Frank Davis was first removed in November 1909 and not when he was permanently removed by the governor on December 7, 1909. When Davis was initially removed, there was more than a year left in his term, and therefore, according to Judge Duncan, a special election should have been held.[1] The day after this decision, coroner Dr. James McGriffen McManus presented himself at the sheriff's office to again assume the position and to take possession of all fees and monies Nellis had collected during his time in office. According to the 1870 state constitution, the county coroner was supposed to assume the sheriff's duties if there was no sheriff. But Nellis refused to relinquish his position as sheriff, showing his commission from Governor Charles Deneen as his authority for remaining in office.[2]

In the midst of the "riot cases," Nellis was now being sued by both the former sheriff Frank Davis and the coroner who would be sheriff, Dr. James McManus. When the mob defendants were acquitted, Sheriff Nellis's reputation was tarnished, and he now faced serious legal troubles.[3] Some alleviation of this dilemma came when Judge Duncan allowed Nellis to appeal directly to the Illinois Supreme Court. Familiar figures were involved with Nellis, the defendant, and Davis and McManus, the plaintiffs. Davis was represented by Judge William S. Dewey (county judges were still allowed to practice law in 1910) and the defense attorney from the riot trial Angus Leek. Dr. McManus was represented by Reed Green, who was

Attorney Reed Green was a lifelong resident of Cairo. From *Memoirs of the Lower Ohio Valley*, 2:222.

Frank E. Davis was permanently removed as sheriff of Alexander County in December 1910. *Cairo Evening Citizen*, August 29, 1910.

another of the defense attorneys in the riot trial. Fred Nellis was represented by John M. Lansden, who was soon to see his *History of the City of Cairo, Illinois* published, containing accounts of the lynchings of 1909 and the attempted lynching of 1910.[4] Representing Alexander County was State's Attorney Alexander Wilson, who now had to work for Nellis's removal from office when he had just tried to get Nellis's defense of the county courthouse legally upheld by the conviction of the mob members.

While awaiting the decision of the Illinois Supreme Court, Nellis was campaigning as the Republican candidate for Alexander County sheriff. His efforts were futile, and he was soundly defeated in the November 1910 sheriff's election by the Democrat Alexander S. Fraser, losing nearly every precinct in the county.[5] Nellis's defeat was probably scant comfort to Frank E. Davis, because the same law that allowed Governor Deneen to remove Davis from office also forbade him to ever run again for sheriff. Davis additionally had political wounds to lick, having been defeated in the September primary in his run for the Republican nomination for state representative by Dr. Hall Whiteaker of Pulaski County and Reuben D. Kirkpatrick of Franklin County.[6] Davis did not even carry his own county of Alexander.

By the time the Illinois Supreme Court decision was issued on February 25, 1911, the status of now former sheriff

Alexander S. Fraser was elected Alexander County sheriff in 1910. From Smith, *History of Southern Illinois*, 643.

Fred D. Nellis was moot, since he had been defeated for office three months earlier. As so often happens, the legal decisions and precedents established by the high court had little effect on the people directly involved but had some far-reaching effect on the law of the state. Davis was permanently out as sheriff of Alexander County by the will of the state legislature and the governor. The Illinois Supreme Court ruled that the mob law of 1905, which was the basis for Davis's removal as sheriff, did not violate the Illinois Constitution or the Fourteenth Amendment of the Constitution of the United States.[7] The ruling showed that the Supreme Court of Illinois in 1910 was not willing to hamper the state legislature when it passed reasonable laws with reasonable purposes. The ruling did establish the precedent that each county sheriff in Illinois was the "chief law enforcement officer of the county." This was cited in numerous cases afterward in Illinois and elsewhere, even after it was no longer true in the majority of situations.[8]

Only two Republicans were defeated among the six candidates for county office in November 1910. One of them was Nellis, who lost his race for sheriff by 1,700 votes. In the elections of the early 1900s, Republican candidates in Alexander County had averaged wins of about 1,400 votes, and yet Nellis lost by considerably more than that number.[9] The soon-to-be former sheriff could console himself with the fact that he had stopped a lynching and upheld law and order, and it no longer mattered if he had been appointed legally or not. Still, it must have been very hard to take. At the time he defended the courthouse, he had said he paid a good price for his job that he might lose in the courts.

McManus's suit against Fred Nellis dragged through Illinois courts for years before it was finally settled by the Illinois Appellate Court in November 1916. At one point, an Illinois circuit court judged that all fees and monies collected by Nellis during his time as sheriff of Alexander County should go to McManus. But finally, the strange nature of the doctor's claims became apparent to the appellate court, and all earlier rulings were reversed.

When the Illinois Appellate Court got the minutes from the Alexander County commissioners' meeting, courtesy of John M. Lansden, Nellis's attorney, it became clear that Dr. McManus did not want to be sheriff at the time Davis was removed. In fact, the records showed that he appeared before the county board saying he wanted to be relieved of the sheriff s duties so that he could give full attention to his extensive practice, and he was losing money "fooling with the sheriff's office."[10] He urged the county commissioners to appoint someone soon. They had three candidates in mind, but only Nellis actually wanted to be sheriff. Then Dr. McManus asserted, "I wish they would hurry up about it. I didn't expect to be kept here this long. . . . You would do me a favor if you would go to the Board and hurry up the appointment. I am losing money."[11] It seems that money was a primary focus for McManus from the beginning, and he decided on the sheriff's office only when Nellis was declared to have been appointed illegally. The appellate court said the test in this case should be whether McManus had any right to the money, and the court ruled that the money did not belong to him.[12]

Dr. McManus never got to be Alexander County sheriff again. That was probably a good thing for Cairo's African American lawmen. McManus had fired every black deputy when he was briefly sheriff, while Fred Nellis had hired black deputies when he was appointed. This was probably for political reasons, but it turned out to be a practical decision. The tiny band of defenders at the Alexander County Courthouse on February 17, 1910, was over half black, and without their stand at the courthouse, Cairo would have likely been again disgraced by yet another lynching.

## CHAPTER EIGHTEEN

# POLITICS AND THE AFRICAN AMERICAN COMMUNITY IN CAIRO

In the weeks after the James-Salzner lynchings, the tolerance of white people for crimes allegedly committed by African Americans was apparently considerably reduced. Willis Leonard Clanahan, formerly of Cairo, stated in his 1909 letter to the *New York Times* that many white people in Cairo had concluded that the only way to control what they perceived as a potentially criminal and violent black population was to frequently resort to lynch law.[1] There is some evidence about the relationship between whites and blacks immediately following the Cairo tragedy of 1909 that should shed some light on whether Clanahan's assertion was true. On the morning after Will James's lynching, black people went about their ordinary lives all over town.[2] Even before many National Guardsmen showed up in Cairo, African Americans hardly seemed terribly afraid.[3] Will "Froggie" James was one of the "floaters" or "transient negroes" that Clanahan discussed in his letter to the *New York Times*, and he boarded in a ramshackle assignation house. Perhaps most black people in Cairo thought white Cairoites would see James as a marginal member of their society, and they probably did. It should be noted that no black person in Cairo publicly defended James's innocence. That defense was offered only by Ida Wells-Barnett of Chicago, who had never met James.

It should also be noted, nevertheless, that there was considerable racial discrimination in Cairo in 1909. The Episcopal reverend George M. Babcock in his sermon following the double lynching pointed out that black people in Cairo had never been welcomed by whites since their migration from the South. He spoke of a people ill housed, ill paid, exploited by politicians, and forced into vice as their most lucrative economic option. According to the priest, Cairo's black "dives" and "hell holes" were profitable not only for certain African Americans but also for certain whites.[4]

Black people in Cairo also had the local Democratic Party in the town and county to be concerned about, as they pointed out to Ida Wells-Barnett when she was there gathering support for Frank Davis's ouster as sheriff. When the Democratic coroner Dr. James McManus was briefly Alexander County sheriff, he fired every black deputy. A deputy position held some prestige and power for black men, and losing it foretold of a worsening racial situation in the city and county should the Democrats come to power in the sheriff's office, which they did in 1910. The new sheriff, Alexander S. Fraser, would again dismiss all African American deputies.

As 1910 approached and the cry for reform in Cairo grew louder, there was also growing evidence that many if not a majority of Cairo's whites saw African Americans as the problem preventing the development of a desirable community.[5] A revealing piece appeared in the *Cairo Bulletin* in early December 1909 that illustrated the difference between how some African Americans perceived race relations in Cairo and how an influential newspaper editor felt toward African Americans. The *Bulletin*'s editor discussed the "strong point" made by Elder Thomas A. Head in his meeting with "the Chicago negress, Mrs. Barnett."[6] Elder Head, who was also a deputy sheriff under Frank Davis and later under Fred Nellis, said at the meeting attended by Ida Wells-Barnett that so far as he knew, no insult had been offered to any "Negro" in Cairo by any white person, showing that there was no race feeling in town. The *Bulletin* commented on Elder Head's declaration by saying that the paper was sorry that Cairo whites could not say the same.

> *It is to be regretted, however, that the same point cannot be illustrated so far as the negroes of Cairo are concerned, for since the lynching two or three respectable young white women have been insulted by members of that class of negro prowlers in the city which seems to be under the protection of the Cairo police department.*[7]

At the very end of December 1909, the *Cairo Bulletin* printed an original song by Edward W. Thielecke that summarized everything the newspaper believed was wrong with city and county officials, the circuit court, and the Cairo police. The song was dedicated to Mayor George Parsons, but there were also verses devoted to black people in Cairo:

> *The negro Honk-a-Tonk is here;*
> *Keep it quiet.*
> *Men and women must have beer;*

*Keep it quiet.*
*The city's dissolute may dance*
*And our black brutes should have a chance;*
*Keep it quiet, keep it quiet.*
*If you raise an awful howl*
*You will your own nest befoul.*
*Keep it quiet. . . .*
*If good women are assailed,*
*Keep it quiet.*
*Negro brutes may not be trailed—*
*Keep it quiet . . .*[8]

Labeling some African Americans in Cairo as "brutes" was certainly a strong indication that the *Cairo Bulletin* was using race as the basis for one of its primary criticisms of community conditions.[9] Corruption and crime were Cairo problems, but the black people dancing in the "honk-a-tonks" and drinking beer were those who attacked women and were under the protection of the Cairo police, according to the *Bulletin*. This was racism. It may have been political racism, because the *Bulletin* was secretly a Democratic newspaper and African Americans voted Republican in Cairo. Indeed, the black vote had made the Republicans in Cairo and Alexander County the majority party for a number of years.[10] But it was racism nonetheless.

Black people in Cairo additionally faced some of the usual problems of African Americans in the twentieth century. For example, the superintendent of Cairo public schools, Professor Taylor C. Clendenen, claimed that between 35 and 40 percent of "negro families had no heads in the lawful sense of the term," apparently meaning there was no male head of household.[11] On the other hand, black men could vote and were represented by African American police officers and sheriff's deputies. Two black doctors lived and worked in Cairo, as did morticians, clergymen, landlords, businessmen, and even some people historians have called upper-class.[12] Certainly the potential for racial conflict was always present, as Sheriff Fred Nellis and his interracial band of black and white deputies found out when they had to open fire on a white lynch mob in 1910.[13] There were, however, a lot of black people in Cairo, and their value was recognized by many white leaders.[14]

A few black men could be brave lawmen and loyal deputies, but what was the status of African Americans in Cairo as a whole in November 1910? Were they better off or worse off after the attempted lynching? There are a few indications of African American status in Cairo in 1910. First, black people were always reminded of their race in the local white press. When an African American was mentioned in the newspaper—for an arrest, for running an assignation house, for dying, for playing baseball, for doing something meritorious—that person was inevitably identified as "negro" or "colored."[15] On the other hand, black people were mentioned in the newspapers constantly. For example, "Cairo's Negro baseball team, Field's Giants," was mentioned in the press even before the team left town to play an important series in Memphis.[16]

Of course there were major differences between Cairo's two dailies on the question of race, as might have been expected since their approaches to other Cairo issues, such as governmental corruption and the justice system, were so different. The *Cairo Evening Citizen* did not use the "N-word"; the *Cairo Bulletin* did.[17] An outline of the *Bulletin*'s latent and sometimes overt racism became quite visible during Fred Nellis's campaign for election to sheriff of Alexander County in 1910.

The *Bulletin*'s attacks against Nellis and black people were probably highlighted a few days before the November 1910 election. Under the headline "Black Brute Insults Girl; Another Anna Pelley Horror Narrowly Prevented Last Night," the daily told of an incident involving Myrtle Broderick, seventeen, who had recently moved from Cape Girardeau, Missouri, and found employment in the linen room at the Halliday Hotel in Cairo. She was leaving the hotel on Ohio Street on the Ohio riverfront when she was "accosted" by a "negro" who said, "Hello Kiddo." Miss Broderick hurried past the man without replying and quickly turned the corner at 4th Street, heading toward Commercial Avenue, which was a main thoroughfare and would have people out and about. She was halfway to the avenue, when the black man reappeared and reportedly said, "Wait a minute, Kiddo!" Now Myrtle Broderick was frightened and ran. The "negro" ran after her and headed her off at the corner of 4th and Commercial, and then "the black brute said, 'I'm going home with you.'"[18] Miss Broderick started screaming and a barkeep from Ladenberger's saloon came running and asked what was going on. The "negro" said, "None of your damned business!"[19] With that the barkeep started toward the man.

The man ran through a nearby saloon and then back out into the street. Several men, including R. F. Briggs of the Ringling Brothers Circus, gave chase as he ran toward Commercial Avenue. They caught the fleeing man and beat him badly before Cairo police sergeant Wilfred French and Officer Jones arrived to take him to the city jail.

There it was learned that his name was Bob Smothers, and he worked as a porter in a saloon on Ohio Street. The *Cairo Bulletin* described him as a "tall, brown fellow."[20] When searched at the police station, two bottles of whiskey were found on his person. Meanwhile, Myrtle Broderick was taken to the Halliday Hotel in shock, according to the newspaper.

The newspaper on the following day in an editorial titled "Cairo and the County" discussed obstacles that the town faced, past and present, and then argued that one of Cairo's obstacles was insurmountable:

> *Cairo has overcome Charles Dickens' assessment of the town, is overcoming the threat of flood, is paving the muddy streets, the city government is getting better after a "hard struggle." We are in a fine way to make our city respected abroad and attentive to would be homemakers and business keepers.*
>
> *One thing remains—"the bad negro." The affair of Saturday night (a black porter accosting a teen-age girl) shows how families would be affected if they wanted to move and considered Cairo.*
>
> *True, there is crime everywhere, and the best that can be hoped for is that criminals will be punished in order that others who are criminally inclined may stand in fear of the law, and the peaceful citizen may be protected.*

The Halliday Hotel was built in 1858 at 2nd and Ohio Streets. It was completely destroyed by fire in 1942. Postcard courtesy of Darrel Dexter.

> *But suppose it were also stated that the element to which the lecherous brutes, "Froggy" James and Bob Smothers belong, and which furnish 85% of all the criminals in this community every year, dominate by an overwhelming majority one of the political parties of this city, the Republican.*[21]

The Republicans, the *Bulletin* asserted, supported the "bad negro" candidate for sheriff of Alexander County, Fred Nellis, who was "their protector."[22]

Then the daily began covering the activities of Democratic attorney Reed Green, who had defended former Cairo policeman Jim Casey, accused of bribe taking, and the rioters who had attacked the county courthouse. Green had also taken Dr. McManus's case to the state courts to try to make him Alexander County sheriff. Reed Green was no longer accused by the *Bulletin* of receiving special privileges from the courts but now became "the Honorable Reed Green."[23] Green traveled to the rural areas of Alexander County, and he, like the *Cairo Bulletin*, was trying to tie Fred Nellis to Will "Froggie" James, the lynched black man and presumed rapist and murderer. The *Bulletin* reproduced Green's speech at Olive Branch, a small town nineteen miles northwest of Cairo, about the upcoming election:

> *The 8th of November next—the day on which the voters of the city and county are privileged to say who shall be their highest law officer during the next four years—is by strange coincidence—the first anniversary of the murder of Anna Pelley by the negro brute "Froggy" James. The people of Cairo will not forget it. The voters of Cairo will keep it in their minds when they mark their ballots on that day. The white voters of Cairo to a man (excepting a few party hacks and their bosses) will do their duty to themselves as men, to the community as citizens, and to their wives and daughters as husbands and fathers. They will repudiate in a manner that will not be misunderstood, the man who comes before them more distinctly, more boldly, more shamelessly than any man dared to stand before—as the candidate and avowed friend of the negro ex-convicts and lechers of Cairo.*[24]

The man Reed Green condemned as the friend of criminals in general and sex criminals in particular was, of course, Sheriff Fred Nellis.

The *Cairo Evening Citizen*, as a usually progressive Republican newspaper, saw the election for sheriff in Alexander County quite differently from

Reed Green and the *Cairo Bulletin*. The *Citizen* stated that if Fred Nellis was defeated, his loss would be chronicled in every newspaper in the country, and editorials without end would be written about Cairo as the town who turned out a sheriff who tried to do his duty.[25] Cairo's evening paper may have been prophetic. In early December 1910, the *Chicago Tribune* printed an article headlined "White Man's Sheriff." The article told how Alexander S. Fraser, Democrat, took office in Alexander County and promised that all "negroes" in the location of the county jail during his term of office would be behind bars.[26]

So there were to be no African American deputies under Alexander Fraser, and regional newspapers started declaring that black people would no longer be a factor in Cairo politics.[27] Every black deputy who had helped defend the courthouse against a mob intent on lynching a couple of purse snatchers was out of a job. There were still black policemen in Cairo, but Cairo's oldest daily, the *Bulletin*, was regularly blasting the Cairo police as corrupt if not actually criminal and charging that the black policemen were the worse of the lot.

Even if the black deputies were half as bad as the *Cairo Bulletin* portrayed them, they were still an important component of Cairo's African American middle class and influential in the black community. For example, Deputy George Jackson had defended Sheriff Frank Davis when he was removed from office by Governor Charles Deneen following the 1909 lynchings in Cairo and tried to get Davis reinstated as sheriff.[28] Cairo would also soon learn that black deputies like George Jackson had law enforcement value that the new white deputies could not match.

The *Cairo Evening Citizen* still recognized the value of the town's black community and spoke against some forms of racial prejudice, as did the prosecution lawyers at the time of the "riot" trial.[29] African Americans could still get a favorable verdict in a trial in Cairo. Officers John Wade and Gus Johnson, black Cairo policemen, were probably guilty of taking payoffs to allow "disorderly houses" to continue operating, but with good representation and the aid of Mayor George Parsons, they were acquitted.[30] Alfred Baltimore, pimp and the prime target of the *Cairo Bulletin*'s campaign against "disorderly houses," was not so fortunate. He was convicted, but it was four black jurors on the panel who convinced the others of a guilty verdict.[31] When a "negro" student at Manning's Bible School in the city was mistakenly identified as a bootlegger and turned over to federal authorities, the outcry from the black clergy had Cairo lawmen retrieve him as the "wrong Arthur Cook."[32]

Economically, Cairo's African Americans were still mostly poor with few exceptions among the clergy and their wives, undertakers, professionals, business and property owners, police, and others working in law enforcement. Politically, Cairo's black clergy and clubwomen had helped the *Cairo Evening Citizen*, the *Cairo Bulletin*, the Pure Ballot League, and the Citizens' League elect a reform ticket of aldermen. Direct black political power in Cairo, however, would soon wane. On March 4, 1913, Cairo voted two-to-one for a commission form of government, with commissioners elected at large. That meant no more representation of blacks in the city government until after a civil rights lawsuit in the 1970s.[33]

In the meantime, crime continued to plague Cairo's African Americans. On May 7, 1910, Mary Lane, an African American prostitute, was killed.[34] She lived at 38th Street and Commercial Avenue in the "corral," a heavily black neighborhood inflamed by a feud involving Josh White, a black storekeeper at 40th Street and Commercial, and Alfred Baltimore, the pimp and "disorderly house" owner and operator at 3815 Commercial. Their disagreement escalated after White secured and brandished a .44-caliber mail-order rifle and was arrested.[35] The feud turned deadly when Mitchell Calhoun killed Mary Lane, with whom he had earlier been arrested and fined five dollars for living with her in a state of adultery. Calhoun confessed at the inquest and named Josh White and his wife, Willie White, as accessories. Calhoun was angry that Mary Lane was working part time as a prostitute for Baltimore, and he asserted that the Whites convinced him that she must be killed for her betrayal.[36] At least that was the *Cairo Evening Citizen*'s published account.

The *Cairo Bulletin* told the tragic tale of Mary Lane and Mitchell Calhoun much differently. Calhoun waived his right to a trial and pleaded guilty before Judge Warren Duncan, was sentenced to life in prison, and each May 7 was to be spent in solitary confinement on bread and water. Before being sent to Menard Penitentiary in Chester, Illinois, Calhoun made an important statement in court, which was published by the *Cairo Bulletin*:

> *I admit I killed Mary. I loved that woman and was jealous of her. I swore to a lie when I said Josh White and his wife put me up to it. They had nothing to do with it. Police Officers Wade and Johnson put me up to saying that. They told me if I did not say that they would form a mob and have me hung. It was because I was afraid of being mobbed that I accused White and his wife.*[37]

Calhoun's shocking confession reveals many of the problems faced by black Cairoites in 1910. The first would be violence, not only from whites but also from fellow African Americans. The next was arbitrary and unjust actions by the Cairo police, especially black police, against African American suspects. Finally, there was pervasive fear of being lynched. The John Pratt purse-snatching case had shown that many of Cairo's whites could be moved to form a murderous mob over some slight offense by a black person.

The murder of John West, the African American "hot tamala peddler," was also fully investigated and reported on in the press. West lived with his mother near Division and Poplar Streets in the "barracks," a part of Cairo dating back to the Civil War's contraband camps.[38] He was found dead on April 23, 1910, lying in the street at Douglas and Cedar with a bullet hole in his back. West's empty tamale heater was found at 14th and Locust Streets, and Officer Frank Hagey and his bloodhounds started there. Cairo had acquired its own dogs after the Anna Pelley murder, and they followed a scent to 10th Street in the railroad yards. A night crew of switchmen was in the yards, and the workers said that two "negroes" had run through the yards at 1:30 a.m. and hopped on a Big Four freight train. Soon, however, the coroner's jury called for the indictment of Harrison Young, James Chambers, Will Evans, and Bettie Mack, alias Moser, all African Americans, for murder or conspiracy to murder. It was at their house at 1313 Cedar Street where West was last seen alive, and the persons named by the coroner's jury had very bad reputations in a bad neighborhood.[39] But they were all eventually released by the grand jury, and the West homicide became another of the unsolved murders in Cairo.

The same day of the coroner's jury's decision concerning the John West killing, evidence of another murder, on April 27, came to light. Minnie Dixon, white, was brought before Judge Whitcamp for killing Luther Davis, black. Davis and his white wife, Mary Davis, had been staying as guests in the Dixon house.[40] Initially, each woman blamed the other for the shooting, saying they had all been playing with the revolver during a drinking bout, but when Davis regained consciousness before he died, he accused Dixon of pulling the trigger. In May, Dixon pleaded guilty to assault with a deadly weapon and was punished with only forty days in the county jail.[41]

Some of the crime problem in Cairo was attributed to the growth in "shack" building in the city from 1900 until the First World War, which was opposed by the African American clubwomen.[42] In those years, Cairo's lumber industry was booming and the town was a railroad center. As the most "southern" of Southern Illinois towns, Cairo demanded, indeed preferred, black janitors, maids, cooks, yardmen, and even cotton choppers and pickers.[43] The job situation attracted black people from all over to Cairo, which was easily accessible by rail and river, and they had to have some place to live. Soon some of Cairo's many Syrian Americans became landlords, throwing up shacks in heavily African American areas of the city. African American entrepreneurs also got into the shack construction and landlord business and found themselves among Cairo's leading black families, at least financially. But these poorly maintained dwellings soon became overcrowded and were recognized as incubators of crime by blacks and whites alike.

Yet black Cairo did have some social standing in the community. Some, such as police officers John Wade and Gus Johnson, were so valued that prominent white Cairoites rushed to their defense when they got into legal trouble. The officers had separately shot and killed four men while in the process of arresting them, and in three instances the slain men were unarmed.[44] When Gus Johnson was indicted by a grand jury for manslaughter in the killing of Napoleon Lipe in 1912, it was the Cairo city council that paid for his legal defense.[45] Indeed, a coalition of black voters and white Republicans would be competitive in Alexander County politics for about

Postcard showing that Cairo was in many ways a southern city. Postcard courtesy of Darrel Dexter.

another forty-five years. By the 1920s, however, there were no more elected African American officials in Cairo itself. Black status, therefore, depended greatly on white goodwill until the 1970s.

Legally, in some instances, African Americans were fairly well protected. Lincoln Wilson, John Pratt's supposed accomplice as a purse snatcher, was released and sent safely on his way, and Josh and Willie White were quickly released from jail when Mitchell Calhoun cleared them. Even Arthur Alexander and Lovie Green—suspects in the Anna Pelley murder—had been let go, although Alexander was warned not to return to Cairo and Green eventually left the city. Still, the situation was bad enough for African Americans in Cairo in 1910 and worsening as the years went by. A lynching and an attempted lynching within a three-month period were not encouraging signs. Overt racism in the "riot" trial and in Sheriff Fred Nellis's resounding election defeat revealed hardening white attitudes toward blacks. Hardest and most troubling for black Cairo must have been the constant barrage of anti-black, if not overtly racist, writings in the *Cairo Bulletin*. Black people were called "lecherous brutes," "black hounds," "arrogant," and "offensively impudent" during the November 1910 election campaign, as well as "moochers," sneaks, thieves, purse snatchers, rapists, and murderers.[46]

After the votes were counted in 1910, Nellis and his supporters filed affidavits alleging illegal voting in some of the precincts. The *Cairo Bulletin* described some of those African American supporters in the following terms: "Tom Clarkson (negro)," keeper of a disorderly house for some years; "C. C. Wilson (negro)," publisher of *Baptist Truth* newspaper; "G. W. Carr (negro)," barber who killed a negro preacher some years ago in a quarrel; "J. H. Stewart (negro) barber and deputy sheriff"; James Dillard, "the negro deputy sheriff who is known as one of the trifling blacks who do not work—notorious as a 'flooence man' and as a dirty political worker"; R. A. Davis, "a negro hanger-on at the sheriff's office"; and "Whit Larry (negro); deputy sheriff and constable—'flooence man' and political corruptionist."[47] In discussing Whit Larry's role in the Nellis campaign, the *Bulletin* used what it saw as black dialect to impress and amuse white readers with Deputy Larry's transgressions. When confronted by a white voter whom Larry had accused of voting illegally, he said,

> *"Ah didn't make no affidavit 'gin you, Boss. . . . Ah don't know nothin' about it. . . . Boss, ah don't know you; never seed you befo'. Ah don't know nothin' about dis. . . . Capt. Nellis give me de papers an' I signed 'em 'cause he tol' me to."*[48]

One may doubt that Deputy Sheriff Whitefield Larry actually talked this way, but there is little doubt of the blatant racism shown in this supposed exchange. Like many, if not most, northern whites, the editor of the *Cairo Bulletin* saw the racial problem simply. That is, the existence of black people in Cairo was the problem. It was not so much what black people did in Cairo, although the *Bulletin* was quick to point out any African American failing; rather, it was what race they belonged to.[49] The *Bulletin*'s editor, Edward W. Thielecke, seems to have done a rough kind of cost/benefit analysis and decided that the large African American population in Cairo was the most serious obstacle to the river city's growth and development. It is known that ten years later, when the black population of Cairo dropped by about 450, according to the 1920 census, the *Bulletin* saw the exodus as an extremely positive development.[50]

Given the hurtful racial stereotyping in the *Cairo Bulletin*, it is surprising that Will Scott was reading that newspaper when he found out about John Pratt's purse snatching and alerted the police to Pratt's plans. The *Cairo Evening Citizen*, in contrast to the *Bulletin*, was one of the major protectors of Cairo's black people. The *Citizen*'s editor and owner, John C. Fisher, was a progressive Republican who seemingly recognized more than the political value of Cairo's black population. Black Cairo had other white protectors in 1910—some for political reasons and others for cultural or intellectual reasons. As this protection waned and anti-black elements in the white population became more ascendant, life for Cairo's African Americans became considerably more difficult.

A symbol of the worsening environment for black Cairo was the arrival in town of James Kimble Vardaman, former governor of Mississippi, to give his lecture "The Impending Crisis," which denounced what he saw as increasing black insolence. He sounded the alarm about a "restless generation of negroes who roamed the roads and posed a threat to white womanhood."[51] This preeminent white supremacist was given what appeared to be a free quarter-page ad in the *Cairo Bulletin* and a write-up headlined, "Governor Vardaman in Great Lecture on 'The Coming Crisis' at Cairo Opera House Next Tuesday Night."[52] Vardaman was known for making such racist statements as, "If it is necessary every Negro in the state will be lynched; it will be done to maintain white supremacy."[53]

The audience at the Cairo Opera House on Commercial Avenue "was as large as any that has ever greeted a lecturer in Cairo, composed of some of Cairo's best citizenship." Mayor Parsons, Professor Clendenen, and Reed Green sat on the stage with Governor Vardaman. The thrust of his speech was that the 15th Amendment to the Constitution, which gave black men the right to vote, should be repealed. He claimed the South was in the process of secretly disenfranchising the black voter, but he wanted it done openly. There were likely no African Americans in the audience that night, but the message reached them loudly and clearly. Anyone hoping for even a slow march toward equality would be up against "Cairo's best citizenship," who were not ready to take steps forward but were actually going in the other direction. In the ten years following Vardaman's appearance in Cairo, the uneasiness with the racial situation became increasingly apparent among a number of the town's black citizens, as Cairo's population increased from 14,548 to 15,203, while the black population dropped by 8 percent from 1910 to 1920.[54]

CHAPTER NINETEEN

# SHERIFF ABNER BANKSON AND THE HOMICIDE OF WILFRED FRENCH

Before leaving office, after his crushing defeat in the November 1910 elections, Alexander County sheriff Fred Nellis possibly saved the life of yet another prisoner entrusted to his care by the police of Cairo, Illinois. This time, however, the suspect was not a black man on the margins of society, such as Will "Froggie" James or John Pratt, or an accused wife killer like Henry Salzner, but an official from a neighboring Illinois county. On December 3, 1910, Pulaski County sheriff Abner C. Bankson of Pulaski County entered the Cairo police station and shot and killed the night sergeant of police, Wilfred French, just before he was to go on duty.[1]

Abner C. "Ab" Bankson was sheriff of Pulaski County, Illinois, from 1906 to 1910. Photo courtesy of Brent Norris.

Abner Cambner "Ab" Bankson was born April 4, 1858, in Pulaski County, Illinois, the son of George W. Bankson and Sarah Jane Kennedy, both from pioneer families in the county. Before being elected to a four-year term as sheriff of Pulaski County in 1906, Bankson was a prominent farmer and stock raiser in the Villa Ridge area, one of the largest landowners, and the father of ten children.[2] He had the reputation of being a friendly, cheerful man and was sometimes a popular sheriff. The number of Bankson supporters increased in Pulaski County following the April 1909 confession of Henry Escue, "a negro aged 23 years," to the murder in the Mounds railroad yards on December 18, 1908, of Charles M. Speikert, an Illinois Central employee. Speikert had been stabbed nine times and "his throat was cut until the head hung to the body by a small piece of flesh."[3] The county's main newspaper, the *Pulaski Enterprise*, stated, "To sheriff A. C. Bankson and his able corps of assistants much credit is due for bringing to judgment many of the criminals this region seems to be afflicted with."[4]

The press outside of Pulaski County was not as supportive, and Bankson was widely condemned for his conduct as a sheriff and as a man. The *Cairo Bulletin* condemned "Ab's" activities in Mounds, Illinois, almost a year before the shooting of French, implying that the citizens of that small town should arrest their county sheriff:

> *Citizens of Mounds are very much aroused over the frequent disorderly outbreaks of Sheriff Bankson and they threaten to make an organized effort to stop him. The sheriff attempted to kill a woman of the town [prostitute] Wednesday evening. This was the second time he used his pistol with murderous intent, having shot W. G. Davis last summer, inflicting a wound in the breast, which narrowly missed proving fatal. The affair of Wednesday was disgraceful, since it was the result of the sheriff's improper relations with the woman he sought to shoot, which had been a scandal in the community for some time. Because of his shameless conduct with this woman, the citizens some time ago succeeded in having the woman run out of town, but the sheriff quietly brought her back after the excitement was over, and has threatened to kill some citizens if they interfere with him.*[5]

The shooting of Wesley G. Davis, a "colored" justice of the peace, occurred on August 24, 1909. Sheriff Bankson had gone to Mounds to serve arrest warrants on several alleged "negro" bootleggers and quarreled with Davis, shooting him twice in the chest. When witnesses arrived, a gun was found in Davis's hand and Bankson claimed self-defense.[6] Bankson surrendered to Pulaski County coroner John Steele, "colored," at the courthouse in Mound City and a petition was soon circulated, asking Governor Charles Deneen to remove Bankson from office, but it was unsuccessful.[7] Davis amazingly survived his wounds, and Bankson, perhaps more surprisingly, appointed him a deputy sheriff after his recovery. Deputy Sheriff Davis was later killed on July 4, 1910, in a shootout on the streets of Mounds while trying to stop three drunken young men from driving their buggy in a "boisterous manner" through the streets of the town.[8]

On Wednesday evening, January 12, 1910, Bankson quarreled violently with "his woman," threatening to kill her supposedly because of his jealousy over her seeing other men. She ran out of the house to a nearby store on Front Street run by Sylvester C. and Elizabeth Hagan and quickly darted out the back. When Bankson came into the store in a fury, he encountered Mary Goe, the wife of Reeder B. Goe, a freight agent for the railroad, and Bankson's hand went to his pocket for his pistol, but then "Ab" luckily recognized that she was not the one he was seeking. Bankson then ran into the street and spotted the fleeing woman and shot at her but missed. The woman's escape sent the sheriff deeper into a rage, which he vented in curses and threats for the future.[9] The sheriff's woman was probably Myrtle Stevenson, also known as Mabel Stevenson, who moved to 13th Street in Cairo and who in January 1910 was fined there for allowing fourteen-year-old boys to use her brothel.[10]

Such behavior, even by a rural sheriff, would be hard to explain, but the *Evening Citizen* attributed Sheriff Bankson's erratic and dangerous actions to alcohol. The *Citizen* claimed that Bankson had been drunk since he was elected.[11] On the night of Sergeant French's killing, the *Daily Free Press* of Carbondale asserted that French had not talked with Bankson at length before the shooting because the Pulaski County sheriff was noticeably under the influence of alcohol when he entered Cairo Police Headquarters.[12] Bankson's friends and family argued that he was a peaceable man when sober, but the *Cairo Evening Citizen* observed that he had not been sober for a long, long time.[13]

Bankson's drinking seemed to be most problematic when coupled with his involvement with prostitutes. Following talk of his possible arrest for disturbances of the peace in Mounds and his attempted shooting of his "favorite harlot" on the street there, Bankson moved his sexual activities largely to Cairo. Early in 1910 the Pulaski County sheriff began to frequent the houses of prostitution lining 13th Street, where his "favorite" now resided. Indeed, if the *Cairo Bulletin* is to be believed, he reconciled with his "woman of the town" and "installed" her in one of the brothels along that street.[14]

According to the testimony of the Cairo police, the conflict with Sergeant French started with an encounter in Myrtle Stevenson's brothel at 212 13th Street on the night of September 23, 1910. Drunk as usual, Bankson created such a disturbance that Mabel Stevenson called the police.[15] Officer Frank Skews responded to the call, and when he found out the problem was created by the Pulaski County sheriff, he turned around and went back to police headquarters for Sergeant Wilfred French. The two Cairo policemen entered the brothel and found Bankson with a gun in his hand, which the quick-thinking sergeant took away from the sheriff.[16] As the two Cairo policemen began marching Bankson toward police headquarters, French decided to give the sheriff a break. French told Bankson that he did not want to make any trouble for him and that Bankson should take the Illinois Central back to Pulaski County, since it was late at night. Upon his release by Sergeant French, the problem drinker Bankson headed not for a railroad depot but for a downtown saloon and began creating disturbances there. Officers Kennedy and Harry Jones were called to one of the saloons, and "Ab" Bankson was taken to the lockup. The next morning the sheriff stood before a judge and was charged with disorderly conduct. He pled guilty and was given a small fine.[17]

Abner C. Bankson's personal and professional problems did not end with drink, sex, and the proclivity for drawing and firing weapons. While in office, the sheriff and collector took $7,846.44 of taxpayers' money as a "loan." To avoid prosecution, Bankson's family took out a second mortgage worth $5,000.00 on 320 acres owned by the sheriff and a first mortgage on another 40 acres. Bankson's son Deputy Sheriff Mannon Bankson then paid the remainder of the amount due in cash.[18]

Bankson fell out of favor with the voters of Pulaski County and did not run for reelection in November 1910. Instead, the Republicans ran his son Mannon Bankson as their candidate to replace Sheriff Bankson. However, Mannon was defeated by an independent, Charles Wehrenberg, in a highly Republican county, no doubt in large part because of his father's growing unpopularity. The *Daily Free Press* of Carbondale commented,

> *On several occasions he has engaged in shooting scrapes in which he was the aggressor, and the general feeling in the Cairo–Mound City neighborhood is that he has been extremely lucky not to have been behind bars long before this time. Sheriff Bankson's term of office expired today, being succeeded as Sheriff of Pulaski County by Chas. Wehrenberg. . . . The defeated Republican candidate was a son of Sheriff Bankson, and his defeat was generally regarded as a rebuke to the elder Bankson.*[19]

The *Pulaski Enterprise* and the Cairo daily newspapers disagreed completely as to Abner C. Bankson's character and possible behaviors. An examination of what exactly happened on December 3, 1910, at Cairo Police Headquarters, just two days before the sheriff's term expired, reveals just how unusual and tragic the event was—the killing of a city policeman by a county sheriff.

About 3 p.m., "Ab" Bankson "came down from Mound City" on the interurban, the rail connecting Cairo and Mound City, and went straight to Brackey Bros. saloon at 3315 Sycamore, in Sergeant French's neighborhood.[20] He stayed there for an hour and a half drinking and then went to Thomas "Tom" Gardner's saloon at 3201 Sycamore, where he was so impaired that he asked the owner-barkeeper to write a check for him. Gardner refused, telling him to write his own check. Bankson stayed in the saloon and was there when Gardner stepped outside to talk to two men. One was Lee Boyd, a foreman at the box mill, and the other was William Henry "Will" French, Sergeant French's brother and the first police officer to arrive on the scene of the Anna Pelley murder.[21] Bankson asked another saloon patron whether one of the men was the night sergeant. The patron replied that French was the sergeant's brother.

Bankson's mention of French and the patron's reply set the sheriff off. He immediately took a streetcar to the vicinity of Cairo Police Headquarters, arriving there shortly after 5 p.m. The following account of the events leading to Sergeant Wilfred French's death was printed with minor variations in both the *Cairo Evening Citizen* and the *Cairo Bulletin*. When Bankson arrived at the police station, he immediately attempted to enter, but the door he tried was locked. Bankson was noticed by the jailer, Melchor Lutz, who let the sheriff into the police facility, even shaking hands with him. Bankson, Lutz, and Officer Lawrence H. Paul sat down to talk. Bankson took out a pair of handcuffs and asked Lutz for a key to fit them, which the jailer did not have. At about that time Cairo police chief James Cowell entered the police station, and Bankson asked him when he was going to get the pistol back that had been seized at the time of his confrontation with Sergeant French in September. Chief Cowell said he didn't know anything about the pistol. Minutes passed, and Sergeant Wilfred French entered. Chief Cowell said, "There's the man who took your pistol. You can talk to him about it."[22]

At that point the Pulaski County sheriff asked French, who was pinning on his badge, "Am I to get that gun by force or by law?" French answered, "We will have to see about that."[23] Also in the police station at the time was street supervisor John Sheehan. Bankson asked him if he had a key to the handcuffs. Sheehan didn't. Bankson then turned to French and inquired if he had a handcuffs key. French replied, "No, I haven't." Bankson then said, "You haven't have you?" and shot at French three times. The gun was later identified as a .32 Colt Special. The first shot hit the sergeant in the back, near the heart, killing him almost instantly. Supervisor Sheehan, who witnessed events leading up to the killing, said it was completely without provocation.[24]

Officer Lawrence Paul was behind Bankson at the time of the shooting and grabbed his arm, which caused the second and third shots to go high into the wall, one about seven and a half feet high and the other about nine feet. Chief Cowell joined Officer Paul in trying to overpower Bankson. The chief hit Bankson about the face with handcuffs, and the sheriff pled, "I'm your fellow officer, don't beat me!"[25] Cowell, Paul, and Lutz subdued Bankson and immediately took him to the county jail. The *Cairo Evening Citizen* stated that Bankson had been in his usual state of mind when talking about handcuffs before French arrived at the police station, although the newspaper admitted Bankson had been drinking heavily.[26] The *Pulaski Enterprise* stated, "Bankson was apparently in a very good humor, and his requests about the keys were made with a smiling face."[27]

The Abner C. Bankson portrayed and condemned in the Cairo dailies would not have been recognized in the *Pulaski Enterprise*—a weekly newspaper printed in the Pulaski County seat of Mound City. The editor of the *Enterprise* found the shooting inexplicable and, in contrast to the Cairo papers' heated discussions of the shooting, engaged in understatement. The *Enterprise* told of Bankson's arrest and the taking of his revolver by the Cairo police and then said "Ab" became "angry" at Sergeant French's refusal to return the gun.[28] The Pulaski County paper went on to say that the shooting came as a "terrible shock" to Mound City and was the sole topic of conversation on the streets. This expression of shock is difficult to understand because the editor of the *Enterprise* must have been aware of Bankson's shooting of Justice of the Peace Wesley G. Davis of Mounds, Illinois, and his attempted shooting of his woman friend also on the streets of Mounds. A possible explanation for the Pulaski paper's soft words concerning the killing was that the county organ was putting itself in a position to aid Bankson in that "court of public opinion" on which the press of the Progressive Era had such an impact.[29]

The *Enterprise* had not a word about "Ab's" former transgressions. Instead the paper focused on "Sheriff Bankson's estimable family"—Mrs. Bankson and her daughters, who had "a large circle of warm personal friends" and were "most highly respected." The *Enterprise* then turned to Mannon Bankson, the ex-sheriff's son, saying he was liked by almost everyone. He was not liked enough by the voters of Pulaski County, however, to elect him sheriff just a few weeks earlier. This was a highly unusual fate for a Republican candidate in Pulaski County at the time. Finally, the Pulaski

County organ discussed "Ab" Bankson's four years as sheriff and his work as a farmer and stock raiser, saying that he "made and held many close friends. To these friends who know him, know his temperament, his good qualities and his faults, this tragedy in Cairo is wholly inexplicable."[30]

Perhaps trying to anticipate Bankson's defense in court, the *Pulaski Enterprise* argued that "no explanation of his deed seems believable save that of insanity." In concluding its editorial, the Pulaski paper spoke of Bankson's awful mental and physical strain for months, during the primary and election campaigns, and of the defeat of his son as "the bitterest disappointment of his . . . life," for which he must have felt largely responsible. The *Enterprise* portrayed a Bankson whom the Cairo newspapers and probably the people of Mounds, Illinois, would not have recognized either. "Who is there humanly wise enough to say, considering Bankson's life long habits and considering these recent heavy burdens thrust upon him, that his mental control did not waver, and even snap and break at almost any moment[?]" the paper asked rhetorically.[31]

"Ab" Bankson seemed to be almost utterly depraved—quick to shoot to kill, an alcoholic, a frequenter of brothels, a keeper of a "harlot," and one who took the people's money while in public office. Indeed, Bankson's behavior appeared to be so extreme that both Cairo daily newspapers seemed to be afraid that the former sheriff was going to mount an insanity defense when brought to trial, and both papers introduced the idea that Bankson had premeditated French's killing. The *Citizen* asked if Bankson had gone to police headquarters with the deliberate intention of killing Sergeant French and pointed out that "Ab" went to Brackey Bros. saloon before going to the police station because he knew French lived in the neighborhood.[32]

The *Cairo Bulletin* was less subtle than the *Citizen*. Cairo's morning daily said that a desire for revenge to the point of insanity "cannot be considered" in the Bankson case. According to the *Bulletin*, there was nothing in the circumstances of that case to suggest that Bankson was insane. What Sergeant French did was to interfere with Bankson's "wild orgies" in a house of ill repute and take away from him a weapon that he had brandished dangerously. The *Bulletin* went on to observe that the temporary insanity defense had been the refuge of many a criminal in the courts of the country. The newspaper added that, even at its best, the theory that a man may be insane on one subject, and only for a moment, while committing a serious crime was manifestly dangerous to society.[33]

In an editorial titled "Insanity or Depravity," the *Bulletin* judged "Ab" Bankson and rejected any pleas he might make.

> *He [Bankson] has been carrying on his drunken orgies in his home county for years, without being made to answer to the law. He had overawed the town and city authorities by his official position, and intimidated them with his gun play, so they dared not even remonstrate with him. Bankson was little, if any, removed from the ordinary town bully, who has grown to be such through the failure of the authorities to take him by the nape of the neck, in time grows more depraved and bolder, claiming as a right what no man may claim, as a privilege in a properly governed community[. He] who recognized no law except his vicious inclinations and resents interference from any source, Bankson claimed the right to do here what he had been doing for years in his home county with little interference, and when Sergeant French gave him to understand that this would not be permitted, he was at first surprised by the officer's temerity; then angered and filled with hate, and finally determined to show the officer that he was not to be hampered with impunity in his gutter-snipe career, adopting the method that is characteristic of bullies generally—cowardly assassination.*[34]

The killing of a police officer by a county sheriff created a sensation in the regional and even the national media.[35] Sergeant French was praised almost unanimously by the newspapers when the crime occurred. The *Daily Free Press* in Carbondale, Illinois, for example, said that French was "one of the most popular police officers on the force and was a most courageous and faithful officer."[36] Sergeant French's hometown paper, the *Cairo Bulletin*, mourned him as an "exemplary young man, an efficient and conscientious police officer."[37] A special session of the Cairo city council was called, at which it was decided that the city of Cairo would pay for Sergeant French's funeral. Police headquarters were to be draped in black in observation of the death of Sergeant French.[38]

Cairo had experienced its fourteenth homicide since the murder of Anna Pelley, only a year and three weeks earlier. The intense light that shone on Cairo following the Pelley murder exposed the corruption of the Cairo police department, and the men of the force were often blamed by the press for much of the violent crime in the city. This time it was one of their own, police sergeant Wilfred V. French, who had been killed. Who was to be the villain this time? Was the assassin, Sheriff Abner C. Bankson, solely to blame, or once again, would the Cairo police force have to bear a part of the guilt?

## CHAPTER TWENTY

# PRETRIAL PUBLICITY AND A CHANGE OF VENUE

As the news of the killing spread in Cairo, crowds began to form that night all over town, particularly around police headquarters.[1] The feeling against Abner Bankson was strong.[2] Alexander County sheriff Fred Nellis, having faced down one mob, which had likely cost him his reelection bid a few weeks earlier, was certainly hoping not to have to do it again. It was decided to take "Ab" Bankson to Murphysboro, Illinois, by buggy as quickly as possible. The Pulaski County sheriff was in the Alexander County jail only five or ten minutes before he was hustled out a side door. Escorting him were Chief Deputy Ben Jones—one of the hardest lawmen in the county—and Deputy John W. Greif.[3] The deputies started down Sycamore Street, and when they reached 34th Street with their prisoner, they encountered a "great crowd." This had been Sergeant Wilfred French's neighborhood. But the crowd let the buggy pass, perhaps because of Deputy Jones's reputation as a known gunman.

At Mounds, they secured another "rig" and Deputy Greif returned to Cairo. A man named Sperley joined Ben Jones and drove the wagon to Jonesboro in Union County, Illinois, thirty miles away.[4] They arrived in Jonesboro at 2:30 a.m. the next day, December 4, where the handcuffed Bankson and Deputy Ben Jones boarded a Mobile & Ohio train for Murphysboro.[5]

With the Pulaski County sheriff safely out of the city, there remained only the task of bringing formal charges against him. This was done quickly by the coroner's jury after a short session. Three witnesses were called—Officer Lawrence H. Paul, street supervisor John Sheehan, and health officer Frank Fitzgerald. There was general agreement that Bankson had asked French for a handcuff key, and when the sergeant said he did not have one, the sheriff started shooting. The coroner's jury concluded that the killing was "without cause or provocation."[6]

The jurors stated their verdict in these words:

> *We the undersigned jurors, sworn to inquire into the death of Wilfred E. French, on oath do find that he came to his death by a bullet wound in the left part of the back . . . caused by a bullet fired from a weapon held in the hands of Abner C. Bankson, who was not justified in the act, and we therefore recommend that he be held without bail until discharged by due process of law. The said shooting took place at police headquarters, No. 1111 Commercial Avenue in Cairo, Alexander County on Saturday, December 3, 1910.*[7]

With Bankson in the Jackson County jail in Murphysboro without bail, there would be a murder trial in the months ahead that would affect Cairo, Alexander County, Pulaski County, and eventually Union County. First, however, Sergeant Wilfred French needed to be buried. French's funeral was held in St. Joseph's Catholic Church in Cairo, with Father James Gillen officiating. Father Gillen was celebrated in the *Cairo Evening Citizen* for his words during the service, which included the following:

The funeral of Wilfred V. French was held at St. Joseph's Catholic Church in Cairo. Postcard courtesy of Darrel Dexter.

> *A crown of sorrows has been placed upon the white haired heads of several parents, a deep wound inflicted upon the hearts of loving brothers and sisters. I hope I do not trespass when at this solemn moment I offer not only my own pity, but the sympathy of the authorities of the city, and, indeed of the whole community, recommending you to the love of God, and the departed to the mercy of our blessed Savior. I will say no more, lest a touch, be it ever so tender, might cause the wounds to hurt and flow again.*[8]

Father Gillen's words of sorrow and pity were then followed by harsh criticism of the men of Cairo in general and those in city government in particular. The priest observed that what he was about to say was in the hearts of everyone in Cairo, but at this particular moment only he could utter them. Father Gillen said, "Must this fair city of ours go ever in garments spattered with blood? Within recent years she has scarcely obliterated the purple stains of one murder when the life stream of another homicide begrimed her."[9] Father Gillen then went on to outline recent assaults and murders in Cairo where due process and the jury system had failed the cause of justice. He spoke of Patrick Doud, another Cairo policeman who was stabbed while on duty. A jury set his assailant free, and by this Doud was branded the criminal.[10] Gillen next exposed an even more heinous miscarriage of justice: "A mother warns her daughter from infamy and the lewd scoundrel shoots her down like a cur by the wayside. Twelve men 'tried and true' under oath adjudged the assassin innocent. Of course the victim was the guilty one."[11] The third victim was a small and weak fisherman who offended another man by something he said. That man hunted the fisherman down as one would a rabbit and shot him with as little remorse as killing an animal. Yet a Cairo jury declared the "hunter" not guilty.[12] Finally, Father Gillen asked, "How is it that murderers in our court are all found innocent, while petty criminals are promptly punished?"[13]

Father Gillen then said, "But this I do know—that if you business and representative men would sacrifice half the time for the welfare of your city in the jury room that you spend in the Commercial Club and lodge rooms, murders would not disgrace the streets of Cairo."[14] The priest was admonishing Cairo men, especially the leaders of business and government, to become jurors. He was not directly denouncing the jury system but was charging that leading Cairo men avoided jury service.

Potential jurors or not, Cairo men had learned of "Ab" Bankson's state of mind once he was safely out of Cairo and locked up in Murphysboro in the Jackson County jail—thought to be the strongest in Southern Illinois. Bankson was interviewed by the *Murphysboro Independent* and made the following statement:

> *I went to Cairo a while back and French arrested me and took my gun. He never gave it back. Saturday I went to Cairo and visited police headquarters, I asked Officer Paul if he had a key that would unlock a pair of handcuffs I had and he said he didn't.*
>
> *Then French came in and I asked him. He swore and said no, then reached across a desk. I thought he was going for his club and I shot him. They've been after me down there and said they'd get me next time I was in Cairo. It was all over politics. French was a good fellow, but we just got in bad with each other.*[15]

The *Cairo Bulletin* seized on Bankson's press statement both to defend Sergeant French and to further condemn and vilify "Ab." According to the Cairo paper, the coroner's inquest had already disproved anything mitigating about Bankson's statement in Murphysboro. First, the *Bulletin* asserted that French was not "addicted to swearing" and was not one to show temper because he was one of the coolest-headed officers on the police force, not to mention being the most pleasant. Second, everyone would admit the sergeant was reaching for something—his star—as he was preparing to go on duty. "That he was reaching for a club to attack Bankson is nonsense," the newspaper declared. "Certainly Bankson did not wait to see if he was or not, but shot him in the back before he could turn around."[16] Third, the Pulaski sheriff had no grounds for a plea of self-defense either in law or in fact.

The *Bulletin* finished its editorial by attacking Bankson's mental state now that he was finally charged with a crime and the character the newspaper believed he had always exhibited. The paper stated, "There seems to have been no expression of regret over what he had done. His talk was of the bravado, the reckless, unfeeling, bluster of the roué and rowdy, whose career had suddenly been cut short by force."[17]

Up in Pulaski County, however, the *Mounds Headlight* portrayed "Ab" Bankson not as a lecher and a hooligan but as just another defendant, innocent until proven guilty, and the paper attacked the *Cairo Bulletin* for calling the county's sheriff a murderer. "*The Bulletin* of Cairo tried Sheriff Bankson for the killing of Officer French almost immediately and found him guilty before it has even heard his side of the story," complained the *Headlight*.[18] Now there were two newspapers in Pulaski County hoping to influence public opinion there in support of any "not guilty" defense Bankson might muster.

If Pulaski County newspapers were trying to save Bankson's body from the gallows and his reputation from the attacks of Cairo newspapers, it seems that no one in Southern Illinois or the region was inquiring into Sergeant French's reputation. On the occasion of the selection of a new "night sergeant" for the Cairo police force, the *Cairo Bulletin* recalled how Sergeant French "gave his life so nobly to the service of his people."[19] Only months before, however, the *Cairo Bulletin* came close to charging Officer French with perjury and police brutality. In December 1909, Wilfred French was partners with Officer James Casey, who was to be charged with taking payoffs to allow "dives" and brothels to continue operating.

In October 1909, before the Anna Pelley assault and the lynchings of Will "Froggie" James and Henry Salzner, President William Howard Taft had visited Cairo, as had President Theodore Roosevelt before him.[20] "Taft Day" was declared in Cairo, and this unusual holiday plus the opportunity to see and hear the president of the United States drew crowds of people into town. Some of them ended up in Gus Bourgois's "dive" at 4th and Ohio Streets. Chief Deputy Thomas Fuller, who in a short time would try to save a black man from being lynched, and Deputy Sheriff James Gilmore entered the Bourgois "joint," following a drunk man off the street. Gus tried to stop Deputy Fuller from going into the back room, where gambling was going on, but the deputy pushed past Bourgois. Upon entering the room, he saw about twenty-five men; a shell game; a craps table, where John W. "Tip" McGlasson was "banking"; and a "chuck-a-luck" wheel, being operated by a man named Beland. Bourgois immediately called Cairo police officer James Casey, who soon arrived to see what he could do to smooth things over.

Charges were brought against Bourgois, McGlasson, and Anson Lynn, who was the "capper" or lure who stood in front of Bourgois's dive, enticing men in by saying, "There's a good game going on inside." The men were convicted in county court in December 1910 and fined, but only after Officer James Casey, who was "seen in confidential consultation with Bourgois and McGlasson before the trial," allegedly perjured himself by testifying that Bourgois had called him on Taft Day because Deputy Gilmore was at his saloon drunk and disorderly.[21] Casey went on to say that Deputy Fuller "was the drunkest man he saw on the streets that day" and was not even able to speak clearly. Casey's testimony was not believed by the jury and was contradicted by Calvin V. Neff, the people's witness, who stated that Fuller was not drunk but "was his usual sober self."[22] Officer French testified that he was in Bourgois's saloon twice that day and saw no gambling going on there. His testimony was contradicted by the Reverend William King, a Methodist Protestant Church minister in Thebes, Illinois, who said he had gone to Bourgois's to eat on Taft Day, wandered into a back room, and saw men gambling. There was talk of perjury charges being brought against Casey and French, but it came to nothing.

French's partnership with Casey could not have been good for his reputation for honesty. The officers were members of the Cairo police force's notorious "kangaroo court." One Saturday night in December 1909, for instance, the two policemen spotted John Smith and a man named Mitchell, "negroes," in the rear of the Marion Hotel on Railroad Street whom they stopped and frisked for concealed weapons. They found none. Officer Casey then searched a nearby wagon bed and found a pistol, "a fine weapon, a .38 Colt—quite a little prize."[23] Casey then slapped Smith in the face and told him to skedaddle, keeping the revolver. Casey later sent word to him that he could have his gun back if he would give Casey fifteen dollars. Smith testified before the grand jury investigating the Cairo police officers that he bought his gun back for ten dollars. A "prominent citizen" witnessed the event and called for a police investigation, but there was none. Abner C. Bankson's pistol, then, was not the first one whose confiscation involved Wilfred French. In fact, the *Cairo Bulletin* claimed on the same day as the murder of French, "Hundreds of pistols have been taken from prisoners during the last several years, which have never been accounted for to the public, but disposed of by the officers to pawn brokers and second-hand dealers for their own profit."[24]

When word of the incident reached the reform-minded *Cairo Bulletin*, an editorial titled "Our Kangaroo Court" was written. The piece said the kangaroo court was usually held at Cairo Police Headquarters, "but any old place will do—at midnight or in the day light, on the open street or in a dark alley."[25] According to the *Bulletin*'s account, the "judges" who administered "justice" were Cairo police officers, and their judgments were binding, merciless, and often extremely brutal—comparable to the Dark Ages.[26]

In the midst of all the complaints against Officer James Casey, Chief Martin Egan planned to transfer him to an uptown beat, but he refused and angrily resigned the force. Casey took to his yacht, made a trip down the Mississippi River, and was gone several weeks. When he returned to Cairo, he demanded to be reinstated to the police force and his old beat. When the mayor and the chief delayed, he threatened, "If they don't put me back on the force, I'll publish the orders the chief gave to his men regarding some of the dives!" Casey was reinstated with what the *Cairo Bulletin* called "greater liberty to do as he pleased."[27]

In January 1910, Officers French and Casey were again involved in extralegal activities. French swore out a warrant against Charley Williams, "negro," for conducting a restaurant without a license. Late at night Casey and French went to Williams's boardinghouse and arrested him. The trio supposedly started toward police headquarters, with French in the lead and Casey bringing up the rear. They had walked only a short distance when Casey, without warning, struck Williams on the head with a club, knocking him down, kicking and cursing him, leaving a scalp wound two inches long. As Williams got to his feet, Casey continued to curse him, saying, "I'll teach you niggers to tell on us before the grand jury."[28] Williams was taken to jail late at night so that he would have to spend at least a night in jail, as no magistrates or justices of the peace were available at that time. He bonded out of jail as soon as possible the next morning. The reason for this arrest was that Charley Williams had been an effective witness against Officer James Casey before the special grand jury formed in November 1909, following Cairo's double lynching.[29] Casey was indicted by that grand jury for bribery. This was police brutality, which Wilfred French certainly condoned if not participated in.

The operations of Officer Casey's kangaroo court and his intimidation of witnesses certainly were not condoned by the *Cairo Bulletin*. This was the age of reform in the United States, and municipal graft and corruption were being seen as barriers to commercial growth and progress in the Progressive Era. In a long and revealing editorial titled "Victims of Graft," the *Bulletin* spelled out what municipal corruption, specifically within the police department, was doing to Cairo.

> *Cairo's "Kangaroo Court" is infamous throughout this section of the country. It has victims in nearly every little town within a radius of a hundred miles of the city and every one of these victims is a "knocker" of Cairo and her people—justly so, from his point of view. The number of victims runs into the hundreds and the stories they have to tell would fill a very large book that*

> *would equal in sensational interest some of the thrilling tales of brigandage of olden times.*
>
> *The "Kangaroo Court" has been a sort of auxiliary institution to the Bourgois "Robbers Den" and one or two others of similar character though less notorious. Strangers who come to the city on business or just for a visit and who were wary enough not to fall victim to the wiles of the Den's "cappers" were frequently "taken care of" by the agents of the "Court," and the result was just the same—they were robbed. Instead of using "knock-out" drops, a favorite and effective means of subduing victims in the "Den," the policeman's club or fist was used, if a threat of "ten days in jail" did not serve the purpose.*
>
> *As a result of this practice persisted in for years, the number of men in the surrounding towns who curse Cairo and her people, and who do much effective work in preventing others from coming here for any purpose is legion, and while it is not possible to estimate the injury that has been done, not only morally, but in a commercial way, it is safe to say that it is very great. This is shown by letters to wholesale firms here, and by reports from travelling men who visit the neighboring towns regularly and come in contact with people there.*[30]

Cairo police officer Wilfred French had participated in these activities, at least as a witness to them. Now he was dead, but his assailant was not in the Alexander County Jail in Cairo but in the Jackson County Jail in Murphysboro. How would the corrupt activities of his fellow officers and his town's infamous reputation as a twentieth-century Sodom affect the chances for a conviction in his killing? Would Abner C. Bankson be hanged or imprisoned for shooting Sergeant French, or would the hatred of Cairo by hundreds if not thousands in the surrounding towns and countryside put Cairo on trial for past and present crimes and not "Ab" Bankson?

Bankson's lawyers asked for and got a change of venue from Alexander County. Perhaps anticipating this development, the *Cairo Bulletin* some weeks earlier had asked that Bankson be returned to Cairo from Murphysboro. The *Bulletin* gave two reasons for bringing Bankson back. The first was that "word has come that he is being visited at Murphysboro by people almost indiscriminately, a practice which has been a source of much evil in such cases in this city."[31] The second reason was that there was literally a "new sheriff in town." Alexander S. Fraser, considered more of a "people's sheriff," had been elected to succeed Fred Nellis and had taken office.[32]

Fraser's new chief deputy was William P. Greaney, who was suspended from the National Guard and undergoing a military court of inquiry for arriving at the courthouse with his company of National Guardsmen five hours after being ordered out by the governor on the night of the attempted lynching of John Pratt and Lincoln Wilson. He was also charged with allowing members of his company to break up chairs in the sheriff's office and for padding the company's payroll.[33] Chief Deputy Greaney's main job for Sheriff Fraser was to be tax collector, and he was given a leave of absence from the Alexander County National Bank to accept the position.[34]

The change of venue was granted by Judge William N. Butler. The *Cairo Bulletin* was often highly critical of Butler's performance on the bench, portraying him as weak or, worse, an active aider of perjurers, witness procurers, and jury packers.[35] Butler gave several reasons for allowing the change of venue. He said that after eliminating all the Cairo people; any "colored people," because they would not be acceptable to the defense lawyers; those legally exempted; those who served on a jury in the past year; and all those who had signed affidavits in the case, there would be virtually no one left. According to Judge Butler, therefore, a jury could not be drawn without great expense.

Expense may not have been Judge Butler's only motivation for granting a change of venue to Union County. His courts in Cairo had seen sensational criminal trials that set free people who had stabbed a policeman, killed a grieving mother, and shot down a poor, weak fisherman. The *Cairo Bulletin* had charged that "his rulings from the bench are open to serious criticism in that they operated in at least two instances, very seriously against the prosecution and correspondingly aided the defense in bringing about verdicts of acquittal."[36] Judge Butler may have feared that another trial at the Alexander County Courthouse in Cairo with a verdict of not guilty would threaten his quickly diminishing reputation and his job. He was already unpopular, since grand juries he had called had indicted men who were accused of participating in the mob that attempted a lynching at the Alexander County Courthouse in February 1910.

Reasons for Judge Butler's granting a change of venue in the Bankson case might not be difficult to ascertain, but why did the people of Cairo not rise in murderous anger to avenge Sergeant French against an unrepentant gun player from a neighboring county? In the same historical era, when an unpopular judge in Council Bluffs, Iowa, granted a change of venue to three accused murderers, the people of Council Bluffs rallied to form a mob that lynched all three suspects before they could be sent out of town to stand trial.[37] In Cairo, the people must have known their city was widely disliked if not hated in Union County, at least since the rape and murder of Anna Pelley in 1909. Miss Pelley was from Union County and working in Cairo when she was killed. Cairo and Alexander County, however, did not have possession of Abner C. Bankson. He was in Murphysboro in Jackson County, where former sheriff Fred Nellis had sent him immediately after Wilfred French was killed, when hostile crowds could have turned into mobs. Not having physical possession of Bankson, it was unlikely that Cairo men would go after him in Murphysboro.

What was happening in Murphysboro at that time and before might have inflamed the attitudes of Cairo men had they known of the events. When Alexander County deputy sheriff Ben Jones gave "Ab" Bankson to Jackson County sheriff Sylvester Hanson on December 4, 1910, Hanson immediately called a photographer to document Bankson's injuries.[38] Sheriff Hanson, however, did not call a doctor, which, if Bankson's injuries were serious, would have been a more logical step than sending for a photographer.

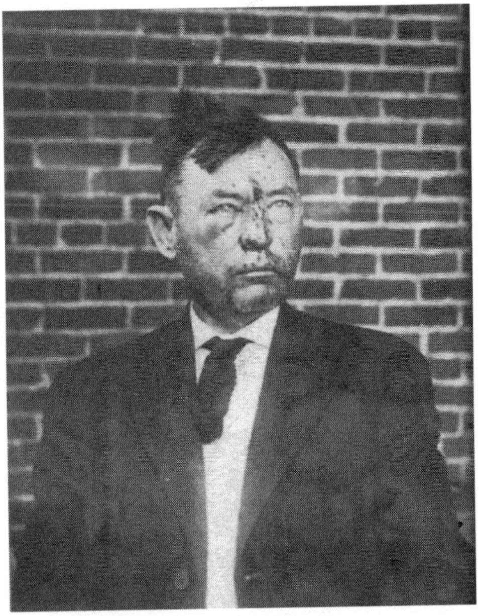

Sheriff Abner Bankson claimed he had this photograph taken to show his family that he had been beaten by the Cairo police, but it became important evidence in his trial. Photo courtesy of Brent Norris.

Then in the middle of December 1910, an article appeared in the Carbondale newspaper titled "Think He Is a Fine Fellow." In the piece, Sheriff Edwards of Jackson County and Deputies White and Roberts said that Bankson was a "fine fellow," pleasant of manner and quiet.[39] There are one or two possible interpretations of what was going on in Murphysboro from December 1910 until June 1911, when Abner C. Bankson was put on trial. One is that "Ab" Bankson, realizing his life was at stake, changed outwardly from an impulsive, unpredictable man to the quiet, "peaceable" man his family described at the time of

Wilfred French's murder. Another interpretation of events in Murphysboro is less charitable. Perhaps the county lawmen in Jackson County quickly came to the support of a fellow sheriff and did everything they could to help him escape the gallows. Might this have been especially true if in the process they could humiliate and make helpless a city police department, and even more satisfying if that department was the one in Cairo? The humiliation and helplessness of the Cairo Police Department would be clearly demonstrated when former sheriff Bankson was tried for the murder of Cairo police sergeant Wilfred French in June 1911.

CHAPTER TWENTY-ONE

# THE TRIAL OF SHERIFF BANKSON

When Abner C. Bankson's trial opened in Jonesboro, the county seat of Union County, Illinois, in June 1911, he was well represented by some of the most successful attorneys in Southern Illinois. This was despite the fact that his family had already paid out enough money to have purchased two of the houses former sheriff Fred Nellis had built in Cairo. The money had been tendered to cover funds that Bankson had borrowed from Pulaski County while sheriff, but somehow additional money was raised for Bankson's legal defense.[1] The lawyers included Louis Marion Bradley

The Union County Courthouse in Jonesboro, where the trial of Abner C. Bankson was held, built in 1858. The streetcar in the picture ran from the courthouse in Jonesboro to the state mental hospital in nearby Anna. Postcard courtesy of Keith Vincent.

of Carbondale, a former state's attorney in Pulaski County; Philetus E. Hileman of Jonesboro; and Carl S. Miller of Mounds.[2] In examining the potential jurors, the defense attorneys asked repeatedly if they believed in "the right of self-defense."[3] All the jurors selected were farmers, except for one veterinarian, who was dependent on farmers for his livelihood.[4] "Ab" Bankson was also a farmer, one who was reputed to have rather large holdings for that time and place, and possibly one whose apparent success fellow agriculturalists might admire.

The prosecuting attorneys in the case were State's Attorney Alexander Wilson of Alexander County; William D. Lyerle, the state's attorney for Union County; James Lingle, also of Union County; and Angus Leek of Cairo. It is interesting and perhaps revealing that Leek was chosen as a prosecutor. He was the city attorney of Cairo and close to George Parsons, the mayor. Indeed, Mayor Parsons had hired him for the prosecution team in an effort to show that the city could care for and protect its employees.[5] Angus Leek had also been one of the defense attorneys who managed to have every defendant charged with mob action in the attack on the Alexander County Courthouse in 1910 declared not guilty. These defendants had been heavily coached, and most of them probably committed perjury.[6] It is likely that Mayor Parsons prevailed on the other prosecutors to take Leek, not only because he was a good lawyer but also because he knew all the tricks that criminal lawyers used to free defendants, even those charged with the most serious crimes. Leek's presence looks like an effort "to set a thief to catch a thief."

Attorney Phil Hileman made the opening statement for the defense. The criminal lawyer was nothing if not audacious in what he delivered. Hileman said he would show that Abner C. Bankson went to the "house" on 13th Street in Cairo on the night of September 23, 1910, solely for purposes connected with his duties as sheriff of Pulaski County. While he was there on official business, two Cairo policemen entered, one of whom was Wilfred French. They accosted Bankson, taking twenty dollars and his gun. According to the lawyer, Bankson assumed he would never get his money back, but he wanted his gun. On December 3, 1910, at 5:15 p.m., looking for a missing key to some handcuffs, he went to Cairo Police Headquarters. According to Bankson, when he asked Sergeant French for the gun French and the other officer had taken, French said he would "fix him" so he didn't need any gun. Bankson said that French then hit him, probably with a pair of brass knuckles, inflicting a wound over his eyes. As "Ab" drew the gun he had on him, he received a violent blow on the back of the head and fired blindly. Bankson "had a perfect right under the law to shoot him [French]," according to Hileman. After the head blow, Bankson remembered little or nothing, except that he was alive but very badly beaten.[7]

Anyone who had read Bankson's statement of early December 1910, either the original in the *Murphysboro Independent* or the quotes in the *Cairo Bulletin* or the *Alton Evening Telegraph*, would have been astonished at this opening statement. When interviewed in Murphysboro, Bankson had said nothing of brass knuckles or beatings or of a threat from Sergeant French. He spoke only of asking for a handcuff key, being denied by two Cairo policemen and believing that French was about to club him. A couple of days after he killed the man, Bankson said in the newspaper interview that French was a "good fellow" and that "we just got in bad with each other."[8] Another statement the former Pulaski County sheriff made in the interview would become the underlying theme of his trial: "They've been after me down there and said they'd get me next time I was in Cairo."[9] Formally and legally, Abner C. Bankson was on trial in Union County, but informally and extralegally, Cairo, Illinois, was on trial.

Alexander County state's attorney Alexander Wilson's opening statement also tried to bring the jurors back to 1910 but with very different intent from what Hileman had suggested. Wilson recalled the facts as they had been generally agreed to at the time of the shooting. That is, in September "Ab" Bankson created a disturbance in a Cairo "bawdy house" on 13th Street, where he had gone for pleasure and not official business. When the police were called, Officer Frank Skews responded. After discovering it was the Pulaski County sheriff disturbing the peace, he went for Sergeant French's help, as French was the highest ranking police official on night duty. Upon reaching the 13th Street brothel, French was forced to disarm Bankson. The sergeant, however, while keeping the sheriff's gun, did not take him into custody but advised him to go home because of the lateness of the hour.[10]

Prosecutor Wilson then brought events up to the evening of December 3, 1910, when Bankson entered Cairo Police Headquarters heavily under the influence of alcohol but apparently in his right mind.[11] Since he was a fellow lawman, the police in the station accorded him a measure of respect, even though he seemed to be asking for a handcuff key over and over again when it was obvious to everyone that none of their keys would fit his cuffs. Bankson even asked the street supervisor about having a key to fit his manacles. Bankson then asked the Cairo chief of police, James Cowell, when he would get his gun back. The chief said to ask Sergeant French and then walked away to his office. Jailer Melchor Lutz talked with Bankson longer than Cowell, but he too retreated to Cowell's private office when Sergeant Wilfred French entered police headquarters.

As soon as French came in, Bankson started asking him questions that centered on the return of his gun. French, in the prosecutor's account, was uncomfortable and did not want to discuss the matter; he tried to put Bankson off by saying he had not decided about the gun and was going to the toilet. When French came back from the restroom and was pinning on his star, Bankson shot him in the back. Officer Lawrence Paul, who was in the room, sprang at Bankson and was immediately joined by Cowell and Lutz, who came out of the private office as soon as shots were fired. The three men struggled to overpower the sheriff, and Chief Cowell got the handcuffs away from Bankson and hit him in the face with them. French was already dead, lying face down, when Cowell and Lutz charged into the room.[12]

In the account published in the *Cairo Evening Citizen*, the jury paid close attention to the "graphic recital by State's Attorney Wilson," while Bankson gave faint smiles to his lawyer Carl S. Miller, who was also from Pulaski County.[13] The *Cairo Bulletin* examined Bankson's behavior in the courtroom even more closely than did the *Citizen*. Cairo's morning paper stated that the former sheriff appeared somewhat nervous, glancing quickly about, whispering frequently to his attorneys, and almost losing control when State's Attorney William D. Lyerle of Union County asked a juror if he had any scruples against the death penalty. The *Bulletin* then judged Bankson's personality based on his appearance in the courtroom, saying he exhibited "temper, and that he is a man to quickly resent an insult, fanciful or otherwise."[14]

William David Lyerle was state's attorney for Union County, Illinois, where Sheriff Ab Bankson's trial was held. From *Standard Atlas of Union County, Illinois*, 65.

If this personality assessment was true, then "Ab" must have been deeply angry at the testimony of the first prosecution witness, special Cairo police officer Frank Skews. The officer said that Bankson was "disorderly and flourishing a weapon" in the house of ill fame on 13th Street and in such bad shape that he and

Sergeant French tried to get him to lie on a couch in the police chief's office, but he refused. Officer Skews affirmed that nothing was taken from Bankson except a pistol and then claimed that he and French had escorted the Pulaski sheriff "downtown," where they all had a drink in a saloon and were treated to cigars by Bankson. According to the *Bulletin*, the defense tried to discredit Officer Skews and his account "without effect."[15] The *Cairo Evening Citizen* also commented on the rigorous cross-examination undergone by Skews and asserted that the defense was unable to confuse him.[16]

The courtroom in Jonesboro was not full on the first couple of days of the trial, but on June 1, 1911, it was "comfortably filled." Perhaps Union County people had heard rumors that both the prosecution and the defense were going to introduce "surprise" witnesses, which they did. The *Cairo Bulletin* also became aware on that day that the Cairo police as well as "Ab" Bankson were on trial in Union County. The sympathy expressed by many in Union County for Bankson was based on

> *alleged misdoings on the part of Cairo's police. Numerous stories are afloat of bad treatment received at the hands of Cairo's constabulary. Of how a friend was arrested, his money and valuables taken by the police, and how they were turned loose minus money, etc., and told to "skidoo" without trial.*[17]

The *Cairo Bulletin* should not have been surprised at the anti-Cairo police sentiment in Union County. A year to the day before Wilfred French was killed, the newspaper featured an editorial on Cairo's "kangaroo court," where out-of-towners were routinely robbed by the Cairo police, and spoke of the deep resentment by people for a hundred miles around against Cairo and its police.[18] The *Bulletin* reporters should have suspected that if the Cairo police were declared guilty in the court of public opinion, then Abner C. Bankson would be not guilty, and it indeed seemed that the people of Union County had already found the Cairo cops guilty.

After State's Attorney Wilson's opening statement, Angus Leek did most of the questioning of the prosecution witnesses. The prosecutors supplied their witnesses with a diagram of Cairo Police Headquarters and asked them to point out locations, showing the position of the furniture and all parties in the building at the time of the shooting, where Bankson stood when he did the shooting, and where French fell. "Ab" Bankson, never one to follow rules scrupulously, got up from his seat and walked in front of the jury, so anxious was he to see the diagram. Even the judge did not ask him to sit down but only to stand aside so that he would not obstruct the jury's view.

After the police headquarters diagram was allowed as evidence, much to the objections of Bankson's lawyers, Dennis Morgan was called to the stand. Morgan was a bartender in the saloon at 34th and Sycamore in Cairo.[19] He testified that Bankson was in the saloon about 4:30 p.m. on the afternoon of December 3, 1910. Bankson had pointed out a man in the bar and asked Morgan if that man was the night sergeant, and Morgan told him that he was not. At that the Pulaski County sheriff had smiled and left the saloon. The man in the saloon at 34th and Sycamore was *William* French, the sergeant's brother and also a Cairo police officer, who testified that about forty minutes after Bankson left, he heard his brother had been killed.[20]

The witness who followed Morgan and French's brother was jailer Melchor Lutz. He brought in the gun that was used to kill French, which was admitted into evidence, as were the two bullets dug out of the wall at the police station in Cairo, which were steel-jacketed. The man who had loaded the weapon that killed French had meant it to do just that.[21] French's coat and vest, with the "telltale" bullet hole in the back, was also placed in evidence.[22] The defense did not contest the clothing.

After the gun, bullets, and uniform were presented, Lutz told his version of the events that led to Sergeant French's death. Lutz admitted letting Bankson into the police station, where the Pulaski County sheriff greeted various police officers and asked around about a key to unlock a pair of handcuffs that he had. According to Lutz, about that time French came in and Bankson greeted him. Sheriff Bankson then asked the sergeant about a handcuff key and levelly asked, "When are you going to give my pistol back?"[23] French replied that he didn't know, or words to that effect. Lutz had retreated to an office by this time; after hearing three shots in rapid succession, he and Chief Cowell rushed out to find Officer Paul struggling with Bankson. As they "got a hold of him," the former sheriff said, "I'm a game man!"[24] Lutz said he had hold of Bankson's right arm when Chief Cowell began striking "Ab" in the face with his own handcuffs, and he had a clear view of the Pulaski County lawman's face during the fight. Lutz declared that there were no wounds on Bankson's face before Cowell struck him. Lutz swore that Chief Cowell, Officer Paul, and he had taken the Pulaski County sheriff to the county jail not five minutes after the shooting. This would mean that the Cairo police had scant time to beat Bankson as he claimed.

When Lutz was cross-examined, he said that Officer Paul and Chief Cowell had hold of Bankson when he joined the fight. The police chief was trying to open the former sheriff's coat to find the gun used in the shooting when Paul told Cowell that the gun was on the floor. The chief had already hit Bankson in the face with the handcuffs he had wrestled away from the sheriff.

Gus Johnson (whom the *Bulletin* identified as a "colored policeman" and the *Citizen* identified by name, assuming its readers would know who he was) followed Lutz for the prosecution. Johnson was the prosecution's surprise witness who revealed that Bankson had asked him when Sergeant French went on duty, and when Johnson told him, he immediately boarded the uptown streetcar, "the same car that passed police headquarters."[25] This established premeditation, or so the prosecution hoped. The *Citizen* asserted, "This is important for the State, as showing that Bankson went to headquarters for the express purpose of meeting French and demanding his gun."[26]

After Gus Johnson came the Alexander County coroner, Dr. James McManus. He testified that he arrived at police headquarters about 5:30 p.m. on the day of the killing and found Sergeant French dead with his head lying at the door to Chief Cowell's office. The coroner said the wound to French was in the left part of the back, about an inch from the spine, and it was a wound sufficient to cause death. Indeed, French was dead when Dr. McManus arrived on the scene. At the scene, the coroner stripped the body and determined that the bullet had passed through the back wall of the chest and the heart.[27]

Chief James Cowell followed Dr. McManus on the stand. His testimony corroborated jailer Melchor Lutz's. Cowell swore that Bankson had been to the Cairo police station at least twice between September 28 and December 3, 1910, and had asked both times for his pistol, "which all the time had been locked in the chief's desk."[28] At each meeting the chief assured Bankson that he would fix it with Sergeant French. Cowell further testified that Bankson had never asked for a cent of money or made any complaint, formal or otherwise. James Cowell stated that Bankson was at police headquarters when he came in on December 3 and that they had a brief conversation about Bankson's confiscated gun. Cowell then went to his office, and the "next thing he heard were shots fired."[29] James Cowell rushed out of his office, and Wilfred French fell dead at his feet. Cowell stepped over the body of his sergeant and saw that Officer Paul was struggling with Bankson. Cowell grabbed the former sheriff and began fighting with him.

Officer Paul then yelled, "I've got his gun," to which the chief replied, "He may have another."[30] It was at this time that Cowell grabbed the handcuffs away from "Ab" Bankson and hit him with them. Cowell could not swear that the Pulaski County sheriff was unmarked before he hit him. The chief said that he was not paying attention to Bankson's face but was trying to keep him from hurting anyone else. As to hitting the sheriff, Cowell said he struck him two or three times. While they were struggling and fighting, the Cairo police chief heard Bankson say, "I'm a brother officer and a game man."[31] As soon as the sheriff was subdued, he was put in handcuffs and Chief Cowell called a patrol wagon. A crowd was already gathering, so the chief started walking Bankson toward the courthouse. A patrol wagon overtook them at 18th and Poplar, and they proceeded to the county courthouse to turn the prisoner over to Sheriff Fred Nellis.

On cross-examination, lawyer Louis Bradley asked James Cowell if on one visit Sheriff Bankson did not say, "They took $20 from me!" The Cairo chief denied Bankson ever said that. Cowell also denied hitting the sheriff on the way to the county jail or that Bankson implored him not to hit him while the sheriff was still at Cairo Police Headquarters. When asked, Cowell stated that he struck Bankson with both hands during the struggle.[32]

Cairo's other police officer on the stand, Lawrence H. Paul, expanded the conversation slightly between Sergeant French and Sheriff Bankson. Paul also recounted the sheriff's unusual behavior of showing a pair of handcuffs and asking everyone for a key—even street supervisor John Sheehan, who would be unlikely to have one. Next, Officer Paul recalled that Bankson had said, "Sergeant, come over here. I want to talk to you," and French replied, "I haven't time now."[33] Bankson persisted, asking the sergeant what he was going to do about the gun. French said he hadn't yet decided and went to the toilet. Officer Paul then recounted French's movements after the sergeant returned from the restroom: French went to a closet, from there to the chief's office, and then to John Sheehan's desk, where he proceeded to pin on his star. At that time Bankson asked French about the handcuff key, and the sergeant replied that he didn't have one to fit Bankson's cuffs. The Pulaski County sheriff said, "You haven't, eh?," jumped to his feet, and shot French in the back.[34]

The state then called John Sheehan, Cairo street supervisor, to the stand. Sheehan said he did not see anyone strike Bankson before the shooting. Sheehan was followed by Frank Fitzgerald, Cairo health officer. The *Cairo Evening Citizen* thought he was an excellent witness for the prosecution.[35] His testimony corroborated the testimonies of Chief Cowell and jailer Lutz as to the main facts. Fitzgerald was outside police headquarters talking with Officer Frank Hagey when the shooting started, and he rushed in, seeing French staggering toward Chief Cowell's office. He testified that he saw Bankson with his arm extended but did not see the pistol. He said that

Officer Paul and jailer Lutz subdued the Pulaski County sheriff and that he personally searched Bankson for the weapon. Officer Paul told him the gun was on the floor where he had knocked it. Fitzgerald said he did not notice Bankson's face at this time. While telephoning for a doctor, he saw Chief Cowell hit Bankson in the face but did not know with what. Finally, his take on Bankson's words were, "I'm a game son of a bitch, I am."[36] During Fitzgerald's testimony, "Ab" Bankson was once again on the move in the courtroom, going to the water pitcher on the judge's bench and taking a tablet from his watch pocket.[37]

Fitzgerald also told the court that he was at police headquarters on one earlier occasion when Sheriff Bankson came in asking for his gun. At that time Chief Cowell told Bankson that if he went at the night sergeant the right way, he would get his gun back. On that occasion Bankson said nothing about money. Fitzgerald identified the gun as a .32-20, loaded with "mushroom" cartridges that expand when they strike.[38] When cross-examined, the health officer stated that he did not see anyone hit Sheriff Bankson in the head, breast, or side or kick or stamp on him, except for Chief Cowell's two strikes to Bankson's face.

Officer Frank Hagey, who swore that he was with Frank Fitzgerald outside the police station at the exact time of the shooting, said that by the time he entered the police station in Cairo, Bankson had been arrested by Officer Paul and jailer Lutz. Hagey went over to Sergeant French's body and lifted his head and then laid it on his arm, as if Wilfred French were resting. Frank Hagey had not said much under oath but was cross-examined nonetheless. Hagey said his chief concern was with French's body, and he did not see Chief Cowell hit Bankson at all. All the prosecution witnesses were rigorously cross-examined, except for Officer Gus Johnson. This probably pleased Officer Johnson, who was likely anxious to leave Jonesboro, Illinois, a "sundown" town, where typically no black person was allowed after dark.[39]

The next day Bankson's defense lawyers began to have their witnesses tell quite a different story from the one the Cairo officials had told. The first person lawyer Carl S. Miller brought to the stand was former Alexander County deputy sheriff Ben Jones, who had for a time been chief deputy under Sheriff Fred Nellis. He was one of the white deputies who had defended the courthouse when it was attacked during the attempted lynching of 1910. The defense wanted Jones to describe Bankson's wounds when the Cairo police brought him to the county jail. Jones said Bankson was "all bloody" on the face and head but that he didn't examine the wounds.[40] His main concern was driving Bankson out of Cairo before mob violence ensued, and so Jones pushed on to Jonesboro in a "buggy" and then boarded a train to Murphysboro, where the prisoner was turned over to Jackson County sheriff Sylvester Hanson. Ben Jones said all the Cairo policemen were "excited" to the point of irrationality when he got the suspect. Ever the faithful subordinate, Jones had driven Bankson to Mounds, Illinois, a distance of about ten miles, in a single "rig" but changed to a double "rig" in Mounds. There Jones allowed William H. Parker, a saloonkeeper, to cash a twenty-five-dollar check for Bankson but did not think his prisoner was rational even then. Then Jones and Bankson got some whiskey from a man named Wehrenberg, likely Charles E. Wehrenberg, whom Bankson would have known well, as he had just defeated his son Mannon Bankson in the sheriff's election the month before.[41]

The *Cairo Evening Citizen* judged Friday a good day for the prosecution "because the evidence in rebuttal was strongly presented and was unshaken by cross examination."[42] Court was adjourned until Saturday morning because several jurors complained they were feeling ill due to the oppressive heat and feared they would break down.

The first witness Saturday morning was former sheriff Sylvester Hanson of Jackson County. Hanson testified that Bankson was turned over to him on the morning of December 4, cut about the face but seemingly not seriously injured.[43] Hanson did not call a doctor for the prisoner and was present when a picture of Bankson was taken.

On a cross-examination, which probably did not help the prosecution, Hanson said there was a small break in the skin between Bankson's eyes, enough to have bled profusely. The former sheriff also said the prisoner had a one-inch gash on the back of his head and that one eye was badly swollen. Hanson admitted that Bankson had not washed his face until a photograph was taken, which Hanson then identified.

Under the heading of "Negro Witness," the *Cairo Bulletin* reported that George Fuqua of Pulaski, Illinois (Bankson's hometown), followed Sylvester Hanson to the stand.[44] According to his sworn testimony, he was an eyewitness to the shooting of Sergeant French at the exact time it happened. Fuqua was employed in the Mobile & Ohio railroad yards in Cairo. On the day of the shooting, he was at his sister's house on 14th Street and decided to walk out to Commercial Avenue, passing by Cairo Police Headquarters just as events came to a head. He said he saw a man hit Sheriff Bankson with what he thought was a pair of brass knuckles, because he saw something shine, and another man hit him on the back of the head. Fuqua then testified that he heard someone yell, "Look out!" and then a single shot was fired. The witness said he didn't stick around after that but went back to the railroad yards, where he heard Sergeant French was dead. Fuqua was asked, on cross-examination, why he heard but one shot. The *Cairo Bulletin* reported that Fuqua said, "I'se gone when dat shot was fired."[45] Under further questioning by the prosecution, Fuqua admitted knowing Bankson for some time and coming to see the prisoner as soon as he was moved to the Jonesboro jail. When asked by the prosecution what he was getting for his testimony, he said that his expenses were being covered.

Nick Morrison of Cairo, who was as usual identified as a "negro," followed Fuqua as a defense witness.[46] Morrison said he "hadn't been around much" for the past six years, meaning in the vicinity of the police station, but claimed to know Chief Cowell and French as the night sergeant, even though he didn't know him by name. Morrison was the defense's "surprise" witness, but he surprised his attorneys by saying that he did not see French strike Bankson. The defense quickly removed Carl S. Miller from the courtroom and brought in the criminal lawyer Phil Hileman. Hileman claimed intimidation of a defense witness, as Alexander County state's attorney Alexander Wilson had questioned Morrison the night before. Wilson, however, established that a prosecutor had a perfect right to question any witness about testimony, and Morrison admitted that Wilson did not threaten him or offer him a reward.

Circuit judge Albert William Lewis of Harrisburg, Illinois, then took over Morrison's questioning, dismissing the jury and warning him about changing his testimony. The witness became "terribly frightened" as the judge commanded him to tell all he knew, the whole truth, without regard to any previous statement made to anyone. Morrison then said some colored men and some white man in Cairo had told him that he had better have nothing to do with the matter and that he had found notes in his keyhole and elsewhere warning him to be careful if he wanted to live in Cairo.[47] Suddenly, Morrison said the statement he made to Carl S. Miller in Mound City was true. The *Cairo Bulletin*'s observation at this point was, "It was evident that the witness was badly scared and thought he would perjure himself if he acted anything contrary to any former statement he had made."[48]

The jury was brought back. Morrison changed his testimony substantially and seemed to have a story all prepared for the occasion. Morrison said he "heard a racket" while between 11th and 12th Streets and rushed to the front of Cairo Police Headquarters, where he looked through the south part of the building front and saw a man staggering. He stated that he had not seen the man before but later learned that it was Sheriff Bankson. Morrison said

Bankson and another man, whom he knew as the night sergeant, "looked like they were angry" and were "squabbling," but neither had a weapon in his hand.[49]

Morrison claimed the night sergeant suddenly struck Bankson, who staggered against the wall and was raising a pistol as the sergeant was going away from him. The witness said all the Cairo men in the police station were going away from Bankson. "The pistol went off," but it looked like the barrel of the pistol was in the sheriff's hand rather than the handle. The witness said he saw a man stagger and a policeman grab Bankson. Morrison explained that he then ran away, hearing two other shots as he ran.[50]

James Lingle, a skilled Union County litigator who had worked on the Cairo attempted lynching cases, cross-examined Nick Morrison. He testified that he had known Frank Fitzgerald since he was a boy but did not recall seeing him at police headquarters at the time of the shooting. The witness also stated he had known "Mr. John Sheehan" for twenty years and didn't see him in the police station "until after the fight." Morrison further said he knew Officer Hagey but did not recall seeing him at police headquarters at the time of the killing, either.[51]

During his testimony, Morrison managed to slam the city of Cairo. According to Morrison, the night before he testified, he was questioned by Alexander County state's attorney Alexander Wilson, who, among other things, assured him that he would be safe in Jonesboro, which was a "sundown town."[52] Morrison observed, "I know it is safer here than in Cairo."[53]

At the end of his cross-examination, Morrison explained how he came to be in Jonesboro testifying for the defense. After saying he witnessed and ran from the shooting, Morrison told a number of people about what had happened. Bankson's defense attorney Carl S. Miller went to Morrison's house the next day and took him to Mound City. Miller paid his fare and gave him some drinking money—a dollar one time and a quarter another. Throughout the cross-examination, Morrison stuck to his second story of events at Cairo Police Headquarters on December 3. The prosecution could not shake his sworn recollection. The *Cairo Evening Citizen* asserted that Morrison was the best defense witness, notwithstanding his changed testimony.[54] At the end of that testimony, Morrison got one final dig in against Cairo and Alexander County. When asked if there was anyone who could directly corroborate his account, Morrison said that Ed Brooks had been with him and could have placed him at the shooting but that Brooks had been shot dead by an Alexander County constable, Jim Dillard, who was now in the state penitentiary.[55]

Ed Brooks, who worked at the Illinois Central roundhouse, was killed by Constable James Dillard on Saturday night, January 28, 1911, as he was entering his house at 312½ 19th Street, near Poplar Street. The shooting seems unconnected to the French homicide. After Dillard's sister had accused Brooks of stealing five dollars from her, Dillard searched Brooks and found nothing but a revolver, which he took. In the argument that followed, Dillard shot Brooks in the breast and he fell dead. Both Brooks and Dillard were identified in the newspaper account as "colored."[56]

The next defense witnesses to testify in the morning session of the circuit court were from Murphysboro, where "Ab" Bankson had been taken immediately after the killing. Dr. Ira W. Ellis gave strange testimony, saying that he found Sheriff Bankson's face bruised but did not examine his head or ask the Pulaski County sheriff to remove his clothes. Dr. Ellis did observe that Bankson had no fractures when he got to the Jackson County jail but was complaining of "hurting" in his breast. Following the seemingly uncurious doctor was Rollie C. Whittenberg, called to identify the photo he took of Bankson on Sunday, December 4, 1910. It showed the sheriff with a swollen right eye, a bruise between the eyes, and a darkened face.

The afternoon session brought another unusual witness for the defense. This was John Moore, who was from Bankson's hometown of Pulaski, Illinois. Moore claimed to have been a former special deputy under Bankson and that he was in Uncle Joe's Saloon in Cairo at 600 Commercial on December 3, 1910.[57] There he met the Pulaski County sheriff between 4 and 5 p.m. and went with him to the Cairo Police Headquarters to get handcuff keys. Moore did not go into the police station with Bankson but stood outside, directly in front, with a "negro" named George Fuqua. From his vantage point, John Moore said he saw Bankson sitting in a chair and appeared to be getting up.

At that moment, Moore said, someone grabbed Bankson and threw him back in the chair and hit him, at which time the Pulaski County sheriff drew his gun but was hit from behind and then hit again on the head when the gun went off. Moore testified that he didn't know the men he said hit Bankson, but he thought they were in police uniforms. Moore did say he saw jailer Lutz (whom he apparently did recognize) with a pair of handcuffs in his hand. Moore said that the man who struck Bankson on the back of the head was larger than himself, who weighed 170 pounds.[58]

This "special deputy" abandoned his sheriff to take the next train home and at the depot learned that Sergeant French had been killed. At the end of his testimony, Moore explained why he was a "special deputy" on that particular day. He swore that Bankson and he were supposed to catch the 5:50 train to Kentucky to retrieve a prisoner, which is strange considering Bankson had only two days left of his term in office. Under cross-examination, Moore could not explain why he abandoned Bankson when the sheriff was obviously in trouble. Incredibly, during the cross-examination, Moore said he had no special interest in the case and had come to testify because he had talked about the situation with Mannon Bankson, the sheriff's son. He did admit that he had frequently visited with the defense attorneys in Jonesboro. As bewildering as Moore's testimony may have been to jurors, it was soon overshadowed when Abner Bankson took the stand in his own defense.

## CHAPTER TWENTY-TWO

# SHERIFF BANKSON ON THE STAND

On the day that Abner C. Bankson was to take the stand in his own defense, June 2, 1911, the courtroom in Jonesboro contained the largest crowd it had seen for many years.[1] He contradicted some of his own witnesses but stuck to his story from start to finish "under one of the most grilling cross-examinations that was ever put to a witness in a murder trial."[2] "Ab" Bankson's account of events, beginning with his being in a "house of ill fame" on 13th Street in Cairo on the night of September 23, 1910, was almost the opposite of the prosecution's case but was somewhat consistent with what the African American defense witnesses had sworn.

If Bankson's testimony was consistent as to the points proving that he was not guilty, it was also confusing. First, Bankson tried for sympathy, saying that he had been in jail since December 3, 1910, that the incarceration had left him a sick man, and that two evenings before he had suffered a "hard night." Next, he defended his presence in a "bawdy house" on September 23, 1910, saying he went to 212 13th Street in Cairo because his neighbor, Hays Graddy, a switch engineer at Mounds, had been killed. A woman had been living with the man Bankson thought had killed Graddy, and Bankson stated that he hoped to find the woman at that address. The name of the woman, according to Bankson, was Edie or Ada.[3]

Bankson's testimony would have already been suspicious had the jurors known the details of the case to which he referred. Hays Graddy was shot in the back of the head on July 19, 1909, at about 2:30 a.m. on the road to Cairo after leaving the Halfway House, a "resort" midway between Cairo and Mound City.[4] The murder occurred in Alexander County, and after the coroner's jury interviewed John Crain, Graddy's companion, they attributed his death to a "person unknown."[5] Unable to testify before the coroner's jury because of a broken leg was Helen Sexton, "a denizen of Thirteenth Street," who was with H. N. Hoopengarner, white, and James Crawford, "colored," when they came upon Graddy and Crain in the road after the shooting. This woman may have been the Edie or Ada to whom Bankson referred, as one of the "roomers" in Myrtle/Mabel Stevenson's house in 1910 was twenty-two-year-old Hellen Kelly, likely the same person as Helen Sexton. (Prostitutes often used many pseudonyms.) The governor offered a $200 reward for the conviction of Graddy's murderer, which may have motivated Bankson to investigate the case, but the murder occurred in Alexander County, outside of his jurisdiction.[6]

As the jurors were trying to follow the Edie/Ada story, Bankson completely changed the subject. He said he knew a man named Skews and a man named Wilfred French, whom he described as "the man that was killed." Bankson identified neither man as a law officer, nor did he say he killed French. At that point the Pulaski prisoner returned to Edie/Ada. With the cooperation of the madam (whom he called the landlady), he could spy on the women of the house and their prospective clients through a peephole in her room. According to Bankson he had somehow identified Edie/Ada and was looking for the man who was "friendliest" to her. To show he was in the "bawdy house" for an official purpose and not an immoral one, Bankson said the surveillance was long, and he admitted he would lie down on the bed in the "landlady's" room from time to time but with his pistol beside him at the ready.[7]

About 11 p.m. or midnight, Officers Wilfred French and Frank Skews entered the room where Bankson was lying down, and he rose up and exclaimed, "Hello, boys! What is it?"[8] Without replying, as attested by Bankson, the two policemen grabbed him and took his gun. Just then the "lady of the house," according to Bankson's testimony, asked the officers, "What are you doing?" Bankson's story at this point went back to him putting his money in different pockets of his clothing, lest he fall asleep and be robbed—five ten-dollar bills in his right pants pocket, three twenty-dollar bills in another, and a twenty in his hand. Why he was holding the twenty in his hand was never explained. Bankson said that French and Skews left with his gun but did not take him into custody. After they left he noticed twenty dollars missing. Bankson claimed he then waited in the brothel about half an hour, apparently having lost all interest in finding a "suspect," and then left on his own and headed toward Commercial Avenue, saying, "In my condition I could not count time."[9]

On his walk up Commercial Avenue, Bankson testified that he saw French and Skews standing in the middle of the avenue. Tramping on past the officers, he went to the police station and said he was "going to make a case with Officer Hagey"[10] but found no one there. This statement was strange and difficult to understand. An empty police station on one of Cairo's crime-filled nights? Next, according to Bankson, he headed straight for the train station to go home after the incident, but somehow he instead ended up in Ashley's downtown Cairo saloon. It was there, said the sheriff, that he discovered three of his ten-dollar bills missing.

On cross-examination Bankson denied that he raised any disturbance in Myrtle Stevenson's "house." He denied that Stevenson phoned the police, saying he would have seen her had she done so since the phone was in the "peep" room. The former sheriff also said it was Stevenson who intervened and told the officers to let Bankson alone. He did admit to being questioned by the Cairo policemen as to his reason for being there and said he told them, "I'm looking for a lost necklace." This lost necklace, reminiscent of Anna Pelley's missing crucifix, had never been mentioned in all the thousands of official and unofficial words written about the Bankson case.[11]

Several days after the incident on 13th Street, the former sheriff said he spoke with Cairo police chief James Cowell and told him that French and Skews had taken his gun and money. Bankson added, "Chief Cowell talked insulting to me."[12] Recall the *Cairo Bulletin*'s earlier observation that Bankson was a man of temper, quick to resent an insult, real or imagined.[13] Later the sheriff talked with Cowell at a saloon on 34th Street in Cairo. According to Bankson's testimony, Cowell said, "Now Bankson, if you get down and beg you will get that gun." "Ab's" reply was that he didn't have to beg for a little $15.50 gun. Bankson said he "applied" to Cowell two or three times for his gun, and "quite a while afterward" asked French for the gun. "Ab" then testified that French said, "There has been too much talk about that gun now. We're on to you," or words to that effect.[14]

Bankson next brought his testimony to December 3, 1910—the day Wilfred French was killed. He said it was his intent on that day to go to Kentucky to seek a "negro" murderer. He asked John Moore, a sometimes deputy of his, to go with him. The two men set up an evening meeting at Uncle Joe's Saloon at 600 Commercial in Cairo, but like much else during his testimony, Bankson didn't remember the exact time of the meeting.[15] After they met, the two men slowly walked up the street, passing "Mr. French" but not speaking. On this cold December day, the sheriff testified, he and Moore walked all the way from 6th and Commercial to 34th and Sycamore—a distance of at least twenty-eight blocks. The sheriff then entered a saloon at that location, where, according to him, he encountered William French, the sergeant's brother. Bankson claimed that he treated William French to a cigar while he had a beer.

The view of "Uncle Joe" Steagala's saloon and hotel taken from Ohio Street and published in the 1904 Cairo city directory. Sheriff Bankson and Deputy John Moore met here before going to police headquarters the night Sergeant French was killed.

After finishing the beer, Bankson said he and John Moore headed for Cairo Police Headquarters. Once again, Bankson claimed an official purpose. He said that since Cairo was larger than Mound City, the Cairo police must have a key to his handcuffs. Bankson said John Moore went with him to the police station but didn't go in. Inside was jailer Lutz, Mr. Sheehan, and "this fellow Paul, I didn't know him"; later Frank Fitzgerald came in. When asked if Cairo police chief James Cowell was present when he entered the police station, Bankson once again said he didn't remember. According to the sheriff's account, however, he asked the chief about his gun, and the reply was "God damn your gun, I don't care about you or your gun."[16]

Just then Sergeant French entered the police headquarters and Chief Cowell said, "There's the man that has your gun; ask him."[17] French was striding to the rear of the police station and Bankson asked him if he would be back "directly," to which French replied that he would. Upon returning from the toilet, Bankson said, French came within three feet of him. The sheriff said he was embarrassed by Chief Cowell's refusal to help him get his gun back. Then, according to the defendant, he asked French about handcuff keys, and when the sergeant said he had none, Bankson said, "Yes, and what about my gun?" The defendant then said French's reply was, "There's nothing doing about your gun," to which Bankson rejoined, "Is that so?" According to the defendant, the Cairo policeman then snarled, "I'll give you something so you won't need another gun," and hit him in the face between the eyes.[18]

The defendant then testified that French hit him between the eyes with what he thought was a pair of handcuffs. The defendant further testified that he fell back and tried to straighten up with his eyes full of blood. Being nearly blind in his left eye, he tried to wipe the blood out of his right eye. At this time, Bankson claimed, he had his gun out and was looking at French. Bankson testified that he said, "Hold up!," but someone hit him from behind on the back of the head.[19] Bankson said when the gun went off, the Cairo people were hitting him everywhere, and he didn't know if his pistol went off once or twice or where its bullets went. The defendant ended this part of his testimony by declaring that he had said, "I'm your fellow officer, don't beat me up."[20]

At that point Bankson declared that if he said, "You can kill me now, I've done what I wanted to," as Lawrence Paul had stated in his testimony, he didn't know what he was saying. Finally, the defendant pled a combination of accidental shooting and self-defense.

> *I shot because that man hit me; I did not shoot intentionally; I didn't shoot at any one; don't know how many times I was struck; I know when they handcuffed me; no one hit me with handcuffs. They took me to the county jail. On the way to the county jail Cowell abused me all the way, calling me all kinds of names, Cowell hit me in the breast. . . . Cowell said: "You God damn son of a bitch. I have a notion to kill you!" I said; "gentlemen pull off these handcuffs, and put me even with you and I'm game all right."*[21]

When asked at the close of the examination whether he intended to kill Officer French, he declared that he did not, that he only drew his gun to protect himself and pulled the trigger when he gripped the gun, as he was hit on the head by someone from behind.[22]

Both Cairo daily newspapers commented on Abner C. Bankson's performance on the witness stand in the Jonesboro courtroom. The *Cairo Evening*

*Citizen* stated that James Lingle of Union County, veteran prosecutor though he was, could not shake the former sheriff's story "on any material point."[23] Bankson, however, was also a problem for his defense attorneys. Frequently when asked to recall events that supported their defense, the defendant would say he didn't remember, as has been previously stressed. Yet when what he remembered seemed important to Bankson himself, "his memory seemed remarkably clear."[24]

The *Citizen* discussed Bankson's testimony in general and sought to gauge its impact upon his murder trial.

> *He was not what was called a good witness, for he talked too much and would not confine his remarks to answers to the questions of the attorneys, but he got a story before the jury that may cast a doubt in their minds as to his innocence of any intent to kill Officer French.*

Commenting specifically on the cross-examination of Bankson, the *Cairo Bulletin* observed that "Bankson was quite verbose in his answers and insisted on telling over again all details and making explanations." The *Bulletin* also noted that the spectators believed the defense was not now one of self-defense but of accidental killing.[25]

At that point the *Cairo Bulletin* covered every inconsistency in Bankson's testimony, taking up two columns in the small type of the time. On cross-examination "Ab" did not remember the name of the suspect he was going after in Kentucky on December 3, 1910. Then he said "De Bean" was the person he was after. Bankson stated he did not tell John Moore their destination, and later he said they were going to Fulton, Kentucky, on a run to look for "some negroes wanted for murder in Mound City." Finally, the defendant said he didn't know how he suspected the man (De Bean) was in Fulton.[26] On the stand, Bankson twice said he didn't remember how many pairs of handcuffs he had. Then he testified that he had three. As to the missing handcuff keys, the defendant said he lost them on the way to Cairo but thought he had them, then noticed them missing in Cairo. Finally he said he really didn't know where he missed them.

The *Bulletin* then turned to Bankson's erratic testimony of going to Cairo on September 23, 1910. First, he said he couldn't remember whom he was seeking as sheriff, then he said he was looking for the "party" that killed Hays Graddy. Second, the defendant said he was looking for the woman connected with the killing but had no particular woman in mind; however, he did find her. Third, Bankson said his defense attorney Phil Hileman knew the name of the man he was seeking. Finally, the defendant said he didn't remember when the crime was committed by the person he was seeking and his woman.[27]

Bankson then said he was not in the brothel on 13th Street on September 23, 1910, to see Myrtle Stevenson, who was probably the "harlot" the *Bulletin* accused him of installing at the "bawdy house" at 212 13th Street, where he was that night. The defendant said he couldn't remember how long he had known Stevenson; he admitted that he went to the "resort" to see her but could not remember how many times. Bankson testified that he didn't know if Stevenson phoned the police or not but denied calling her on the night of September 23, 1910, from a saloon on 8th and Commercial in Cairo and calling her "ugly names," as other witnesses had testified.

The defendant at that point told of the money allegedly taken from him by Sergeant French. The total amount he had when accosted by the Cairo policemen was $130. Bankson said he had five $10 bills in his right pocket, three $20 bills in his left pocket, and a $20 bill in his hand. He claimed that the policemen got $50 and his gun, although earlier he had claimed he was missing just $20. How would they have done this? Would the police have taken both twenties from his left pocket, but only one ten from his right pocket? Or could they have taken the twenty from his hand, one twenty from his left pocket, and one ten from his right pocket? It is reasonable to assume that if the police were going to take any money, they would take it all.

"Ab" Bankson testified that the police had his gun and that he saw Officer Skews later and asked for it back. As to Sergeant French, the defendant said the officer did not ask him to lie down at police headquarters on September 23, nor did the sergeant advise him to go home. When Bankson was asked where he spent the balance of the night, the defense objected and it was sustained.

Abner Bankson spent three hours on the stand testifying in his own defense, a risky and perhaps desperate move on the part of his defense attorneys. Observers in the courtroom said he was not a good witness because he talked too much and did not restrict his answers or comments to the questions he was asked. The purpose of his testimony was to cast doubt in the mind of at least one juror that he intentionally killed Wilfred French. If his testimony was not successful in this endeavor, he could face a public hanging. Bankson said he did not intend or desire to kill French, that he pulled his gun in self-defense, and that it went off only when he was hit on the back of the head. He concluded by testifying that he never even said a hard word to anyone in Cairo Police Headquarters and "I never had a fuss in Cairo in my life." The question was, would the jury believe him?

## CHAPTER TWENTY-THREE

# THE VERDICT

After showing how inconsistent and confusing Abner Bankson's testimony was, the *Cairo Bulletin* made a prediction that proved to be correct—that is, there would be a hung jury or an acquittal. The people in Union County must have also believed that the prosecution was defeated, because when rebuttal testimony was offered the day after Bankson's testimony, there was only a "very small crowd when the crier convened court Saturday morning." The first witness called was Cairo jailer Melchor Lutz, who explained an amended "map" of Cairo Police Headquarters. Lutz denied that Cairo police chief James Cowell had struck the defendant while escorting him between the Cairo police station and the county jail. Following Lutz to the stand was Chief Cowell himself, who was also asked whether he hit Bankson after he had been subdued. Prosecution lawyers objected to the question, which was sustained. When asked, Cowell denied cursing Bankson just prior to Wilfred French being killed.[1]

After Lutz and Cowell testified, Frank Fitzgerald, the city health officer, took the stand. He had substantiated Officer Lawrence H. Paul's and street supervisor John Sheehan's testimony before the coroner's jury a few days after the shooting. Fitzgerald had been in and out of the police station and thought Bankson was talking with the Cairo lawmen pleasantly enough when he stepped outside to speak with Officer Frank Hagey. Outside he heard three shots and ran in only to turn Sergeant French on his side and call a doctor. Having been about eight feet north of the police station as the shooting occurred, he adamantly argued that John Moore of Pulaski County, a defense witness, had been nowhere in sight at that time. Fitzgerald also said he did not see the two "negroes," George Fuqua and Nick Morrison, who had claimed to have seen the shooting, and stated that "Morrison's reputation for veracity was bad." On cross-examination Fitzgerald positively reiterated that they were not there.[2]

Officer Frank Hagey, who Fitzgerald testified was standing with him in front of the police station when the shooting occurred, echoed the health officer's statement that there was no one else standing outside Cairo Police Headquarters looking in. Officer Hagey was followed by John Bland McElligot, who testified that he was going north on Commercial Avenue when the three shots were fired and had reached a point just south of the police station. McElligot saw officers outside, just north of police headquarters, but saw no one else or anyone running across the street. After McElligot came Robert H. Baird, a grain inspector, who was walking with McElligot. Baird testified that he did not see Nick Morrison, George Fuqua, or John Moore in front of the building or anyone running across the street from the scene. He did see Officer Hagey and Frank Fitzgerald running into the police station immediately after he heard shots. Baird himself then fled the scene.[3]

Two witnesses, Peter Day and Charley Williams, corroborated Fitzgerald's testimony concerning Nick Morrison's truthfulness. Day said Morrison had worked for him for six years and stated that Morrison's reputation for veracity was bad; Charley Williams said it was "very bad." The attempt to impeach the most damning defense witness continued when Ben Bradley took the stand. Bradley was a police constable living at 504 Douglas Street, next door to Morrison at 502 Douglas Street. Bradley swore under oath he saw Morrison standing on his porch at 5:45 p.m. on December 3, 1910, so he couldn't have been blocks away at the police station.[4]

After Bradley came a surprise prosecution witness, Enos L. Cauble. Young Cauble was working at Corzine's livery stable in Jonesboro, where Alexander County deputy sheriff Ben Jones stopped with Abner C. Bankson after their long journey from Cairo. Enos Cauble heard Bankson say, "All I hated is that I didn't get the other damn son of a bitch."[5] Cauble's testimony might have been somewhat discounted, because he claimed Sheriff Fred Nellis was with Deputy Jones and the prisoner Bankson, when it had been established that Nellis was back in Cairo at the time.

Following the rebuttal testimony, the *Cairo Evening Citizen* declared the prosecution had delivered "proof" of certain facts in the case. It said that Chief Cowell's rebuttal testimony showed conclusively that Sergeant French had not spoken roughly with an oath to Sheriff Bankson at police headquarters and that Cowell had not struck the sheriff on the breast while taking him to the county jail. The newspaper claimed that the prosecution further proved by the testimony of Frank Fitzgerald and Frank Hagey that John Moore, George Fuqua, and Nick Morrison were not in front of police headquarters just before the shooting, which was substantiated by the new witnesses, John McElligot and Robert Baird. The *Citizen* also emphasized Morrison's reputation for not telling the truth.[6]

Judge Albert Lewis had allowed Nick Morrison to change his testimony with decided favor to the defense. Did either of the Cairo newspapers condemn him for this? On the contrary, the *Cairo Bulletin* even praised Lewis's conduct of the proceedings: "Not once during the whole trial was there a single exception to any ruling of the court. The court was eminently fair to both sides on all questions and won the admiration of the crowd by his quiet, gentle dignity."[7]

Following the rebuttal testimony, State's Attorney William D. Lyerle of Union County gave one of the closing arguments for the prosecution. The argument from the lawyer and Baptist minister was biblical. Lyerle said that law was from God, given to Moses on Mount Sinai, and that the Bible was filled with injunctions to obey the law and punish all offenders. Lyerle declared that Bankson's crime was grave and willful. Trying to anticipate the defense, Lyerle said that they would try to assassinate the character of the prosecution witnesses, as many of them were associated with the liquor trade—bartenders, saloonkeepers, and the like. The state's attorney said that these were the natural witnesses in a case involving Abner C. Bankson because he frequented such places. "The state is compelled to go to the resorts the defendant frequented for the story of the causes that led up to the crime," he reasoned.[8]

After Lyerle came the Carbondale defense lawyer, Louis M. Bradley, and the jury paid him "close attention." First, Bradley explained the law of self-defense to his own satisfaction. Second, he claimed that Bankson was being "framed" by the Cairo police. Third, trying to be eloquent, he called Cairo police chief Cowell "a cowardly puppy" for hitting Bankson when two men were holding him. Finally, Bradley became bitter, denouncing the Cairo police as liars and thieves. According to the *Cairo Bulletin*, Bradley's arraignment of the Cairo police was "terrific."[9]

Perhaps realizing that Bradley's total condemnation of the Cairo police was swaying a jury that didn't need much convincing to free "Ab" Bankson, Alexander County state's attorney Alexander Wilson told the jurors that they were now officers of the law. Wilson said that the jurors should withhold judgment until they had heard the court's interpretation of the law. Then the Cairo prosecutor went through a graphic description of French's killing, stressing this was a human being and a policeman who was shot down. Finally, Wilson commended French's fellow officers for the way they handled an extremely difficult situation totally by the law.[10]

Carl S. Miller of Mounds followed Alexander Wilson. Miller at the time was considered one of the best attorneys in Pulaski County. As Bradley had done, Miller attacked the Cairo police. Bradley had called them liars, and Miller charged that they were "coached" liars. Miller charged that the testimony of the Cairo policemen "tracked too closely."[11] Bradley had stressed Bankson's right to self-defense, and Miller tried to combine a self-defense argument with an accidental killing argument and then demonstrated how a blow on the back of the head would cause someone grasping a pistol with tense nerves and muscles to naturally pull a trigger. With irrelevance to Sergeant French's killing, Miller then began a discussion of the Cairo police's protection of "dive" saloons and bawdy houses. He was trying to put Cairo and the city's police on trial. His closing words were novel. Miller said that if any one of the jurors had reasonable doubts, then the entire jury must vote to acquit.

Another prosecutor, Angus Leek, of Cairo, came after Miller. The *Cairo Bulletin* said he made a defense of the Cairo police with "vim and vigor," but Leek should have known the Cairo police weren't legally on trial, and his words on their behalf played into the hands of the defense. Still, Leek did his best to remind everyone that "Ab" Bankson was the sole individual on trial. With biting sarcasm, he described Bankson's general behavior and his particular actions that led to Wilfred French's death. Leek ended his arguments at 4:15, and the jury was allowed to rest.[12]

The last defense attorney to argue was Phil Hileman of Jonesboro. Already well known as a man who could free an indicted person by swaying a jury at the last minute, Hileman, according to the *Cairo Bulletin*, was "brilliant" and gave the best effort of his life. Criminal lawyer Hileman took up where the other defense attorneys had left off. In his one-hour-and-ten-minute argument, he put the Cairo police in particular and Cairo government in general on trial and completely neglected to discuss whether his client was innocent or guilty. Instead, Hileman spoke of the police officer's oath to uphold the law. Yet here was Cairo with "rowdy houses" allowed to run in open violation of the law and with the consent of the police. The Cairo police were violating their oaths.[13]

At exactly 8:23 p.m., James Lingle, a seasoned prosecutor, reminded a packed courtroom, with people standing in the aisles, that Abner C. Bankson was the only one on trial—not Officer Skews or Chief Cowell or any other Cairo policeman.[14] Lingle dominated the room as none of the other lawyers had done and used few notes. Lingle made a last-ditch attempt to have the jury convict Bankson. In this last closing argument, Lingle spoke of mob law and how often it occurred because juries failed to do their duty and protected offenders. He spoke of the United States boasting of an advanced civilization while the country led the world in murders—1,500 a year. Criminal lawyer Phil Hileman jumped to his feet to object to this but was overruled by Judge Lewis. Attorney Lingle went on, trying to explain to the jury how difficult prosecution had become because all the evidence was a matter of public record, while the machinations of the defense were hidden from the people until the trial. The prosecution, Lingle said, could not bring the body of the murdered officer into court, nor could his aged mother attend the trial to excite the sympathy of the jury. Then James Lingle picked up Sergeant French's uniform coat and dramatically pointed to the hole in the back, referring to it "as a silent, truthful, and incorruptible witness." At that point Lingle said, "Do not cheapen and belittle the law of self-defense by a verdict supporting such a plea, when the victim has been shot in the back." According to the *Cairo Bulletin*, special prosecutor Lingle then went through the defense point by point and "riddled" the plea of Bankson's lawyers in his analysis of the testimony. The *Bulletin* also declared that before Lingle's closing argument, most of the spectators expected an acquittal, but now there was some doubt.[15]

The *Cairo Bulletin*, however, must have known that there was little doubt, if any, that Bankson would be found not guilty. The Cairo newspaper had hired two prominent Union County men to cover the trial for the daily—Edgar A. Davie of Anna and Edward Lee of Jonesboro.[16] In the beginning of the article covering the closing arguments of attorneys Phil Hileman and James Lingle, the *Bulletin* had written of a "report" that the jury was eleven to one in favor of acquittal, which was exactly the case when the verdict was released.[17] The *Bulletin* claimed that Judge Lewis had given strong instructions to the jurors that no word of their deliberations should "leak out" and had appointed men to guard the jury who would enforce this instruction.[18] This was perhaps true, yet Davie and Lee got information from someone even before the final closing arguments as to how the jury stood.

The jury was out for almost three days—sixty-five hours.[19] From the beginning of deliberation, or even before, however, eleven jurors were in favor of acquittal and only one wanted Bankson found guilty. There matters stood until the morning of June 6, 1911. After a breakfast for the jury, the lone dissenter assented to the will of the eleven. At 8:30 a.m., Judge Albert W. Lewis polled the jury, received the jurors' verdict, discharged them, and adjourned court.[20] Bankson was released immediately. His family, who had stayed at the courthouse for the whole sixty-five hours, met him with tears.

## CHAPTER TWENTY-FOUR

# THE ANALYSIS OF THE VERDICT AND ITS CONSEQUENCES

The former sheriff and his family took a train from Jonesboro, which, as it passed through the town of Ullin in Pulaski County, was greeted by a "great crowd" with flags and people shouting congratulations to "Ab" Bankson. When the train arrived in Pulaski, Illinois, Bankson's hometown, he was given an ovation by the people. Some must have wondered at the time how Bankson went from the father of a defeated candidate, himself disgraced, to a killer-hero to many of his fellow citizens in Pulaski County.

Cairo's evening newspaper, the *Cairo Evening Citizen*, did not wonder. A lengthy article on the front page of the paper, not the editorial page, outlined what the editors believed had set Bankson free. Near the end of the article the entire jury system was called into question.

> *It cannot be said that the case of the prosecution was not presented as strongly as it could be. Every scrap of evidence that could be introduced was presented, and the whole course of events was traced from the beginning of the trouble on Sept. 23, to the closing of the tragedy on Dec. 3, where Wilfred French was shot down in police headquarters.*
>
> *The defense had a powerful advantage which they made the most of in the feeling which had spread all over the country surrounding Cairo against the police force of Cairo. Whether one will agree that the feeling is justified or not, this sentiment is very strong and the defense had little trouble in appealing to the prejudices of the jurors that Bankson was the victim of a plot.*
>
> *We cannot but regard the verdict as other than a gross miscarriage of justice, and an added reason why our imperfect and antiquated jury system should be overhauled if not abandoned entirely.*

> *Verdicts like this do very much toward creating disrespect for law.*[1]

This was an extremely serious statement for the *Citizen* to make and a departure from earlier views expressed during the Cairo lynchings of 1909 and the attempted lynching of 1910. During those terrible and tragic events the Cairo newspaper was always supportive of law, order, and due process of law.[2] The *Citizen* had equated the vigilantism of 1909 and 1910 with mob rule. The paper had wanted Will "Froggie" James tried for the rape and murder of Anna Pelley in 1909 and did not expect him to be lynched. The paper applauded the quick but legal justice when John Pratt was sent to prison for twenty-eight years for purse snatching. The *Citizen* supported unconditionally Sheriff Fred Nellis when he defended with about a dozen men the same John Pratt from an armed lynch mob in 1910. Mob violence and general lawlessness, according to the newspaper, were destroying any positive reputation Cairo had and were costing the town investment and growth. The position of the *Citizen* from 1909 to the summer of 1911 had consistently been toward more respect for law rather than less. The paper over and over again called for laws on prostitution and gambling to be enforced to the letter in Cairo, and the *Citizen* called for new ordinances to control alcoholic beverages in the community and prevent the further spread of vice.

The *Cairo Evening Citizen* had been a voice of reform and due process of law in Cairo, but the killing of a police sergeant in police headquarters by a rural alcoholic sheriff without any punishment was too much for the newspaper. There had been too many unpunished murders in Cairo in the town's recent history. The *Citizen* viewed the French killing as a catalyst for disrespect of law bordering on contempt.

As might have been expected, the *Cairo Bulletin* was more extreme than the *Citizen* in condemning the freeing of Abner C. Bankson. The *Bulletin* referred to attorney James Lingle's waving of Wilfred French's clothing—"showing where the bullet from Bankson's pistol entered through the back and killed the man who had worn them"—a "silent and incorruptible" witness to the killing. The *Bulletin* raged that "a silent and incorruptible witness did not count as much as did witnesses, who can talk and who will lie themselves black in the face, if they are not already black by nature." Having condemned the defense witnesses of both races as liars, the *Bulletin* went on to sarcastically describe the Union County jury: "There are at least nine farmers in Union county who believe that a man killer may set up and maintain a plea of self-defense, even when he has shot his victim through the back."[3] The newspaper contrasted these men with most of the other farmers in Union County, who were intelligent enough to tend to their crops after a rain.

The next day, the *Cairo Bulletin* printed another editorial concerning the Bankson verdict. By then the paper must have had inside information on the jury deliberations, because the editorial declared that hostile feelings toward Cairo had largely shaped the verdict. Judging also from the arguments of the defense attorneys, the *Bulletin* charged that deep hostility toward the river city made the defense case.

> *One may almost declare that Bankson was not on trial at all, and the killing of Officer French was a trifling circumstance hardly worth considering in connection with the case; that the real culprit and prisoner at the bar was the police department of Cairo—and it was found guilty.*[4]

The *Bulletin* editors admitted that some of the victims of Cairo police misconduct resided in Union County, as well as in other counties in Illinois and surrounding states. Some of those who felt they had a grievance against the Cairo police, according to the *Bulletin*, came to the town to have "what they are pleased to call a good time, indulging in conduct that they would not dare to indulge in at home."[5] Bankson was such a man, the newspaper declared. He was different, however, from most of the others looking for a good time in Cairo. First, the paper argued, he was treated more leniently than the majority of offenders. Second, Bankson had no more respect for the people of his own community than for the people of Cairo. Indeed, the *Bulletin* emphasized Bankson's "disgraceful episodes, including several attempts to kill people who dared protest against his conduct," and pointed out that "Ab's" behavior had scandalized and outraged people in Pulaski and Alexander Counties for years. Bankson's conduct as a private roué and a public rowdy should have been as much before the jury in Union County as the past misconduct of the Cairo police.[6]

In the *Pulaski Enterprise*'s account of the Bankson not-guilty verdict, the misconduct of the Cairo police very much affected the jury. The *Enterprise* stated, "The evidence of the Cairo police seems to have been of little benefit to the prosecution, leaving them with little or no convincing testimony."[7] In other words, the jury did not believe a word of what the Cairo officers said. Set free by that jury, the *Enterprise* declared that "Mr. Bankson" was greeted by his faithful family and relatives, who had not left the courthouse day or night during the trial, with congratulations and tears. Then the weekly said

Bankson was met tearfully by many friends in Ullin and Pulaski. Continuing in this sentimental mode, the *Enterprise* described the Bankson greeters in Pulaski: "Everybody had a smile on their faces for they knew he was a free man and had proved himself clear in a hard fought trial."[8] Regardless of who the victim and his colleagues were, Abner C. Bankson had killed a man. The Pulaski County newspaper made "Ab's" return appear to be a celebration of the freeing of a wronged and beloved county citizen, not a lecher and a thug, as he was portrayed in the *Cairo Bulletin*.

Which newspaper was closer to the truth about Bankson, the *Bulletin* or the *Enterprise*? A letter to Carbondale's *Daily Free Press* by Mrs. L. M. Bradley, the wife of one of Bankson's defense attorneys, written before he was retained, could present a rather clear idea of "Ab's" general character and behavior at the time of the killing. Mary E. Williamson Bradley was a native of Mound City, Illinois, and an active prohibitionist. In the fall of 1907, Mound City had been voted "dry," and the saloons were closed. In the fall of 1909 another vote was scheduled to see if Mound City would be "dry" or "wet." Mrs. Bradley went home to fight for prohibition and was helped by bands of local schoolchildren who passed out anti-saloon tracts. Mrs. Bradley was then approached by Bankson, who told her she was wrong in what she was doing and making a great mistake. She listened to Bankson, having heard he was a very rich farmer in the prime of life, with a fine family and many friends. He was also the sheriff of Pulaski County. She may have heard also that he shot people who angered him, and this included women, although she did not mention "Ab's" gunplay in the letter.[9]

As an ardent prohibitionist, Mrs. Bradley was trying to contrast the man who had accosted her in Mound City in 1909 with the jailed Abner C. Bankson of February 10, 1911, the date of her letter:

> *A few weeks ago, that same man was brought to our Jackson county jail, to save him from a Cairo mob.*
>
> *After weeks of a drunken debauch, he shot and killed a man—his friend.*
>
> *His oldest daughter has, since, gone insane, because of this terrible deed and danger to her father.*
>
> *His money is gone—gone into saloons.*
>
> *His wife and younger children are broken-hearted, desolate, and disgraced. And he is a financial and mental wreck.*[10]

Mrs. Bradley may have had occasion to regret the letter to the editor when her husband, Louis Marion Bradley, became one of Bankson's defense lawyers. The letter, however, gives her appraisal of Bankson as generally similar to those found in the Cairo newspapers. That is, he was an alcoholic who stayed drunk for weeks and engaged in debauchery while in that state. Bankson was a killer, one who had murdered a man who tried to show him friendship. "Ab" was a terrible father who had driven his daughter to a state of mental illness because of the many horrible things he had done and disgraced his family by those acts. Finally—and this may have been most significant to the prohibitionist woman—Bankson's frequenting of saloons had ruined him financially as well as mentally.

Mrs. Bradley was trying to convey a moral lesson about the dangers of drink and the saloons that provided it. She was also giving a portrait of a man who was a danger to himself and to others, a man who was careless of the consequences that his actions had on others, especially his own family. Mrs. Bradley blamed the behavior on alcohol, but it cannot be totally explained by alcoholism. The man was dangerous and unpredictable, drunk or sober, especially to those who tried to help him.[11]

If there was ample evidence that Abner C. Bankson was a dangerous man, and that Sergeant French was not the first person "Ab" had shot with lethal intent, why did the Union County jury proclaim him "not guilty"? Was it because the jury's hostility toward Cairo and the Cairo police was so great that the jurors almost completely failed to consider French's killing and instead concentrated on prosecuting the Cairo police, as suggested in the *Cairo Bulletin*? Or, more charitably, did the jurors actually believe in a conspiracy by the Cairo police, as suggested by the *Cairo Evening Citizen*? If so, what could it have been?

There are a number of ways of evaluating the Union County jury's behavior. The first would be that the jurors did believe in a conspiracy on the part of the Cairo police. Surely, though, it was not to steal twenty dollars (a sum attested to by Bankson's own witnesses) or fifty dollars (the amount Bankson swore to, surprisingly, on the stand) and a .32-caliber revolver. But if not theft, what could have been the motivation of the Cairo police? Was it to humiliate and get rid of a sheriff from a neighboring county who was becoming a public nuisance? If that were so, why didn't Officers French and Skews arrest Sheriff Bankson on 13th Street on the night of September 23, 1910, which, according to both Skews and Bankson, they did not?

Were the Cairo policemen so clever that they were setting a long-range trap for "Ab" Bankson? The jury had heard testimony that Bankson came to police headquarters in Cairo two, three, or perhaps more times asking for his gun back. Thus it was reasonable for the Cairo policemen to expect him to return again to request his pistol. Did Chief Cowell and Sergeant French plot to give Bankson such a beating when next he entered police headquarters that he not only would be humiliated but also would be unlikely to frequent Cairo again? And would the plot be more likely to succeed because the Bankson family had been repudiated by Pulaski County voters in the recent November election? Did the police see their chance when Bankson was once again picked up on 13th Street on the night of December 3, 1910, knowing that his pattern was to go drinking around town for several hours after being released and then come ask for his gun?

If the Cairo police were plotting, it went tragically wrong when "Ab" Bankson managed to pull out a gun and kill Sergeant French. Probably, however, there was no plot. "Ab" Bankson may have been a public nuisance, but he was less likely to threaten the Cairo authorities now that he and his son were no longer Pulaski County lawmen. The Cairo police had larger problems to deal with than Bankson. The crime rate was high, mob violence could break out at any time, and it was widely held that Cairo streets were not safe at night.[12] Sergeant French may have hit Bankson in the head and sworn at him, and even stolen his gun, but these acts were probably not planned and should not have cost him his life.

Sergeant French was no angel and was at least a passive participant in gun theft and police brutality.[13] Bankson came to Cairo Police Headquarters looking for trouble, and he found it. It is more likely that he planned to shoot Wilfred French than that the Cairo Police Department plotted to give him a beating. And if the Cairo Police Department was as corrupt and brutal as Bankson and his attorneys claimed, would officers have not shot and killed Bankson when they got his gun away from him? They would have no fear of indictment, because vigilantism had never been punished in Cairo during the previous year and a half.[14] Finally, if the Cairo police were so lawless, why did they give Bankson over to Sheriff Fred Nellis and not wait for the mob, described by the righteous Mrs. Bradley, to become better formed? "Ab" Bankson could thank Providence, prejudice, and good criminal lawyers for his freedom.

If there was no plot against Sheriff Abner C. Bankson on the part of the Cairo Police Department, what role did prejudice possibly play in causing a Union County jury to turn Bankson loose? The answer to such a question would involve where Cairo stood in the estimation of the people in the surrounding counties, particularly in Illinois. First, consider Union County, where the jury declared Bankson not guilty. This was the home of Anna Pelley, who was raped and murdered in Cairo in November 1909, just nineteen months before.

The crime against Miss Pelley in Cairo had so inflamed Union County that thousands of men scoured the countryside between Anna-Jonesboro and Karnak looking for her suspected killer, Will "Froggie" James.[15] Even before the rape and murder, the town of Anna had a reputation of not liking "negroes" and did not "permit them to reside there," other than the fifty or so who were inmates at the state mental hospital in the town.[16] Ten African Americans were allowed to work at the rock quarry about a mile east of Anna until the day of the lynching. That night the managers of the "rock crusher" asked for deputies to protect their property and workers "but soon found that Anna was very much shy on men who would take the responsibility of protecting a nigger."[17] When a group of men from Anna marched to the quarry, the "negroes" had advance warning and "left for the woods and have not been heard of in that vicinity at last count."[18] The *Jonesboro Gazette* claimed that they "went to points where a nigger is more welcome. And we're much obliged to the managers of the crusher if they will confine their force to whites in the future."[19]

About 37 percent of Cairo's population in 1911 was black. This could not have been pleasing to the people in Union County's largest town, Anna. Cairo was where a poor white shopgirl could be sexually assaulted and strangled by a black man. For many if not most people in Union County, Cairo was a town whose people and police could not control their African American population.[20] Cairo even had black policemen, who could and did arrest white men.

It was the relationship between blacks and whites in Cairo that chiefly concerned Union County's oldest weekly newspaper, the *Jonesboro Gazette*, at the time of the attempted lynching in 1910. "The situation in Cairo is deplorable," it stated. "That unfortunate city has a problem on its hands, which we fear must be worked out in blood and tears. The insolence of negro criminals in choosing Cairo for their field of operations after the events of a few short weeks ago must be hard to brook."[21] The *Gazette* also had forcefully given its opinion of Cairo at the time of the lynching of Will "Froggie" James and Henry Salzner: "That town needs a cleaning from top down to the bottom up, and all Southern Illinois should unite in demand that it purge itself."[22]

The rare positive statement about Cairo appeared in the *Jonesboro Gazette* only after Will James was lynched. In an editorial titled "Well Done Cairo," the Union County weekly praised the vigilantism.

> *There was wild work in Cairo on the night of Nov. 11. But it was good work, well performed. Never was a mob more orderly, quiet, intent upon the business in hand—putting to death a beast who had no right to live. . . . After the lynching of those two, the state militia came, a whole regiment, and the other Negro beast, [Arthur] Alexander, has cheated justice, it is to be feared forever. He was found and arrested but put at once under the protection of the militia . . . , also the nigger accomplice, [Lovie] Green. . . . There are more details of the horrible outrage of the night of Nov. 8 that are too horrible to print, too awful to be uttered above a whisper. It is well that the white man became a law unto himself under such circumstances, for otherwise there would be no protection for white women abroad.*[23]

So there it was in black and white for Union County residents to read, that Cairo was rife with "negro" crime and white women were unsafe. Cairo, "the Crime Stained City," was only "partially redeemed" by a black "beast" being killed by white vigilantes, not by anything the police had done.[24] Thus, might the trial of Abner C. Bankson be a chance for twelve Union County men to show Cairo, especially its police force, what they thought of the town?

The other significant Union County newspaper, the *Anna Democrat*, agreed with its Jonesboro neighbor that the state militia protected only the guilty. The Anna newspaper called the double lynching in Cairo "a slight provocation." "Besides this act of calling out troops, every time a mean nigger kills somebody, simply encourages them to keep it up," stated the paper. "They know they had to be protected, penned up and well fed and then stand a chance of defeating justice when their cases come up for trial in the courts."[25] The *Democrat* went on to argue that the shielding of the guilty was especially true in Republican counties and towns (of which Alexander County and Cairo were examples) where the vote of the African American race was considered an asset.

When it came to "Ab" Bankson, however, protecting the guilty did not particularly concern the *Anna Democrat*. In an editorial titled "Cairo," which was reprinted in its entirety in the *Pulaski Enterprise*, the Anna paper began, "You have this week, in Union County reaped of the first fruits of the harvest of your unholy sowing. . . . You have lost this case because of the unsavory reputation of your officers of the law."[26]

Upholding the honor of Union County juries, the *Anna Democrat* argued that they had always been "strong" in the defense of law officers. Then, just as "Ab" Bankson's defense attorneys had done, the Anna newspaper attacked the Cairo police: "Only a small percent of the infamous charges made against your police force crept into the trial of this case, but there was enough of it, when added to the dexterous management of the defense to destroy your case."[27] The "dexterous defense," according to the *Democrat*, was showing "your police force to be so rotten that its members were unworthy of belief. . . . The verdict could not have been averted."[28]

The Anna weekly warned against abuse of the jury, as the *Cairo Bulletin* had done. The *Democrat* proclaimed if everyone in Union County had been divided up into twelves, each group would have brought in a not-guilty verdict long before the actual jury did. Commenting on the intense local interest, Anna's press proclaimed, "There have been few cases tried in Union County where the verdict was so eminently satisfactory. . . . The defendant was a stranger to our people, but the reputation of the police force of Cairo was not."[29]

As always seemed to be the case in the early years of the twentieth century, when Cairo was discussed in another town's press, race was brought into the discussion. "There are few places in Union County where a negro is allowed to live. Our people have but little use for a negro, and yet the defense pitted a negro against your police force and created a reasonable doubt in the minds of the jury," stated the *Anna Democrat*.[30] At that point the *Democrat* surveyed Cairo's recent history, saying that during Cairo's 1909 and 1910 mob violence, police officers did not intervene and a company of militia did nothing. After the first incidence of mob violence the governor of Illinois removed the county sheriff from office, and after the second he had charges brought against the militia captain. In the *Democrat*'s account, the "best people" "lionized" the sheriff and the captain "bought them diamonds." During the second mob action, there was a sheriff "who kept his oath and defended his prisoner and your best citizens damned him and defeated him."[31]

With liberal use of the N-word and admitted "little use for a negro," it was odd for the *Democrat* to criticize Cairo people for defeating a sheriff at the polls who defended African American prisoners. It seemed, however, that the purpose was to kick Cairo when the town was down, not to be consistent or even logical in presentation. The *Democrat*, perhaps unwittingly, confirmed what the *Cairo Bulletin* had charged. That is, Bankson's guilt or innocence was beside the point of his Union County trial; the *Bulletin* did not say Bankson was guilty or innocent but rather that the reputation of the Cairo police deprived the prosecution of even a chance for a conviction.

Having blasted the Cairo Police Department as a pack of liars, the *Democrat* added charges of police brutality, saying if members of the Cairo press knew the methods used to obtain convictions in Alexander County, they would be appalled. The Anna weekly then coupled the Cairo newspapers with their police as deserving of criticism. The *Democrat* snarled sarcastically, "Your newspapers have discovered that the reputation of your police force was the cause of the verdict, but they charge that the jury was prejudiced thereby."[32] Then the Anna weekly admitted that the jury *was* prejudiced against the Cairo police officers: "The jury weighed your police in the balance of equal justice and from the evidence concluded that its members were not worthy of belief."[33]

The *Anna Democrat*, echoing the criminal lawyers at the Bankson trial, claimed the Cairo cops were unworthy of belief because they violated their oath by allowing brothels such as the one at 212 13th Street to exist.

> *That each of them took an oath to enforce the law. That under our statute that place was an outlaw. That every day it continued your police were perjurers. That is, they would commit perjury to enable that place to continue its debauchery; they would commit perjury to hang a man who killed their commander.*[34]

Whatever the "oath defense" lacked in logic, either in court or in the *Anna Democrat*, it revealed once again what prosecutor James Lingle, also of Union County, had said in his final argument—the Cairo police were on trial as much as or more than Abner C. Bankson. The jury was prejudiced against Cairo in general and its police in particular, and if the *Anna Democrat* and the *Jonesboro Gazette* truly reflected public opinion, they were agreeing with most of the people in Union County. Ending the scathing editorial titled "Cairo," the Anna weekly made one final observation concerning the river city: "Your reputation is a stench and whether or not it is true, it is here and you should make some effort to remove it instead of making so many efforts to make it worse."[35]

Since the *Pulaski Enterprise* reprinted this utter condemnation of Cairo and the Cairo police, it is safe to assume that the opinions expressed were shared by that weekly. The thoughts of most of the people of Pulaski County must have also been quite negative toward the river city, if the crowds celebrating Bankson's not-guilty verdict are any indication.[36] Some of the largest crowds in the county's history to that point turned out to celebrate the release of a "cop killer." Was it that the crowds were so happy that their former sheriff was free, or that his freedom was an ultimate reproof to the river city and to the Cairo police?

The Cairo Police Department certainly had problems in 1911. The officers made up a corrupt police force in a corrupt town. They had over sixty retail liquor establishments to patrol and two blocks on both sides of 13th Street filled with "bawdy houses," and the prostitution problem was spreading to other streets in town.[37] The murder rate in Cairo compared to any western town and was growing worse under Mayor George Parsons's administration, according to the *Cairo Bulletin*.[38] Women did not go out alone at night unless they were armed or extremely brave.[39] As the distinguished local attorney and author John M. Lansden said, Cairo in 1911 had a "hard name."[40] And, the Cairo policemen were hard men. One regional newspaper called them "corrupt and brutal."[41] In an environment of heavy alcohol use, vice, and gambling, would the Cairo officers not have to be tough to the point of brutality? In a fifteen-year period, three Cairo officers were killed in the line of duty. Being a Cairo police officer was not a job for someone who could not face violence.

So the Cairo police took shortcuts in protecting themselves and their town, and they may also have augmented their meager pay by relieving Cairo's many drunks of whatever money they had on them when they were put in the city jail. Cairo was a "wide-open" town, and police behavior both reflected that fact and was influenced by it. A rough town made for rough police justice, sometimes administered directly by the police. In 1910 and 1911 the Cairo police were particularly concerned with rural men, such as "Ab" Bankson, bringing their guns into town, which could only add to the worrisome death toll.[42] If some farmer pulled a gun on them and they took it away, as alleged in the Bankson case, it was not unlikely that the Cairo police would beat the gun player.[43] Thus, several if not many rural Southern Illinoisans had reason to fear and loathe the Cairo police and Cairo.

Cairo, therefore, faced a dilemma. The town wanted to grow and prosper. Businessmen wanted to attract people from counties such as Union and Pulaski into town. The attractions, however, were of a wrong kind to build a safe and well-thought-of community. The major attractions to Cairo were alcohol—one could get a drink at any time of day or night—followed by prostitution, with dozens of "houses of ill fame" on 13th Street and elsewhere in Cairo. Since the officials stayed in power and individually prospered because of the trade in alcohol and vice, Cairo's "wide-open" status was not likely to change.

"Wide-open" Cairo not only attracted rural people with drink and sex but also was easily accessed by them. Many major railroads passed through Cairo: the Illinois Central, the Mobile & Ohio, the Big Four, the New York Central, and the Missouri Pacific. If a farmer or a townsman got on the IC in Anna or the M&O in Jonesboro, he could be in Cairo in thirty minutes for little money.[44] Passenger trains ran frequently, so the wait for one would not be long. Union County residents could be on 13th Street quite soon, depending on how many saloons they stopped at on the way. For Pulaski County residents it would be even easier to come to Cairo. They could get on the IC in Mounds and get off at 10th Street in Cairo, three blocks from 13th, in ten minutes. More convenient and cheaper was the interurban, a streetcar-like conveyance that ran from Cairo to Mounds to Mound City and back again.

People from Union and Pulaski Counties, therefore, could easily go to Cairo to drink, have sex, and even gamble without fear of the home folks knowing about it. Could they not have a positive image of the town in something of the way contemporary Americans have of Las Vegas? Some probably did. Cairo, however, was a dangerous place. One could get "cleaned out" by dishonest gamblers, be beaten up by crooked and fearful cops, be shot or stabbed in a saloon, be fed a "Mickey" in the same place, be "rolled"—that is, have one's money stolen—in a "bawdy house," or perhaps contract a sexually transmitted disease.[45] So the people of Union and Pulaski Counties had little reason to like Cairo or wish the town and its police force well, especially if they were "country folk," such as the Union County farmers on the jury who acquitted "Ab" Bankson, or "hicks" who were targeted by the "tinhorn" gamblers, bad barkeeps, and malicious madams.[46]

Was the negative opinion of Cairo shared by people in Union and Pulaski Counties likely to have been Cairo's image statewide or even nationwide? Probably it was. Cairo had recently received publicity across the country as a city of lynching and mob violence in 1909 and 1910. The newspaper reporters who covered Cairo during the lynchings and mob violence of 1909 and the attempted lynching of 1910 had discovered a city awash in alcohol, teeming with prostitutes, and possessing a race problem. These newsmen made no secret of Cairo's shortcomings in the material they wrote while they were in town. Cairo's bad reputation spread and grew worse.

Cairo's bad reputation, especially with respect to race and lawlessness, affected both white and black Cairoites. Perjury, for example, seemed to come easily to Cairo witnesses when they appeared in court. Was Nick Morrison really in front of the Cairo police station the exact moment when

"Ab" Bankson shot Wilfred French? We have reason to at least doubt it, since it was confirmed only by men who were associates of Bankson and by his defense lawyers. The year before, all the men in the attempted lynch mob who were indicted by a grand jury had precisely the same story, which was confirmed by everyone testifying in their behalf.[47] Was this a unique moment in American judicial history, where every witness gave the same true testimony, or, as seems more likely, clever coaching of the witnesses by skilled lawyers? If black people, such as Morrison, could be bought to testify falsely in court and black votes could be bought to elect city and county officials, why worry about protecting these and their other civil rights? If lynchings and attempted lynchings went totally unpunished in Cairo, in a town that was apparently already unusually lawless, why would individuals bring their business to Cairo? Even if one worked in Cairo, might it be possible because of good transportation to live somewhere else?

In 1911, Cairo's reputation grew worse, and the town's prospects for success and progress dimmed. The trees were being cut out of Southern Illinois with the consequent effect on the lumber industry, and railroad transportation was becoming less important. The same could be said of river traffic. Always a problem, flooding and seepage into the town during high water became particularly severe during the 1912–13 floods. Both floods broke railroad levees and inundated the drainage district, which contained much

Resentment of Cairo by other towns in the region is old and was expressed in this 1913 Max Stein postcard titled "Flooded to save Cairo, Ill." Postcard courtesy of Darrel Dexter.

of Cairo's industry, including Sears Roebuck Illinois Lumber Manufacturing Plant.[48] Fear of flooding would always make Cairo an unattractive place for factories. Finally, the alcohol trade may not have been particularly good for Cairo's reputation, but it was the major dollar earner for Cairo. In one holiday week, Cairo had recently shipped 200,000 express orders of wholesale liquor.[49]

A long, slow, agonizing decline for Cairo was beginning, with the town more and more dependent on an economy of retail alcohol and vice, with all their attendant problems. Eventually, in the mid-1950s the town would be "cleaned up," with at least gambling and prostitution banished. By then, however, it was probably too late. Major factories had already closed and the population had declined by about 3,500 people. Cairo's racial problems had become very serious and in the 1960s would explode into violence, or what the *Washington Post* called "race war."[50]

What of Cairo police chief James Cowell and the other survivors of "Ab" Bankson's shooting in Cairo Police Headquarters on December 3, 1910? Chief Cowell was fired as chief of police in May 1911, even before the Bankson trial commenced. Mayor Parsons and the city council, over the strenuous objections of Alderman C. V. Neff, reappointed the former corrupt police chief Martin S. Egan.[51] There was, however, an opening as night sergeant with Wilfred French's death. This was filled by James Cowell, who must have thought over and over about the evening when his predecessor was gunned down right in police headquarters. Perhaps Father James Gillen at St. Joe's had the best question concerning the future of Cairo, Illinois, when he said at Sergeant Wilfred French's funeral, "Must this fair city of ours go ever in garments spattered with blood?"

# CONCLUSION

If Cairo was to be forever bloodstained, as charged by one of the river city's own Catholic priests, many local people and state and national observers would always see Anna Pelley's murder and Will "Froggie" James's lynching as the most unforgettable of times when blood flowed in the town. The national press coverage and comments on Cairo's double lynching became part of what student of American lynching Ashraf H. A. Rushdy called the "discourse of lynching."[1] According to him, it was during the "Age of Lynching," 1890 to 1940, that American lynching took on its most brutal form, occurred most regularly, and assumed great prominence and importance in American culture, becoming a gauge of that culture. Rushdy emphasized in his work the importance in American culture of lynching as a spectacle.[2] The double lynching of Will James (black) and Henry Salzner (white) was certainly a spectacle. An estimated 10,000 people attended the James lynching either as participants or spectators. Blazing lights were turned on, James was lifted up a number of times for the mob to see, and he was drawn up by a rope around his neck from a decorative steel arch on Cairo's most prominent street corner. When the rope broke and James fell, his body was dragged toward the river and then riddled with hundreds of bullets. Finally, his heart was cut out, his hanging rope soaked with his blood, and his body burned.

James's lynching was sanctioned by local newspapers and several other papers across the country because there seemed to be little doubt that he had raped and murdered Anna Pelley. Her rape received particular comment both locally and in the outside press. Local newspapers defended her honor and purity. The *Belleville News-Democrat*, for example, wrote of a "virgin girl," an "innocent girl outraged by a fiend."[3] Even though Anna Pelley was twenty-four years old at the time of her death and it may have been widely known in the community that she had a relationship with a Cairo policeman (and perhaps there was speculation about the extent of that relationship),[4] she was portrayed as a "girl" defending her honor and not as a woman defending her life. She was, after all, murdered.

The Cairo Police Department and members of the Cairo City Council, 1910. From the author's private collection.

Why would newspapers both in Cairo and elsewhere emphasize the rape instead of the murder? It may have been because in the "discourse of lynching" in America, sexual assault was considered the most important criminal activity justifying lynching. There was a "rape myth" abroad in the United States that broadcast the idea that the only way to protect white girls from rape was to lynch rapacious black "fiends," "brutes," and "beasts."[5] The southern lecturer and writer Rebecca Latimer Felton called for lynchings in the thousands to protect white women's chastity.[6] U.S. senator Ben "Pitchfork" Tillman declared he would rather have his daughters devoured by wild animals than raped by a "black fiend."[7]

Despite America's obsession with rape by African Americans, only about 25 percent of black men lynched were even accused of rape. Almost 30 percent of black lynching victims were charged with murdering whites, as Anna Pelley had been murdered. The largest percentage of black people lynched were murdered for minor offenses such as theft, "sassiness," or other breaches of the American racial code.[8] The rape myth, however, was powerful and widely believed by white Americans. It had animated the lynch mobs in Springfield, Illinois, in 1908 and in Cairo in 1909. Anna Pelley's rape was an actual fact; she had been sexually assaulted. Thus, the local newspapers could use a readily available justification for mob action and attract sympathetic support regionally and even nationally for the town's lynchings.

The Cairo lynchers and their apologists could also count on the support of Americans who believed that justice was widely being cheated or fatally delayed and that reliance on due process of law was becoming increasingly futile in the United States because of criminals in the guise of lawyers, packed juries, weak judges, and state governors who issued pardons.[9] In the days immediately following Cairo's double lynching there were some racially charged discussions in the Cairo press, but the majority of the rhetoric was directed at the denial of justice in the river city's recent past.

Even one of the ministers who spoke on the Sunday following Cairo's double lynching declared that the failure of the courts to deliver righteous judgments caused the people to take vengeance into their own hands, and editor Edward W. Thielecke of the *Cairo Bulletin* not only condemned judicial incompetence but also called city and county officials corrupt "weaklings."[10] Letters from ordinary Cairo citizens to the press echoed complaints with local officials and the courts. One of these especially blasted juries as composed of "illiterate, incompetent, weak unsophisticated men who are hunted up by the hirelings of the officers and made jurors, who weigh the evidence, but who are not competent to judge it and are easily swayed by lawyers, who scorn and laugh at justice."[11]

Did that person who wrote to the Cairo daily newspaper know what he was talking about? The same themes were repeated by another correspondent with the daily. The next letter writer had no doubt of either Will James's or Henry Salzner's guilt of "crimes unspeakably horrible."[12] The writer, however, pointed out that the evidence against both men was largely circumstantial and that both could have been freed, since such miscarriages of justice had happened before in Cairo. The correspondent also observed that "the strongest evidence will avail nothing against unscrupulous lawyers and packed juries."[13]

The last word on the subject of justice denied in Cairo and Alexander County at the time of the double lynching might have come from E. A. Burnett, the former editor and publisher of the *Cairo Bulletin*. In a letter to that paper, Burnett said, "The court history of several years was evidence enough to show the day was coming when Judge Lynch would hold court in Cairo."[14] Burnett then mentioned "quibbling lawyers and packed juries." Finally, the former editor wrote that he and the present editor both knew if James and Salzner had been tried and convicted, there would have been appeals, new trials, and the final freedom of the pair.[15]

Cairoites and former residents seem to have been in considerable agreement at the time that the double lynching of 1909 was justified because of the town's legal history. Killers were set free, killings went unpunished, and cases such as Henry Salzner's seemed to never come to trial. Even if this was a sincere expression of Cairo sentiment because of victims left unavenged, it was still convenient justification for mobbing after the fact. This defense of mob action was so common at the time that it became part of Rushdy's "discourse of lynching."[16] It was there to be used, and the Cairo daily newspapers used it to an extent to justify their townsmen and others killing two men without due process of law.

No direct local affirmation of the concept of popular sovereignty, with respect to the James and Salzner lynchings, has come down to us, but one emanating from the *Bellville News-Democrat* approvingly reprinted in the *Cairo Bulletin* stated the principle in rather extreme terms and thus bears repeating:

> *What is the sense in raving and panting against a people, vulgarly called a mob, who have temporarily taken the law into their own hands and avenged an awful crime and meted out rough justice? They are the state. . . . They have performed the supremest function of organized society.*[17]

Most of the Cairo people who either participated in the town's double lynching or witnessed the acts would have perhaps not have been sophisticated enough to argue popular sovereignty as the sufficient reason for their actions. A year later, however, when Cairo men voted not to elect a sheriff who had resisted with gunfire a lynching attempt, it was affirmed that a majority of the electorate believed "the people" (whoever they might be) had a right to take the law into their own hands. Even before this clear expression of popular will, every man charged with rushing the Alexander County Courthouse with the purpose of lynching purse snatchers was found not guilty by a Cairo jury. Thus, the "rough justice" approved by the *Belleville News-Democrat* was supported by a rough political theory of popular sovereignty, which if it could not be articulated by many of the people who believed it was nevertheless real.

Also real was racial conflict in Cairo in 1909 and 1910. A lynching of a black man and the attempted lynching of two more African Americans in those years are certainly proof. Were these outbreaks of mob violence, however, proof of the use by Cairo whites of organized terrorism to control black people and others who deviated from community standards, which has been so often mentioned in studies of American lynching?[18] This may be doubted from the existing evidence, although if Sheriff Fred Nellis and his interracial group of deputies had not fired on the mob of attempted lynchers in 1910 and driven them off, such racial terrorism might have become an active tool for white supremacy in Cairo.

If the Cairo lynchings and attempted lynching were not based on terrorism designed to control the town's black population, does it mean that white Cairo saw little or no reason for the controlling of black Cairo? The answer would have to be no. Of Cairo's two daily newspapers, the *Cairo Bulletin* had the largest circulation, and it charged that 85 percent of all criminals in the river city were black and that African Americans dominated the local Republican Party. The *Cairo Bulletin* then argued that the Republican organization protected the "bad" African Americans and celebrated the activities of attorney Reed Green. Green, according to the *Bulletin*, in the 1910 election campaign charged Sheriff Fred Nellis (Republican) with being the "avowed friend of negro ex-convicts and lechers of Cairo."[19]

The *Cairo Bulletin* was consistently anti-black and often overtly racist and some years later applauded the fact that the African American portion of the river city's population was dropping.[20] The newspaper's solution to the racial problem, however, was not terrorism—the *Bulletin*'s support for the lynchings of 1909 was certainly not unqualified, and the paper condemned the attempted lynching of 1910. The *Cairo Bulletin* wanted to control black people politically by defeating the local Republican Party in elections. The *Bulletin*'s reasoning was that if the county sheriff and other local Republicans no longer protected and extended a measure of equality to African Americans, the town would no longer be attractive to black in-migration. What little power black people had in Cairo was largely political. Reduce that significantly, and control and suppression of the African American community would follow.[21]

With black political power in Cairo under attack in 1909–10 by whites seeking greater control of African Americans in the river city, partisan elections proved to be too uncertain as a means for the white majority to dominate the black minority politically and in other ways. In 1913 the commission form of government was introduced as a reform measure. The four commissioners and the mayor were elected at large from throughout the city, which meant that the white majority would always elect each commissioner and the mayor.[22] Now black political power was indirect and could only be funneled through white politicians, chiefly Republicans. Even before this destruction of largely independent black politics in Cairo, the usual problems associated with a white majority–black minority electorate were already present. Black votes were being bought, and as seen in the trial of former sheriff Abner C. Bankson, African Americans were being encouraged to commit perjury for financial gain.[23]

Whether because of the loss of political power or because greater opportunity seemed to be looming in Chicago and East St. Louis, less than a day's train ride away, Cairo's African American population declined by 434 persons when the next census figures were revealed in 1920.[24] Black people in Cairo were voting with their feet and were apparently looking for greater opportunity and equality elsewhere. Did the decline of black Cairo portend a decline of all Cairo?

Certainly there were signs of stress in Cairo in 1909–10, even as the town continued to grow into the next decade. The dilemma for Cairo during the Progressive Era was that the town's growth and prosperity depended on its alcohol sales, as well as on a widespread and notorious population of prostitutes and gambling. The existence of the latter two was greatly corrupting, since they were illegal and the alcohol trade would become illegal with Prohibition ten years later. The police had to be paid off and the city council placated also with monies. Crime and violence in the form of lynchings, attempted lynchings, and killings plagued the town. Cairo was known as a "wide-open" town and suffered the consequent extremely bad publicity that such a status entailed. And in addition to Cairo's growing reputation for lawlessness, the city faced economic decline brought on by changes in railroad and river traffic and the dwindling lumber industry in Southern Illinois.[25]

The river city was also a repository for much of the state and national media's more virulent condemnation. White Cairo was branded by the *Chicago Tribune* as a nest of "river rats" and the creator of a "crazed, brutalized, inhuman mob."[26] The *New York Times* referred to the 1909 lynchings as "an orgy of blood and murder."[27] The *St. Louis Post-Dispatch* saw "madness" and "barbarism" in the double lynching.[28] The lynchings were called "human savagery" and examples of "human degradation."[29] Even southern newspapers publicized Cairo as lawless. As might have been expected, black Cairo fared worse in the American press than even white Cairo. Will James was characterized as a "brutal negro," a "black brute," "a brute in human form," and a "cowardly coon."[30] Cairo's African Americans were described as "the cheeky niggers down there, the rankest in the state of Illinois."[31]

Why did the Belleville newspaper find black people in Cairo "cheeky" and the "rankest" in Illinois? It was probably because Cairo African Americans had built a community with considerable racial pride and some accomplishment. Cairo blacks also had great influence in the Republican Party in their city and in Alexander County, and their votes allowed that party to either dominate or compete successfully with local Democrats. The Belleville paper was a Democratic organ, and it would have had as little liking for Republicans as it apparently had for African Americans.

About three months after such editorials appeared in the *Belleville News-Democrat*, in February 1910 the attempted lynching in Cairo occurred. If anything, the press reaction was more extreme than it had been to the double lynching of 1909. Leading American newspapers criticized Sheriff Fred Nellis's use of black deputies to defend the courthouse, either not realizing or not caring that it was those lawmen who likely were the ones who fired into the lynch mob and drove it off.[32] Once again Cairo's white people were described extremely negatively: "And from every dive and den in Cairo went up the endorsing cheers of thugs and hoodlums."[33] These "thugs and hoodlums" in Cairo were now seen in their nation's press not only as thwarted lynchers but also as hardcore potential rioters who would attack Cairo's black community and drive out the town's African Americans.[34]

Throughout February 1910 and beyond, the extreme criticism and negative coverage of Cairo continued unabated. The town was called a "lynching center," a "mob-ridden city," and a place where the mob spirit never died.[35] The *Cairo Bulletin* summarized the media's treatment of the river city by bemoaning the fact that "Cairo's name has been dragged in the mire from ocean to ocean and from the lakes to the gulf; a community to be shunned who would live in peace and prosper."[36] Cairo was presented as a town seething with racial tensions, awash in alcohol, teeming with prostitutes, and inhabited by whites who were barbaric river rats and by brutish blacks prone to raping white girls. The media characterized Cairo as an exceptionally bad place, inhabited by exceptionally bad people.

Such coverage persisted throughout the twentieth century and continues into the twenty-first. In 1954, *Life* magazine, then America's most popular periodical, highlighted a four-foot neon arrow that pointed to the home of a local white attorney, David Lansden, who was using his legal expertise to foster integration of the Cairo schools. The flashing sign was placed there by a neighbor to point out the target for those throwing rocks and bricks at Lansden's house or otherwise vandalizing it.[37] In the 1960s, 1970s, and 1980s, the *New York Times* put Cairo's racial troubles into the nationally read newspaper, and the *Washington Post* proclaimed race war in the river city.[38] A recent offering on the Internet proclaimed its findings in a piece on Cairo: "Death by Racism."[39]

These were simplistic portraits of a racially troubled community, and they singled out one suffering town unfairly. There was white racism in

Cairo in 1909–10 and throughout the twentieth century. White racism, however, was not confined to Cairo, and it was not even particularly brutal there, even in 1909–10. In Springfield, Illinois, in 1908, there was arson and looting and white lynch mobs fighting the police and the National Guard and killing several African Americans. In Cairo in 1909, mobs melted away when the soldiers came and the police emerged. One black person and one white person were lynched, but there were no fires and no looting. Cairo, Illinois, failed to solve its racial problems in the 1960s and 1970s, but so did the entire United States. They are not yet resolved.

How then did racial problems in Cairo affect the town's future, and did they, as the American media has usually charged, cause Cairo's drop in population from 15,203 in 1920 to an estimated 2,200 today? It should be kept in mind that towns never identified as particularly racially troubled all along the Ohio River valley have drastically lost population in the last hundred years. For example, Mound City, a town not ten miles from Cairo, has shrunk from a thriving United States naval base during the Civil War to a town of about 450 people. Indeed, there are now only about 5,500 people in all of Pulaski County.[40] Another river town, Thebes, Illinois, on the Mississippi—twenty-five or so miles from Cairo—was in deep distress as early as 1958, with stores closed, streets empty, and relief checks said to be the largest source of local income.[41] Long before the severe racial problems of the late 1960s and early 1970s, Cairo had already lost 15 percent of the town's population. Indeed, as one author pointed out, all of Southern Illinois was "somewhat south of prosperity," with the city of Centralia losing 15 percent of its population between 1940 and 1950, like Cairo. In the same census period, other Southern Illinois cities experienced significant declines in population: Johnston City, 17 percent; Zeigler, 16 percent; Salem, 15 percent; and West Frankfort and Eldorado, 8 percent.[42] Economics probably had more to do with the river town's decline than any other factors, including extremely unfavorable media attention and racial conflict. Cairo, Mound City, and Thebes were rapidly losing people and jobs even before Cairo and America's racial conflict became inflamed in the 1960s, but so was all of Southern Illinois.

What then does race and racism in Cairo have to do with the town's growth and success throughout the twentieth century and into the twenty-first? Every community south of the "dead line," where no black people were supposed to live—Cairo, Mounds, Mound City, Olmstead, Ullin, Tamms, Joppa, and Metropolis—has experienced economic distress at least since the late 1950s.[43] Many of the towns have been reduced to mere hamlets.

Racism is everywhere in Illinois, as Dr. Martin Luther King Jr. found when he tried to champion equal housing in the neighborhoods of Chicago.[44] In Southern Illinois, however, racial *strife* is not everywhere—in many places there simply are no African Americans.

It may be remembered that the woman for whose rape and murder Will "Froggie" James was lynched in Cairo in 1909, Anna Pelley, was from Anna, and Sheriff Abner Bankson of Pulaski County was tried for the killing of Sergeant Wilfred French in the sister town of Jonesboro. Anna and Jonesboro were "sundown towns" with no black residents in 1909–10, or even well into the twentieth century. By 2000 the official population of Anna was 5,190. By that time Cairo's population had dropped to below 4,000, where it once had been easily twice that of Anna and Jonesboro combined. Is it a coincidence that white Anna-Jonesboro grew, albeit slowly, in the ninety years between 1910 and 2000 and an interracial Cairo declined to the point of extinction in the same time period? The town that survived nicely through the twentieth century was all white. The town that increasingly was seen as dying a slow, painful death had 37 percent black people in 1909–10, and the small population that remains today is 71 percent African American and only 29 percent white. Cairo tried to imitate another Mississippi River town, Hannibal, Missouri, by inviting tourists to its restored 1867 custom house and historic library, but as pointed out by *Time* magazine in an article in 2000, which devoted considerable sympathetic space to Cairo, in Hannibal during the Tom Sawyer festival there were lots of little Toms and Beckys running around but no ("Nigger") Jims.[45]

So in the twentieth century in Illinois, it appears that having the black race in a town penalized the community because of what Saul Alinsky theorized as the 5 percent threshold of white interracial tolerance. If the community was above 5 percent African American, outside white people did not want to move in. In 1909–10, Cairo was about 37 percent black, which dropped significantly in later decades, but by 1950 the town had again become 37 percent African American. Why this jump after Cairo's black population had declined at Cairo's apogee in 1920? One source argued that in the 1930s and 1940s, Illinois established a much better welfare system than either Kentucky or Missouri, and this created a rush of poor people, most of them African Americans, across the Ohio and Mississippi Rivers to Cairo, especially from Southeast Missouri.[46]

How could there be such an occurrence in the state of Illinois, where a town such as Anna, which effectively banned black people, did well, while Cairo—the town that had been white and black from the beginning of the twentieth century—became nearly a ghost town by the twenty-first? James W. Loewen in his *Sundown Towns: A Hidden Dimension of American Racism* points out that there was never any sanction or enforcement against sundown towns in Illinois or nationally.[47] When even temporary black workers were driven out of Anna-Jonesboro in 1909 on the occasion of Anna Pelley's rape and murder, no one was arrested, and neither the state nor the federal government interfered.[48] So for the next ninety years the white people of Anna-Jonesboro were free to work at the Anna State Hospital in town or to commute a few miles to Carbondale for employment with Southern Illinois University, which was an Illinois institution receiving federal aid. Anna-Jonesboro, however, was not the only Southern Illinois town that faced no repercussions for going "sundown." As late as 1954, following a murder and an attempted rape by two black men in Vienna, Illinois, the small African American community within the town that dated back to the Civil War was burned out, with people running for their lives. The 2000 census recorded one black resident in Vienna, but the town also has a medium security prison for the locals to work in provided by the state of Illinois.[49]

The most egregious example of the federal government's indifference to the existence of communities from which African Americans were excluded, and one that involved Cairo, occurred in the 1970s. The Southern District of Illinois federal court held sessions in East St. Louis and Cairo, Illinois, from about the end of the Civil War through the 1960s. But in the 1970s the Cairo sessions were moved to Benton, Illinois, which was long known as a sundown town and was unapologetic about it.[50]

It must be admitted that the racial upheavals in Cairo, particularly in the 1960s and 1970s, were very detrimental to the town, if not fatal. In the twentieth century, virulent racists such as the bombers of the 1950s and the "White Caps" of the 1960s were present in the town. Nevertheless, one may legitimately question if the media coverage of the racial conflict, which presented images of racist villains and suffering black people, harmed the river town more than the actual events. One may also legitimately speculate, given the 5 percent black population threshold identified by Saul Alinsky, if Cairo ever would have been attractive to a large majority of white Americans in the twentieth century. As late as 2005, one scholar remarked that people were moving out of Springfield, Illinois, because the population was by then 15 percent black.[51]

Finally, we should remember the concept of multiple causation, a concept apparently neglected by many writers and critics discussing Cairo. Cairo is constantly threatened by the Ohio and Mississippi Rivers, and in 2011 a flood threatened the town with destruction.[52] The Corps of Engineers decided to save Cairo by blowing levees protecting farmlands; the next time, they might not do so. Cairo is not the only town along the Ohio and Mississippi Rivers suffering dire economic distress and severe population loss as the nation's commerce has been increasingly funneled along the highways and through the air. Cairo, however, justly or not, is probably the most notorious.

This work began by discussing lynching in America and how Cairo's lynchings in 1909 might be related to this terrible American practice. Orlando Patterson, a historical sociologist, has identified the American South as the fountainhead of lynching because of slavery, segregation, and evangelical religion.[53] His idea of an ultraviolent American South is echoed by Christopher Waldrep, a lynching scholar.[54] Ashraf H. A. Rushdy maintains that lynching is an American social institution developed from colonial theories of popular sovereignty.[55] Donald Mathews, a historian of religion, has suggested that lynching is particular to Christians—a type of violent Eucharist, especially if burning of the victim is involved.[56]

These scholars certainly are not entirely mistaken. Most lynchings in the nineteenth and twentieth centuries took place in the South, as do the most murders per capita today.[57] In the same vein, America in the nineteenth and twentieth centuries witnessed the most lynchings in the world, depending on how one defines lynching. Last, most of the persons who lynched other people in the nineteenth and twentieth centuries in America professed to be Christians. The problem one sees with these kinds of analyses is that they introduce a kind of inevitability into American lynching. If lynching and violence are part of southern culture, then an imperative is presented. One logical conclusion to this would be to theorize that southerners cannot help it, and thus while lynching as such has mostly been eliminated, nothing can be done about the violence. If Americans are prone to a violent, misguided form of popular sovereignty, then might there also be a mass movement of attacks on illegal aliens or other unpopular groups, as has already begun on a small scale? Finally, there are billions of Christians in the United States and around the world. Even if we consider just evangelicals in this country, do we expect that religion will cause these Christians to be more likely to commit heinous crimes, if it is believed that faith impelled them to do so in the past?

The problem with theories of lynching, one might observe, is that they excuse to some extent personal responsibility. If southern evangelical Christians were driven to torturing, mutilating, hanging, and burning black people by Walter White's "hellfire" preachers, then their behavior is somewhat excused.[58] The same would be true of Americans intoxicated by democracy to the point they feel they can take the law into their own hands. Laying collective guilt on southerners, Americans, and Christians for lynching may be convenient, but is it fair and just? If everyone is responsible for lynching, then at some level no one is responsible. We would do well to remember that even in Cairo in 1909, fewer than fifty men planned Will James's lynching. These are the persons guilty of homicide, not all the other Americans, southerners, and Christians in existence on that terrible day.

In Cairo, Illinois, in 1909–10, therefore, who were the lynchers? We know of only one for certain: "Mr. Logan" of Logan and Cox. This was George William Logan, a grocery man, who lived on 9th Street in Cairo.[59] He was the only Cairo resident identified by name to the press by Sheriff Frank Davis.[60] After the lynching, he returned to Warrensburg, Missouri, the place of his nativity.

There are better records of the defendants in the "riot trials" after the 1910 attempted lynching in Cairo. The accused included Frank J. Gorman, bartender and alderman of the Fifth Ward; James B. Scott, blacksmith; George B. Walker, printer and publisher of the Cairo city directory, 1908–9; Sam Wissinger, watchman for the Mobile & Ohio Railroad; Camelous O. Foster, deputy circuit clerk; Oliver P. Hurd Jr., lumberman and alderman in 1911; James M. Davidge, constable; James L. Casey, private detective and former policeman; John Maloney, blacksmith and wagon maker; and William C. Charles, owner of a livery and feed stable. The most immediate fact that emerges from this list is that all of the men charged in the "riot trial" were known residents of Cairo, not outsiders, Kentuckian or otherwise.[61] It could be speculated that Kentuckians, Missourians, and people from Southern Illinois were not involved in the attempted lynching, as they had been in the double lynching, because a purse snatching did not draw them into action as did a rape and murder.

The list of those on trial for riot in 1910 also reveals that two Cairo aldermen were probably involved in the attempted lynching—Frank Gorman and Oliver P. Hurd Jr. Indeed, Hurd may have been elected alderman on the strength of his participation in or leadership of the attempted lynching. Gorman and Hurd were not the only city or county officials indicted for rioting. Camelous O. Foster was the deputy circuit clerk, standing trial where he usually worked for the people. Also on the defendants list was a present and former law officer, a railroad worker, and two blacksmiths and a liveryman who apparently owned their own businesses. Finally, there was the printer and publisher of the Cairo city directory, George B. Walker, and, as might have been expected, John Maloney, blacksmith and wagoner, the brother-in-law of Rosa Maloney, the victim of the purse-snatching.

With the exception of Hurd and possibly Gorman, the men who attempted to lynch the African American John Pratt in Cairo, Illinois, in 1910 were laborers, small businessmen, or local government employees. Following the double lynching of 1909, a letter to the *Cairo Bulletin* expressed thanks that the Cairo lynch mob had found a leader so that Will "Froggie" James could be successfully killed.[62] Was that leader Frank Gorman, already a well-known Cairo politician, or Oliver P. Hurd, who was involved in Cairo's second largest business enterprise, lumber? Or was the leader of the lynch mob Alex Halliday, a member of Cairo's most prominent family who was killed during the lynching attempt in 1910? History has not yet revealed who the leader or leaders of the 1909 Cairo lynchings were. It is even possible that there were two or more lynch mobs—the larger mob lynching Will James and another one lynching Henry Salzner.[63]

Even if the politician Gorman or the lumberman Hurd were the leaders of a mob or mobs, either at the double lynching of 1909 or at the attempted lynching of 1910, the whole group of men on trial for the attempted lynching of 1910 were fairly ordinary. The only defendant who stands out somewhat would be the former crooked cop, James L. Casey. His involvement with gamblers and prostitutes, however, was certainly not atypical for this historical time or for a Cairo police officer. The question then emerges, what made this group of ordinary Cairo men believe they had the right to kill a man without due process of law? We know from other cases of mob violence and murder at the time, especially in Springfield, Illinois, in 1908, that the men would have had little fear of being successfully prosecuted.[64] We also know that this particular group of men was astonished when the sheriff and his deputies fired on them to protect two purse-snatching black men from being lynched.[65] Their interviews with two Indiana newspapers revealed that the attempted lynchers of 1910 wanted to lynch the "negroes quietly," as if the unlawful taking of a black man's life was not particularly important. An oral history interview taken from a former African American teacher in Cairo in the 1970s, Hattie Kendrick, revealed that a white woman she knew was incensed that Alex Halliday had been killed, because he and his companions were just out for a little "fun."[66] The Cairo white woman had told Kendrick that

> *Captain Nellis killed himself in Cairo when he caused that white man to be killed and laid out in the snow all night. You see, it wasn't supposed to be anything; it was just a crowd of young people having fun. He told them not to come any closer; he just jumped the fence and was shot. It was ridiculous; they were just having fun.*[67]

Had lynching become so common in the United States in 1909–10 that the young "smart set" considered it "fun" to participate in killing people? There is no doubt that lynching was common in the United States from 1890 to 1940. An average of one lynching per week occurred in the country for fifty years.[68] Had lynching, however, become so commonplace in America that there was no longer any stigma attached to it? Reading this work, one would have to say no. Certainly neither the editor of the *Cairo Evening Citizen* nor the editor of the *Cairo Bulletin* took either the double lynching in 1909 or the attempted lynching of 1910 lightly because of the negative consequences to Cairo. Both men knew lynching was wrong for Cairo.

The editors also tried to blame the double lynching, particularly Henry Salzner's killing, on outsiders. Kentuckians, in the *Bulletin*'s account, even had to find someone from Cairo to identify Salzner before he was removed from his cell in the Alexander County Courthouse. It is known that a very large crowd or mob from Paducah, Kentucky, Mrs. Salzner's hometown, was cheered when it arrived by train immediately before Will "Froggie" James was killed. It may be recalled that bloodhounds were brought down from Harrisburg, Illinois, to smell the gag in Anna Pelley's mouth and try to track her murderer. Once the dogs left and the word got out, crowds boarded trains and headed for Cairo.[69]

The appearance in Cairo on November 11, 1909, of the people from Harrisburg and Paducah eager to kill men brings up one of the older theories about American lynching. In one of MacKinlay Kantor's books, *Missouri Bittersweet*, he gives a historical account of a lynching in Maryville, Missouri, on January 12, 1931, in which a black man named Raymond Gunn was burned to death for attacking and killing a white schoolteacher.[70] Kantor spoke of the out-of-towners involved and said lynchings always attracted itinerant sadists who either took over or tried to take over the killing process.[71] In *Missouri Bittersweet* these were mysterious men whom no one knew but who always seemed to appear when a lynching threatened.

Are Kantor's observations the key to understanding not only the Maryville lynching but also all or most lynchings in the "Age of Lynching," including the ones in Cairo, Illinois? That is, in that historical time, were sociopaths waiting to appear at any incipient lynching, ready to turn it into an orgy of torture, mutilation, and burning? The Cairo double lynching obviously had its share of outsiders, and probably of sadists too. How else could one explain the taking of pieces of James's body to distribute as souvenirs and soaking ropes with his blood? Salzner's blood was also needlessly spilled and his body mutilated. Nevertheless, it is doubtful that such disturbed individuals led the lynchings in Cairo or in many other places. Will "Froggie" James's lynching was headed by Cairo men who believed they had a right to take men's lives.

At the time, if one had asked the editor of the *Cairo Bulletin* why James and Salzner were lynched, he would have said it was because Cairo and the judicial circuit had become corrupt and too many men had gotten away with murder. The townspeople could not take a situation where justice was delayed or denied any longer.[72] If one had asked the editor of the *Cairo Evening Citizen* what caused Cairo's double lynching in 1909, he would probably have said that the Cairo people supported it and that officials who had made the lynchings possible would also be supported by the people. If the editor of the *Belleville News-Democrat*, who so liberally used the N-word, was asked why the lynchings, he no doubt would have said that it was the will of the people and that African Americans had to be controlled—indeed, suppressed.[73]

It is pure speculation as to what "Mr. Logan," the only Cairo man clearly identified as a key figure in Will "Froggie" James's lynching, believed concerning the Cairo double lynching in particular and lynching in general. This would also be true of the defendants in the "riot trials" following the attempted lynching of 1910. We may, however, assume that Aldermen Gorman and Hurd were not stupid men and that they knew above everything else that whatever they did, they would probably never be convicted in a court of law. What they did not count on was Sheriff Fred Nellis's use of deadly force to defend his prisoners, and so Alex Halliday was killed. If lynching was ever "fun" for the young members of the Alexander Club, such as Halliday, it was no longer.

This then appears to be an important factor in American lynching in the "Age of Lynching." Lynching participants did not fear legal retribution at the local, state, or national level. Sheriffs such as Fred Nellis and their deputies had to possibly risk their lives and certainly their elections to defend prisoners. The American law courts could do little with lynch mob members. In Cairo in 1909, such people became "persons unknown to us." In 1910 they became defendants and probably perjured themselves, as did their supporters, and the local jury set them free. In the murder trial of Sheriff Bankson, perjury also seemingly abounded, and the jurors deliberated with prejudice and arrived at a verdict that would have been hard to justify legally. They took the law into their own hands as much as the lynchers did in Cairo on November 11, 1909.

These Cairoites were a lawless group in 1909–10, but so were Americans in general. Something had to be done because law and especially order was always breaking down.[74] In Cairo the commission form of government was introduced. Now four commissioners and a mayor dealt with 14,000 people, where before 14 aldermen had each dealt with a few hundred. Other towns and cities adopted the city manager form of local government. Americans had to be controlled better. Mob rule seemed to be always lurking nearby, ready to bring disaster and disgrace on any locality.

Ida B. Wells-Barnett was the foremost crusader against lynching in America during the nineteenth and twentieth centuries. Photo courtesy of University of Chicago Library.

The Cairo double lynching of 1909 and the attempted lynching of 1910 were disasters for Cairo, and certainly the national media never forgave the town or forgot the incidents. The heroes of those years were Ida Wells-Barnett and Fred Nellis, though both were flawed, one by the need to stand alone when cooperation might have been better and the other by the taint of corruption. Hattie Kendrick said in an interview, "We don't know whether Captain Nellis loved the Negroes so much that he wanted to preserve their lives or if Captain Nellis wanted to preserve his job."[75] Like many brave men, Fred Nellis's actions were not rewarded at the time and not well remembered afterward, especially by the minority race.

Ida Wells-Barnett has fared much better, as historians and other writers have discovered her life and work and lauded them in the main. The original source of much of this adulation was her autobiography, which one of her children finally got published sometime after her death. In that work, she perhaps summarized the historical significance of the Cairo double lynching: "That was in 1909, and from that day until the present there has been no lynching in the state."[76] Lynch law was to have a place no more in Illinois.

APPENDIXES

NOTES

WORKS CITED

INDEX

# APPENDIX A: HOMICIDES IN CAIRO, ILLINOIS, 1900–1912

## Reported in the *Cairo Evening Citizen*

## Compiled by Darrel Dexter

| *Accused* | *Date* | *Location* | *Weapon/ Cause* | *Deceased* | *Outcome* |
|---|---|---|---|---|---|
| **1900** | | | | | |
| The People | Apr 20 | county courthouse | rope | Riley Powell (white) | legal hanging |
| Boy "Dutchy" (w) | Jun 2 | boat on Ohio River | gun | Dr. A. F. Schrader (w) | |
| Ira Ewing (black) | Oct 6 | Smith Bros. wagonyard | knife | Henry Moore (b) (alias Brown) | fled |
| Simon Webb (b) | Nov 7 (died Nov 12) | | whip | Katie Webb (b) | |
| **1901** | | | | | |
| Charles Rucker (b) | Jan 13 | 14th & Washington, saloon of Henry Zerfass | gun | Dan Buckner (b) | 35 years |
| William Grimes (w) | (died Feb 16) | Farmers Saloon | hatchet | Walter Moore (w) | self-defense |
| Harvey Eddington (w) (alias Henry Edington) | Mar 25 | shanty boat on Ohio River | gun | Mrs. Harvey Eddington (w) | |
| Sam C. Brown (w) | Apr 26 | 220 20th St. | knife | William Nourse (w) | |
| L. D. Stovall (b) | Aug 3 | 34th St. | gun | Major Parrott (b) | self-defense |

| Accused | Date | Location | Weapon/Cause | Deceased | Outcome |
| --- | --- | --- | --- | --- | --- |
| **1902** | | | | | |
| Frank Shaw (b) | Nov 4 (died Nov 8) | Commercial & 5th St., Anderson Field's place | pistol | Wallace Stovall (b) | |
| **1903** | | | | | |
| Thomas O'Neil (w), William Grimes (w) | Sep 30 | Washington Ave. (Brewery Saloon) | gun | Cornelius Sheehan (w) | self-defense |
| Sol. Edwards (b) | Oct 24 | 211 19th St. | gun | Mrs. Sol. Edwards (b) | suicide |
| **1904** | | | | | |
| Belle Mason (w) | Feb 9 (died Feb 10) | 4th on Commercial | gun | John Green | acquitted |
| Frank Lewis (b) | Apr 7 | Wild Cat Chute | | Mr. Sullivan? | |
| Bob Williams (b) | July | Stone Depot | | John Blackman (b) | killed |
| Bob Miller (b) | Aug 5 | upper Poplar | gun | Amos Gibson (b) | |
| Unknown man (w) | Aug 23 | ladies' room, IC depot | knife | Sam Higgerson (b) | fled |
| Henry Agson (b) | Sep 18 (died Sep 19) | Big Four crossing near Washington | gun | George Zook (w) | life sentence |
| Charles Bradley (b) | Sep 25 (died Sep 28) | 19th St. | drill | Fred Whitcamp (w) | life sentence |
| Unknown man (w) | Oct 9 | 13th & Commercial | gun | Thomas Trennery (w) | |
| Snappy Jackson (b) | Oct 21 | Bell's saloon on Commercial above 2nd St. | gun | Bob Williams (b) | fled |
| **1905** | | | | | |
| Shorty Carr (b) | Jan 22 | 17th St. | gun | Wm. Major Green (b) | exonerated |

| *Accused* | *Date* | *Location* | *Weapon/Cause* | *Deceased* | *Outcome* |
|---|---|---|---|---|---|
| Charlie Williams (b) | Apr 14 | Ky. House, 406 Ohio St. | gun | William Parr (w) | exonerated |
| A. B. Douglas (w) | Apr 14 | Ky. House, 406 Ohio St. | gun | William Parr (w) | acquitted |
| John Sims (b), Sid Matthews (b) | May 30 | Commercial near 11th | gun | Wade Hampton (b) | |
| Mr. Rogers (b) | Jul 20 | 24th St. | knife | Jim Caruthers | self-defense |
| Joe Thomas (b) | Jul 28 | Future City, above bridge | knife | Frank Whitehead (b) | captured |
| Harry Taylor (b) | Aug 6 | 20th St. near Poplar | knife | Alex McGee (b) | |
| George Martin (b) | Sep 16 (died Sep 18) | 6th & Commercial | gun | W. O. Bruce (w) | 18 years |
| Alvin Guymon (w) | Sep 17 (died Jan 27, 1906) | Commercial between 4th & 5th | gun | Al Anderson (w) | fled |
| Bob Perry (b) | Oct 29 | 18th St. | knife | C. Horn (b) | |
| Lethea Hines (b) | Nov 6 | 218 33rd St. | gun | Garfield Hines (b) | self-defense |
| Will Van Buren (b) (alias Buckner) | Nov 18 | Thomas residence | gun | Lena Thomas (b) | accidental |
| Bud Dawson (b) | Dec 10 | 33rd & Commercial | knife | George Phillips (b) | |
| **1906** | | | | | |
| Henry Green (w) (alias Hill) | Jan 12 | 2202 Sycamore | shot | Thomas Guinn (w) | not guilty |
| Ed Pearson (b) | Jan 31 | 20th & Walnut | knife | Oscar Thomas (b) | |
| Charles Crook (w) | Feb 6 | Park Ave. between 33rd & 34th | gun | Ralph Orr (w) | |
| Richard Buckner (b) | Feb 26 (died Feb 27) | Smith Bros. Saloon, 13th & Poplar | gun | Jesse Speed (b) | fled |

| *Accused* | *Date* | *Location* | *Weapon/Cause* | *Deceased* | *Outcome* |
|---|---|---|---|---|---|
| Guy E. Smith (w) | Mar 2 (died Mar 6) | 28th & Sycamore | gun | Otto Boershal (w) | 14 years |
| Pink Christian (b) | Mar 11 | 24th & Poplar | knife | William Gusby (b) | penitentiary |
| Sadie Hardin (b) (alias Pride) | Apr 5 | 2nd & Commercial outside Corner Saloon | gun | Sam Brown (b) (alias Hump Brown) | 16 years |
| J. F. Cannady (w) | May 7 | IC yards near Stone Depot | gun | Webb White (w) | justified |
| Lenn Armstrong (b) (alias Clem Armstrong) | Aug 5 | drainage district | gun | Henry Williamham (b) (alias Willingham) | killed |
| John Wade (b) (police officer) | Aug 18 | Sycamore & 38th | gun | Lenn Armstrong (b) | exonerated |
| Ed Maley (w) | Aug 24 | Maley's Saloon, Lower Ohio | gun | Patrick Vhey (w) (alias Paddy Fay) | self-defense |
| Unknown | Aug 30 | Big Four crossing bridge | coupling pin | Ben Pettigrew (b) | |
| John Williams (b) | Sep 16 | lower Commercial, Richard Taylor's saloon | gun | Bruce Hardin (b) | penitentiary |
| Unknown (w) | Oct 8 (died Nov 1) | Steagala Hotel on Ohio levee | knife | W. A. Lawrence (w) | |
| John Lewis (w) | Oct 12 | houseboat on Ohio River | gun | Will Thomas (w) | self-defense |
| Luther Davis (b) | Nov 4 | Egan's saloon, 33rd & Commercial | gun | John Williams (b) (alias Kit) | self-defense |
| **1907** | | | | | |
| Richard Williams (b) (alias Nub Williams) | 1907 | 14th & Ohio | gun | Mr. Curtis (b) (died in Chester) | 18 years |
| Oscar Moore (w) (aliases "Hog" & "Lion") | Feb 10 | M&O sand house near roundhouse | gun | Henry Tice (b) | |

| *Accused* | *Date* | *Location* | *Weapon/Cause* | *Deceased* | *Outcome* |
|---|---|---|---|---|---|
| Marvin Boren (w) | Mar 21 | outside 235 13th St. | knife | Patrick Doud (w) (police officer) | not guilty |
| Joseph Causey (w) | May 16 | 26th & Poplar, Wooden's store | gun | George Wooden (b) | not guilty (all-white jury) |
| Unknown (b) | May 17 (died Jul 9) | lumberyard near 10th St. | club | Oliver "Al" Abbott (w) | |
| Dore Green Johnson (w) (police officer) | May 30 (died Jun 1) | 10th St. | gun | Frank James (b) | justified |
| Fred Korn (w) | Jun 18 | IC depot | gun | David Bharam (b) | not guilty (all-white jury) |
| Albert Jeans (b) | Jul 16 (died Jul 19) | Wild Cat Chute | knife | Andrew Jackson (b) | self-defense |
| Louis James (b) (alias Nellum) | Aug 10 | 17th & Commercial | pick | Patrick Dougherty (w) | death, new trial |
| John R. Ford (w) | Oct 30 | Riddle's saloon, corner of 8th & Commercial | gun | John W. Lewis | not guilty |
| Unknown (w) | Nov 5 | 10th St. sewer outlet | thrown over wall | day-old infant (w) | |
| **1908** | | | | | |
| John Wade (b) (police officer) | Jan 20 | 32nd & Commercial | gun | Lee Griggs (b) | justified |
| Oliver Welch (b) | Mar 2 | 515 15th St. | lamp & chair | Levange Welch (b) | life |
| M&O brakeman | Mar 16 (died Mar 22) | M&O bridge near Sycamore | thrown off train | Casey Rickets (b) | |
| Lena Dickmeyer (w) | Apr 9 | disorderly house, 1710 Cedar | gun | Walter Watts (w) | |

| *Accused* | *Date* | *Location* | *Weapon/Cause* | *Deceased* | *Outcome* |
|---|---|---|---|---|---|
| William Walker (b) | Apr 18 | north side 33rd St. near Poplar | knife | Tom Price (b) (alias Matt Price) | 45 years |
| Ambrose Beecher (b) | Apr 30 | Singer plant | gun | Clyde Williams (b) | reformatory |
| Joe Causey (w) | Aug 15 | 30th & Commercial | gun | Fred Williams (b) | |
| Frank Jackson (b) | Sep 2 | 510 12th St. | gun | Lonny Calvin (b) (alias Lonnie Cavander) | escaped jail |
| Nancy Brooks (b) | Sep 5 | 231 21st St. | knife | Amelia Brooks (b) | 45 years |
| Margie Allen (b) (stepson of deceased) | Sep 14 | 221 22nd St. | gun | Chas. Newells (b) (alias Nevell) | justifiable |
| John Williams (b) | Sep 20 | Sycamore St. | gun | Walter McCall (b) | killed |
| Walter McCall (b) | Sep 20 | Sycamore St. | gun | John Williams (b) | killed |
| Drew Marshall (w) | Oct 2 | 217 34th St. | gun | Mrs. Frank Bechtel (w) | suicide |
| Walter Davidge (w) | Oct 6 | 25th & Walnut St. near high school | gun | Eugenie McClarney (w) | not guilty |
| James Walton (b) | Dec 7 | 22nd & Poplar | gun | Orville Warrick (b) (alias Dick Woods) | self-defense |
| Unknown (b) | Dec 25 | Dick Taylor's saloon, lower Commercial | gun | Riley Bradley (b) | |
| **1909** | | | | | |
| Alfred Baltimore (b) | Jan 15 | 3109 Commercial, Ellis's tenement | gun | George Bradley (b) (ex–police officer) | justified gunplay |
| Effie Finney (b) | Feb 3 | 229 22nd St. tenement | gun | Charley Hudson (b) (alias Louis Hudson) | self-defense |

| *Accused* | *Date* | *Location* | *Weapon/Cause* | *Deceased* | *Outcome* |
|---|---|---|---|---|---|
| James Cammon (b) (alias Jim Campbell) | Feb 12 | M&O bridge | gun | Josh A. Askew (w) (alias A. S. Askew) | life sentence |
| Chas. Turner (b) | Mar 18 | 222 25th St. | knife | Missouri Overby (b) | fled |
| Chas. Lee Russell (b) (alias Chas Allen) | Apr 14 (died Aug 13) | 32nd & Poplar | gun | Robert Taylor (b) (alias Will Latimore) | fled |
| Andrew Price (b) | Apr 14 (died Apr 15) | Nero Hall on Poplar St. | gun | Joseph Mason (b) (alias "Cute Kid") | 14 years |
| Will Thompson (b) | Apr 24 | | gun | Bob Rogers (b) | exonerated |
| Gus Johnson (b) (police officer) | May 29 | 19th & Commercial | gun | Frank Conners (b) | exonerated |
| Phillip Herron (b) | May 22 (died Jun 9) | 314 21st St. | gun | Lizzie Jenkins (b) | 14 years |
| Jim Thomas (b) | Jun 20 | Halfway House | gun | William Johnson (b) | self-defense |
| Odessa "Bessie" Scott (b) | Jul 17 (died Jul 25) | "house" on Poplar near 30th St. | razor | Faithy "Fay" Blake (b) | penitentiary |
| Peter Hall (w) (son of deceased) | Jul 19 | 16th St. | gun | Annie Hall (w) (mother of accused) | accidental |
| Cora Kizer (b) | Jul 26 | 217 5th St. | gun | Sylvester Grundy (b) | self-defense |
| Minnie Clifton (b) (alias Mit Norris), Ollie Watson (b) | Jul 27 | 520 18th St. | gun | Henry Stanley (b) | |
| Henry Salzner (w) | Aug 7 (died Aug 19) | Lancaster tenement, 208 16th St. | hatchet | Mary Salzner (w) | lynched |
| Will Moore (b) (alias Calhoun) | Oct 18 | 530 17th St. | gun | Lena Taylor (b) (alias Allen) | |
| Russell Jos. Barbee (w) | Oct 28 | 213 7th St. | gun | Frank Tracey (w) | |

| *Accused* | *Date* | *Location* | *Weapon/Cause* | *Deceased* | *Outcome* |
|---|---|---|---|---|---|
| Will James (b) (alias "Froggie" James) | Nov 9 | alley between 25th & 26th | strangled | Anna Pelley (w) | lynched |
| Unknown (w) | Nov 11 | arch at 8th & Commercial | guns | Will James (b) (alias "Froggie" James) | |
| Unknown (w) | Nov 11 | Washington & 21st St. | rope | Henry Salzner (w) | |
| Henry Small (b) | Nov 17 | 1909 Poplar, Will Walker's barber shop | gun | Will Polk (b) | life sentence |
| Nelse Valentine (b) | Dec 25 (died Jan 15, 1910) | Smith Bros. Saloon | gun | Alfred Miller (b) (alias Buddy Warner) | life sentence |
| **1910** | | | | | |
| John Mitchell (w) | Jan 1 | 330 33rd St. | gun | Harry Smith (w) | |
| Martha Jones (b) | Feb 5 | Commercial Ave. near 15th St. | gun | Will Jones (b) | 25 years |
| Unknown deputy | Feb 17 | county courthouse yard | gun | Alex "Spinney" Halliday (w) | |
| Harrison Young (b), James Chambers (b), Will Evans (b), Bettie Moser (b) | Apr 23 | Douglas & Cedar ("the barracks") | gun | John West | |
| Minnie Dixon (w) | Apr 27 | Cedar between 12th & Douglas | gun | Luther Davis (b) (alias Geo. Davis) | 40 days |
| Mitchell Calhoun (b) | May 7 | 38th & Commercial | gun | Mary Lane (b) (alias Annie Payne) | life sentence |
| Fred Ragland (b) | Jul 31 | Future City | gun | Louis Levey (b) | fled |
| James White (w) | Oct 8 | 401 Commercial, William McCann's saloon | gun | Fred Otterson | fled |

| *Accused* | *Date* | *Location* | *Weapon/Cause* | *Deceased* | *Outcome* |
|---|---|---|---|---|---|
| William Hackney | Nov 20 (died Nov 21) | Nordman's old mill near Mississippi levee | gun | Andrew J. Walder (alias Jack Walder) | life sentence |
| Abner C. Bankson (w) | Dec 3 | 1111 Commercial, Cairo Police Headquarters | gun | Wilfred French (w) | not guilty |
| **1911** | | | | | |
| Luther Shad | 1911 | | | | Pontiac Boys Reformatory |
| James Dillard (b) (constable) | Jan 28 | 312½ 19th St., near Poplar | gun | Ed Brooks (b) | 14 years |
| James Dyson (b) | May | Planters Hotel | bottle | James White (b) | Pontiac Boys Reformatory |
| Al Moore (b) (alias "Toothless") | Jul 24 | on Rees Lee on Ohio River at Cairo Harbor | capstan bar | Will Turner (b) (alias Will Moore) | fled |
| Ben Bradley (b) (former police officer) | Sep 8 | 530 Douglas | gun | Henry Smith (b) (alias Small) | |
| Lee Folds (b) | Sep 18 | Halliday brickyard near 21st & Mississippi levee | bat | Jack Taylor (w) | exonerated |
| Elmer Yanders (w) (alias Pollock) | Oct 13 | 28th St. | gun | Lula Wright (w) | suicide |
| John B. Arntzen (w) (ferry boat captain) | Oct 29 (died Oct 31) | 1900 Washington, Rudy Laurent's saloon | gun | Louis Voight | self-defense |
| Albert Johnson (b) (alias Sonny Johnson) | Nov 17 | steamer John A. Wood at Cairo Point | gun | John Thomas (b) (alias Brock) | 14 years |

| *Accused* | *Date* | *Location* | *Weapon/Cause* | *Deceased* | *Outcome* |
|---|---|---|---|---|---|
| **1912** | | | | | |
| Chas S. McCann (w) | Jan 24 | 6th & Commercial, Meyers Bros. Saloon | gun | Bennie Lampert (w) (alias Hollingshead) | 14 years |
| Gus Johnson (b) (police officer) | Jan 27 (died Jan 28) | Washington Ave. at corner of 28th | gun | Napoleon Lipe (b) | exonerated |
| Cal Nickerson (b) (alias Nichols, alias Carrel Johnson) | Mar 12 (died Mar 14) | 411 Commercial, John Durrah's barbershop | gun | Eli Bobo (b) | 14 years |
| Philip W. Harlan (w) | Mar 18 (died Mar 19) | 418 Commercial, Green Tree Hotel | knife | S. F. George (w) | self-defense |
| John Mason (b) | May 8 | 40th & Sycamore near Big Four crossing | gun | Albert Lipe (b) | fled |
| Richard Anderson (b) | Sep 8 | 3301 Commercial at D. W. McPherson's saloon | gun | Louis Oliver (b) | |
| Bill Noise (b), two unknown men (b) | Nov 19 (died Nov 20) | 12th & Washington | | Nagib Mallouf (w) | |
| Sam Foree (b) (alias "Cat") | Dec 14 | 14th & Washington | gun | "Babe" Barney (b) | |

# APPENDIX B: CAIRO INTENTIONAL HOMICIDE RATES, 1890–1912

## Compiled by Darrel Dexter

The intentional homicide rates for Cairo, Illinois, were determined by using statistics from homicides reported in the *Cairo Bulletin* and the *Cairo Evening Citizen* for the years 1890 to 1912 and population numbers from the federal census reports. Accidental homicide and suicide numbers were not included. The homicide rate is the number of homicides per 100,000 people.

| *Year* | *Est. Population* | *No. of Homicides* | *Homicide Rate* |
|---|---|---|---|
| 1890 | 10,324 | 1 | 9.69 |
| 1891 | 10,548 | 3 | 28.44 |
| 1892 | 10,772 | 4 | 37.13 |
| 1893 | 10,997 | 3 | 27.28 |
| 1894 | 11,221 | 6 | 53.47 |
| 1895 | 11,445 | 4 | 34.95 |
| 1896 | 11,669 | 6 | 51.42 |
| 1897 | 11,893 | 3 | 25.22 |
| 1898 | 12,118 | 3 | 24.76 |
| 1899 | 12,341 | 6 | 48.62 |
| 1900 | 12,566 | 4 | 31.83 |
| 1901 | 12,764 | 5 | 39.17 |
| 1902 | 12,952 | 1 | 7.72 |
| 1903 | 13,160 | 2 | 15.20 |
| 1904 | 13,358 | 9 | 67.38 |
| 1905 | 13,556 | 12 | 88.52 |
| 1906 | 13,754 | 16 | 116.33 |
| 1907 | 13,952 | 11 | 78.84 |
| 1908 | 14,150 | 16 | 113.07 |
| 1909 | 14,348 | 22 | 153.33 |
| 1910 | 14,548 | 10 | 68.74 |
| 1911 | 14,613 | 9 | 61.59 |
| 1912 | 14,679 | 8 | 54.50 |

## NOTES

### Preface

1. Rushdy, *American Lynching*, 69–93.

2. Goldsby, *Spectacular Secret*, 9. Professor Goldsby expressed similar sentiments in her complicated and enlightening work, asserting that lynching was a topic that should not have existed. She found lynching's cruelties so great as to often have exceeded her own interest in coming to understand the act as an object of knowledge.

### Introduction

1. The 1910 federal census records Cairo's population as 14,548, the third largest community in the region behind Evansville, Indiana, with 69,647, and Paducah, Kentucky, with 22,760. The population of other neighboring communities: Cape Girardeau, Missouri, 8,475; Marion, Illinois, 7,093; Carbondale, Illinois, 5,411; Charleston, Missouri, 3,144; Anna, Illinois, 2,809; Vienna, Illinois, 1,124 (Thirteenth Census of the United States Taken in the Year 1910, Volume II Population Alabama–Montana [Washington, D.C.: Government Printing Office, 1913]).

2. *New York Times*, November 13, 1909, 10; Lantz, *Community in Search of Itself*, 51.

3. *New York Times*, November 19, 1909, 10.

4. Ibid.

5. Paul Laurence Dunbar High School opened in Washington, D.C., in 1870 and was the first black public high school in the nation. Sumner High School, at 19th and Walnut Streets in Cairo, Illinois, claimed to be the oldest black high school because it was a Freedmen's Bureau school for "colored pupils" and became a public school when "negroes were given the ballot" (*Cairo [Ill.] Evening Citizen*, Monday, August 3, 1908; Friday, August 21, 1908). Giddings, *Ida*, 483–87; *New York Times*, November 13, 1909, 10; *Fort Wayne (Ind.) Journal-Gazette*, November 13, 1909, 1.

6. Author's conversation with the treasurer of the city of Cairo, Illinois, Preston Ewing, November 18, 2014.

7. Duster, *Crusade for Justice*, 312.

8. Lantz, *Community in Search of Itself*, 50.

9. Strout, *Maud*; Lantz, *Community in Search of Itself*, 50.

10. Lantz, *Community in Search of Itself*, 50.

11. Ibid., 4.

12. Ron Powers, *Far from Home*, 11.

13. *Cairo Evening Citizen*, February 12, 1910, 4.

14. Author's conversation with Lieutenant Paul E. Echols, Carbondale, Illinois, April 5, 2013.

15. Rushdy, *American Lynching*, 69–122.

16. Loewen, *Sundown Towns*, 48, 141, 173–74, 306–7, 494.

17. *Chicago Tribune*, February 19, 1910, 10; *Paducah (Ky.) Evening Sun*, April 1, 1909, 4; *Portsmouth (Ohio) Daily Times*, February 21, 1910, 1; *Chicago Post* as quoted in *Cairo Evening Citizen*, February 23, 1910, 2. The *Sun* suggested that the former inhabitants of Paducah's "bawdy houses," who had been driven out of town, moved to Cairo (*Paducah Evening Sun*, June 12, 1909, 4).

18. Berg, *Popular Justice*, 87–88; *Cairo (Ill.) Bulletin*, April 4, 1910, 4.

19. Waldrep, *Night Riders*, 146–49.

20. *Chicago Tribune*, July 4, 1910, 5.

21. Waldrep, *Night Riders*, 7.

22. My father, Thomas Beadles, who was born in Cairo in 1910, told me that his father, Jess Beadles, manager of the Thomas McFarland Lumber Company, had to pay black people from Mississippi for some weeks so they could buy food before they were fit enough for most of the work in the lumber mill.

23. Lantz, *Community in Search of Itself*, 45.

24. Ibid.

25. *Cairo Bulletin*, October 10, 1910, 2.

26. *Cairo Evening Citizen*, July 22, 1910, 5.

27. Lantz, *Community in Search of Itself*, 50.

28. Cartwright and Jordan, *Between Two Rivers*.

29. Lansden, *History of the City of Cairo*, 49, 58–62; *Paducah Evening Sun*, June 14, 1909, 4.

30. Lansden, *History of the City of Cairo*, 49, 58–62.

31. Steffens, *Shame of the Cities*. The book is a collection of muckraking articles originally published in *McClure's* magazine in 1904.

32. Southern, *Progressive Era and Race*; Loewen, *Sundown Towns*.

33. Southern, *Progressive Era and Race*, 162.

34. Walling, "Race War in the North."

35. *Chicago Tribune*, November 13, 1909.

36. Waldrep, *Many Faces of Judge Lynch*, 6.

37. Loewen, *Sundown Towns*, 62.

38. Saul David Alinsky was the author of *Rules for Radicals*, his 1971 book of advice to community organizers on how to unite and empower low-income communities.

39. Frisbe, *Alley in Chicago*, 121.

40. *Cairo Bulletin*, February 19, 1910, 1.

41. Ibid.

42. Ibid., February 21, 1910, 1; January 3, 1910, 2.

43. Ibid., February 21, 1910, 1.

44. Ibid., October 31, 1910, 2; November 5, 1910, 2.

45. *Waterloo (Iowa) Times-Tribune*, November 17, 1909, 1; *Cairo Evening Citizen*, January 3, 1910, 4; *Cairo Bulletin*, December 26, 1909, 10.

46. *Cairo Bulletin*, November 30, 1909, 4; November 19, 1909, 1; November 27, 1909, 4; December 1, 1909, 4.

47. *New York Times*, November 13, 1909, 7.

48. Ibid., November 15, 1909, 8.

49. Ibid., November 19, 1909, 10.

50. Reid, *River City*, 76–77.

51. *Cairo Bulletin*, November 22, 1909, 2.

52. Goldsby, *Spectacular Secret*.

53. Waldrep, *Many Faces of Judge Lynch*, 2–4.

54. Rushdy, *American Lynching*, 72; Equal Justice Initiative, *Lynching in America*, 7–9.

55. "Lynchings by Race and Year, 1882–1968."

56. Ibid.; Southern, *Progressive Era and Race*, 135.

57. *New York Age*, January 27, 1910, 4.

58. "Lynchings by Race and Year, 1882–1968."

59. Equal Justice Initiative, *Lynching in America*, 17.

60. *Cincinnati Enquirer*, November 13, 1909, 1; *Cairo Bulletin*, November 12, 1909, 1; November 13, 1909, 1.

61. Berg, *Popular Justice*, 87–88; *Cairo Bulletin*, April 4, 1910, 4.

62. Equal Justice Initiative, *Lynching in America*, 10; Gibson, "Negro Holocaust," 1.

63. Ashraf, *American Lynching*, 71.

64. Equal Justice Initiative, *Lynching in America*, 10.

65. Joanne Wheeler, "Together in Egypt: A Pattern of Race Relations in Cairo, Illinois, 1865–1915," in Burton and McMath, *Toward a New South*, 110–11; Powers, *Far from Home*, 122–23.

66. *Cairo Evening Citizen*, May 7, 1910, 8.

67. *Cairo Bulletin*, November 19, 1909, 3.

68. Wheeler, "Together in Egypt," 121.

69. *Cairo Evening Citizen*, April 23, 1910, 1; May 7, 1910, 8; *Cairo Bulletin*, October 30, 1910, 2; October 31, 1910, 2; December 3, 1909, 6; December 15, 1909, 2.

70. *New York Times*, November 12, 1909, 1; *Fort Wayne Journal-Gazette*, November 18, 1909, 2; *Chicago Tribune*, November 13, 1909, 10; *Cairo Evening Citizen*, January 8, 1910, 1.

71. Goldsby, *Spectacular Secret*, 21.

72. Quoted in Waldrep, *Many Faces of Judge Lynch*, 133.

73. Quoted in Southern, *Progressive Era and Race*, 31.

74. *Cairo Evening Citizen*, November 9, 1909; *Cairo Bulletin*, November 10, 1909.

75. Wheeler, "Together in Egypt," 119–21.

76. Loewen, *Sundown Towns*, 48.

77. *Cairo Bulletin*, November 15, 1909, 2–3.

78. Raper, *Tragedy of Lynching*, 13–14.

79. *Cairo Bulletin*, November 19, 1909, 8; *Cairo Evening Citizen*, May 19, 1910, 1; *Cairo Bulletin*, April 15, 1910, 2; *Cairo Evening Citizen*, April 13, 1910, 5.

80. *Chicago Tribune*, November 9, 1910; *Daily Free Press* (Carbondale, Ill.), November 21, 1910, 2.

81. *Cairo Bulletin*, October 31, 1910, 2.

82. Powers, *Far from Home*, 7–8, 122–24. I personally remember the drinking fountains labeled "For Colored Only" in the old courthouse in Cairo, as well as the "colored" benches.

83. Ibid., 126.

84. Ibid.; Loewen, *Sundown Towns*, 513.

85. Gibson, "Negro Holocaust," 4.

86. Goldsby, *Spectacular Secret*, 35, 288–94.

87. Pfeifer, *Rough Justice*, 122–47.

### 1. Anna Pelley's Life and Death

1. Joseph Pelley enlisted in Company H, 25th North Carolina Regiment of the Confederate Army, on July 15, 1861.

2. *Jonesboro (Ill.) Gazette*, November 12, 1909.

3. *Daily Free Press*, February 11, 1903, 1.

4. *Cairo Bulletin*, December 15, 1910. 4.

5. *Daily Herald* quoted in ibid.

6. *Chicago Tribune*, February 18, 1910, 2. Joseph Pelley Jr. was born November 6, 1876, in Anna and died May 3, 1940, from injuries sustained in a tornado.

7. *Jonesboro Gazette*, November 11, 1910.

8. Ella Dolan and Anna Pelley had much in common. Both were daughters of Irish immigrants, clerks in a dry goods store, and single young women.

9. *Chicago Herald*, November 12, 1909, 17.

10. *Waterloo Times-Tribune*, November 12, 1909, 1.

11. *Cairo Evening Citizen*, November 9, 1909.

12. Ibid., 1.

13. *Cairo Bulletin*, November 10, 1909, 1. The urban press of the era was almost always sensational in its coverage of rapes that led to lynchings; see Rushdy, *American Lynching*, 75. In the Pelley case it was the *Inter Ocean* (Chicago), November 11, 1909, 1, that discussed the state of Anna's "nude body," as did the *Chicago Tribune*, November 12, 1909, 1.

14. *Cairo Bulletin*, November 10, 1909, 1; *Waterloo Times-Tribune*, November 12, 1910, 1.

15. *Cairo Bulletin*, November 10, 1909, 1.

16. *Waterloo Times-Tribune*, November 12, 1909, 1; *Cairo Evening Citizen*, November 9, 1909, 1.

17. *Cairo Evening Citizen*, November 9, 1909.

## 2. The Crime Investigation

1. *Cairo Evening Citizen*, November 9, 1909, 1; *Waterloo Times-Tribune*, November 12, 1909, 1.

2. *Cairo Bulletin*, November 10, 1909, 1.

3. Ibid.; Harvey and Harvey, "Reliability of Bloodhounds in Criminal Investigations," 811–16. The Harveys' article states that the potential error rate of a veteran bloodhound-handler team is low and can be a useful tool for law enforcement.

4. *Chicago Herald*, November 12, 1909, 17; *Washington Post*, November 13, 1909, 1.

5. *Cairo Evening Citizen*, November 10, 1909, 3. The 1909 Cairo city directory lists Arthur Alexander and his residence at 2515 Poplar; see *Walker's Cairo City Directory for 1908–9*. Will James was not listed.

6. *Cairo Bulletin*, November 10, 1909, 1.

7. Ibid.

8. *Cairo Evening Citizen*, November 10, 1909, 1.

9. Dray, *At the Hands of Persons Unknown*, 173; Lansden, *History of the City of Cairo*, 272.

10. *Fort Wayne Journal-Gazette*, November 13, 1909, 1.

11. *New York Times*, November 12, 1909, 1.

12. *Cairo Bulletin*, November 11, 1909, 1.

13. Ibid.

14. Ibid., November 10, 1909, 1.

15. Ibid., November 11, 1909, 1.

16. Ibid., November 10, 1909, 1.

17. The *Cairo Bulletin* identified him as Ed Thomas, alias Will Thomas, but the *Cairo Evening Citizen* gave his name as Sam Mosby, who worked at Woodward's Warehouse (*Cairo Evening Citizen*, November 10, 1909, 1).

18. *Cairo Evening Citizen*, November 10, 1909, 3; December 10, 1909, 1; January 10, 1910, 6. Arthur Alexander had three little sisters, Bertha, twenty-one, a schoolteacher; Somy, seventeen; and Frankie, twelve.

19. Ibid., November 10, 1909, 1–3.

20. Ibid., 1.

21. Ibid.

22. Ibid., November 11, 1909, 1.

23. *Chicago Tribune*, November 11, 1909, 7.

## 3. The Flight and Pursuit of Will "Froggie" James

1. *Cairo Evening Citizen*, November 11, 1909. "McDaniel's automobile" was likely the one purchased in Chicago in April 1906 by Leo McDaniel, proprietor of McDaniel's Hay and Grain business, and was at the time "one of the finest, if not the finest automobile in Cairo" ("Cairo Will Have Another Auto," *Cairo Bulletin*, Thursday, April 12, 1906).

2. *Cairo Evening Citizen*, November 11, 1909.

3. Ibid., 1.

4. *Chicago Tribune*, November 11, 1909, 1.

5. *Cairo Bulletin*, November 11, 1909, 1.

6. Ibid.

7. *Waterloo Times-Tribune*, November 12, 1909, 1; *Cedar Rapids (Iowa) Evening Gazette*, November 12, 1909, 9; *Inter Ocean*, November 11, 1909, 1.

8. *Cairo Bulletin*, November 11, 1909, 1.

9. *Fort Wayne Journal-Gazette*, November 18, 1909, 2.

10. *Cairo Bulletin*, November 11, 1909, 1.

11. Ibid.

12. Ibid.

13. Rushdy, *American Lynching*, 69–93; Dray, *At the Hands of Persons Unknown*, 222–23.

14. *Cairo Bulletin*, November 11, 1909, 1.

15. Ibid.

16. Ibid.

17. Ibid.

18. Ibid.

19. *Inter Ocean*, November 11, 1909, 1.

20. *Cedar Rapids Evening Gazette*, November 12, 1909, 9.

21. *Atlanta Constitution*, November 11, 1909, 1.

22. *Cairo Evening Citizen*, November 11, 1909, 1.

23. *Fort Wayne Journal-Gazette*, November 18, 1909, 2.

24. *Cairo Evening Citizen*, November 11, 1909, 1.

25. Ibid.

26. *St. Louis Post-Dispatch*, November 12, 1909.

27. *Cairo Evening Citizen*, November 11, 1909, 1; *Washington (Ind.) Democrat*, November 12, 1909, 1.

28. *Cairo Evening Citizen*, November 10, 1909.

29. Ibid., November 11, 1909, 1.

30. *Daily Free Press*, November 11, 1909, 1; *Inter Ocean*, November 12, 1909, 1.

31. *Daily Review* (Decatur, Ill.), November 12, 1909, 1. The newspaper report claimed that several of Anna Pelley's brothers were in the mob, but although at least one brother, Joe Pelley, had been in the mob the day before, it seems more likely they were attending their sister's funeral services in Cairo and in Anna most of the day on Thursday.

32. *Cairo Evening Citizen*, November 11, 1910, 2.

33. *St. Louis Post-Dispatch*, November 12, 1909.

34. Ibid., February 10, 1910, 2.

35. *Waterloo Times-Tribune*, November 12, 1909, 1.

36. *Daily Review*, November 12, 1909, 1.

37. This man was identified by Sheriff Frank E. Davis as "Mr. Logan of Cox & Logan" in his statement to the *Citizen* (*Cairo Evening Citizen*, extra, November 12, 1909). Logan confirmed that he was present but stated he was not a leader of the mob and was not there to lynch Froggie James (*Cairo Evening Citizen*, November 13, 1909). Despite the fact the sheriff "recognized the Cairo crowd," he was more than reluctant to provide names.

38. *Cincinnati Enquirer*, November 13, 1909, 1.

## 4. The Lynchings of Will "Froggie" James and Henry A. Salzner

1. *Fort Wayne (Ind.) Weekly Sentinel*, November 17, 1909, 2.

2. *Daily Review*, November 12, 1909, 1.

3. *Cedar Rapids Evening Gazette*, November 12, 1909, 9; *Washington Democrat*, November 12, 1909, 1.

4. *Cincinnati Enquirer*, November 13, 1909, 1.

5. *St. Louis Post-Dispatch*, November 12, 1909.

6. *Inter Ocean*, November 12, 1909, 1.

7. *Chicago Tribune*, November 12, 1909, 1–2.

8. *Fort Wayne (Ind.) Daily News*, November 12, 1909, 12.

9. *Inter Ocean*, November 12, 1909, 1.

10. *Waterloo (Iowa) Reporter*, November 12, 1909, 1.

11. *Cairo Evening Citizen*, November 11, 1909, 1.

12. *Cairo Bulletin*, November 12, 1909, 1.

13. *St. Louis Post-Dispatch*, November 12, 1909. The Egyptian Hustlers was an organization of traveling salesmen who held conventions in Southern Illinois towns each year.

14. Ibid.

15. *Inter Ocean*, November 12, 1909, 4.

16. *Cincinnati Enquirer*, November 13, 1909, 1.

17. *Inter Ocean*, November 12, 1909, 1.

18. *St. Louis Post-Dispatch*, November 12, 1909, 1.

19. *Cairo Evening Citizen*, November 11, 1909, 10.

20. *Cairo Bulletin*, November 12, 1909, 1. In other accounts of Will James's lynching, much is made of the female role in it. Newspapers spoke of "500 women" pulling the rope that was to hang James (*Waterloo Times-Tribune*, November 12, 1909, 1; *Portsmouth Daily Times*, November 12, 1909, 1; *Fort Wayne Weekly Sentinel*, November 17, 1909, 2). Further, the lone woman on the train to Belknap was pointed out (*Washington Democrat*, November 12, 1909, 1). One explanation came from the *Jonesboro Gazette*, which stated that reports of Cairo women pulling the rope were utterly and ridiculously false; the *Gazette* blamed the misinformation on a "reckless and indifferent" Associated Press reporter (*Cairo Evening Citizen*, December 11, 1909, 5). The *Cairo Bulletin* mentioned women in the lynch crowd as spectators only, and the *Cairo Evening Citizen* did not comment on the gender composition of the crowd.

21. *New York Times*, November 12, 1909, 1.

22. *Cairo Evening Citizen*, November 11, 1909, 10.

23. *Jonesboro Gazette*, November 19, 1909.

24. *Cincinnati Enquirer*, November 13, 1909, 2; *Fort Wayne Daily News*, November 12, 1909, 17; Senechal, *Sociogenesis of a Race Riot*, 54.

25. Ruel Hindman interview, Shawnee Community College, Oral History Project, November 14, 1975, 27, http://www.shawneecc.edu/student-resources/library/local-history-project/ruel-hindman-interview. In his interview, Hindman recalled that when he was eight years old, he and his older brother went to meet the train returning to Anna from Cairo with citizens of Anna who had been in the mob. He said he never saw the body part that Anna, Illinois, men brought back to town to prove they had lynched Will James. He thought it was a leg. The *Jonesboro Gazette* stated that "souvenirs, such as pieces of rope and pieces of a burnt negro's bones are quite plentiful here" (November 19, 1909).

26. *Cairo Evening Citizen*, November 11, 1909, 10.

27. *St. Louis Post-Dispatch*, November 12, 1909.

28. *Cairo Evening Citizen*, November 11, 1909, 1.

29. *Cairo Bulletin*, November 12, 1909, 1.

30. *St. Louis Post-Dispatch*, November 12, 1909.

31. *Fort Wayne Weekly Sentinel*, November 17, 1909, 2.

32. "Coroner's Jury Held Henry Salzner for Wife's Death," *Cairo Evening Citizen*, August 21, 1909.

33. *Oskaloosa (Iowa) Daily Herald*, November 12, 1909, 1. Henry's father, William Franklin Salzner, a native of Germany, was a fur and hide merchant in Cairo in 1909 and had been a junk dealer in Anna. Henry's mother, Emily Jane Hollick Salzner, was from Pope County, Illinois. Mrs. Henry Salzner's maiden name was Mary E. Jones; she was born in February 1883 at Bird's Point, Missouri, the daughter of Henry H. Jones, a carpenter, and Clara Jones, a native of Ireland. She married W. M. Brown, a caulker in Paducah, Kentucky, on December 24, 1903. This marriage ended by divorce or the death of her husband, and in 1906 she married Henry A. Salzner in Cairo, Illinois. She had worked as a maid in the Salzner home before they married. The 1909 Cairo city directory lists Henry Salzner's photographic studio at 1701 Commercial (*Walker's Cairo City Directory for 1908–9*, 232). Henry and Mary Salzner had two children, Fred A. Salzner, who was born June 27, 1906, in Cairo, Illinois, and committed suicide on January 20, 1931, in Chaffee, Missouri, and William H. Salzner, who was born December 19, 1907, in Cairo and died June 12, 1971, in Detroit, Michigan.

34. "Death and Sheriff Stood at Bedside, Henry Salzner Arrested on Charge of Murder When Wife's Soul Fled," *Cairo Evening Citizen*, Thursday, August 19, 1909.

35. *Chicago Tribune*, November 12, 1909, 1.

36. *Logansport (Ind.) Reporter*, November 16, 1909, 6.

37. Ibid.

38. *Inter Ocean*, November 12, 1909, 1.

39. *Logansport Reporter*, November 16, 1909, 6.

40. *Daily Review*, November 12, 1909, 12; *Cairo Bulletin*, November 12, 1909, 1.

41. *Waterloo Times-Tribune*, November 12, 1909, 1.

42. *St. Louis Post-Dispatch*, November 12, 1909.

43. *Cairo Bulletin*, November 12, 1909, 1.

44. *Cairo Evening Citizen*, November 11, 1909, 9.

45. At that time it was not unusual for jailers and sheriffs to reside in an area of the jail or courthouse with their family.

46. *Cairo Bulletin*, November 12, 1909, 1; *Cairo Evening Citizen*, November 11, 1909, 9.

47. *Chicago Tribune*, November 12, 1909, 1.

48. *Cairo Evening Citizen*, November 11, 1909, 9; *Cairo Bulletin*, November 13, 1909, 1.

49. *Cairo Bulletin*, November 12, 1909, 1.

50. *St. Louis Post-Dispatch*, November 12, 1909.

51. *Chicago Tribune*, November 12, 1909, 2; *San Francisco Chronicle*, November 12, 1909, 1. Goldsby in *Spectacular Secret* argues that the urban American press trivialized lynching in the United States by sensationalizing it, as did the *Chicago Tribune* and the *Cincinnati Enquirer* in their accounts (12–16).

52. *Chicago Tribune*, November 12, 1909, 1.

53. *Cairo Evening Citizen*, November 11, 1909, 9.

54. *Cincinnati Enquirer*, November 13, 1909. 1

55. *Waterloo Times-Tribune*, November 12, 1909, 1; *Oskaloosa Daily Herald*, November 12, 1909, 1; *Portsmouth Daily Times*, November 12, 1909, 1. In the Midwest the feeling was widespread that justice delayed was justice denied, that slow justice was no justice (Pfeifer, *Rough Justice*, 25).

56. *Daily Review*, November 12, 1909, 1; Giddings, *Ida*, 483.

## 5. A Third Lynching Prevented

1. *Cairo Evening Citizen*, November 12, 1909.

2. *Cairo Bulletin*, November 12, 1909, 1. In the terrible lynchings and

race riot in 1908 in Springfield, Illinois, that city's mayor, Roy Reece, had been attacked and had to be rescued by his friends (Senechal, *Sociogenesis of a Race Riot*, 31).

3. "Reports of Riots at Cairo, Illinois, November 12, 1909," 41.

4. *Cairo Bulletin*, November 13, 1909, 1.

5. *Waterloo Times-Tribune*, November 12, 1909, 1. Two members from the Newton company, Private Ira Chrisman and Sergeant Sidney R. Ellis, were court-martialed for having failed to report for riot duty in Cairo on November 12 ("Another Result of Cairo Lynching," *Cairo Evening Citizen*, January 4, 1910).

6. "Reports of Riots at Cairo, Illinois, November 12, 1909," 38–45.

7. *Fort Wayne Weekly Sentinel*, November 17, 1909, 2.

8. *Waterloo (Iowa) Evening Courier*, November 12, 1909, 1.

9. *Oskaloosa Daily Herald*, November 12, 1909, 1.

10. *Cairo Evening Citizen*, Friday, February 18, 1910.

11. *Inter Ocean*, November 12, 1909, 1; *Chicago Tribune*, November 12, 1909, 1.

12. Southern, *Progressive Era and Race*, 162.

13. *Cincinnati Enquirer*, November 13, 1909, 2.

14. *Alton Evening Telegraph*, November 12, 1909, 11; *Fort Wayne Daily News*, November 12, 1909, 1.

15. *Cairo Bulletin*, November 12, 1909, 2.

16. Ibid.

17. *Inter Ocean*, November 12, 1909, 4.

18. *Daily Review*, November 12, 1909, 12.

19. *Waterloo Evening Courier*, November 13, 1909, 1.

20. *Cairo Bulletin*, November 14, 1909, 1.

21. *Waterloo Evening Courier*, November 13, 1909, 1.

22. *Chicago Tribune*, November 13, 1909, 1.

23. *Waterloo Evening Courier*, November 13, 1909, 1.

24. *Chicago Tribune*, November 13, 1909, 1.

25. "Reports of Riots at Cairo, Illinois, November 12, 1909," 41.

26. *Logansport Reporter*, November 13, 1909, 6. When Sheriff Davis initially fled Cairo with Will James, the destination might have been Kankakee—the northern part of Illinois was thought to be at least less anti–African American than the rest of the state. Alexander, however, never went to Kankakee, as stated in the Waterloo newspaper.

27. Ten companies of National Guardsmen were sent to Cairo following the November 11, 1909, lynchings. On November 13, seven of them were ordered home.

## 6. The National Spotlight on Cairo

1. *New York Times*, November 13, 1909, 6.

2. *Washington Post*, November 13, 1909, 7.

3. Ibid.

4. *New York Times*, November 13, 1909, 7.

5. Ibid., November 15, 1909, 8.

6. Ibid.

7. Ibid. It is uncertain whether Mayor Parsons slept through the lynchings, but the mob's initial plan to parade James by Parsons's house at 604 28th Street was decided against, and he was taken directly to 8th and Commercial.

8. Ibid.

9. There were 6,300 African Americans in Cairo in 1900 and 109,000 African Americans in the state of Illinois, meaning 5.78 percent of the state's African American population lived in Cairo.

10. *New York Times*, November 19, 1909, 10.

11. "Obituaries and Death Notices from Cairo." There were five homicides in Cairo in November and December 1909, bringing the total to twenty-two in 1909.

12. *Cairo Bulletin*, November 12, 1909, 1–2.

13. *Chicago Tribune*, November 15, 1909, 6.

14. The last previous public hanging in Cairo was December 29, 1899, when William Martin was executed for the murder of Joe Landum on October 8, 1899 (*Cairo Citizen*, January 4, 1900).

15. *Cairo Bulletin*, November 15, 1909, 5.

16. *Chicago Tribune*, November 13, 1909, 10; Rushdy, *American Lynching*, 73.

17. *Boston Herald* quoted in *Washington Post*, November 15, 1909, 6.

18. *Springfield Republican* quoted in *Washington Post*, November 15, 1909, 6.

19. Waldrep, *Many Faces of Judge Lynch*, 6.

20. Pfeifer, *Rough Justice*.

21. *New Orleans Times-Democrat* quoted in *Washington Post*, November 15, 1909, 6.

22. *Memphis Commercial-Appeal* quoted in *Cairo Bulletin*, November 18, 1909.

23. *New York Age*, November 18, 1909, 1. The prediction of the newspaper proved true and Alexander County was forced to pay $5,000 to the two children of Henry Salzner, who had been lynched. It could not be proven that Will "Froggie" James left any children, so no payment had to be made to the one who claimed to be his child.

24. *St. Louis Post-Dispatch* quoted in *Cairo Bulletin*, November 16, 1909, 2. Removal of a black prisoner from a city when a mob was threatening was the preferred method of dealing with such a situation at the time (Southern, *Progressive Era and Race*, 134–35; Senechal, *Sociogenesis of a Race Riot*, 26–27). Davis was simply doing what other midwestern sheriffs had done.

25. *St. Louis Post-Dispatch* quoted in *Cairo Bulletin*, November 16, 1909, 2.

26. *Bloomington Pantagraph* and *Champaign Gazette* quoted in *Daily Review*, November 13, 1909, 8.

27. Quoted in *Cairo Bulletin*, November 16, 1909, 2.

28. Quoted in ibid., November 18, 1909, 4.

29. *Belleville News-Democrat* quoted in *Cairo Bulletin*, November 15, 1909, 2. In Pfeifer's study of Iowa lynchings, the frustration with the mechanics of due process was often given as justification for the act (Pfeifer, *Rough Justice*, 111–15). Ray Stannard Baker, in what was considered the classic study of race in America at the time, accepted the myth that lynching occurred because of the inefficiency of the justice system (Southern, *Progressive Era and Race*, 58–59).

30. *Muncie Press* quoted in *Cairo Bulletin*, November 18, 1909, 4.

31. Ibid.

32. *Belleville News-Democrat* quoted in *Cairo Bulletin*, November 16, 1909, 1. It is almost as if Ashraf H. A. Rushdy had read this editorial before writing *American Lynching*. He may have read similar editorials that argued that the people are the power behind the government and can therefore elect or empower themselves to enforce justice in their own way (Rushdy, *American Lynching*, 140–44). The whole concept of "rough justice" is examined at length by Michael J. Pfeifer in his work of the same name.

33. Rushdy, *American Lynching*, 70.

34. *Cairo Bulletin*, November 15, 1909, 1; Pfeifer, *Rough Justice*, 111. In neighboring Iowa, newspapers often railed against bad juries and defense attorneys.

35. *Cairo Bulletin*, November 15, 1909, 3. An oral history source from 1975 tells of a black servant called to stay with a white family while the man of the house went to participate in the lynching. This gives some concrete evidence that white women in Cairo were not encouraged to participate (Hattie B. Kendrick interview, Shawnee Community College, Oral History Project, August 18, 1975, http://www.shawneecc.edu/student-resources/library/local-history-project/hattie-kendrick-interview). Only one woman participant is mentioned in the *Cairo Evening Citizen* (November 11, 1909, 10) and none in the *Cairo Bulletin*.

36. *Cairo Bulletin*, November 15, 1909, 3; Goodwin, *Bully Pulpit*, 258–59.

37. *Cairo Bulletin*, November 15, 1909, 1.

38. Ibid., 3.

39. Ibid.

40. Ibid.

41. Ibid.

42. *Chicago Tribune*, November 15, 1909, 6.

43. *Inter Ocean*, November 15, 1909, 8.

44. *Los Angeles Herald*, November 15, 1909, 2.

45. *Chicago Tribune*, November 15, 1909, 6; *Inter Ocean*, November 15, 1909, 8; *Los Angeles Herald*, November 25, 1909, 2. Goldsby argues that the wire services so controlled information in the United States at the time that anti-lynching activists like Ida B. Wells-Barnett were forced to use other forms of communication, such as pamphlets, to reach black audiences with something approaching the actual facts of a lynching (*Spectacular Secret*, 101).

46. The Springfield, Illinois, race riot and lynchings of 1908 seemed to have the greatest possible impact in Illinois and throughout the country and were referred to time and again both by the Cairo press and nationally. It is sometimes argued that the Springfield riot, coming as it did in Lincoln's hometown, catalyzed African America to expand the civil rights struggle (Southern, *Progressive Era and Race*, 162).

47. *Cairo Bulletin*, November 15, 1909, 2.

48. Ibid.

## 7. The Removal of Sheriff Frank E. Davis

1. *Cairo Evening Citizen*, November 3, 1906.

2. Ibid.

3. The election results gave Davis 2,432 votes for county sheriff and his Socialist opponent, James B. Stewart, only 166 (*Cairo Evening Citizen*, November 3, 1906, 9; November 6, 1906).

4. The death certificate of James McGriffen McManus, Ancestry.com, https://search.ancestry.com/cgi-bin/sse.dll?indiv=1&dbid=2542&h=1545423&usePUB=true&_phsrc=Raf6467&_phstart=successSource&requr=2550866976735232&ur=0&lang=en-US, accessed October 9, 2016.

5. *Chicago Tribune*, November 19, 1909, 6.

6. *Cairo Bulletin*, November 19, 1909, 8.

7. *Inter Ocean*, November 19, 1909, 3.

8. *Cairo Bulletin*, November 23, 1909, 6.

9. *Cairo Evening Citizen*, November 11, 1909, 6.

10. *Cairo Bulletin*, December 10, 1909, 4.

11. Goodwin, *Bully Pulpit*, 58–59.

12. *Cincinnati Enquirer*, November 13, 1909, 1; *Washington Post*, November 13, 1909, 1.

13. *Washington Post*, November 13, 1909, 1.

14. *Cairo Evening Citizen*, November 30, 1909, 1.

15. See Giddings, *Ida*.

16. Duster, *Crusade for Justice*, 312.

17. Schechter, *Ida B. Wells-Barnett and American Reform*, 140. Wells recalled that Thomas A. Head was an African Methodist Episcopal preacher, but he was likely Baptist as he was editor of the *Baptist Truth*, a religious newspaper published in Cairo. His father, Franklin Head, was also a Baptist minister in Madison County, Missouri, from where the Reverend T. A. Head moved to Cairo before 1900.

18. Thomas A. Head's son, Pearl Head, was an office worker for Dr. William H. Field, an African American physician in Cairo, and later became a mail carrier.

19. Giddings, *Ida*, 484–85.

20. Duster, *Crusade for Justice*, 312.

21. John C. Lewis and his wife, Cordelia C. Lewis, were both natives of Kentucky and teachers in the public school at Cairo. The 1915 Cairo city directory lists them still living at 612 12th Street and John as principal of Sumner High School (*Cairo Illinois City Directory 1915*, 229).

22. Duster, *Crusade for Justice*, 313.

23. Ibid.; Giddings, *Ida*, 285, 485.

24. Duster, *Crusade for Justice*, 313.

25. Giddings, *Ida*, 486.

26. "Resolutions Adopted by Cairo Negroes," *Cairo Evening Citizen*, December 1, 1909, 1.

27. *Cairo Evening Citizen*, December 2, 1909, 1. In her autobiography, Wells-Barnett called George Jackson an "Uncle Tom." A couple of months later he would be one of the county deputies who defended a black prisoner at the courthouse with deadly force. The prisoner was not lynched.

28. *Cairo Bulletin*, December 4, 1909, 2.

29. Ibid.; *Cairo Evening Citizen*, December 2, 1909, 1.

30. *Cairo Bulletin*, December 4, 1909, 2.

31. Giddings, *Ida*, 486.

32. *Cairo Evening Citizen*, November 30, 1909, 1.

33. Thomas Winton Warrick, a native of Hickman, Kentucky, had left Cairo and moved to Springfield before 1910, where he was a clerk in a department store and later appointed a clerk at the State House.

34. *Cairo Bulletin*, December 2, 1909, 1. It had been established that James had delivered ice regularly to the house where Anna Pelley lived. Three sets of bloodhounds were given the gag found in the dead woman's mouth, and all tracked to Will James at Lovie Green's dwelling, at his workplace, and finally to the city jail. Ida Wells-Barnett, however, never admitted that any black suspect who was lynched was guilty (Waldrep, *Many Faces of Judge Lynch*, 122–23). Of course, it is possible that the Cairo police framed Will James as a convenient suspect, as Atlanta detectives were to do later with Leo Frank (Dinnerstein, "Fate of Leo Frank").

35. *Cairo Bulletin*, December 2, 1909, 1.

36. Ibid. Obviously there was a split in Cairo's black community between supporters and opponents of Frank Davis. There was no voice from the black community involved in running either of Cairo's daily newspapers, so we have only the white version of the division among black people, and little of that. Two of Davis's strongest supporters were George Jackson and Thomas A. Head. Both were deputy sheriffs under Davis, and both briefly lost their jobs when Dr. McManus became sheriff.

37. Quoted in Duster, *Crusade for Justice*, 315.

38. Dray, *At the Hands of Persons Unknown*, 176.

39. *Nebraska State Journal* (Lincoln), December 13, 1909, 4.

40. *Cairo Evening Citizen*, December 2, 1909, 3.

41. Ibid.

42. *Muscatine (Iowa) Journal*, November 12, 1909, 1.

43. Seng, "Cairo Experience."

44. *Cairo Bulletin*, December 18, 1909.

45. Ibid. The case was People ex rel. Davis v. Nellis, 249 Ill. 12, 23 94 N. E. 165, 169 (1911).

46. *Cairo Evening Citizen*, December 8, 1909, 2.

47. Ibid., December 9, 1909, 2. The *Evening Citizen* was a staunch Republican paper, especially of the reform or progressive wing of the party.

48. Goldsby, *Spectacular Secret*, 101.

49. Duster, *Crusade for Justice*, 319–20; Dray, *At the Hands of Persons Unknown*.

50. Dray, *At the Hands of Persons Unknown*, 176; Giddings, *Ida*, 487.

51. *Cairo Evening Citizen*, December 21, 1909, 4.

52. "Troops Rushed to Vienna to Check Mob," *Cairo Evening Citizen*,

January 12, 1910, 1. The accused were brothers Hosea Lee Taborn and Perry Taborn and also Alexander Jenkins of Carrier Mills, Saline County, Illinois. The cases against Perry Taborn and Jenkins were dropped, and sixteen-year-old Hosea Lee Taborn pled guilty to manslaughter and was sentenced to the penitentiary (*Cairo Evening Citizen*, June 4, 1910).

## 8. Lovie Green and Her House

1. *Cairo Bulletin*, November 27, 1909, 4.

2. The 1908–9 Cairo City Directory lists a "colored" restaurant owned by F. Robertson at 2503 Commercial near 26th Street, which is likely where Lovie Green worked (*Walker's Cairo City Directory for 1908–9*, 233).

3. "Lovie Green Came before Committee," *Cairo Evening Citizen*, Tuesday, November 30, 1909.

4. *Cairo Bulletin*, November 15, 1909, 1.

5. Waldrep, *Many Faces of Judge Lynch*, 3.

6. Ibid.

7. *Cairo Evening Citizen*, November 10, 1909, 3.

8. *Cairo Bulletin*, November 19, 1909, 4.

9. Ibid., December 29, 1909, 6.

10. Owen Evers and Malcolm Beck interviews, Shawnee Community College, Oral History Project, April 1975, 5–6, http://www.shawneecc.edu/LIBRARY/history/oevers-5.asp. Pelley's suitor, according to Owen Evers, a prominent educator in Pulaski County from the 1940s to the 1960s, was Cairo police sergeant Wilfred French. In a conversation with Jay Manus, a student of the Cairo lynchings, Manus revealed that Anna Pelley had a lawman lover, but it was not Sergeant French.

11. *Jonesboro Gazette*, November 19, 1909, 2.

12. *Cairo Bulletin*, December 9, 1909, 1.

13. "Negress Involved in James' Case Dead," *Cairo Evening Citizen*, December 8, 1910.

14. *Cincinnati Enquirer*, November 13, 1909, 2.

15. *Cairo Evening Citizen*, November 30, 1909, 2.

16. Ibid. Luther Lewis was indicted for murderous assault on his wife, Annie Epps Lewis, in January 1910, but after she visited him in jail, she agreed to drop the complaint (Alexander County Circuit Court Criminal Records 44th day October Term 1909, January 8, 1910, 83; *Cairo Evening Citizen*, Tuesday, January 25, 1910).

17. Thirteenth Census of the United States, 1910 Population, Alexander County, Illinois, City of Cairo, 4th Ward, District 8, Thirteenth Street,

Ancestry.com, https://www.ancestry.com/interactive/7884/31111_4327545-00825?pid=4250124&treeid=&personid=&rc=&usePUB=true&_phsrc=Raf6535&_phstart=successSource.

18. *Cairo Bulletin*, December 1, 1909, 4.

19. Ibid., November 19, 1909, 4; April 5, 1910, 3; *Cairo Evening Citizen*, May 7, 1910, 8.

20. *Cairo Bulletin*, November 27, 1909, 4.

21. *Cairo Illinois City Directory 1915*, 335.

## 9. The Grand Jury's Report and Coroner's Verdict

1. *Cairo Bulletin*, December 8, 1909, 1, 4.

2. Ibid., December 13, 1909, 1.

3. *Cairo Evening Citizen*, December 14, 1909, 8.

4. Ibid.

5. Ibid., January 8, 1910, 1.

6. *Muscatine Journal*, November 12, 1909, 1.

7. Ibid., 7.

8. *Cairo Evening Citizen*, January 5, 1910, 1.

9. Ibid., January 25, 1910, 1. The jury was composed of W. H. Simpson, foreman; William Magner; George J. Fischer; A. S. Magner; A. E. Guilliams; and Albert Hurst.

10. *Cairo Bulletin*, January 9, 1910, 8. Alexander County Circuit Court Criminal Records 44th day October Term 1909, January 8, 1910, 84.

11. *The Standard* (Ogden, Utah), January 11, 1910, 7.

12. *Cairo Bulletin*, January 11, 1910, 8.

13. Ibid., January 13, 1910, 1.

## 10. The Anna Pelley and Mary E. Salzner Memorials

1. "Suggests Monument to Miss Pelley," *Cairo Evening Citizen*, November 13, 1909.

2. *Cairo Bulletin*, November 17, 1909, 8.

3. *Syracuse (N.Y.) Herald*, October 14, 1934, 3. On February 8, 1937, John Jeremiah Pelley's picture was on the cover of *Time* magazine. In the accompanying article, Pelley was called "the most popular man in American railroading" and an industrial statesman. His "amazing" career in railroading was described, but there was no mention of his murdered sister, Anna, or of the lynching in Cairo ("Business and Finance: All Aboard!").

4. *Cairo Bulletin*, November 17, 1910, 8.

5. Ibid., November 15, 1909, 2. This editorial was later discussed in James W. Loewen's *Sundown Towns*, and he commented, "Neither editor saw any irony in using a symbol of a lynching rope as a celebration of 'law and order'" (175).

6. *Cairo Evening Citizen*, November 16, 1909, 1; *Cairo Bulletin*, February 4, 1910, 2.

7. *Cairo Evening Citizen*, January 24, 1910, 8.

8. "Will You Give to Erect a Monument to Miss Pelley," *Cairo Evening Citizen*, November 18, 1909.

9. "Buys Monument for Mrs. Salzner," *Cairo Evening Citizen*, November 23, 1909. The committee was composed of Mrs. Louis Zanone, Charles Lancaster, Dr. J. T. Walsh, Mrs. A. Comings, and Mrs. George B. Magee.

10. *Cairo Bulletin*, November 24, 1909, 6.

11. Ibid., December 12, 1909, 2.

12. Ibid., December 18, 1909, 1.

13. *Cairo Evening Citizen*, December 17, 1909, 1; December 18, 1909, 18.

## 11. Liquor, Vice, and Corruption in Cairo

1. *Daily Review*, December 9, 1909, 1.

2. *Cairo Evening Citizen*, December 13, 1909, 9.

3. *Waterloo Times-Tribune*, November 17, 1909, 1.

4. "Reports of Riots at Cairo, Illinois, November 12, 1909," 39.

5. *Cairo Evening Citizen*, December 15, 1909, part 2, 7.

6. Ibid.

7. Ibid., January 3, 1910, 4.

8. *Cairo Bulletin*, December 26, 1909, 10.

9. Ibid., December 17, 1909, 2.

10. Ibid., November 16, 1909, 4.

11. *Walker's Cairo City Directory for 1908–9* lists sixty-nine saloons and nine beer agents and depots. This did not include restaurants, many of which also served alcohol. Thirty saloons were along Commercial Avenue alone.

12. *Cairo Bulletin*, December 14, 1910, 4.

13. Ibid., January 15, 1911, 2.

14. *Cairo Evening Citizen*, February 12, 1910, 4.

15. *Daily Telegram's Cairo City Directory for 1904*, 228.

16. Lansden, *History of the City of Cairo*, 227.

17. *Louisville Courier-Journal* quoted in *Cairo Bulletin*, November 17, 1909, 3.

18. Lantz, *Community in Search of Itself*, 65–87.

19. *Cairo Evening Citizen*, January 10, 1910, 8.

20. *New York Times*, November 13, 1909, 7.

21. *Cairo Bulletin*, November 28, 1909, 6.

22. *Daily Telegram's Cairo City Directory for 1904*, 56; "Prominent Citizen Has Passed Away," *Cairo Evening Citizen*, June 24, 1909, 1.

23. *Cairo Bulletin*, November 28, 1909, 6.

24. *Cairo Evening Citizen*, January 20, 1910, 6. Dave (also known as David or Davis) Ross was a pimp and was indicted twice for keeping a "house of ill fame" in February and March 1910 (Alexander County Circuit Court Criminal Records 21st day February Term 1910, March 28, 106 and 112).

25. *Cairo Evening Citizen*, January 20, 1910, 6; Alexander County Circuit Court Criminal Records 21st day February Term 1910, March 28, 106. A. B. Arey was fined twenty-five dollars at the same time for keeping a disorderly house at 2814 Poplar, where boys age eleven to seventeen were allowed to frequent and purchase beer at the bar.

26. *Cairo Bulletin*, January 22, 1910, 1.

27. *Cairo Evening Citizen*, February 1, 1910, 4.

## 12. Corruption and Reform

1. *Cairo Bulletin*, November 20, 1909, 8. Establishing "Law and Order Leagues" following racial or urban disturbances was common (Senechal, *Sociogenesis of a Race Riot*, 178–79).

2. *Cairo Bulletin*, November 24, 1909, 1.

3. Ibid.

4. Ibid., November 28, 1909, 4.

5. Ibid., November 20, 1909, 4.

6. Ibid., November 19, 1909, 1.

7. Ibid., December 15, 1909, 2.

8. Ibid., November 27, 1909, 4.

9. Ibid., December 1, 1909, 4.

10. Ibid., November 27, 1909, 4

11. Ibid., November 28, 1909, 4.

12. Ibid., December 28, 1909, 6.

13. *Cairo Evening Citizen*, November 17, 1909, 4.

14. *Cairo Bulletin*, November 18, 1909, 2.

15. Ibid., November 29, 1909, 5.

16. Ibid., December 6, 1909, 4.

17. Ibid., December 28, 1909, 6.

18. Ibid., November 25, 1909, 2; December 16, 1909, 2.

19. Ibid., December 16, 1909, 2.

20. *Herrin Promoter*, December 14, 1909, quoted in *Cairo Bulletin*, December 16, 1909, 2.

21. *Cairo Bulletin*, November 18, 1909, 6; December 19, 1909, 4. William Polk was described as "an industrious negro barber." He was reportedly a member of the 25th Infantry Regiment of African American soldiers stationed at Fort Brown in Brownsville, Texas, who were accused of shooting to death a white bartender and wounding a policeman on August 13, 1906. Polk was on guard duty and was wounded in the leg when the mob attacked (*Cairo Evening Citizen*, November 18, 1909, 1; November 22, 1909). President Theodore Roosevelt had all 167 soldiers dishonorably discharged without a trial, but they were posthumously exonerated in 1972 and President Nixon changed their military records to reflect an honorable discharge.

22. "Henry Small Pleads Guilty to Murder," *Cairo Evening Citizen*, January 5, 1910.

23. *Centralia Sentinel* quoted in *Cairo Evening Citizen*, November 20, 1909.

24. Ibid.; Alexander County Circuit Court Criminal Records 44th day October Term, January 8, 1910, Special Grand Jury Report, 83.

25. *Cairo Bulletin*, November 19, 1909, 8.

26. Ibid.

27. Ibid.

28. Ibid., November 18, 1909, 4.

29. Ibid., November 30, 1909, 2.

30. Ibid., December 16, 1909, 2.

31. "Henry Small Taken to Chester Today," *Cairo Evening Citizen*, January 12, 1910.

32. *Cairo Bulletin*, November 12, 1909, 1.

33. Ibid., 2.

34. Ibid., November 13, 1909, 4.

35. Ibid.

36. Ibid., December 10, 1909, 4.

37. Ibid.

38. Ibid.

39. Ibid., November 13, 1909, 4; November 17, 1909, 3; November 22, 1909, 4; December 10, 1909, 4; December 12, 1909, 4.

40. Ibid., December 26, 1909, 6.

41. Ibid.

42. Ibid., January 3, 1910, 4.

43. *Herrin (Ill.) News* quoted in ibid.

## 13. A New Sheriff, a Purse Snatching, and Another Lynch Mob

1. *Cairo Evening Citizen*, December 15, 1909, part 2. Sheriff Davis was permanently removed by order of the governor on December 7, 1909, and his term of office ended December 5, 1910.

2. Ibid. For twelve or so years I lived in the fine two-story house Captain Nellis built at 3014 Washington in Cairo.

3. Ibid., December 24, 1909, 1; December 27, 1909, 4; December 29, 1909, 1.

4. Ibid., February 14, 1910, 1.

5. *Cairo Bulletin*, January 22, 1910, 1.

6. Ibid., February 17, 1910, 2.

7. *Cairo Evening Citizen*, February 21, 1910, 2.

8. *Cairo Bulletin*, February 18, 1910, 6. For a biography of William Thomas Scott, see Mouser, *Black Gambler's World.*

9. *Cairo Evening Citizen*, February 18, 1910; *Cairo Bulletin*, February 18, 1910, 6.

10. *Cairo Bulletin*, February 18, 1910, 6; February 19, 1910.

11. *Chicago Tribune*, February 18, 1910, 1. This story was attributed to Sheriff Nellis in *Cairo Bulletin*, February 18, 1910.

12. *Chicago Tribune*, February 18, 1910, 2. There might have been a distant relationship between William E. Maloney and Anna Pelley, as both of their parents were natives of Ireland, but they were not closely related.

13. "Mob's Joan of Arc Boasts She Knew of Lynch Plot," *St. Louis Post-Dispatch*, February 19, 1910, 2. Maloney later denied the report and said the statements in the *Post-Dispatch* were false (*Cairo Bulletin*, February 22, 1910, 1).

14. *Cairo Evening Citizen*, February 21, 1910, 3.

15. *Cairo Bulletin*, February 20, 1910, 1.

16. *Cairo Evening Citizen*, February 18, 1910, 1.

17. Ibid., February 21, 1910.

18. Ibid. Benjamin F. Thompson served as a private in the Civil War in Company I, 97th Illinois Infantry, and was discharged for cataracts, deafness, chronic constipation, hemorrhoids, and exposure and hardship while on duty.

19. *New York Times*, February 20, 1910. 5.

20. *Chicago Tribune*, February 18, 1910, 2.

21. *Cairo Evening Citizen*, May 8, 1910, 1.

22. Ibid., February 21, 1910, 3.

23. *New York Times*, February 20, 1910, 5.

24. *Cairo Evening Citizen*, February 21, 1910, 5.

25. *St. Louis Post-Dispatch*, February 19, 1910. Albert Frost was identified in the newspaper as a deputy, but he later testified that he was not at the courthouse on the night of the assault (*Cairo Bulletin*, February 19, 1910).

26. *Cairo Evening Citizen*, February 21, 1910, 3.

27. Ibid., July 19, 1910, 1.

28. *St. Louis Post-Dispatch*, February 19, 1910.

29. *Cairo Evening Citizen*, July 19, 1910, 1.

30. *New Castle (Pa.) News*, February 18, 1910, 9; *Fort Wayne Daily News*, February 18, 1910, 13.

31. *St. Louis Post-Dispatch*, February 19, 1910.

32. *Cairo Evening Citizen*, February 18, 1910, 1; *Indianapolis News*, February 18, 1910, 1. Several other papers had this account, and this was probably because the *Citizen* was their source.

33. *Cairo Bulletin*, February 18, 1910, 1.

34. Ibid.

35. *Cairo Evening Citizen*, February 18, 1910, 1.

36. *Cairo Bulletin*, February 21, 1910, 3; *Daily Review*, February 22, 1910, 1; *New Castle News*, February 18, 1910, 1; *Indianapolis News*, February 18, 1910, 1.

37. *Daily Review*, February 22, 1910, 1.

38. *Chicago Tribune*, February 18, 1910, 1.

39. *Portsmouth Daily Times*, February 18, 1910, 1.

40. *Cairo Evening Citizen*, February 21, 1910, 5.

41. *Cairo Bulletin*, February 19, 1910, 1. The newspaper said Halliday could have lived only a few moments after being shot.

42. *Chicago Tribune*, February 18, 1910, 2.

43. *Altoona (Pa.) Mirror*, February 19, 1910, 3.

44. *Cairo Evening Citizen*, February 18, 1910, 1.

45. *St. Louis Post-Dispatch*, February 19, 1910.

46. *Cairo Evening Citizen*, February 18, 1910, 1.

47. Ibid., February 19, 1910, 1.

48. Ibid., February 18, 1910, 1; Alexander County Circuit Court Criminal Records 5th day February Term 1910, February 18, 97.

49. *Cairo Evening Citizen*, February 19, 1910, 1.

50. *Cairo Bulletin*, February 21, 1910, 1.

51. *Cairo Evening Citizen*, February 18, 1910, 1.

52. *St. Louis Post-Dispatch*, February 19, 1910.

53. Ibid.

54. *Cairo Evening Citizen*, February 20, 1910, 1.

55. Allen and Als, *Without Sanctuary*, 168–69.

56. *New York Times*, February 21, 1910, 7.

57. Rushdy, *American Lynching*, 69–93.

58. Ibid.

59. Ibid.

60. *St. Louis Post-Dispatch*, February 19, 1910, 2.

61. Ibid.

62. *Nebraska State Journal*, February 19, 1910, 1.

## 14. Another Coroner's Inquest and Investigation

1. The jury consisted of John L. Parham, Charles F. Miller, A. J. Rees, M. F. Kelly, Gus Osterloh, and Joseph E. Greaney (*Cairo Bulletin*, February 18, 1910).

2. *Cairo Evening Citizen*, February 19, 1910, 1. A compelling aside from the same issue of the *Citizen*, possibly giving insight into the general condition of "wide-open" Cairo in 1910, is the mention of one of the other convicts on the train to Chester besides John Pratt: "Nels[e] Valentine for life for murder of Buddy Warner, one of his companions, on Christmas day over a can of beer." At the coroner's inquest, Nelse Valentine "seemed wholly indifferent as to his fate and grinned or laughed when some of the negro witnesses expressed themselves." The newspaper concluded, "He is a very good specimen of the lowest type of vicious and reckless negro" (ibid., January 17, 1910).

3. Ibid., February 19, 1910, 1.

4. Ibid., February 21, 1910, 3.

5. "Defense Offers Its Evidence," *Cairo Bulletin*, July 21, 1910, 4.

6. *Cairo Evening Citizen*, February 21, 1910, 3.

7. *Altoona Mirror*, February 19, 1910, 3.

8. *Cairo Evening Citizen*, February 18, 1910, 1.

9. Ibid., February 19, 1910, 2; *Cairo Bulletin*, February 19, 1910.

10. *Cairo Evening Citizen*, February 21, 1910.

11. "Testimony before Coroner's Jury," *Cairo Evening Citizen*, February 21, 1910; *Cairo Bulletin*, February 22, 1910, 1.

12. *Logansport (Ind.) Pharos*, February 19, 1910, 1.

13. *Cairo Evening Citizen*, February 19, 1910.

14. Ibid., February 22, 1910, 1.

15. *Cairo Bulletin*, February 21, 1910, 1.

16. *Cairo Evening Citizen*, February 18, 1910, 1.

17. The Halliday family built and owned several mansions in Cairo, most notably Riverlore Mansion on Washington Avenue. Civil rights activist Hattie Kendrick once said the Hallidays and Cairo were synonymous (Hattie B. Kendrick interview, Shawnee Community College, Oral History Project, August 18, 1975, http://www.shawneecc.edu/student-resources/library/local-history-project/hattie-kendrick-interview).

18. *Cairo Evening Citizen*, February 21, 1910, 1. In contrast, the *Daily Free Press* claimed "Cairo Negroes" made an "insulting demonstration" when the funeral train passed a "colored crowd" (February 21, 1910, 7).

19. *Cairo Evening Citizen*, February 18, 1910, 4.

20. Ibid.

21. Ibid.

22. *Cairo Bulletin*, February 22, 1910, 1.

23. Ibid., February 21, 1910, 1.

24. *Daily Review*, February 22, 1910, 1.

25. Ibid.

26. *Indiana (Pa.) Gazette*, February 21, 1910, 8.

27. *Fort Wayne Daily News*, February 28, 1910, 8.

28. *Atlanta Constitution*, February 20, 1910, 6; *Bisbee (Ariz.) Daily Review*, February 20, 1910, 1; *Washington Post*, February 21, 1910, 1; *New York Times*, February 21, 1910, 2; *Nebraska State Journal*, February 21, 1910, 1; *San Francisco Chronicle*, February 21, 1910, 6; *Daily Herald* (Arlington Heights, Ill.), February 25, 1910, 7.

29. *Cairo Bulletin*, February 19, 1910, 1; February 20, 1910, 5.

30. "Two Tenements Destroyed by Fierce Blaze, Some Suspicious Circumstances," *Cairo Evening Citizen*, Saturday, January 8, 1910. The tenements were owned by R. Redman and Angus Leek.

31. "Another Fire That Looks Like Work of Fire Bug," *Cairo Evening Citizen*, January 29, 1910. The tenements were owned by E. A. Smith, Charles Lancaster, and John M. Lansden.

32. Ibid.

33. Ibid., February 14, 1910.

34. "Firebug Landed behind Bars," *Cairo Evening Citizen*, March 3, 1910.

35. *Cairo Bulletin*, May 13, 1910, 6.

36. Ibid., February 21, 1910, 7.

37. *New York Times*, February 21, 1910, 7, quoted in *Cairo Evening Citizen*, February 22, 1910, 6.

38. *Louisville Courier-Journal* quoted in *Cairo Bulletin*, February 22, 1910, 2.

39. Ibid.

40. *Chicago Tribune*, February 19, 1910, 10.

41. *St. Louis Star* quoted in *Cairo Evening Citizen*, February 22, 1910, 6.

42. *St. Louis Republic* quoted in *Cairo Evening Citizen*, February 22, 1910, 6.

43. *Denver Republican* quoted in *Cairo Evening Citizen*, February 23, 1910, 2.

44. *New York Age*, February 24, 1910, 1; Southern, *Progressive Era and Race*, 87.

45. *New York Age*, February 24, 1910, 4.

46. Ibid.

47. *Fort Wayne Daily News*, February 19, 1910, 8.

48. *Fort Wayne Weekly Sentinel*, February 23, 1910, 6.

49. *St. Louis Globe-Democrat* quoted in *Cairo Evening Citizen*, February 22, 1910, 6.

50. *Chicago Post* quoted in *Cairo Evening Citizen*, February 23, 1910, 2.

51. *Denver News* quoted in *Cairo Evening Citizen*, February 23, 1910, 2.

52. *Mansfield (Ohio) News Journal*, February 18, 1910, 4.

53. *Cairo Evening Citizen*, February 21, 1910, 2.

54. Ibid.

55. *Cairo Bulletin*, February 21, 1910, 2.

56. *Cairo Evening Citizen*, February 21, 1910, 2.

57. Ibid., February 23, 1910, 2.

58. Ibid., February 19, 1910, 2; *Daily Review*, February 22, 1910, 1.

59. "Where Citizens Can Aid," *Cairo Evening Citizen*, February 19, 1910, 2.

60. *Cairo Evening Citizen*, February 19, 1910, 6.

61. Ibid.

62. Ibid.

## 15. The Cairo Police and a New Reform Effort

1. *Cairo Bulletin*, February 21, 1910, 1.

2. Ibid., January 5, 1910, 2.

3. Ibid., February 21, 1910, 1.

4. Ibid.

5. Ibid.

6. Senechal, *Sociogenesis of a Race Riot*, 82.

7. Ibid. Cairo alderman Leo McDaniel told the *Moberly (Mo.) Monitor* that Negroes snatched white girls on the street, hugged and kissed them, and then grabbed their purses (February 20, 1910, 2).

8. *Cairo Evening Citizen*, February 24, 1910, 1.
9. Ibid., February 25, 1910, 1.
10. Ibid., February 26, 1910, 1.
11. Ibid.
12. Ibid.
13. Ibid., February 28, 1910, 1.
14. Ibid., March 1, 1910, 1.
15. Ibid., March 5, 1910, 4.
16. *Cairo Bulletin*, March 5, 1910, 4. Policemen who did resist mobs such as the February 1910 one in Cairo faced threats to their own lives (Pfeifer, *Rough Justice*, 33).
17. *Cairo Evening Citizen*, March 9, 1910, 1.
18. *Cairo Bulletin*, March 9, 1910, 4.
19. *Cairo Evening Citizen*, March 9, 1910, 2.
20. Ibid., 4.
21. *Cairo Bulletin*, March 6, 1910, 4.
22. *Cairo Evening Citizen*, March 10, 1910, 2.
23. Ibid.
24. Ibid., March 25, 1910, 4.
25. Ibid., March 14, 1910, 7.
26. *Cairo Bulletin*, March 17, 1910, 4.
27. *Cairo Evening Citizen*, April 2, 1910, 1.
28. Ibid., April 11, 1910, 4.
29. *Cairo Bulletin*, March 8, 1910, 3; March 17, 1910, 8.
30. *Cairo Evening Citizen*, March 17, 1910, 1.
31. Ibid.
32. Ibid.
33. *Cairo Bulletin*, March 18, 1910, 2.
34. Ibid., March 20, 1910, 2.
35. Ibid., 4. The "panel game" involved wall panels that opened while the victim was involved with the "wenches" and then his belongings were searched and any valuables stolen.
36. Ibid., 4; March 23, 1910, 2.
37. *Cairo Evening Citizen*, March 28, 1910, 1; *Cairo Bulletin*, March 29, 1910, 5.
38. *Cairo Evening Citizen*, March 28, 1910, 1. In all, sixteen people were indicted for either leasing or operating a "house of ill fame." Alexander County Circuit Court Criminal Records 21st day February Term 1910, March 28, 109–10.

39. *Cairo Evening Citizen*, January 16, 1909.

40. Ibid., March 29, 1910, 2. Three members of the grand jury owned property on which brothels were operated. Thus, they were indirectly ruling against themselves. *Daily Free Press*, March 29, 1910, 2.

41. *Cairo Evening Citizen*, March 29, 1910.

42. Ibid., March 28, 1910, 5.

43. Ibid., March 17, 1910, 2.

44. Ibid., March 30, 1910, 6.

45. *Cairo Bulletin*, March 30, 1910, 6.

46. Ibid.

47. The grand jury consisted of Charles Cunningham (foreman), M. C. Metzger (clerk), J. P. Schuh, A. B. Howland, G. W. Buchanan, James Curry, Henry Zerfass, W. M. Hurt, H. C. Steinel, D. K. Brown, Rolla H. Spann, James Hileman, Thomas J. Kerth, Peter Day, John C. Gholson, W. L. Duncan, John T. Boyd, A. B. Turner, A. Kaufman, C. C. Miller, and W. B. Huette (ibid., March 29, 1910, 1).

48. *Cairo Evening Citizen*, March 28, 1910, 5.

49. Ibid.

50. Ibid.

51. Ibid.; Alexander County Circuit Court Criminal Records 21st day February Term 1910, March 28, 108.

52. *Cairo Evening Citizen*, March 28, 1910, 4.

53. *Fort Wayne Daily News*, February 19, 1910, 1; *Indianapolis News*, February 19, 1910, 1.

54. *Fort Wayne Daily News*, February 19, 1910.

55. *Cairo Evening Citizen*, March 29, 1910, 2.

56. Quoted in ibid., March 28, 1910, 6.

57. *Cairo Bulletin*, March 6, 1910, 4.

58. Ibid.

59. *Cairo Evening Citizen*, April 6, 1910, 2.

60. Ibid.; April 16, 1910, 5.

61. Ibid., April 6, 1910, 2.

62. Ibid., April 19, 1910, 2.

63. *Cairo Bulletin*, March 22, 1910, 2.

64. Mount Lebanon is in modern-day Lebanon, and many of Cairo's "Syrian colony" were actually Lebanese.

65. *Cairo Bulletin*, March 22, 1910, 2.

66. *Cairo Evening Citizen*, October 12, 1910. His son, Shirley G. Maloof,

remained in Cairo and paid his father's fine and fees, which amounted to about forty-six dollars.

67. *Cairo Bulletin*, March 22, 1910, 4.

68. Ibid., 2.

69. Ibid., April 2, 1910, 4.

70. *Cairo Evening Citizen*, April 19, 1910, 2.

71. Ibid., April 20, 1910, 1.

72. Ibid., 2.

73. Ibid.

74. Ibid.

75. Ibid., March 4, 1910, 1.

## 16. The Riot Cases

1. The jury consisted of Claude McRaven of McClure; Blaine Caldwell of Thebes; T. J. Williams and J. H. Griffin of Cairo; J. B. Branson of Sandusky; William Holl Powless and James Dunning of Diswood; S. H. Cox and J. T. Tinsley of Delta; W. S. Hurston and J. S. Hill of Elco; and Eli Dickson of Tamms (*Cairo Bulletin*, July 19, 1910).

2. June C. Smith served as state's attorney for Marion County, Illinois, from 1904 to 1908 before becoming assistant Illinois attorney general in 1909. From 1941 to 1947 he served on the Illinois Supreme Court and was elected chief justice.

3. *Cairo Evening Citizen*, May 10, 1910, 1.

4. Ibid., July 19, 1910, 1. The *Cairo Bulletin* had earlier charged that the circuit court was "very deferential" to Reed Green (March 17, 1910, 6).

5. *Cairo Evening Citizen*, May 8, 1910, 1.

6. "Court Declares Grand Jury Was Illegally Drawn," *Cairo Evening Citizen*, May 11, 1910, 1; "Important Day in Circuit Court," *Cairo Bulletin*, May 12, 1910, 6.

7. *Cairo Evening Citizen*, May 8, 1910, 1.

8. Ibid., July 19, 1910, 5.

9. Alexander County Circuit Court Criminal Records 21st day February Term 1910, March 28, 105.

10. *Cairo Evening Citizen*, July 19, 1910, 5.

11. Ibid., July 21, 1910, 1.

12. Ibid.

13. What were the lieutenant and captain doing in a bar across the street from the Alexander County Courthouse when the sheriff and his men were

still under siege in that building and Alex Halliday was lying dead in the snow?

14. *Cairo Evening Citizen*, July 21, 1910, 1.

15. Ibid.

16. Ibid., July 22, 1910, 5.

17. *Cairo Bulletin*, July 22, 1910, 4.

18. *Cairo Evening Citizen*, July 22, 1910, 5.

19. Ibid.

20. Ibid., 2.

21. Ibid.

22. Ibid.

23. *Cairo Bulletin*, July 23, 1910, 6.

24. Ibid.

25. *Muldrow (Okla.) Press*, July 29, 1910, 1.

26. Ibid.

27. Senechal, *Sociogenesis of a Race Riot*, 170–73. Abraham Raymer, a recent Russian Jewish immigrant, was convicted of stealing the sword of Major Otis Duncan of the Illinois National Guard.

28. *Cairo Bulletin*, July 23, 1910, 2. This was juror William Holl Powless of Diswood, Illinois.

29. *Cairo Evening Citizen*, July 23, 1910, 2.

30. *Cairo Bulletin*, July 23, 1910, 2.

31. Ibid.

32. *Cairo Evening Citizen*, July 29, 1910.

## 17. The Contest for Alexander County Sheriff in Court and at the Polls

1. *Cairo Evening Citizen*, July 23, 1910, 1.

2. *Daily Free Press*, July 14, 1910, 2.

3. *Cairo Evening Citizen*, July 23, 1910, 5.

4. Ibid., 1.

5. Ibid., November 8, 1910, 1; November 12, 1910, 1.

6. Ibid., September 16, 1910, 1.

7. People ex rel. Davis v. Nellis, 249 Ill. 12, 23 94 N.E. 165, 169 (1911).

8. See especially Ruehman v. Sheahan, Nos. 93-4031, 94-1333, 34 F. 3d 525, United States Court of Appeals, Seventh Circuit; argued April 19, 1994, decided September 6, 1994.

9. *Cairo Evening Citizen*, November 12, 1910, 1.

10. Appellate Court of Illinois, Fourth District, McManus v. Nellis, 203 Ill. App. 108 (1916).

11. Ibid.

12. Ibid.

## 18. Politics and the African American Community in Cairo

1. *New York Times*, November 13, 1909, 7.

2. Ibid., November 12, 1909, 7.

3. *Waterloo Evening Courier*, November 12, 1909, 1.

4. *Cairo Bulletin*, November 15, 1909, 1.

5. Rushdy, *American Lynching*, 89.

6. *Cairo Bulletin*, December 3, 1909, 6.

7. Ibid., December 6, 1909, 2.

8. Ibid., December 29, 1909, 2.

9. Goldsby, *Spectacular Secret*, 21.

10. *Cairo Bulletin*, December 23, 1909, 6.

11. Ibid., February 14, 1910, 6. Clendenen based his statistics on information he gathered from the school census. An examination of the 1,507 households in the 1910 federal census headed by a "black" or "mulatto" reveals that 30 percent were headed by females. The federal census statistic applies to all households, whereas the school census refers only to households with school-age children.

12. Giddings, *Ida*, 482.

13. *Cairo Evening Citizen*, February 21, 1910, 5.

14. Ibid., February 21, 1910, 2.

15. Ibid., January 22, 1910, 1; February 16, 1910, 1; February 21, 1910, 1; February 28, 1910; May 14, 1910, 6.

16. Ibid., May 14, 1910, 6; *Cairo Bulletin*, July 23, 1910.

17. *Cairo Bulletin*, July 23, 1910, 6; March 6, 1910, 4.

18. Ibid., October 30, 1910, 1.

19. Ibid.

20. Ibid.

21. Ibid., October 31, 1910, 2.

22. Ibid.

23. Ibid.

24. Ibid.; "At Olive Branch," ibid., October 31, 1910, 6.

25. *Cairo Evening Citizen* quoted in *Cairo Bulletin*, November 5, 1910, 2.

26. *Chicago Tribune* quoted in *Cairo Bulletin*, December 9, 1910, 3.

27. *Chicago Tribune*, November 9, 1910, 3; *Daily Free Press*, November 21, 1910, 2.

28. *Cairo Evening Citizen*, December 2, 1909, 1.

29. Ibid., February 21, 1910, 2; July 22, 1910, 2.

30. Ibid., May 19, 1910, 1.

31. *Cairo Bulletin*, April 15, 1910, 2.

32. *Cairo Evening Citizen*, April 13, 1910, 5.

33. Loewen, *Sundown Towns*, 513.

34. *Cairo Evening Citizen*, April 23, 1910, 1–2; May 7, 1910, 1.

35. Ibid., March 2, 1910, 1; Alexander County Circuit Court Criminal Records 21st day February Term 1910, March 28, 110; March 28, 106.

36. *Cairo Evening Citizen*, May 7, 1910, 1.

37. *Cairo Bulletin*, May 12, 1910, 6; Alexander County Circuit Court Criminal Records 4th day May Term 1910, May 12, 118.

38. *Cairo Evening Citizen*, April 23, 1910.

39. Ibid., 1.

40. Ibid., May 7, 1910, 8.

41. Ibid., May 13, 1910.

42. Ibid., March 10, 1910, 2.

43. Loewen, *Sundown Towns*, 463.

44. *Cairo Evening Citizen*, August 20, 1906; January 20, 1908; May 31, 1909; January 29, 1912.

45. Ibid., May 15, 1912.

46. *Cairo Bulletin*, October 31, 1910, 2; November 5, 1910, 2.

47. Ibid., November 4, 1910, 1.

48. Ibid.

49. Senechal, *Sociogenesis of a Race Riot*, 176.

50. Loewen, *Sundown Towns*, 463.

51. Ibid.

52. *Cairo Bulletin*, May 12, 1910, 5; May 13, 1910, 2.

53. Tolnay, *Festival of Violence*, 25.

54. Lantz, *Community in Search of Itself*, 51–52.

## 19. Sheriff Abner Bankson and the Homicide of Wilfred French

1. *Cairo Evening Citizen*, December 4, 1910, 1.

2. *Pulaski Enterprise* (Mound City, Ill.), May 29, 1931, 1. Abner C. Bankson was married twice, which further increased his alliances with Pulaski

County families. He married first on December 10, 1876, Julia Lurah Snell, the daughter of James H. Snell and Elizabeth Bettis. He married second on May 22, 1883, Laura B. Curry, the daughter of James Curry and Martha E. Rogers.

3. Ibid., December 25, 1908, 1.

4. Ibid., April 30, 1909, 1.

5. *Cairo Bulletin*, January 14, 1910, 2.

6. *Cairo Evening Citizen*, August 25, 1909.

7. Ibid.

8. *Pulaski Enterprise*, July 8, 1910; *Cairo Evening Citizen*, July 5, 1910.

9. *Cairo Bulletin*, January 14, 1910, 8.

10. She may also be the same person as Mabel Stevens, alias Cooper, alias Roberts, who kept a house on 13th Street in Cairo and was tried in federal court on charges of white slavery. She was accused of enticing seventeen-year-old Robbie Augustus Malpas to Cairo from Union City, Tennessee, with a promise of a job as a telephone operator but instead brought Malpas to her house and told the girl to "entertain" men. Stevens was found guilty and sentenced to two years in federal prison in Lansing, Kansas. Her attorney was Philetus E. Hileman (*Cairo Evening Citizen*, September 20, 1911; October 6, 1911, October 7, 1911; October 9, 1911; October 10, 1911). For obvious reasons, prostitutes often went by several names and pseudonyms.

11. Ibid., December 4, 1910, 4.

12. *Daily Free Press*, December 5, 1910, 3.

13. *Cairo Evening Citizen*, September 24, 1910, 4; December 4, 1910, 4.

14. *Cairo Bulletin*, December 4, 1910, 2.

15. *Cairo Evening Citizen*, December 4, 1910, 1; *Daily Free Press*, December 5, 1910, 3.

16. *Cairo Evening Citizen*, September 24, 1910, 4.

17. Ibid., December 4, 1910, 1.

18. Ibid., March 3, 1911, 1; *Daily Free Press*, December 24, 1910, 3.

19. *Daily Free Press*, December 5, 1910, 3.

20. *Cairo Evening Citizen*, December 4, 1910, 1. Brackey Bros. Saloon was owned by Edward J. and Henry L. Brackey (*Walker's Cairo City Directory for 1908–09*, 46, 88).

21. Policeman Wilfred V. French had three brothers living in 1910, William Henry "Will" French, also a Cairo city policeman; Wenceslaus Lavin "Winslow" French, a professional baseball player; and Wilburn T. French, a bartender.

22. *Cairo Evening Citizen*, December 4, 1910, 1.

23. *Cairo Bulletin*, December 6, 1910, 6. The *Citizen* did not mention Bankson asking about a gun.

24. *Cairo Evening Citizen*, December 4, 1910, 1.

25. Ibid.

26. Ibid.

27. *Pulaski Enterprise*, December 9, 1910, 1.

28. Ibid.

29. Goodwin, *Bully Pulpit*, 467–68.

30. *Pulaski Enterprise*, December 9, 1910, 1. In 1914 Mannon Bankson was elected sheriff of Pulaski County (*Cairo Bulletin*, December 3, 1914).

31. *Pulaski Enterprise*, December 9, 1910, 1.

32. *Cairo Evening Citizen*, December 4, 1910, 1.

33. *Cairo Bulletin*, December 6, 1910, 2.

34. Ibid.

35. *Logansport Reporter*, December 6, 1910, 2; *Arizona Republican* (Phoenix), December 4, 1910, 4; *Indianapolis Star*, December 4, 1910, 23; *Riverdale (Ill.) Pointer*, December 9, 1910, 2.

36. *Daily Free Press*, December 6, 1910, 2.

37. *Cairo Bulletin*, December 4, 1910, 2.

38. *Cairo Evening Citizen*, December 4, 1910, 1.

## 20. Pretrial Publicity and a Change of Venue

1. *Cairo Evening Citizen*, December 4, 1910, 1.

2. *Waterloo Times-Tribune*, December 4, 1910, 16; *Logansport Reporter*, December 6, 1910, 2; *West Bend (Iowa) Journal*, December 5, 1910, 2.

3. *Cairo Bulletin*, December 5, 1910, 6.

4. Ibid. The man was likely Frederick W. Sperle, who was a bartender in a saloon in Mounds, Illinois, in 1910.

5. *Daily Free Press*, December 6, 1910, 2.

6. Ibid., December 6, 1910, 2.

7. *Cairo Evening Citizen*, December 4, 1910, 1.

8. Ibid., December 7, 1910, 1.

9. Ibid.

10. Policeman Patrick J. Doud was stabbed to death just before midnight on March 21, 1907, by Marvin Boren. Doud tried to arrest Boren for creating a disturbance at the brothel of Alice Parham at 235 13th Street. Boren was married to a niece of former Cairo mayor Claude Winter. Boren testified that Doud struck him three times with his club before he stabbed him in self-defense (ibid., March 22, 1907; March 23, 1907; July 15, 1907). Boren

was charged with murder, but when the case came to trial, he was acquitted (ibid., July 17, 1907).

11. Ibid., December 7, 1910, 1. The priest referred to the murder of Eugenie McClarney on October 6, 1908.

12. This is a reference to Will Thomas, who was shot and killed by John Lewis on October 12, 1906. They were both fishermen. The two had argued in the morning and Lewis had clubbed Thomas's wife, accusing her of keeping a "bad house," and slapped her four-year-old daughter. Thomas, "under influence of liquor," met Lewis in the afternoon and said, "If you're going to kill me, do so now." They exchanged gunfire. Contradictory testimony was given as to who fired first. Lewis ran to his houseboat on the Ohio River, and when Thomas followed, the fatal shot was fired by Lewis as Thomas entered his door (ibid., October 12, 1906). Lewis claimed self-defense (ibid., October 13, 1906).

13. Ibid., December 7, 1910, 1.

14. Ibid.

15. *Murphysboro Independent* quoted in *Cairo Bulletin*, December 8, 1910, 2; also quoted in *Alton (Ill.) Evening Telegraph*, December 6, 1910, 9.

16. *Cairo Bulletin*, December 8, 1910, 2.

17. Ibid.

18. *Mounds Headlight* quoted in *Cairo Bulletin*, December 20, 1910, 2.

19. *Cairo Bulletin*, December 23, 1910, 4.

20. Lansden, *History of the City of Cairo*, 267.

21. *Cairo Bulletin*, December 1, 1909, 4.

22. Ibid., 4; December 2, 1909, 2.

23. Ibid., December 3, 1909, 2.

24. Ibid.

25. Ibid.

26. Ibid.

27. Ibid., December 6, 1909, 2.

28. Ibid., January 13, 1910, 2.

29. Ibid.

30. Ibid., December 4, 1910, 2.

31. Ibid., December 20, 1910, 2.

32. Ibid., December 16, 1910, 5.

33. *Cairo Evening Citizen*, August 10, 1910; August 19, 1910. Greaney survived the military inquiry in December 1910, was reelected captain of Company K in January 1911, and resigned in September of the same year (ibid., December 15, 1910, 1; January 6, 1911, 1; September 28, 1911).

34. "Capt. Greaney Gets Leave of Absence to Become Chief Deputy," *Cairo Evening Citizen*, November 10, 1909, 1.

35. *Cairo Bulletin*, December 9, 1909, 4; Alexander County Circuit Court Criminal Records 2nd day February Term 1911, February 14, 139.

36. *Cairo Bulletin*, December 9, 1909, 4.

37. Pfeifer, *Rough Justice*, 52.

38. *Cairo Evening Citizen*, June 2, 1911, 1.

39. *Daily Free Press*, December 15, 1910, 7. Bankson's significant change in behavior might simply be because "Ab" sobered up.

## 21. The Trial of Sheriff Bankson

1. *Cairo Evening Citizen*, March 3, 1911, 1.

2. *Cairo Bulletin*, May 30, 1911, 1.

3. *Cairo Evening Citizen*, May 30, 1911, 1.

4. The jurors were John C. Jean of Lick Creek; Herbert S. Hardin of Cobden; Lee Medlin of Dongola; W. J. Johnson of Progress; Charles Wesley McCommons of Dongola; Eric Smith of Alto Pass; Frank Hubbs of Anna; Otis J. Lewis of Jonesboro; Oscar H. Ferrell of Cobden; W. J. Ira of Cobden; Dennis Bevel of Cobden; and Harry W. Gunn of Cobden (*Cairo Bulletin*, June 1, 1911, 1).

5. *Cairo Evening Citizen*, January 4, 1910, 6.

6. Ibid., July 23, 1910, 2.

7. Ibid., May 30, 1911, 1.

8. *Murphysboro Independent* quoted in *Cairo Bulletin*, December 8, 1910, 2; also quoted in *Alton Evening Telegraph*, December 6, 1910, 9.

9. *Cairo Bulletin*, December 8, 1910, 2.

10. *Cairo Evening Citizen*, May 30, 1911, 1.

11. Ibid.

12. Ibid.

13. Ibid.

14. *Cairo Bulletin*, May 31, 1911, 1.

15. Ibid., June 1, 1911, 1.

16. *Cairo Evening Citizen*, June 1, 1911, 1.

17. *Cairo Bulletin*, June 2, 1911, 1.

18. Ibid., December 3, 1909, 2; December 4, 1909, 2; January 13, 1910, 2.

19. The *Cairo Evening Citizen* reported that Dennis Morgan was a bartender in Gardner's saloon, but listed the address as 34th and Sycamore (*Cairo Evening Citizen*, June 1, 1911). Morgan was likely a bartender in the

Brackey Bros. saloon, identified as being at 34th and Sycamore in an earlier edition of the paper (*Cairo Evening Citizen*, December 4, 1910). This 1910 issue also reported that Sheriff Ab Bankson visited both saloons on the night Wilfred French was killed.

20. *Cairo Bulletin*, June 2, 1911, 1.

21. *Cairo Evening Citizen*, June 1, 1911, 1; *Cairo Bulletin*, June 2, 1911, 1.

22. *Cairo Bulletin*, June 2, 1911, 1.

23. Ibid.

24. *Cairo Evening Citizen*, June 1, 1911, 1.

25. *Cairo Bulletin*, June 2, 1911, 1.

26. *Cairo Evening Citizen*, June 1, 1911, 1.

27. Ibid.

28. *Cairo Bulletin*, June 2, 1911, 1.

29. *Cairo Evening Citizen*, June 1, 1911, 1.

30. Ibid.

31. Ibid.

32. Ibid.

33. Ibid.

34. *Cairo Bulletin*, June 2, 1911, 1.

35. *Cairo Evening Citizen*, June 2, 1911, 1.

36. Ibid.

37. *Cairo Bulletin*, June 2, 1911, 1.

38. *Cairo Evening Citizen*, June 2, 1911, 1.

39. Loewen, *Sundown Towns*, 5.

40. *Cairo Bulletin*, June 3, 1911, 1.

41. *Cairo Evening Citizen*, June 3, 1911, 1.

42. Ibid.

43. *Cairo Bulletin*, June 3, 1911, 1.

44. Ibid.

45. Ibid.

46. Morrison was identified as "Dick" Morrison in the *Cairo Bulletin* and "Nick" Morrison in the *Cairo Evening Citizen*. The 1900 census lists Nick Morrison as a laborer living on Jefferson Street in Cairo, Illinois (Twelfth Census of the United States, Alexander County, Illinois, City of Cairo, Ward 1, Ancestry.com, https://www.ancestry.com/interactive/7602/4113692_00773?pid=52959767&backurl=https://search.ancestry.com/cgi-bin/sse.dll?indiv%3D1%26dbid%3D7602%26h%3D52959767%26tid%3D%26pid%3D%26usePUB%3Dtrue%26_phsrc%3DRaf6548%26_phstart%3Dsuccess

Source&treeid=&personid=&hintid=&usePUB=true&_phsrc=Raf6548&_phstart=successSource&usePUBJs=true).

47. *Cairo Bulletin*, June 3, 1911, 1.

48. Ibid.

49. Ibid.

50. Ibid., 6.

51. Ibid., 1.

52. Loewen, *Sundown Towns*, 5.

53. *Cairo Evening Citizen*, June 2, 1911, 1.

54. Ibid.

55. *Cairo Bulletin*, June 3, 1911, 6. James Dillard was an African American constable who lived in the Sixth Ward of Cairo on 21st Street with his wife, Annie.

56. "Coroner's Jury Probes Death of Ed Brooks," *Cairo Evening Citizen*, January 30, 1911.

57. "Uncle Joe" Joseph Steagala owned 600–602 Commercial Avenue, where he operated two saloons and a hotel.

58. *Cairo Bulletin*, June 2, 1911, 1.

## 22. Sheriff Bankson on the Stand

1. *Cairo Bulletin*, June 3, 1911, 6.

2. *Cairo Evening Citizen*, June 3, 1911, 3.

3. *Cairo Bulletin*, June 3, 1911, 6.

4. *Pulaski Enterprise*, Friday, July 23, 1909, 1

5. *Cairo Evening Citizen*, July 31, 1909.

6. *Pulaski Enterprise*, August 20, 1909, 1.

7. *Cairo Bulletin*, June 3, 1911, 6.

8. *Cairo Evening Citizen*, June 3, 1911, 3.

9. Ibid.

10. Ibid.

11. *Cairo Bulletin*, June 3, 1911, 6.

12. Ibid.

13. Ibid., May 31, 1911, 1.

14. *Cairo Evening Citizen*, June 3, 1911, 3.

15. Bankson frequently answered "I can't remember" during his cross-examination. Indeed, one of the headlines in the *Bulletin*'s front-page story was "I Can't Remember" (June 4, 1911, 1).

16. *Cairo Evening Citizen*, June 3, 1911, 3; *Cairo Bulletin*, June 3, 1911, 6.

17. *Cairo Evening Citizen*, June 3, 1911, 3.
18. Ibid., 1.
19. Ibid.
20. *Cairo Bulletin*, June 3, 1911, 1.
21. Ibid.
22. *Cairo Evening Citizen*, June 3, 1911, 1.
23. Ibid., 3.
24. Ibid.
25. *Cairo Bulletin*, June 4, 1911, 1.
26. Likely the name was "DeBeau," as among the assassins of Bankson's deputy, Wesley G. Davis, on July 4, 1910, were two brothers, Thelbert DeBow and Jake DeBow, one of whom "disappeared" after the shooting (*Pulaski Enterprise*, July 8, 1910).
27. *Cairo Bulletin*, June 4, 1911, 1.

## 23. The Verdict

1. *Cairo Bulletin*, June 4, 1911, 1.
2. Ibid.; December 6, 1910, 6.
3. *Cairo Evening Citizen*, June 3, 1911, 1; *Cairo Bulletin*, June 4, 1911, 8. (The *Bulletin* incorrectly identified the witness as Robert Pair, but the *Citizen* used his correct name, Robert H. Baird, in its report.)
4. *Cairo Bulletin*, June 4, 1911, 8.
5. Ibid.
6. *Cairo Evening Citizen*, June 3, 1911, 1.
7. *Cairo Bulletin*, June 4, 1911, 8.
8. Ibid.
9. Ibid.
10. Ibid.
11. Ibid.
12. Ibid.
13. Ibid., June 5, 1911, 1.
14. Ibid.
15. Ibid.
16. Ibid., June 7, 1911, 2.
17. *Cairo Evening* Citizen, June 6, 1911, 1.
18. *Cairo Bulletin*, June 6, 1911, 1.
19. *Elgin (Ill.) Echo*, June 15, 1911, 2.
20. *Cairo Evening Citizen*, June 6, 1911, 1.

## 24. The Analysis of the Verdict and Its Consequences

1. *Cairo Evening Citizen*, June 6, 1911, 1.

2. For an explanation as to how popular support for due process of law was eroding at the time, see Pfeifer, *Rough Justice*, especially "The Revolt against Due Process," 94–121.

3. *Cairo Bulletin*, June 7, 1911, 2.

4. Ibid., June 8, 1911, 2.

5. Ibid.

6. Ibid.

7. *Pulaski Enterprise*, June 9, 1911, 1.

8. Ibid.

9. *Daily Free Press*, February 10, 1911, 2.

10. Ibid.

11. *Cairo Bulletin*, December 4, 1910, 2. The *Bulletin* said that Sergeant French was the victim of the mistaken theory that the man known to become criminal when drunk, yet deliberately gets drunk, is not responsible for his conduct; the blame is on the whiskey.

12. *New York Times*, November 13, 1909, 7.

13. *Cairo Evening Citizen*, March 5, 1910, 1.

14. Ibid., December 2, 1910, 3; July 3, 1910, 1.

15. *Waterloo Times-Tribune*, November 12, 1909, 1.

16. *Cairo Bulletin*, November 15, 1909, 1.

17. *Jonesboro Gazette*, November 19, 1909.

18. Ibid. One year later, A. Ney Sessions, a lawyer and owner of the *Anna Democrat*, employed an African American man as a hostler in Anna who was threatened with dynamite if he did not leave. Sessions offered a $1,000 reward for the arrest and conviction of the parties involved, but "behind it was the tradition that Anna shall not become the home of a negro" (*Cairo Evening Citizen*, November 21, 1910). Sessions was ironically the administrator of the estate of Joseph Pelley, the father of Anna Pelley.

19. *Jonesboro Gazette*, November 19, 1909.

20. Ibid., February 25, 1910, 2.

21. Ibid.

22. Ibid., November 12, 1909, 2.

23. Ibid., November 19, 1909, 2.

24. Ibid.

25. *Anna Democrat* quoted in *Cairo Bulletin*, January 15, 1910.

26. *Anna Democrat*, June 9, 1911, quoted in *Pulaski Enterprise*, June 16, 1911, 4.

27. Ibid.

28. Ibid.

29. Ibid.

30. Ibid.

31. Ibid.

32. Ibid.

33. Ibid.

34. Ibid.

35. Ibid.

36. *Cairo Evening Citizen*, June 6, 1911, 1.

37. Ibid., January 3, 1910, 4; January 10, 1910, 4; *Cairo Bulletin*, February 13, 1910, 4.

38. *Cairo Bulletin*, December 30, 1909, 2.

39. *Mansfield News Journal*, February 18, 1910, 1.

40. Lansden, *History of the City of Cairo*, 277.

41. *Jonesboro Gazette*, June 9, 1911, 3.

42. *Cairo Evening Citizen*, March 16, 1910, 6; April 6, 1910, 2.

43. *Jonesboro Gazette*, June 9, 1911, 3.

44. *Cairo Evening Citizen*, May 21, 1910, 2.

45. *Cairo Bulletin*, November 20, 1909, 8; November 21, 1909, 2; November 27, 1909, 4; February 7, 1910, 4.

46. Ibid., November 30, 1910, 4; December 29, 1909, 2; January 7, 1910, 2.

47. Ibid., July 23, 1910, 2.

48. Lantz, *Community in Search of Itself*, 139–40.

49. *Cairo Bull*etin, December 26, 1910, 10.

50. David Marniss and Neil Henry, "Race 'War' in Cairo," *Washington Post*, March 22, 1987.

51. *Cairo Bulletin*, May 5, 1911.

## Conclusion

1. Rushdy, *American Lynching*, 69–122.

2. Ibid., 91.

3. *Belleville News-Democrat* quoted in *Cairo Bulletin*, November 16, 1909, 1.

4. The author's conversation with Jay Manus, a student of the Cairo lynching of 1909, June 30, 2014.

5. Goldsby, *Spectacular Secret*, 21.

6. Waldrep, *Many Faces of Judge Lynch*, 133.

7. Southern, *Progressive Era and Race*, 31.

8. Ibid.

9. Pfeifer, *Rough Justice*, 25, 27, 53, 111; Southern, *Progressive Era and Race*, 58–59.

10. *Cairo Bulletin*, November 15, 1909, 2.

11. Ibid., 1.

12. Ibid.

13. Ibid., 3.

14. Ibid., November 19, 1909, 8.

15. Ibid.; Rushdy, *American Lynching*, 83.

16. Rushdy, *American Lynching*, 107–8.

17. *Cairo Bulletin*, November 16, 1909, 1.

18. See especially Rushdy, *American Lynching*, 84–85; and Goldsby, *Spectacular Secret*, 102–3.

19. *Cairo Bulletin*, October 31, 1910, 2.

20. Loewen, *Sundown Towns*, 463.

21. In researching Cairo's double lynching in 1909, the attempted lynching, and the killing of Sergeant French by Sheriff Bankson in 1910, I discovered a rich political and social life for Cairo's black community. Growing up in Cairo in the 1940s and 1950s, I don't remember black Republicans holding meetings to screen candidates but rather black Republicans, and Democrats too, going to back doors to be paid for their vote. My father served on many juries, which many times had black criminal defendants, but by that time there were never any black jurors. By the time I left for Decatur, Illinois, in 1959, racial relations were rapidly deteriorating in Cairo, especially after attempted peaceful school desegregation in the early 1950s failed badly, with local white men indicted for bombing homes and businesses of NAACP members.

22. Lantz, *Community in Search of Itself*, 139–40.

23. *Daily Review*, February 22, 1910, 1; *Indiana Gazette*, February 21, 1910, 8; *Cairo Bulletin*, June 7, 1911, 2.

24. Loewen, *Sundown Towns*, 463.

25. Brownell, *Other Illinois*, 9.

26. *Chicago Tribune*, November 13, 1910, 10.

27. *New York Times*, November 15, 1909, 8.

28. *St. Louis Post-Dispatch* quoted in *Cairo Bulletin*, November 16, 1909, 2.

29. *Springfield Republican* quoted in *Washington Post*, November 15, 1909, 6.

30. *Bloomington Pantagraph* quoted in *Daily Review*, November 13, 1909, 8; *Peoria Journal* quoted in *Cairo Bulletin*, November 16, 1909, 2; *Southern Illinois Herald* quoted in *Cairo Bulletin*, November 18, 1909, 4; *Belleville News-Democrat* quoted in *Cairo Bulletin*, November 15, 1909, 2.

31. *Belleville News-Democrat* quoted in *Cairo Bulletin*, November 15, 1909, 2.

32. *New York Times*, February 21, 1910, 7, quoted in *Cairo Evening Citizen*, February 22, 1910, 6; *Louisville Courier-Journal* quoted in *Cairo Bulletin*, February 22, 1910.

33. *Fort Wayne Daily News*, February 19, 1910, 8.

34. *Atlanta Constitution*, February 20, 1910, 6; *Bisbee Daily Review*, February 20, 1910, 1; *Washington Post*, February 21, 1910, 1; *New York Times*, February 21, 1910, 2; *Nebraska State Journal*, February 21, 1910, 1; *San Francisco Chronicle*, February 21, 1910, 6; *Daily Herald*, February 25, 1910, 7.

35. *St. Louis Globe-Democrat* quoted in *Cairo Evening Citizen*, February 22, 1910, 2; *Mansfield News*, February 18, 1910, 4.

36. *Cairo Bulletin*, February 21, 1910.

37. *Life*, February 1, 1954, 25. *Life* said David Lansden, a white NAACP lawyer, and at whose home was pointed the neon arrow, "was the only white man in Cairo, Ill., who had come out against segregating Negroes in the city's schools"; three out of four letters to the editor on Cairo supported Lansden ("Letters to the Editors," *Life*, February 22, 1954, 10). David Lansden was a grandson of John M. Lansden, author of *A History of the City of Cairo, Illinois*.

38. See especially *New York Times*, November 9, 1970, 30; and David Marniss and Neil Henry, "Race War in Cairo," *Washington Post*, March 22, 1987.

39. "Cairo, Illinois—Death by Racism."

40. U.S. Census Bureau estimate, https://www.census.gov/quickfacts/fact/table/pulaskicountyillinois/PST045218, accessed February 23, 2019.

41. Brownell, *Other Illinois*, 21–22.

42. Ibid., 10.

43. Ibid., 107.

44. Branch, *At Canaan's Edge*, 511. Involved in an open housing march in Chicago's Gage Park, which was viciously attacked by a white mob, Dr. King said, "I have never in my life seen such hate. Not in Mississippi or Alabama."

45. "Life on the Mississippi."

46. Cartwright and Jordan, *Between Two Rivers*.

47. Loewen, *Sundown Towns*, 140.

48. Ibid.

49. Ibid., 10.

50. Ibid., 444.

51. Ibid., 95.

52. Cartwright and Jordan, *Between Two Rivers*.

53. Patterson, *Rituals of Blood*, 208, 218.

54. Waldrep, *Many Faces of Judge Lynch*, 6.

55. Rushdy, *American Lynching*, 152–55.

56. Donald G. Mathews, "Lynching Is Part of the Religion of Our People," in Schweiger and Mathews, *Religion in the American South*, 155, 163, 181.

57. Waldrep, *Many Faces of Judge Lynch*, 6.

58. Rushdy, *American Lynching*, 131.

59. His identity is verified by an item in the *Cairo Evening Citizen* of December 23, 1907, which stated "George Logan of the firm of Cox & Logan" was called to Warrensburg, Missouri, to attend the funeral of his father, Albert B. Logan, an attorney. He and his family are listed in the 1910 census of Cairo, living on 9th Street in Cairo's Third Ward. Thirteenth Census of the United States, 1910 Population, Alexander County, Illinois, City of Cairo, Ancestry.com, https://www.ancestry.com/interactive/7884/31111_4327545-00792?pid=130058433&treeid=&personid=&rc=&usePUB=true&_phsrc=Raf6537&_phstart=successSource, accessed February 23, 2019.

60. *Muscatine Journal*, November 12, 1909, 1.

61. *Cairo Bulletin*, November 19, 1909, 8.

62. Ibid., November 15, 1909, 1.

63. *Cairo Evening Citizen*, November 11, 1909, 9; *Cairo Bulletin*, November 12, 1909, 1.

64. Senechal, *Sociogenesis of a Race Riot*, 168–73.

65. *Fort Wayne Daily News*, February 19, 1910, 1; *Indianapolis News*, February 10, 1910, 1.

66. Hattie B. Kendrick interview, Shawnee Community College, Oral History Project, August 18, 1975.

67. Ibid.

68. Rushdy, *American Lynching*, 75.

69. Conversation with Jay Manus (student of the Cairo double lynching of 1909 and the attempted lynching of 1910), June 30, 2014.

70. Kantor, *Missouri Bittersweet*. He is probably best known for his novel *Andersonville*, for which he won the Pulitzer Prize for fiction in 1956.

71. Ibid., 153.

72. *Cairo Bulletin*, November 15, 1909, 2.

73. *Belleville News-Democrat* quoted in *Cairo Bulletin*, November 15, 1909, 2; November 16, 1909, 2.

74. Wiebe, *Search for Order.*

75. Hattie B. Kendrick interview.

76. Duster, *Crusade for Justice*, 319.

## WORKS CITED

### Newspapers


*Alton (Ill.) Evening Telegraph*

*Altoona (Pa.) Mirror*

*Arizona Republican* (Phoenix)

*Atlanta Constitution*

*Belvidere (Ill.) Daily Republican*

*Bisbee (Ariz.) Daily Review*

*Cairo (Ill.) Bulletin*

*Cairo Citizen*

*Cairo Evening Citizen*

*Cedar Rapids (Iowa) Evening Gazette*

*Chicago Herald*

*Chicago Tribune*

*Cincinnati Enquirer*

*Daily Free Press* (Carbondale, Ill.)

*Daily Herald* (Arlington Heights, Ill.)

*Daily Review* (Decatur, Ill.)

*Elgin (Ill.) Echo*

*Fort Wayne (Ind.) Daily News*

*Fort Wayne Journal-Gazette*

*Fort Wayne Weekly Sentinel*

*Indiana (Pa.) Gazette*

*Indianapolis News*

*Indianapolis Star*

*Inter Ocean* (Chicago)

*Jonesboro (Ill.) Gazette*

*Logansport (Ind.) Pharos*

*Logansport Reporter*

*Los Angeles Herald*

*Mansfield (Ohio) News Journal*

*Moberly (Mo.) Monitor*

*Muldrow (Okla.) Press*

*Muscatine (Iowa) Journal*

*Nebraska State Journal* (Lincoln)
*New Castle (Pa.) News*
*New York Age*
*New York Times*
*Oskaloosa (Iowa) Daily Herald*
*Paducah (Ky.) Evening Sun*
*Portsmouth (Ohio) Daily Times*
*Pulaski Enterprise* (Mound City, Ill.)
*Riverdale (Ill.) Pointer*
*San Francisco Chronicle*
*The Standard* (Ogden, Utah)
*St. Louis Post-Dispatch*
*Syracuse (N.Y.) Herald*
*Washington (Ind.) Democrat*
*Washington Post*
*Waterloo (Iowa) Evening Courier*
*Waterloo Reporter*
*Waterloo Times-Tribune*
*West Bend (Iowa) Journal*
*West Point (Iowa) Journal*

## Books

Allen, James, and Hilton Als. *Without Sanctuary: Lynching Photography in America.* Santa Fe, N.M.: Twin Pines Press, 2000.

Berg, Manfred. *Popular Justice: A History of Lynching in America.* Chicago: Ivan R. Dee, 2011.

Branch, Taylor. *At Canaan's Edge: America in the King Years.* New York: Simon and Schuster, 1998.

Brownell, Baker. *The Other Illinois.* New York: Duell, Sloan and Pearce, 1958.

Burton, Orville Vernon, and Robert C. McMath Jr., eds. *Toward a New South.* Westport, Conn.: Greenwood Press, 1982.

Dray, Phillip. *At the Hands of Persons Unknown: The Lynching of Black America.* New York: Random House, 2002.

Duster, Alfreda M., ed. *Crusade for Justice: The Autobiography of Ida B. Wells.* Chicago: University of Chicago Press, 1970.

Equal Justice Initiative. *Lynching in America: Confronting the Legacy of American Terror, Summary.* Montgomery, Ala.: Equal Justice Initiative, 2015.

Frisbe, Margery. *An Alley in Chicago: The Life and Legacy of Monsignor John Egan.* Franklin, Wis.: Sheed and Ward, 2002.

Giddings, Paula J. *Ida: A Sword among Lions.* New York: HarperCollins, 2008.

Goldsby, Jacqueline. *A Spectacular Secret: Lynching in American Life and Literature.* Chicago: University of Chicago Press, 2006.

Goodwin, Doris Kearns. *The Bully Pulpit: Theodore Roosevelt, William Howard Taft, and the Golden Age of Journalism.* New York: Simon and Schuster, 2013.

*The Governors of Illinois, 1818–1918.* Springfield: Illinois State Journal Company, 1918.

Hofstadter, Richard. *The Age of Reform.* New York: Vintage Books, 1955.

Kantor, MacKinlay. *Missouri Bittersweet.* Garden City, N.Y.: Doubleday, 1969.

Lansden, John M. *A History of the City of Cairo, Illinois.* 1910. Reprint; Carbondale: Southern Illinois University Press, 1976.

Lantz, Herman R. *A Community in Search of Itself: A Case History of Cairo, Illinois.* Carbondale: Southern Illinois University Press, 1971.

Loewen, James W. *Sundown Towns: A Hidden Dimension of American Racism.* New York: Touchstone, 2005.

*Memoirs of the Lower Ohio Valley: Personal and Genealogical with Portraits.* 2 vols. Madison, Wis.: Federal Publishing Company, 1905.

Mouser, Bruce. *A Black Gambler's World of Liquor, Vice and Presidential Politics: William Thomas Scott of Illinois, 1839–1917.* Madison: University of Wisconsin Press, 2014.

*Official Directory of the Fortieth General Assembly of Illinois.* Springfield: Press of Illinois State Journal, 1897.

Patterson, Orlando. *Rituals of Blood: Consequences of Slavery in Two American Centuries.* Washington, D.C.: Civitas, 1998.

Perrin, William Henry, ed. *History of Alexander, Union and Pulaski Counties, Illinois.* Chicago: O. L. Baskin and Co., 1883.

Pfeifer, Michael J. *Rough Justice: Lynching and American Society, 1874–1947.* Urbana: University of Illinois Press, 2006.

Poor, Henry V. *Poor's Manual of the Railroads of the United States 1903.* New York: H. V. Poor, 1903.

Powers, Ron. *Far from Home: Life and Loss in Two American Towns.* New York: Random House, 1991.

Raper, Arthur F. *The Tragedy of Lynching.* Chapel Hill: University of North Carolina Press, 1933.

Reid, Larry. *River City: A Discovery of Cairo, Illinois.* New York: Exposition Press, 1966.

"Reports of Riots at Cairo, Illinois, November 12, 1909." In *Biennial Report of Adjutant General 1909–1910*. Springfield: Illinois State Journal, 1914.

Rushdy, Ashraf H. A. *American Lynching*. New Haven: Yale University Press, 2012.

Schechter, Patricia A. *Ida B. Wells-Barnett and American Reform, 1880–1930*. Chapel Hill: University of North Carolina Press, 2001.

Schweiger, Beth Barton, and Donald G. Mathews, eds. *Religion in the American South: Protestants and Others in History and Culture*. Chapel Hill: University of North Carolina Press, 2004.

Senechal, Roberta. *The Sociogenesis of a Race Riot: Springfield, Illinois, in 1908*. Urbana: University of Illinois Press, 1990.

Smith, George Washington. *A History of Southern Illinois*. Chicago: Lewis Publishing Company, 1912.

Southern, David W. *The Progressive Era and Race: Reaction and Reform, 1900–1917*. Wheeling, Ill.: Harlan Davidson, 2005.

*Standard Atlas of Union County, Illinois*. Chicago: George A. Ogle and Co., 1908.

Steffens, Lincoln. *The Shame of the Cities*. New York: McClure, Phillips and Co., 1904.

Strout, Richard Lee, ed. *Maud*. New York: Macmillan, 1939.

Tolnay, Stewart Emory, and E. M. Beck. *A Festival of Violence: An Analysis of Southern Lynchings, 1882–1930*. Urbana: University of Illinois Press, 1995.

Waldrep, Christopher. *The Many Faces of Judge Lynch: Extralegal Violence and Punishment in America*. New York: Palgrave Macmillan, 2002.

———. *Night Riders: Defending Community in the Black Patch, 1890–1915*. Durham: Duke University Press, 1993.

Wiebe, Robert H. *The Search for Order, 1877–1920*. New York: Hill and Wang, 1967.

## Journal and Magazine Articles

"Business and Finance: All Aboard!" *Time*, February 8, 1937.

Dinnerstein, Leonard. "The Fate of Leo Frank." *American Heritage*, October 1996, 98–108.

"Dynamite Arrow." *Life*, February 1, 1954, 26.

Harvey, L. M., and J. W. Harvey. "Reliability of Bloodhounds in Criminal Investigations." *Journal of Forensic Science* 48, no. 4 (July 2003): 811–16.

"Letters to the Editors." *Life*, February 22, 1954, 10.

"Life on the Mississippi: An Eye Opening Journey about America's River of Dreams." *Time*, July 10, 2000, 30–37.

Seng, Michael P. "The Cairo Experience: Civil Rights Litigation in a Racial Powder Keg." *Oregon Law Review* 61, no. 285 (1982): 285–315.

Walling, William English. "A Race War in the North." *The Independent*, September 3, 1908, 529–34.

## Internet and Film

"Cairo, Illinois—Death by Racism." Legends of America. http://www.legendsofamerica.com/il-cairo.html, accessed June 24, 2017.

Cartwright, Jacob, and Nick Jordan, dirs. *Between Two Rivers*. Manchester, UK: Wurstundgritz, 2012. Documentary.

Gibson, Robert A. "The Negro Holocaust: Lynching and Race Riots in the United States, 1880–1950." Yale-New Haven Teachers Institute, 1978–2016. http://teachersinstitute.yale.edu/curriculum/units/1979/2/79.02.04.x.html, accessed June 30, 2017.

"Lynchings by Race and Year, 1882–1968." The Charles Chesnutt Digital Archive. http://www.chesnuttarchive.org/classroom/lynching_table_year.html, accessed June 30, 2017.

"Obituaries and Death Notices from Cairo, Alexander County, Illinois, Newspapers, 1848–1909, 1912, 1918." Transcribed by Darrel Dexter. Genealogy Society of Southern Illinois. http://www.rootsweb.ancestry.com/~ilgssi/Cairo.html, accessed December 28, 2016.

## Alexander County, Illinois, Court Records

Alexander County Circuit Court Criminal Records 44th day October Term 1909, January 8, 1910, 83–84.

Alexander County Circuit Court Criminal Records 5th day February Term 1910, February 18, 1910, 97.

Alexander County Circuit Court Criminal Records 21st day February Term 1910, March 28, 1910, 105, 106, 107, 108, 109, 110, 112.

Alexander County Circuit Court Criminal Records 4th day May Term 1910, May 12, 1910, 118.

Alexander County Circuit Court Criminal Records 2nd day February Term 1911, February 14, 1911, 139.

## City Directories

*The Cairo Illinois City Directory 1915*. Vol. 5, The Delta Series. 1915.

*Daily Telegram's Cairo City Directory for 1904*. Cairo, Ill.: E. E. and C. M. Ellis, 1904.

*Walker's Cairo City Directory for 1908–9*. Cairo, Ill.: George B. Walker, 1909.

# INDEX

John A. Beadles not only has taught in high schools, colleges, and universities since 1964, retiring in 2012, but has written articles and a book. Early in his career he taught at Decatur Lakeview and Pontiac Township High Schools in Illinois and at Bishop DuBourg High School in Missouri. As a college instructor Beadles was a teaching assistant at Syracuse University and taught at Cazenovia College for Women, Lane College, State University of New York at Geneseo, St. Louis Community College at Meramec, and Kennesaw State University. He also served as Comprehensive Employment and Training Act (CETA) supervisor of the local history project for the five southernmost counties of Illinois, from which his previous book, *A History of Southernmost Illinois*, emerged.